Phonics Lessons

Letters, Words, and How They Work

Contents

LS Letter/Sound Relationships

SP Spelling Patterns

HF High Frequency Words

WM Word Meaning

WS Word Structure

WSA

Word-Solving Actions

Phonics: Why and How

Welcome to *Phonics Lessons: Letters, Words, and How They Work, Grade 2,* a collection of one hundred minilessons. These brief minilessons (so-called to emphasize their targeted focus in both content and delivery) enable you to help children attend to, learn about, and efficiently use information about letters, sounds, and words. While the lessons are most appropriate for second graders, they also work for first graders who have developed control of related principles and for third graders who need this content. The lessons take into account what children already know and help them acquire the knowledge and concepts they need to learn next. You may connect the lessons to word solving in reading and writing across the language and literacy curriculum or use them as prototypes for other phonics minilessons that you design yourself. Most important, each lesson is organized around a language principle—an essential understanding about language and how it works—thus enabling you to plan and teach efficiently and systematically.

Why Teach Phonics?

The true purpose and promise of phonics instruction is to expand and refine children's reading and writing powers. In the complex processes of reading and writing, letters, sounds, and words are the keys to help children grasp and use language as a tool. Most children acquire this tool and learn how to use it at school under the guidance of a skilled teacher who provides a wide range of learning opportunities. While this volume focuses on children's learning about letters, sounds, and words, *phonics is not a complete reading program, nor is it even the most important component of a reading program.* The lessons here enhance but do not take the place of experiences with real texts. Phonics instruction as described here takes only about ten or fifteen minutes of explicit teaching each day, with students spending an additional fifteen to twenty minutes a day applying, sharing, and evaluating what they have learned.

What's the Best Way to Teach Phonics?

Children learn phonics best as part of a wide range of engaging literacy experiences accompanied by rigorous teaching. As teachers work alongside readers and writers, they demonstrate effective behaviors, draw attention to important information, and prompt children to use their knowledge. The great majority of time in the classroom is devoted to reading and writing continuous text. Children learn to solve words "on the run" while reading for meaning and writing to communicate. The curriculum is content rich and includes a range of instructional approaches, from demonstration and explicit teaching to supporting children's independent work.

In the arguments about what constitutes effective instruction, two issues often arise:

- Should instruction be *explicit,* that is, focused directly on language elements, or *implicit,* that is, embedded in the processes of reading and writing?
- Should we teach children directly or allow them to discover or generalize essential concepts for themselves?

These two areas of tension make designing instructional programs in literacy quite a challenge.

Children learn much more than we teach them; they often astound us with the creativity of their insights. One goal of our teaching is to help children become active examiners and analyzers of print. We want them always to be searching for connections and patterns, to form categories of knowledge, and to have a store of examples to which they can refer.

In the tug-of-war between direct teaching and discovery, going to extremes can be dangerous. Leaving everything to discovery will almost surely mean that many children will not attend to or acquire the understanding they need. Yet assuming that children learn only through direct teaching may lead us to neglect the power of the learning brain, that is, the excitement that makes learning real.

We believe that well-planned and organized direct teaching of language principles is critical but that our lessons must also contain an element of inquiry. In these minilessons, the principle is stated in simple language appropriate for use in the classroom, but the children are also encouraged to categorize words, notice features of letters and words, and search for examples. In any lesson, you decide whether to state the principle first and then generate examples that will make it clear, always leaving room for children to notice more about letters, sounds, and words, or to show some clear examples first and invite children to make connections and generalizations. The combination of discovery and direct teaching makes learning efficient; teaching prompts discovery.

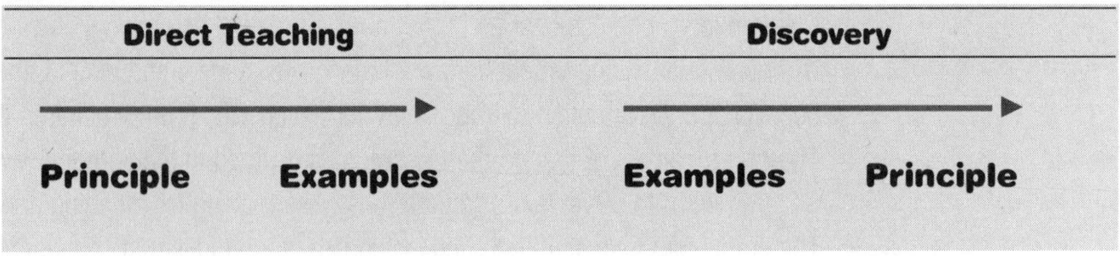

Direct Teaching		Discovery	
Principle →	**Examples**	**Examples** →	**Principle**

The Word Study Continuum

The Word Study Continuum is the key to the phonics minilessons. You will use it, in concert with the Month-by-Month Planning Guide, the Lesson Selection Map, and continuous, informed assessment, to guide your work over the course of a school year. The Continuum comprises nine Categories of Learning. (In second grade, however, we address only six categories, as most second graders will control the first three categories.) Each category showcases multiple principles your children will develop over time. The Continuum represents a comprehensive picture of linguistic knowledge that children develop over time. While there are easier and more complex concepts within each category, we are not suggesting that there is a rigid sequence. Instead, we want to help children develop their abilities along a broad front, often using and learning about several different kinds of information simultaneously. The Continuum gives us as teachers an extensive and organized understanding of the body of knowledge that forms the foundation for expert word solving.

As we set out to construct this Continuum, we examined a wide range of research on language and literacy learning, and we asked both teachers and researchers for feedback. At the heart of literacy is a process in which children use what they know about the language they speak and connect it to print (Clay 1991). As teachers, we are simultaneously helping children expand their oral language capabilities while we work with them on the understandings needed for literacy. The semantic, syntactic, and phonological systems of language all contribute to literacy learning. Readers must understand the relationships between language and the graphic symbols that represent sounds and words (Moats 2000). Decades of research have shown that when they are meaningfully engaged in using print, children develop awareness of these relationships early (Read 1971; Treiman 1985). It is especially important that children develop awareness of the phonological system, learn about letters, and develop understanding of sound-to-letter relationships and of words and how they work (see Adams 1990; Armbruster, Lehr & Osborn 2001; Clay 1991, 1998, 2001; Juel 1988; Juel, Griffith & Gough 1986; Moats 2000; National Institute of Child Health and Human Development 2001; Pressley 1998; Snow, Burns & Griffin 1989). Our task as teachers is to organize our own knowledge and design systematic ways to present the information to children and help them use it for reading and writing. We found surprising agreement on the knowledge needed to become an expert word solver. It represents an inventory of knowledge that, together, will form a strong foundation for becoming literate.

Let's look at the nine Categories of Learning in more detail.

Nine Categories of Learning

Early Literacy Concepts

Typically, second graders will have established early literacy concepts. Therefore, we do not include minilessons for this category. If you have a small group of children who are still learning, use interactive writing with them daily and, if time permits, use minilessons from Grade 1.

Phonological Awareness

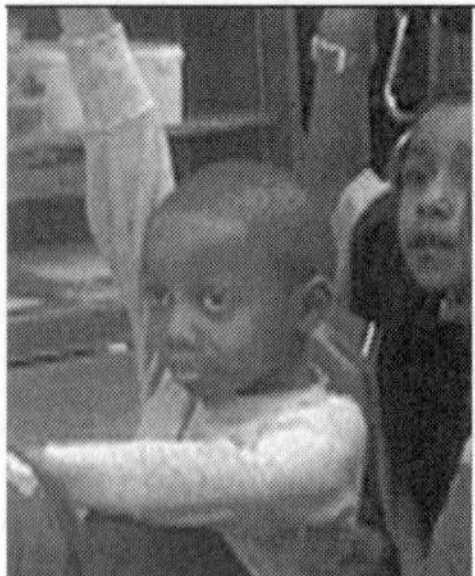

Most second graders will be sophisticated in hearing and manipulating sounds. Therefore, we do not include minilessons for this category. For second graders who need a review, you can work with them in small groups to provide the explicit instruction that will help them learn quickly. Most second graders will still be noticing syllables in multisyllable words, complex onsets and rimes, and individual sounds in longer and more complex words. Also, second graders delight in lyrical language and are still learning about the sounds of words as they contribute to poetry and literature. They will need help in recognizing alliteration, subtle rhymes, and onomatopoetic words. Songs, rhymes, and poetry provide students with the background and examples they need to participate fully in your minilessons in this area. They will enjoy word play that focuses on sounds.

Letter Knowledge

Most second graders are thoroughly familiar with letters and can recognize and write them automatically. Therefore, we do not include minilessons for developing letter knowledge. Children who have low letter knowledge or have trouble recognizing and using letters quickly and automatically will profit from participating in the Buddy Study System using very simple words; in the process of exploring words, they will learn how to look at letters and eventually recognize them automatically.

Letter/Sound Relationships

Second graders will be learning more complex relationships between letters, letter clusters, and sounds. They will expand their knowledge of the ways various sounds are represented by consonant and vowel patterns. Your minilessons in this area will help students have an organized view of the tools of literacy.

Spelling Patterns

The patterns in regularly spelled words are helpful to children, but second graders will be expanding their knowledge of how words "look" so that they develop a sense of the common and less common patterns. Second graders will still be exploring and expanding their knowledge of phonograms and words with reliable letter-sound correspondence. They will also extend this knowledge to irregular words.

High Frequency Words

Children need to expand their knowledge of high frequency words, learning those that are more difficult. High frequency words are also learned in many other components of the language and literacy framework, especially guided reading. Second graders should add continuously to the list of high frequency words they can recognize quickly.

Word Meaning

Children need to know the meaning of the words they are learning to read and write. It is important for them to expand their vocabularies constantly as well as develop a more complex understanding of words they already know. This section of the Continuum for Grade 2 describes understandings related to the development of vocabulary words with multiple meanings, homophones, antonyms, and synonyms.

Word Structure

Word structure involves the underlying rules for understanding both simple and complex patterns in words, including syllables, contractions, compound words, plurals, prefixes, affixes, possessives, and abbreviations.

Word-Solving Actions

Word solving refers to the strategic actions that readers take when they use their phonics knowledge while reading or writing continuous text. These strategies are "in-the-head" actions that are invisible, although we can infer them from some overt behavior; for example, children will sometimes make several attempts at words, revealing their hypotheses. Or, children may work left to right on a word (sometimes called "sounding out"). They may also make connections with other words. Good readers tend to use these in-the-head word-solving actions in connection with meaning and knowledge of language so that the reading is smoother, makes sense, and is accurate. They are fitting all systems together. In all grade levels, it is important for children to understand that every bit of information they learn is highly useful in literacy processes.

Learning Your Way Around the Minilessons

We have designed these minilessons so that as you use them, you will always consider the particular children you teach. You will decide which lessons to use and whether or not to modify them to meet the needs of your particular students. Certainly, you will note the connections you can make to your own students' discoveries and learning about letters, sounds, and words across the Language and Literacy Framework. Although we present the lessons in a standard format, each one is inherently different because of the conversations you will have with the children you teach. Your students will offer their own examples and make their own connections, and you will enrich their learning as you acknowledge and extend their thinking.

We have included a generous sampling of lessons in six of the nine Categories of Learning. Our goal is to provide clear prototypes from which you can create your own lessons, (see *Teaching Resources,* Blank Lesson Template) using the Word Study Continuum, that will develop the understanding your students need to experience over time. Within each category, the lessons are numbered for ease of reference, *but we are not implying an unalterable sequence.* Nevertheless, if you are new to teaching or have not taught phonics before, you may want to follow this sequence, because within each learning category we have clustered principles from easier to harder. But easy and hard are relative terms; they refer to students' previous experience, and only you as a teacher know the children's learning background. As you implement these lessons, you will not only learn more about children's development of word-solving strategies but you will also gain invaluable insight into our English linguistic system. Ultimately, feel confident in building your own sequence of explicit lessons that moves your students systematically toward a flexible and powerful range of strategies.

Each lesson title reflects the content of the lesson. The subtitle indicates the type of activity children will do in the Apply section.

GENERATIVE LESSONS provide a recurring structure you can use with similar items within a knowledge set, for example, to teach consonant clusters. As children acquire knowledge, they build systems for similar learning that accelerate the learning.

All materials needed for TEACH, APPLY, and SHARE sections of the lesson are listed. Specific materials (word cards, activity templates, etc.) are provided as reproducibles in the accompanying binder, *Teaching Resources.* If children are rotating through a center, you need only enough materials for one small group to work with at a time. If they are working individually, as partners, or in simultaneous small groups, you will need additional materials.

Generative Lesson

early
mid
late

17

Identifying Words with ai, ay, ee, ea, oa, ow

Crazy Eights

What do your students already know, and what do they need to learn next? Your insights about your own students will guide your choice of lessons and help you plan instruction that targets your students' learning needs.

Consider Your Children

Once children have learned to play this card game, they will be able to apply the routine with four of the six new patterns at a time. They should have good control of common long and short vowel patterns and initial consonant clusters and digraphs. They should also have a repertoire of known words with vowel patterns.

Working with English Language Learners

English language learners may need support in a small group to understand the rules of Crazy Eights and play it successfully. Quickly go over the words you use for examples to be sure they can read and understand them.

You Need

- Pocket chart.

From *Teaching Resources:*

- Pocket Chart Word Card Template, to create word cards for *rain, pail, day, pay, meet, feet, seat, beat, boat, soap, snow, row.*
- Directions for Crazy Eights.
- Crazy Eights Game Cards made from the previous lesson's word cards (Lessson LS 16) and Deck Card Template:

13 cards of each of four selected vowel patterns.

4 cards with a Crazy Eight on them.

Understand the Principle

Children need to learn that there are many common vowel patterns, or *vowel teams,* in words. These vowel patterns are best learned as part of phonograms or rimes.

Explain the Principle

“Some vowels go together in words and make one sound.”

“When there are two vowels *(ai, ay, ee, ea, oa, ow),* they usually make the sound of the name of the first vowel *(rain, day, meet, seat, snow).*”

LS 17 LETTER/SOUND RELATIONSHIPS

CONTINUUM: LETTER/SOUND RELATIONSHIPS — RECOGNIZING AND USING LETTER COMBINATIONS THAT REPRESENT LONG VOWEL SOUNDS

135

We help you understand the language principle underlying each minilesson so you can teach with clarity and a well-defined purpose.

Typically, it takes several years for young children to learn English as a second language and to learn to read, write, and think consistently in their new language. As you adjust the lesson for English language learners, your instruction becomes clearer and more explicit in ways that help all your students. (See Guidelines: Working with English Language Learners.)

Each lesson highlights a key principle from the Word Study Continuum.

Concise, clear language “rings inside students' heads.” Avoid jargon and technical labels; use a common language that enables you to reach your readers and writers simply and easily. Sometimes you will show children examples and invite them to think of the principle; other times, you will state the principle, give a few examples, and invite the children to add examples. You determine which approach will be more effective.

Modify the steps for implementing the lesson to fit your own group of children. Much will depend on your children's experience and how well you have taught routines.

plan

teach

We take you through the lesson step by step, suggesting effective language you might use. Sometimes, the lesson is oral only, without written examples. Make frequent use of the pocket chart to hold pictures, letters, and words (or use chart paper on an easel). Occasionally, you may write the principle on the chart before the lesson and generate examples with children during the lesson.

In each Teach section, we provide a sample chart that you and your children might create. Some depict the chart in process; some depict the final result.

Explain the Principle

"Some vowels go together in words and make one sound."

"When there are two vowels (*ai, ay, ee, ea, oa, ow*), they usually make the sound of the name of the first vowel (*rain, day, meet, seat, snow*)."

rain day meet seat boat snow
pail pay feet beat soap row

1. Explain to the children that you are going to tell them about more vowel patterns they will see in words.
2. Place in six columns the word cards for *rain* and *pail*, *day* and *pay*, *meet* and *feet*, *seat* and *beat*, *boat* and *soap*, and *snow* and *row*.
3. Read each word pair and ask the children to notice the vowel sound they hear and the two letters that make the sound.
4. Explain that some vowels go together in words and make one sound. They usually make the sound of the first vowel.
5. Invite the children to give one more example for each pattern. If they suggest a word that has a different pattern, write it off to the side and explain the pattern.
6. Tell the children they are going to play the Crazy Eights card game. Here's how it works. Give each player eight cards and place the remaining deck face down, with one card turned face up beside the deck. The first player reads the card that is face up, puts down a card with the same vowel sound, and reads it. The discarded card can match a word with the same vowel sound (an *ai* word can match an *ai* word or an *ay* word, and vice versa). If the player doesn't have a card that will match, he can discard a Crazy Eight card, which functions as a free card. Otherwise the player draws a card until he finds a match to put down. The first player to discard all cards wins the game.
7. Demonstrate and explain the game with two children until everyone understands how to play the game.

We repeat the principle in language suitable for children that you may refer to during your teaching.

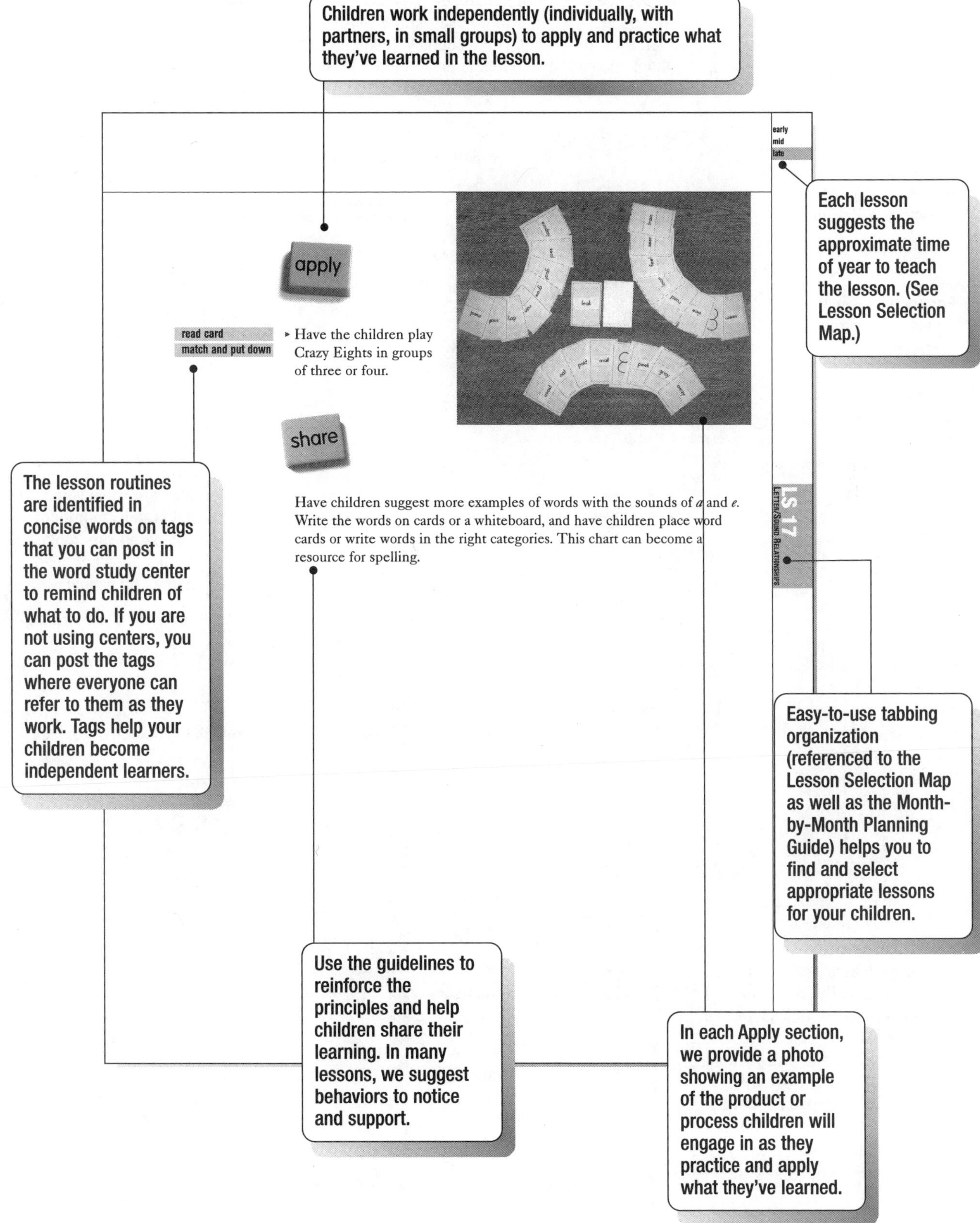

Children work independently (individually, with partners, in small groups) to apply and practice what they've learned in the lesson.
early
mid
late
Each lesson suggests the approximate time of year to teach the lesson. (See Lesson Selection Map.)
apply
read card
match and put down
▸ Have the children play Crazy Eights in groups of three or four.
share
Have children suggest more examples of words with the sounds of *a* and *e*. Write the words on cards or a whiteboard, and have children place word cards or write words in the right categories. This chart can become a resource for spelling.
LS 17
Letter/Sound Relationships
The lesson routines are identified in concise words on tags that you can post in the word study center to remind children of what to do. If you are not using centers, you can post the tags where everyone can refer to them as they work. Tags help your children become independent learners.
Easy-to-use tabbing organization (referenced to the Lesson Selection Map as well as the Month-by-Month Planning Guide) helps you to find and select appropriate lessons for your children.
Use the guidelines to reinforce the principles and help children share their learning. In many lessons, we suggest behaviors to notice and support.
In each Apply section, we provide a photo showing an example of the product or process children will engage in as they practice and apply what they've learned.

Connect learning across the Language and Literacy Framework through interactive read-aloud, shared reading, guided reading, interactive writing, and independent writing. Your observations across learning contexts will help you think of specific connections you can bring to your children's attention; add your own notes to enhance the lesson.

We provide a variety of useful bibliographies in *Teaching Resources.*

For each lesson, we provide two suggested read-aloud titles chosen specifically to support the principle and work of each lesson.

Link

Interactive Read-Aloud: Read aloud books that use words containing long vowel patterns, such as

- ***Madeline and the Bad Hat*** by Ludwig Bemelmans
- ***Horton Hatches the Egg*** by Dr. Seuss

Shared Reading: Select poems that contain some words with long vowel patterns, such as "Row, Row, Row Your Boat," "The Bear," "Slowly, Slowly," and "Sneeze on Monday" (see *Sing a Song of Poetry*). Have children locate and highlight two or three words containing a specific pattern.

Guided Reading: During word work, use magnetic letters to make three or four words with long vowel patterns. Have the children write some of these words.

Interactive Writing: When the children are constructing a word with a long vowel pattern, prompt them to think of another word with the same pattern: "Do you know a word like that?"

Independent Writing: Encourage the children to reread their writing and check for the correct spelling of the long vowel patterns in the editing process.

Expand the Learning

Repeat the lesson with a different deck of cards incorporating the two patterns not used in the first deck and eliminating two of the originally used patterns. (Each deck features only four patterns at a time.)

Connect with Home

Send home the deck of Crazy Eights cards so that the children can play the game with family members.

If children need more experience, you can repeat the lesson format using these suggestions for variations, different examples, or more challenging activities.

These are not homework assignments; rather, they are ways you can help family members and caregivers make connections between home and school.

assess

- Dictate six to ten words with long vowel patterns and note how many of them the children control.
- Notice the children's use of long vowel patterns in their writing.

Assess the impact of the minilesson and application in ways that are informal and integral to the work children are doing. For some lessons, we suggest using the more formal and systematic procedures in the Assessment Guide (in *Teaching Resources*) to help you determine children's needs for further lessons.

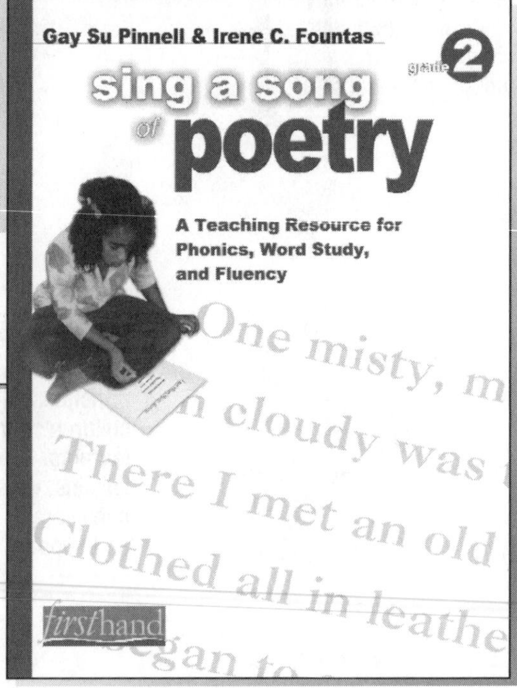

Gay Su Pinnell & Irene C. Fountas
grade 2
sing a song of poetry
A Teaching Resource for Phonics, Word Study, and Fluency
One misty, m
cloudy was
There I met an old
Clothed all in leathe
firsthand

Available separately: *Sing a Song of Poetry* provides reproducibles of hundreds of your favorite rhymes, songs, and poems that will help children use and enjoy oral and written language.

Teaching Resources is your comprehensive professional resource for everything from diagnostic assessment to a Consonant Cluster Linking Chart.

Gay Su Pinnell & Irene C. Fountas

grade 2

phonics lessons

TEACHING RESOURCES

- *Assessment Guide*
- *Materials & Routines*
- *Games*
- *Templates*
- *Lesson Word Cards*
- *Category Word Cards*
- *Bibliographies*

Assessment

Lesson Word Cards

Materials & Routines

Category Word Cards

Games

Bibliographies

Templates

The Assessment Guide includes more formal, performance-based Assessment Tasks across the Categories of Learning.

We've provided a variety of bibliographies listing hundreds of books categorized for ease of use. They include Language Play, Rhymes, Poetry, and Read-Alouds.

You will find descriptions of and directions for the materials and daily routines most important for your classroom. These are comprehensive lists of the hands-on materials and activities that undergird effective teaching.

Additionally, look for word cards, templates, and reproducibles to make an array of your own cards and ready-to-use booklets. We include game materials and directions for Lotto, Crazy Eights, Concentration, and Follow the Path. We also provide numerous reproducibles for student activities.

Essential Literacy Concepts Every Second Grader Should Know

The lessons in this book show you how to provide very basic information about linguistic principles, but we also expect and encourage second grade students to use their knowledge across all activities in the Language and Literacy Framework. For us as teachers, it is essential to have in mind some basic concepts that are important for second graders to learn during a year of instruction. There will always be individual variation, but these goals help us to construct an efficient and organized curriculum that will serve as a foundation for good teaching.

We'll explore six different important areas of word learning, each of which is essential for becoming a skilled user of written language. We emphasize that these principles are learned and enriched in *both* direct word study and in reading/writing continuous text.

More extensive discussions of second grade learners may be found in Pinnell & Fountas (1998, Chapters 9 and 19), and Fountas & Pinnell (1996, Chapter 2). The expectations inherent in these descriptions are consistent with recommended literacy standards for kindergarten through third grade (New Standards Primary Literacy Committee).

Phonemic Awareness

Second graders will have consolidated their knowledge of sound patterns in words, including rhymes, syllables, and regular spelling patterns. Phonemic awareness is usually no longer an issue; most second graders can make complex connections between words by noticing sound patterns. They are still expanding their appreciation of the phonology of language and enjoy word play and the sounds of poetry and sensory language, in the process learning more about how words work. You may have a few second graders who need support in exploring the sounds of the language.

Letters and Sounds

Second graders have also consolidated their knowledge of relationships between letters and sounds. They know regular letter-sound correspondences but they also understand that there is not a direct one-to-one relationship between letters and sounds in English words. While many words have regular spellings (for example, *pig* and *cat* have three letters and three sounds), most spellings are more complex, for example:

- *Ride* has four letters and three sounds.
- *Might* has five letters and three sounds.
- In *partner* the sound of *a* and *e* are influenced by *r*.

Second graders are learning how to map the sounds of the language onto the print system and to expand their understandings to accommodate how words *look*. For example, the sound of /a/ can be represented by the letter *a*, as in *make*, by *-ea*, as in *steak*, by *-ey*, as in *hey*, by *-ay*, as in *today*, and by *eigh-*, as in *eight*. Further, some of these letter clusters (vowel diphthongs) may be connected to other sounds: *freak, instead, bread, plead.* These are all patterns that second graders may encounter in reading or use in writing, and second graders are ready to understand the more complex letter-sound relationships that exist.

Second grade is a time when children are "tidying up" their knowledge of consonant clusters, including the more complex and less frequently used ones, for example, *spl-, thr-, sch-, tw-, squ-, scr-*. They also learn more about the varied sounds that can be associated with the vowels, and they learn about vowel clusters or "diphthongs," such as *-ea, -ai, -oa*. They learn more about the role of "silent" letters in words, explore how vowels sound in combination with *r*, and understand *y* as a vowel. Much of this learning is accomplished by looking at letter-sound relationships within words as children explore them in categories.

Phoneme Chart

We examine forty-four phonemes. The actual sounds in the language can vary, as dialect, articulation, and other factors in speech vary. The following are common sounds for the letters listed.

Consonant Sounds

b /b/ box	**n /n/ nest**	**ch /ch/ chair**
d /d/ dog	**p /p/ pail**	**sh /sh/ ship**
f /f/ fan	**r /r/ rose**	**wh /hw/ what**
g /g/ gate	**s /s/ sun**	**th /th/ think**
h /h/ house	**t /t/ top**	**th /TH/ the**
j /j/ jug	**v /v/ vase**	**ng /ng/ sing**
k /k/ kite	**w /w/ was**	**zh /zh/ measure**
l /l/ leaf	**y /y/ yell**	
m /m/ mop	**z /z/ zoo**	

Vowel Sounds

/ă/ hat	**/ā/ gate**	**/o͞o/ moon**	**/û/ bird**
/ĕ/ bed	**/ē/ feet**	**/o͝o/ book**	**/ə/ about**
/ĭ/ fish	**/ī/ bike**	**/ou/ house**	**/ä/ car**
/ŏ/ mop	**/ō/ boat**	**/oi/ boy**	**/â/ chair**
/ŭ/ nut	**/ū/ mule**	**/ô/ tall**	

Reading Words

Second graders have consolidated their knowledge of regular letter-sound correspondences in one- and two syllable words and are expanding their ability to use this knowledge, as well as their knowledge of consonant clusters in multisyllable words. They also are learning to recognize and solve less regular words with more complex spelling patterns.

They are expanding their knowledge to a wider range of letter clusters and patterns in words and can recognize and use word parts. Their recognition of high frequency words expands rapidly because they have developed systems for remembering the features of words. They are growing in their understanding of inflectional endings and their role in verb tense. They can solve many words with affixes (prefixes and suffixes).

Through their reading, they learn to decode new words but they also expand their knowledge of word meanings. By the end of second grade, they will recognize or be able to solve (both decoding and understanding) the full range of words usually found in texts at approximately level I to M (see Fountas & Pinnell, 1999).

Good second grade readers are aware when they do not understand the meaning of a word, and they know how to search for more information. They are able to make connections between words by thinking about the way they sound and look and what they mean, and they know how to form

Literacy Concepts Every Second Grader Should Know

Phonemic awareness—most second grade children are still expanding their ability to:

- Appreciate and play with rhyme and rhythm.
- Hear parts of words and manipulate them—onsets, rimes, syllables.
- Enjoy the sounds of language in poetry and well-written texts.
- Appreciate language play.

Letters and Sounds—most second grade children are still expanding their ability to:

- Recognize and use the more complex consonant clusters at the beginning, middle, and end of words.
- Understand irregular sound correspondences, for example *–eigh-* for /ā/.
- Recognize when letters are "silent."
- Understand the variety of sounds connected to the five main vowels.
- Understand *y* as a vowel.
- Understand vowel combinations.
- Understand and recognize the sounds connected to vowels in words with *r.*

Reading Words—most second grade children are still expanding their ability to:

- Recognize and solve most irregularly spelled words.
- Recognize and solve words with complex spelling patterns.
- Know regular letter-sound correspondences and use them to recognize or solve regularly spelled one- and two-syllable words.
- Recognize letter clusters and other patterns in words to solve them.
- Know the meaning of a wide range of words that they meet in reading texts at second grade level.
- Realize when they don't know the meaning of a word and engage in a search for more information.
- Connect words by their meanings.
- Connect words with similar word patterns—diphthongs, special vowel spellings, and word endings.
- Understand and manipulate words by adding or deleting affixes or changing tenses.
- Understand plurals.
- Realize that there can be more than one meaning for words and that two words can mean the same (synonyms) or the opposite (antonyms).
- Realize that words can be connected by the way they sound or look (homonyms).
- Realize the functions of parts of speech—nouns, verbs.
- Recognize quickly and automatically most of the words that they meet in reading texts at second grade level (approximately level I to M).

Writing Words—most second grade children are still expanding their ability to:

- Write a large number of high frequency words quickly and automatically.
- Write words automatically with regular letter-sound relationships and with spelling patterns they know.
- Internalize spelling rules from looking at words in categories.
- Apply affixes—including simple prefixes and suffixes—in spelling words.
- Spell words with inflectional endings.
- Know many irregular words, the spelling of which must be memorized.

- Demonstrate clear logic in their attempts to spell words so that incorrectly spelled words are close to conventional.
- Recognize when a word is incorrectly spelled.
- Know words that must be capitalized.
- Know most frequently used abbreviations and how to punctuate them.

Processing Strategies in Reading—most second grade children are still expanding their ability to:

- Apply reading strategies to longer stretches of texts and to more difficult texts.
- Recognize a large number of high frequency words and many multisyllable words while reading continuous text.
- Use a range of word-solving strategies to take words apart while reading for meaning.
- Recognize and solve words while at the same time maintaining fluency and phrasing by using their knowledge of language and of punctuation.
- Notice and use punctuation cues (commas, periods, question marks, and quotation marks) to assist in phrased reading.
- Use letter-sound knowledge and visual features of words to self-monitor and self-correct their reading.
- Use word solving strategies in combination with sense of language and meaning in a smoothly orchestrated system.
- Realize when they do not comprehend and go back to search for clarification through examining words, sentences, or longer stretches of text.
- Understand how a text is organized as a way of checking on accuracy and understanding.
- Learn more about decoding new words from the act of reading.
- Expand vocabulary through their reading.

Processing Strategies in Writing—most second grade children are still expanding their ability to:

- Spell correctly in their writing the words they know, including those recently studied and learned.
- Produce writing that is mostly conventionally spelled.
- Write words easily and fluently so that they can produce longer pieces of text.
- Make connections between the texts that they hear read aloud or read for themselves and their own writing, including the use of a variety of words and literary language.
- Select appropriate words, for example, transition words and phrases, in the production of varied sentence patterns in their writing.
- Make word choices that convey their intended meaning and make their writing interesting.
- Acquire and use technical words to make their writing more accurate.
- Use simple punctuation (periods, question marks, exclamation marks, quotation marks) in their writing.
- Use a range of word-solving strategies while writing continuous text.
- Use resources (such as word walls and charts) to assist in the production of writing.
- Use capitalization correctly in sentence structure.
- Proofread and edit their writing.
- Revise their writing, including word choice and sentence construction, to make it more interesting or clear.

categories that help them internalize principles about how words work. They realize that a word can have more than one meaning and that two words may mean the same (synonyms), mean the opposite (antonyms), or sound the same but have different meanings (homonyms).

Writing Words

Second graders are expanding their knowledge of the high frequency words they can write and by the end of the year have made good progress on producing with conventional spelling hundreds of the most frequently used words in English. They write words fluently, with efficient and legible handwriting, and they use their knowledge of letter-sound relationships and word parts to make good attempts at spelling new and more complex words.

Processing Strategies in Reading

Second graders are ready to spend a great deal of time reading, applying their existing strategies to longer stretches of print and more challenging texts. They are expanding their ability to take words apart, using a range of word solving skills, while reading for meaning. They use visual features of print, punctuation, meaning, and language syntax within a smoothly operating system that is always directed toward comprehending. Their comprehension includes a range of "in the head" strategies, for example:

- Solving words.
- Monitoring and self-correcting reading (using various sources of information).
- Gathering and searching for essential information.
- Predicting what will come next within a word, within phrases, and across a text.
- Maintaining fluency and phrasing.
- Adjusting reading for different purposes and to the structure of different texts.
- Making connections between the text and their own personal experience, other texts they've read, and their knowledge of the world.
- Inferring, or going beyond the words of a given text to know what is implied but not stated.
- Summarizing, or accumulating information in summary form so that it can be remembered and applied to reading the rest of the text.
- Synthesizing, or adjusting their own knowledge as they learn from the text.
- Analyzing, or examining literary elements of text (such as language features).
- Criticizing, or making judgments about any aspect of the text.

The true purpose of phonics is to enable the reader to use word solving while reading for understanding. Through applying strategies to reading continuous texts, students will greatly accelerate their reading powers, with most children reading level L or M with fluency and understanding by the end of the year. They will automatically recognize and know (or figure out) the meaning of most of the words in these texts. They will also begin to understand more sophisticated uses of language, such as idioms, vocabulary words that are seldom used in oral language, literary phrases, and metaphor.

Processing Strategies in Writing

As writers, second graders produce longer pieces of text that contain a large proportion of conventionally spelled words. They can quickly access known words and write them fluently; they are expected to accurately spell words they know and/or are studying in the spelling curriculum.

Their writing is legible because they have internalized efficient habits of handwriting, and they can check their writing for accurate spelling. They are becoming more interested in the craft of writing, which involves attention to word choice, sentence structure, and voice. They make connections between their own writing and the texts that they hear read aloud or read for themselves, and that includes the use of a greater variety of words and of literary language. They are learning to select appropriate words, for example, transition words and phrases, in the production of varied sentence patterns in their writing, and they may learn and use technical words. Within a smooth writing process, children employ a range of word-solving techniques. They understand conventions such as capitalization. They further develop proofreading, editing, and revising skills, and they expand their use of resources such as word walls, charts, and other reference materials to help them spell words while writing.

What to Do If Children Are Learning to Speak English

You are likely to have many children in your class who can speak not only one language but are learning a second or even a third language. If English is an additional language, then it will be important that you understand and value the child's expansion of both home and school languages. Usually, it takes several years for young children to learn English as a second language and to become able to read, write, and think consistently in their new language.

You will want to adjust your teaching to make sure that English language learners have access to everything you can help them learn about letters, sounds, and words. Often, these adjustments are minor and easy to implement, but they are necessary to promote learning on the part of these students. In addition, many of these adjustments will help *all* of the children in your classroom because you will be making instruction more explicit and clear.

Following, we have placed some general suggestions for each of four areas—oral language, reading, writing, and phonics instruction. It is obvious that these four areas overlap and are interconnected. Work in one area will tend to support learning in all other areas as well. Each lesson in this book has specific suggestions for helping English language learners acquire understanding of the principles.

Guidelines: Working with English Language Learners

Oral Language

1. Show children what you mean when you give directions. You may need to act out certain sequences of action and have children do it while you coach them. Have them repeat directions to each other or say them aloud as they engage in the activity. Support them during their first attempts rather than expecting independence immediately.
2. Give English language learners more "wait and think" time. You could say, "Let's think about that for a minute" before calling for an answer. Demonstrate to students how you think about what you are going to say.
3. Paraphrase and summarize for students. Repeat the directions or instructions several different ways, watching for feedback that they understand you. Paraphrase until you can see that they understand.
4. Use pictures and objects that children understand and can connect to their homes and neighborhoods. At the same time, avoid examples that may be completely strange to children and to which they have difficulty bringing meaning.
5. Use short simple sentences in shared reading, interactive writing, and oral conversations. Avoid complex, embedded sentences that children will find hard to follow if they are just learning English. When a complex sentence is used (for example, in read-aloud or shared reading), watch for evidence of confusion on the part of students and paraphrase with simpler sentences when necessary.
6. Bring the children's familiar world into the classroom through family photos, holiday souvenirs, and objects from home. Expand the children's world by bringing in other objects that will give them new experiences.
7. Demonstrate using language structures while talking about familiar topics. Involve children in games that require repeating these simple language structures, for example: "My name is _____." "_____ has two brothers." "I like to eat _____." "Josiah likes to (verb)."
8. Make instruction highly interactive, with a great deal of oral language surrounding everything children are learning.
9. Expand the activities using children's names. Learn how to pronounce children's names as they say them in their own language. Be sure that you are pronouncing all children's names correctly and clearly as you draw their attention to the particular word that is a child's name. Help children learn the names of other children in the class by using them in sentences and placing them on charts.
10. Engage English language learners in repeating and enjoying songs, rhymes, and repetitive chants. Incorporate body movements to enhance children's enjoyment of poetry and help them to remember and understand the language better.

Reading

1. Provide an extensive collection of simple alphabet books so that children can encounter the same letters, in the same sequence, with picture examples in different texts.
2. Read aloud often to students; in general, it is wise to increase the amount of time that you read aloud and discuss books with students. Be sure that the material you are reading to students is comprehensible, that is, within their power to understand with your support.
3. Stick to simple and understandable texts when you read aloud to students. Watch for signs of enjoyment and reread favorites. Rereading books to children will help them acquire and make use of language that goes beyond their current understandings.
4. Be sure that children's own cultures are reflected in the material that you read aloud to them and that they read for themselves. They should see illustrations with people like themselves in books as well as their own culture reflected in food, celebrations, dress, holidays, everyday events, and so on.
5. Understand that shared reading involves children in a great deal of repetition of language, often language that is different from or more complex than they can currently use in speech. This experience gives children a chance to practice language, learn the meaning of the words, and use the sentence structure of English.
6. Use a shared reading text over and over, inserting different names or different words to vary it. Rhythmic and repetitive texts are beneficial to English language learners. This repetition will give children maximum experience with the syntax of English and will help them to develop an implicit understanding of noun-verb agreement, plurals, and other concepts. Once a text is well known in shared reading, it can serve as a resource to children. Revisit shared reading texts for examples of language structure and for specific words and their meaning.
7. Include English language learners in guided reading groups, even if you have to begin with very simple texts. Guided reading is a very valuable context for working with English language learners because you can scaffold their reading and their language through an introduction that clears up confusion and you can observe them closely to gain information as to the accuracy and ease of their reading. Through observation and discussion, you can find what is confusing to them and respond to their questions.
8. Be sure to use oral language, pictures, concrete objects, and demonstration when you introduce stories to help children untangle any tricky vocabulary or concepts. When they are reading in texts for themselves in guided and independent reading, they may encounter words that they can "read" (that is, pronounce using phonics skills) but do not understand.
9. In guided reading, help children relate new words to words they already know. During and after reading, check with children to be sure they understand vocabulary and concepts; build into lessons a time when children can bring up any words they did not know.
10. Include word work on a regular basis in the guided reading lessons. Make strong connections to what they have been learning in phonics and word study.

Writing

1. Value and encourage children's drawing, as it represents thinking and connects their ideas to early writing. Spending a few moments drawing may help them more easily form the language they need.
2. Have children repeat several times the sentence they are going to write so that they will be able to remember it. If the sentence is difficult to remember, that may be a sign that it is too complex for the present level of language knowledge; consider simplifying the structure or rephrasing the sentence so that it is easier. It is beneficial to work in interactive writing with small groups of Grade 2 English language learners.
3. Focus on familiar topics and everyday experiences in interactive writing so that children can generate meaningful sentences and longer texts. Reread the piece of interactive writing many times, encouraging fluency as children gain control over the language.
4. Guide children to produce some repetitive texts that use the same sentence structure and phrases over and over again, so that children can internalize them.
5. Know that once a text has been successfully produced in interactive writing and children can easily read it, this text is a resource for talking about language—locating specific words, noticing beginning and ending sounds, noticing rhymes, and so on.
6. Encourage English language learners to write for themselves. Demonstrate how to think of something to write and repeat it so that you remember it. Demonstrate how to say words slowly, providing more individual help and demonstration if needed. Accept language that is not perfect English grammar; children will gradually expand their knowledge.
7. Surround children's independent writing with a great deal of oral language. Talk with them and help them put their ideas into words before they write. Encourage them to tell their stories and share their writing with others and extend their meanings through talk.
8. Provide a great many models of writing for English language learners—interactive writing, shared reading, charts about people in the room or experiences. Encourage them to reread and revisit these models to help them in their writing. In the beginning, they may use phrases or sentences from charts around the room, varying their own sentences slightly. Gradually, they will go beyond these resources, but models will be a helpful support for a time.
9. Learn something about the sound systems of the children's first languages. That knowledge will give you valuable insights into the way they "invent" or "approximate" their first spellings. For example, notice whether they are using letter/sound associations from the first language or whether they are actually thinking of a word in the first language and attempting to spell it.
10. Accept spelling that reflects the child's own pronunciation of words, even if it varies from standard pronunciation. Notice the strengths in the child's attempts to relate letters and sounds. Show that you value attempts rather than correcting everything the child writes.

Phonics and Word Study

① Use many hands-on activities so that children have the chance to manipulate magnetic letters and tiles, move pictures around, and work with word and name cards.

② Be sure that the print for all charts (ABC charts, name charts, shared writing, picture and word charts, etc.) is clear and consistent so that children who are working in another language do not have to deal with varying forms of letters.

③ Make sure your English language learners are not sitting in an area that is peripheral to the instruction (for example, in the back or to the side). It is especially important for these learners to be able to see clearly and hear all instruction.

④ Provide a "rehearsal" by working with your English language learners in a small group before you provide the minilesson to the entire group. Sometimes they may find it more difficult than other children to come up with words as examples; however, only a few minutes (for example, thinking of *s* words) will help these learners come up with responses in whole-group settings. It will not hurt them to think about the concepts twice because that will provide greater support.

⑤ Use real objects to represent pictures and build concepts in children's minds. For example, bring in a real lemon that children can touch and smell rather than just a picture of a lemon. When it is not possible to use real objects to build concepts, use clear pictures that will have meaning for children. Picture support should be included whenever possible.

⑥ Be sure to enunciate clearly yourself and accept children's approximations. If they are feeling their own mouths say the sounds (or approximations), they will be able to make the connections. Sounds and letters are abstract concepts, and the relationships are arbitrary. It will be especially complex for children whose sound systems do not exactly match that of English. They may have trouble saying the sounds that are related to letters and letter clusters.

⑦ Accept alternative pronunciations of words with the hard-to-say sounds and present the written form to help learners distinguish between them. Minimal pairs (sounds that are like each other, have similar tongue positions, and are easily confused, such as *s* and *sh, r* and *l, sh* and *ch, f* and *v*) are often quite difficult for English language learners to differentiate. English language learners often have difficulty with inflected endings *(s, ed).*

⑧ Speak clearly and slowly when working with children on distinguishing phonemes and hearing sounds in words, but do not distort the word so much that it is unrecognizable. Distortion may confuse English language learners in that it may sound like another word that they do not know.

⑨ Use the pocket chart often so that children have the experience of working with pictures and words in a hands-on way. They can match pictures with words so that the meaning of words becomes clearer.

⑩ Work with a small group of English language learners to help them in the application activity and make your instruction more explicit. Notice concepts that they find particularly difficult and make note to revisit them during word work.

Inside the Classroom: Organizing to Teach

As the schedules demonstrate, ideally, your explicit phonics lessons are embedded in a rich language and literacy framework that offers an organized combination of experiences, each of which contributes uniquely to children's literacy development. We describe a Language and Literacy Framework for Grade 2 that features three blocks for learning: Language and Word Study, Reading Workshop, and Writing Workshop

Language and Literacy Framework

BLOCKS & ORGANIZATION	BEGINNING OF YEAR CURRICULUM COMPONENTS	KEY TRANSITIONS	END OF YEAR CURRICULUM COMPONENTS
Language and Word Study Whole Group	Interactive Read-Aloud Language and Word Play Phonics/Word Study • Minilesson • Active Exploration • Application • Connection to Reading and Writing *Select from:* • Modeled/Shared Reading • Modeled/Shared/ Interactive Writing • Handwriting • Interactive Edit	*From short texts that can be read in one lesson to longer texts that require sustained reading for longer periods of time and over several days or a week.* *From oral to mostly silent reading.* *From daily, active exploration of Word Study principles to learning spelling words in a more formal study system.*	Interactive Read-Aloud/ Literature Discussion Word Study Minilesson/ Buddy Study Spelling System *Select from:* • Modeled/Shared-Reading • Modeled/Shared Interactive Writing • Handwriting • Interactive Edit
Reading Workshop Small-Group and Individual Work	Guided Reading Independent Work (centers or individual seats) Sharing and Evaluation	*From several shorter independent work activities in reading workshop to longer periods of independent reading and writing.* *From a variety of active centers that involve talk with others to longer, sustained individual work on reading and writing.*	Guided Reading Independent Reading • Minilesson • Reading and Conferring • Sharing and Evaluation Work at Quiet Literacy Centers or Silent Independent Work at Seats
Writing Workshop Whole-Group, Small-Group, and Individual Work	Minilesson Independent Writing and Conferring Interactive Writing or Guided Writing (small group) Sharing and Evaluation	*From a classroom hum of soft voices to longer periods of engaged silence while working.*	Minilesson Independent Writing and Conferring Guided Writing Sharing and Evaluation

Language and Word Study

The language/word study block includes a variety of activities designed to immerse children in language and help them learn about it. We recommend about thirty to forty-five minutes for the language/word study block, and you will usually be working with the entire group.

Interactive Read-Aloud By hearing written language read aloud, children learn about the structure, or syntax, of written language, which is different in many ways from oral language. Reading aloud is very important for second grade children because the language structures and vocabulary that you meet in books are foundational not only for learning to read for themselves but for expanding their comprehending strategies as they move into more complex texts.

Phonics/Word Study During the language/word study block, you can take the opportunity to provide a brief, lively minilesson on some principle related to the use of letters, sounds, or words.

The minilesson is followed by an application activity that involves exploration of the principle. The minilessons in this volume are examples of minilessons that are appropriate for second grade children. You will want to select many of the easier concepts from the continuum for children who are less experienced and move on to the more challenging concepts if your group, in general, is more advanced.

The Buddy Study Spelling system involves children in a more formal word study process. It is used along with the minilesson. Each child has a "buddy" who is similar in spelling/reading ability.

This system is described in detail in *Word Matters* (Pinnell & Fountas, 1998). The five days of word study activities begin with a minilesson focusing on a spelling principle. See *Teaching Resources* for basic framework and forms. Lessons outlining the Buddy Study Spelling System can be found in the "Word-Solving Actions" section.

Modeled/Shared Reading Most second graders no longer need the very basic understandings that kindergarten and first grade children acquire through shared reading, but, as children become more competent in reading for themselves, shared reading still offers opportunities to enjoy the sound of language, to use structures unique to written language, and to support phrased, fluent reading.

Modeled/Shared/Interactive Writing Modeled writing involves demonstrating the writing process for children. Teachers often "think aloud" about any aspect of writing, for example, word selection, message composition, layout of print, punctuation, word solving, and text organization.

Shared writing involves the composition of a common text by a group of children. Guided by the teacher, they are able to participate in the writing process to develop a meaningful text that may be any genre, for example, a letter, description, story, label, sign, or note.

Interactive writing involves a "sharing the pen" process in which children make contributions by coming up to the easel and writing some words and letters (for a detailed description, see McCarrier, Pinnell, & Fountas, 2000). In second grade you will use interactive writing in a small group for children who are having difficulty with writing and need the "hands-on" support of this transition tool. You can also use interactive writing with small groups of children who need more support in developing their writing strategies—both in composing and in constructing messages.

Handwriting A five- to ten-minute minilesson once a week on letter formation will improve the legibility of student work. The handwriting lesson includes demonstation and guided practice. For example, one student can write on a chalkboard or flipchart while the others work on their own. Then the children spend time practicing formation of letters, words, and sentences.

Interactive Edit An interactive edit is a brief activity (typically no more than five minutes long) that focuses on conventions. You work with dictated sentences that present appropriate challenges related to capitalization, punctuation, grammar, or spelling. You can have one child write it correctly on the easel for all to see while the rest use clipboards, or you can display the sentences on a chart, having the students copy and edit them individually or as partners.

Reading Workshop

At the beginning of the year, your reading workshop block includes guided reading and independent learning activities, but by the end of the year, children will be spending most of their time reading silently. We recommend about sixty minutes for reading workshop.

Guided Reading Guided reading involves small-group instruction within which teachers provide specific instruction on effective reading strategies. For a detailed description of guided reading, see Fountas & Pinnell (1996) and Pinnell & Fountas, (1998, Chapter 18).

Small reading groups are homogenous in terms of students' development of a reading process at a particular point in time. Using a gradient of texts organized according to level of difficulty, you select a book that is within the learners' control but offers a small amount of challenge. You introduce the book, and then each member of the group reads the text softly (or silently) to himself.

While children are reading, you have the opportunity to observe for effective behaviors (including, *but not limited to,* application of phonics principles) and to interact briefly with children. These interactions can support their application of principles you are teaching in word study. Following the reading, you discuss the meaning of the story and teach for processing strategies.

Independent Work While you are working with a small group of children in guided reading, the other children are engaged in a variety of independent activities. Many teachers like to use "centers," which means that children are working with materials in designated areas of the room.

Other teachers prefer to work with the whole class on most activities or for children to work on the same activity at their desks or tables—individually, with a partner or as a small group. Either option is effective, as long as children are engaged in active, interesting, and effective reading, writing and word study options. *The minilessons in this book can be used with either option.*

Think Book As children move through second grade, they can make greater use of writing for a variety of purposes—taking notes, using writing to organize thinking, writing down simple and helpful rules and principles, making lists, and so on. A new item for second graders is a *Think Book,* which helps children become accustomed to using notebooks and journals.

Suggestions for Managing and Using Centers for Word Study

- Clearly organize supplies so that only one kind of material is in a single container.
- Label supplies with both words and pictures.
- Using words and pictures, label the place on the shelf where the container is stored.
- Have all supplies that children will need for a given activity organized and available.
- Teach children routines for getting and returning materials.
- Establish and explicitly teach the routines that will be needed for a learning activity.
- Post simple directions in the center using both words and pictures.
- Limit the number of routines children are expected to follow—a few essential activities can be varied to explore different principles (for example, sorting).
- Stick to a predictable, consistent schedule.
- Introduce only one new application activity each day—typically, children will engage in one activity related to a principle over a period of three to five days.
- Place needed resources (charts, word wall) on the wall near the center so that they will be available.
- "Walk through" the activity so that you can accurately estimate the time it will take.
- Allocate an appropriate amount of time for selected activities and teach children the routines so that they can perform them at a good rate.
- Teach children to speak softly while working independently and model this behavior by speaking softly yourself.
- Have regular meetings with children to self-evaluate the productivity of work in the word study center.

The Think Book is an individual notebook that may be used for particular purposes at any time during the day, for example, to respond to interactive read-aloud, write notes for a piece of writing, or make quick sketches for later discussion. Teach children how to keep the Think Book in a special place and use it *only* when you directly ask them to write something. By using this notebook, children will be building a foundation for using notebooks and journals for reading and writing in grades 3–6.

Sharing and Evaluation At the end of the reading period, you may want to have a brief whole group time so that children can share some of the writing or their discoveries in the word study center.

Writing Workshop

The writing workshop involves a minilesson on some aspect of writing, a time when children work on their own writing with teacher support, and a sharing time. We recommend about sixty minutes.

Minilesson A writing minilesson is designed to demonstrate specific principles related to the conventions and craft of writing. The first minilessons of the year will be procedural in topic, for example, showing children how to use the paper and other writing materials.

Independent Writing and Conferring Children write independently while you interact with individuals and sometimes with small groups, helping them clarify and expand their messages. Individual conferences are a good time to remind children of what they have learned in the word study minilessons. You will also gather very valuable information that will help you select and design effective and timely word study minilessons. Writing is important for second grade children because they using all of the word, letter, and sound knowledge that they have accumulated to increase their understanding of spelling principles but also because they are expanding their ability to express ideas through writing.

Guided Writing Most second grade students can work more independently in writing than can younger children because they can spell so many words. They also will have learned how to use resources such as the word wall, personal dictionaries, and high frequency word lists. When students have learned the routine of working independently and silently, you can begin to bring together small, needs-based groups to work on specific aspects of writing.

Interactive Writing Use interactive writing for small groups of students who still need considerable help in producing a piece of writing. Bringing them together in a small group makes it possible to explicitly teach the concepts they need to know; the group support of interactive writing helps them to go beyond the writing that they could do alone.

Sharing and Evaluation In a brief sharing period at the end of the time, children can discuss their writing. Along with a discussion of the meaning and voice of the stories children write, you can take this opportunity to reinforce the learning in your word study minilesson.

Phonics Minilessons That Really Work

Organization, Space, and Materials Make a Difference

When you teach a minilesson, it is very important to do so in a clearly defined space in which all children can see and hear easily. They should be able to sit comfortably on the floor without touching other children. You will want an easel, a small white dry-erase board, markers, magnetic letters, and a vertical magnetic board. You will also need a pocket chart on which you can post letters or words on cards large enough for the whole group to see. The name chart, Alphabet Linking Chart, and Consonant Cluster Linking Chart are useful tools to have nearby, close enough for you to point to. Children should be able to see the word wall from where they sit.

Basic Principles: Designing/Implementing Effective Minilessons

Designing Effective Minilessons

- Focus on one principle that is appropriate and useful for your children at a particular point in time.
- State the principle in simple, clear terms.
- Think of a few good examples in advance so that you have them ready to show the children.
- Have in mind why you selected the minilesson, which probably will help you connect it to children's work in other components of the language/literacy framework; make connections explicit.
- Have in mind how you can connect your minilesson principle to the children's names (on the name chart).
- Design an application activity that children can do independently (after being taught routines) and that will be productive in their learning.
- Design multilevel activities that permit advanced children to go beyond the given activity and make more discoveries and allow children who are less experienced to complete the minilessons.

Implementing Effective Minilessons

- Have all materials organized and quickly available.
- Be sure that all children can see and hear as you demonstrate the principle or write examples on a chart.
- Make a clear statement of the principle as you begin the lesson, or clearly state the principle at the end as children come to their own conclusions from examples.
- Use a conversational rather than a lecture style. Promote interaction so children can be active, engaged learners.
- Invite interaction so that children bring their own knowledge to bear on the application of the principle.
- Invite children to connect the principle and examples to their names; use names as examples when possible.
- Share examples and add examples from children (if children are unable to provide some examples, then either the principle is not clearly stated or it is too difficult).
- Keep minilessons brief; a few examples are enough.
- Make connections to previous word study minilessons or understandings and discoveries made in any other component of the Language and Literacy Framework.
- Check for understanding by asking children to locate and talk about examples.
- Summarize the minilesson by returning to the principle and stating it again.
- Place an example on the word wall for the children's response when teaching minilessons on words.
- Demonstrate the application activity explicitly so that you know children can perform it independently.
- Provide all necessary materials for the application activity in one place—for example, the word study center or a clearly defined and organized materials center.
- Convene children for a brief sharing period so that they can comment on what they have learned and you can reinforce the principle again.

We recommend using black or dark-colored markers on white or cream-colored chart paper. You may want to use colored transparent highlighter tape to emphasize certain words or letters, but, in general, it is better not to clutter up the examples with color-coding, which is usually a distraction for children. Also, it may confuse them; we want them to look at the distinctive features of letters—not the color! A random assortment of colors increases the appeal of tasks with magnetic letters without creating an identifier that may act as a distractor. If you have set up centers in your classroom, be sure that all the necessary materials are readily available in the word study center where students will use the application. If students work at their own tables, arrange materials in a central area or on each table. If the activity is new or difficult, place a model in clear view so that children can check their results. For additional information about the materials, read the Materials & Routines in *Teaching Resources*.

Classroom Routines for Effective Teaching

Routines refers both to the basic routines of how to live and learn in the classroom (where to store materials or how to participate in a class meeting, for example) and to a series of instructional procedures such as making words, sorting words, and playing word study games that children will use again and again as they learn a range of concepts. Teach the routines carefully when you first begin using word study minilessons. First, demonstrate the activity precisely, and then have everyone do it at once. If you run into a logistical problem (not having enough magnetic letters, for example), ask children to take turns with a partner or in a small group and check each other. When you know that children can perform the routine on their own, then they can work individually, as partners, or in groups. (You will need to demonstrate the activity again in relation to the particular principle you are exploring in the minilesson.) For a comprehensive overview of routines, see the descriptions and directions in *Teaching Resources;* additionally, you will find many references to routines in the Month-by-Month Planning Guide.

Consider Your Language and Delivery

Minilessons should be conversational. You will want to state the principle clearly at the beginning of the lesson (or at the end, if you think it is appropriate for students to derive it through inquiry and example). Your tone should be that of *I'm going to show you something interesting about how words work* or *What do you notice about these words?* Invite children to make connections to words they know. Invite them to contribute further examples and recognize and praise their thinking even if the examples don't quite fit. Always try to understand their thinking and build on a partially correct response. Help them clarify their suggestions as necessary.

Remember that a minilesson is *brief.* Don't let it go on too long. Depending on the particular principle, you'll need only a few examples to make an understanding clear. Your goal is for students to integrate some of these examples into their own thinking so they can connect them to new learning when they

Options for Application Activities

1. **Present the minilesson to the entire class, and then involve all children simultaneously in the application activity. They can work individually or with partners as you circulate around the room. Immediately follow the activity with sharing and evaluation.**
2. **Present the minilesson to the entire class, but involve children in application activities in small groups that you supervise. Have the rest of the children involved in independent reading/writing activities. Follow the activity with sharing as soon as all groups have worked with you.**
3. **Present the minilesson to the entire class and explain the application activity. Have children complete it first (simultaneously for the whole group) and then move to another independent activity. Work with small groups in guided reading or writing while children work independently.**
4. **Present the minilesson to the entire class and explain the application activity. On the same day, have children rotate to a word study center to complete the activity. Have a brief sharing and evaluation at the end of the period.**
5. **Present the minilesson to the entire class and explain the application activity. Over several days, have children rotate to a word study center to complete the activity. Have a brief sharing at the end of each day. Ask the children who participated to talk about what they learned.**

are working on their own. At the end of the minilesson, summarize the understanding you are trying to instill and take another moment to restate the principle. If appropriate, place an example on the word wall. Then explain and demonstrate the application activity.

So What Did We Learn? Sharing and Evaluation

After independent work, convene a brief sharing period in which children can discuss the principle and share their examples. This community meeting is a good way to ask children to evaluate themselves. You can ask how many completed the activity and ask them to self-evaluate their work. Recognizing their independent work gives it value and emphasis. If you have made a chart, refer to it again and restate the principle. You may want to add some of their examples. Recognize children's thinking as they share their ideas. Make further connections with reading and writing in other components of the Language and Literacy Framework.

Do this to find out what they learned.

Your Essential Tools for Teaching

Phonics Lessons and *Teaching Resources* comprise multiple tools that work together to support your teaching. The tools are:

- The Lesson Selection Map
- The Assessment Guide (in *Teaching Resources*)
- The Month-by-Month Planning Guide
- The Word Study Continuum: Systematic Phonics and Spelling

The Lesson Selection Map

The Lesson Selection Map catalogs all Grade 2 lessons by Continuum category and suggested time of year (early, middle, or late). In creating this Map we considered how children's experience is likely to build throughout the year as a result not only of the direct teaching of principles related to letters, sounds, and words but also of their daily experiences hearing written language read aloud and participating in shared, independent, and guided reading and interactive, guided, and independent writing.

Again, this Map is not a rigid sequence; it is a continuum of easier to harder principles. It will help you think in broad strokes about the program you are designing for the children in your classroom, which must always be considered in light of your observations and assessments of what your students know and can do at any given point. If children are very knowledgeable and experienced, you may decide that some lessons can be abbreviated or omitted. You will also want to design more lessons on principles children need (see *Teaching Resources,* Lesson Template). If children are very inexperienced in a given area, lessons may need to be repeated using different examples.

A whole year of lessons may seem overwhelming; however, keep in mind that:

- Any one lesson takes ten to fifteen minutes or less.
- Some lessons can be skipped or shortened.
- Some lessons will go very quickly because children have acquired most of the requisite knowledge already through reading and writing in the classroom.

Even if you do not use all the lessons, reflecting on the Map will help you be aware of the entire body of knowledge that is important for second graders to acquire as a foundation for literacy learning.

The Map contains two kinds of information:

- Using the rows, you can take one category of the Continuum and follow children's development of a principle from easier to harder throughout the year. For example, lessons on word structure begin with syllables and plurals. You'll help your students become more sensitive to the structure of words by having them identify syllables and contractions and listen for the patterns in words. Later in the year you will give closer attention to prefixes, suffixes, plurals and the like in words and help your students develop insights into the structure of words by identifying and manipulating these parts. Each category of the Continuum offers room for growth throughout the year.
- You can look down the columns to get a sense of the understanding children are building across the entire continuum. Working across categories, you ensure that children not only develop their word solving strategies but also continually add to the list of high frequency words they can read automatically.

Look at the Map both ways. Your students might be more advanced in one area than another. It is obvious that planning a program is not always neat and tidy; however, the concept of easier to harder, in combination with assessment, should allow you to design an efficient program that:

- Makes the most of what children know by allowing them to work at the edge of their knowledge.
- Ensures clear, explicit teaching and meaningful practice to deepen conceptual knowledge.
- Ensures that principles do not have to be taught again and again.
- Does not blindly demand that you spend time on exercises teaching what children already know.

Here are some easy directions for using the Map as a practical tool in lesson planning:

- Reproduce a copy of the Map to keep in the front of your lesson-planning book. (Another copy of the Map is included in *Teaching Resources.*)
- When you have used a lesson, highlight it on the Map or place a check on the line next to it.
- Write additional lessons that you design and implement in the empty spaces in each section. (See Lesson Template in *Teaching Resources.*)
- Make notes about adaptations that are helpful to your children because of their native language, background, or culture.
- If you determine that children do not need a particular lesson because they have learned the principle in some other context, cross out the line or highlight it in another color.

Used in this way, the Map becomes a record as well as a planning tool, because you will know at a glance what you have taught (or determined not to be necessary) and what you need to consider teaching next.

Grade 2 – Lesson Selection Map

Letter/Sound Relationships LS

early

___ **LS 1** Recognizing Beginning Consonant Clusters with *r* (Make-Say-Check-Mix)
___ **LS 2** Identifying Words with Short Vowel Sounds (Making Words)
___ **LS 3** Identifying Words with Long Vowel Sounds (Making Words)
___ **LS 4** Identifying Long and Short Vowel Sounds in Words (Vowel Concentration)
___ **LS 5** Recognizing Beginning Consonant Clusters with *s* (Make-Say-Check-Mix)
___ **LS 6** Recognizing Beginning Consonant Clusters (Closed Word Sort)
___ **LS 7** Recognizing Words with Vowels and *r* (Word Grid Game)
___ **LS 8** Identifying the *y* Sound in Words (Two-Way Sort)
___ **LS 9** Identifying Words with the *oo* Vowel Team (Two-Way Sort)

mid

___ **LS 10** Recognizing Ending Consonant Clusters (Go Fish)
___ **LS 11** Noticing Double Consonants in the Middle of Words (Follow the Path)
___ **LS 12** Identifying Medial Consonant Sounds and Letters (Matching Words)
___ **LS 13** Summarizing Consonant Digraphs (Blind Sort)
___ **LS 14** Recognizing Consonants with Two Sounds: *c*, *g*, and *th* (Two-Way Closed Sort)
___ **LS 15** Summarizing Consonants with Two Sounds: *c*, *g*, and *th* (Concentration)

late

___ **LS 16** Recognizing and Using *ai, ay, oa, ee, ea, ow* Vowel Combinations (Making Words)
___ **LS 17** Identifying Words with *ai, ay, ee, ea, oa, ow* (Crazy Eights)
___ **LS 18** Recognizing *st* Consonant Clusters in Words (Blind Sort)
___ **LS 19** Recognizing *mp, nd, nk, nt* Ending Consonant Clusters (Lotto)
___ **LS 20** Recognizing Beginning and Ending Consonant Clusters (Dominoes)
___ **LS 21** Recognizing *ou, ow*, and *aw* Vowel Sounds (Crazy Eights)
___ **LS 22** Learning the Sound of *a* as in *Cake* 1: *a-e, ay, ai* (Blind Sort)
___ **LS 23** Learning the Sound of *a* as in *Cake* 2: *ea, ey, eigh, aigh* (Blind Sort)

Spelling Patterns SP

early

___ **SP 1** Learning a Variety of Word Patterns (Making Words)
___ **SP 2** Learning Onsets and Rimes: *-ack, -ick* (Word Sort)
___ **SP 3** Learning the Silent *e* Pattern (Making Word Pairs)
___ **SP 4** Learning Onsets and Rimes: *-ame, -ate, -ake* (Three-Way Word Sort)
___ **SP 5** Learning Onsets and Rimes: *-ice, -ide, -ine* (Three-Way Rhyme Sort)

mid

___ **SP 6** Learning Onsets and Rimes: *-obe, -oke, -ore, -ope* (Making Words)
___ **SP 7** Learning Onsets and Rimes: *-ing, -ink* (Lotto)
___ **SP 8** Learning Patterns with Double Letters (Making Words)
___ **SP 9** Learning Patterns with *ee* Double Vowels (Follow the Path)
___ **SP 10** Learning Patterns with *oo* Double Vowels (Say and Sort)
___ **SP 11** Learning Onsets and Rimes: *-ail, -ain, -an* (Three-Way Word Sort)
___ **SP 12** Learning Onsets and Rimes: *-ight* (Follow the Path)

late

___ **SP 13** Learning about CVVC Patterns (Making Words)
___ **SP 14** Summarizing Phonograms (Building Words)
___ **SP 15** Summarizing Spelling Patterns with *a* (Building Words)
___ **SP 16** Recognizing Patterns with Ending Consonant Clusters (Say and Sort)
___ **SP 17** Learning about Vowel Combination Spelling Patterns (Go Fish)

High Frequency Words HF

early

___ **HF 1** Learning High Frequency Words 1 (Make-Say-Check-Mix)
___ **HF 2** Learning High Frequency Words 2 (Lotto)
___ **HF 3** Learning High Frequency Words 3 (Follow the Path)

mid

___ **HF 4** Learning High Frequency Words 4 (Concentration)
___ **HF 5** Learning High Frequency Words 5 (Word Sort)
___ **HF 6** Learning High Frequency Words 6 (Word Search)

late

___ **HF 7** Learning High Frequency Words 7 (Word Ladders)
___ **HF 8** Learning High Frequency Words 8 (Go Fish)
___ **HF 9** Learning High Frequency Words 9 (Word Search)

Word Meaning WM

early

___ **WM 1** Recognizing and Using Synonyms (Concentration)

___ **WM 2** Recognizing and Using Antonyms (Concentration)

mid

___ **WM 3** Exploring Synonyms and Antonyms (Lotto)

___ **WM 4** Exploring Simple Homophones 1 (Sentence Pictures)

___ **WM 5** Exploring Simple Homophones 2 (Word Grids)

late

___ **WM 6** Exploring Simple Homographs (Sentence Pictures)

___ **WM 7** Learning about Words with Multiple Meanings (Sentence Pictures)

Word Structure WS

early

___ **WS 1** Recognizing Compound Words (Making Words)

___ **WS 2** Making Compound Words (Word Match)

___ **WS 3** Forming Possessives (Making Sentences)

___ **WS 4** Recognizing Syllables in Words with Double Consonants (Word Puzzles)

___ **WS 5** Forming the Past Tense by Adding *ed* 1 (Say and Write)

___ **WS 6** Forming the Past Tense by Adding *ed* 2 (Three-Way Sort)

___ **WS 7** Recognizing Syllables in Words (Syllable Sort)

___ **WS 8** Identifying Syllables in Words (Syllable Lotto)

___ **WS 9** Forming Plurals with *s* and *es* (Say and Sort)

mid

___ **WS 10** Understanding Contractions of *am, is,* and *will* Phrases (Contraction Lotto)

___ **WS 11** Forming Contractions of *not* and *are* Phrases (Contraction Concentration)

___ **WS 12** Summarizing Contractions *(am, is, will, are, not, have, had)* (Word Sort)

___ **WS 13** Forming Comparisons with *-er, -est* (Word Pictures)

___ **WS 14** Forming Past Tense: Double the Consonant and Add *ed* (Making Words)

___ **WS 15** Adding *-er* and Doubling the Consonant (Making Words)

___ **WS 16** Adding Suffixes to Words Ending in *y* (Make and Write)

___ **WS 17** Forming Past Tense: Summary for *ed* Words (Three-Way Sort)

___ **WS 18** Forming New Words: Summary for Adding *s, ed, ing* (Make and Write)

___ **WS 19** Forming Plurals with Words Ending in *y* (Make and Write)

___ **WS 20** Forming Abbreviations (Abbreviation Lotto)

late

___ **WS 21** Adding *-er* to Words Ending in *y* (Suffix Lotto)

___ **WS 22** Forming Comparatives with *-er* and *-est* (Say and Sort)

___ **WS 23** Forming Plurals for Words Ending in *f* (Make and Write)

___ **WS 24** Changing Spelling to Form the Plural (Lotto)

___ **WS 25** Making Plural Forms: Summary (Sort and Write)

___ **WS 26** Recognizing Closed Syllables (Taking Words Apart)

___ **WS 27** Recognizing Open Syllables (Taking Words Apart)

___ **WS 28** Recognizing Open and Closed Syllables (Say and Sort)

Word-Solving Actions WSA

early

___ **WSA 1** Learning How to Learn Words: Buddy Study 1 (Choose, Write, Build, Mix, Fix, Mix)

___ **WSA 2** Learning How to Learn Words: Buddy Study 2 (Look, Say, Cover, Write, Check)

___ **WSA 3** Learning How to Learn Words: Buddy Study 3 (Buddy Check)

___ **WSA 4** Learning How to Learn Words: Buddy Study 4 (Making Connections)

___ **WSA 5** Learning How to Learn Words: Buddy Study 5 (Buddy Test)

___ **WSA 6** Recognizing and Using Syllables (Syllable Race)

___ **WSA 7** Making Connections Between Words That Start the Same (Making Connections)

___ **WSA 8** Making Connections Between Words That End the Same (Make and Write)

mid

___ **WSA 9** Making Connections Between Words with the Same Pattern (Pattern Highlight)

___ **WSA 10** Using Word Parts to Solve Words (Word Ladders)

___ **WSA 11** Using What Is Known to Solve Words (Word Race)

___ **WSA 12** Using Letter Clusters to Solve Words (Word Grid Game)

___ **WSA 13** Adding Letters to the Beginning and End of Words (Making New Words)

late

___ **WSA 14** Removing Letters from the Beginning and End of Words (Word Pairs)

___ **WSA 15** Connecting Words That Sound the Same but Look Different (Homonym Lotto)

___ **WSA 16** Connecting Words—Same Spelling, Different Meaning (Concentration)

The Assessment Guide

There is a time to use systematic, planned tasks that are designed to gather information about particular aspects of children's growing word knowledge. Performance-based assessment may involve observation, but it also includes more formal structured experiences in which the tasks are standardized. Standardization of the procedure creates a reliable assessment situation that is more objective than daily ongoing observation. The goal is to get a picture of what each student can do independently. Usually, you do not actively teach during a performance-based assessment, but you may make teaching points after the neutral observation.

The Assessment Guide includes more formal, performance-based Assessment Tasks across the nine Categories of Learning (six for second grade). You can use these tasks in multiple ways: as diagnostic tools to determine what your students know and need to know; as monitoring tools to help you keep track of your teaching and your students' learning; and as documentation of the teaching and learning you and your students have accomplished over time. You and your colleagues may even decide to place some of the summary sheets in your children's permanent cumulative folders as a way to create a schoolwide record of the phonics and word study program.

As noted, the opportunities for informal assessment are embedded in each lesson in the Assess feature. Look for more formal assessment opportunities across the second grade's six Categories of Learning in the Assessment Guide inside *Teaching Resources.*

The Month-by-Month Planning Guide

The Month by Month Planning Guide outlines and describes a year of instructional contexts and ways to organize that instruction—whole-group, independent, and small-group work. It also lists the instructional routines (which include everything from where to store supplies to how to play Syllable Lotto) you will need to teach so that children will be able to complete the application activities. Although you'll teach only a few new routines each month, children's knowledge accumulates. Once a routine (sorting, for example) has been learned, children can use it again and again in different ways. Finally, our yearly plan suggests specific lessons by month, from easier to harder, and lists specific competencies that you can determine through observation and assessment. These simple assessments of what children can do will help you identify children who are having more difficulty and may need repetition or additional word study work in a small group.

This yearly plan is a ladder of support as you work with children over time. Don't worry if your group does not progress in precisely the same way this plan implies. They may learn more rapidly in one area than another, but referring to the plan will help you reflect on areas where you need to invest more instruction.

If you are new to teaching (or new to teaching in this area), you may want to follow this month-by-month plan closely. You will learn from the experience and over the year will begin to see how you can adapt the plan for greater effectiveness with your own students and also how you can teach more efficiently.

Here's a more detailed look at how the year is broken up and the progression of activities.

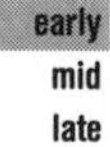

Early Second Grade

At the beginning of the year, most second graders have consolidated their understanding of the phonological system of the language and can use this knowledge as a tool for expanding their knowledge of how sounds and letters work together in words. They recognize and can write most of the simple high frequency words and have developed systems for learning more. They can easily use letter-sound information to take words apart in reading, that is, "phonics," and to construct words in writing, "spelling," but they still have far to go in terms of sophisticated understandings of how words work. The early second grade lessons include some information that children may well have acquired in Grade 1, and you may want to skip them or review the information only briefly. Others in this early category are designed so that if children need more experience, you can repeat with different examples or extend them for deeper learning. In other words, you can move through these lessons quickly or spend more time, depending on your observation and assessment of children's growth.

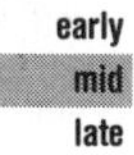

Middle Second Grade

The middle lessons represent a substantive body of knowledge that helps second graders develop the understandings they need to solve the more complex words they meet in texts and spell the wider range of words they need to express themselves in writing. This category includes some very systematic, step-by-step explorations of spelling patterns and word structure. Here, also, you will find generative lessons that can be repeated with different examples to give children more practice if needed. Also, if you think they need more work on a principle, you can expand the learning as guided in that section of the plan.

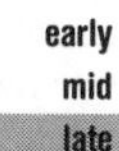

Late Second Grade

Later lessons expand children's knowledge to more complex principles. We have included here some advanced principles that you may decide are too difficult for your second graders at this time. Nevertheless, they provide for the range of learning needs that may be found in Grade 2.

Month-by-Month Planning Guide – September

In September your primary goal is to establish the organization of the classroom, the learning environment, and the feeling of community in the classroom. Review the schedule with children so that they know what is expected of them throughout the day and help them learn how to listen and participate. Explain and demonstrate routines; have children self-evaluate after the lesson and at group share.

Lessons in September focus on concepts that children may have learned in first grade but need to summarize and systematize. As a teacher, you will observe children and decide which concepts they need to work on and which they need only reminders of. Whatever students know, you will continue to work on high frequency words, constantly adding to the words students know and in the process helping them develop systems for learning words.

A goal for September is establishing the routines for the Buddy Study System, which you will be using all year. First, you will want to establish the structure of the word study block, which includes a lesson, word study application, and group share. Take as many days as you need for students to understand the structure so that they easily go from the lesson to the application activity and know that they should be thinking about discoveries that they can share when the class meets at the end of the period. When you are helping students learn the Buddy Study System, you will also be using a lesson based on a principle of word study. Select principles that you think will be clear to students while at the same time you demonstrate routines for the Buddy Study System. We have suggested some principles for September, and any of these would be appropriate for your focus: short vowel sounds, word patterns, beginning consonant clusters, high frequency words, compound words.

In September you will want to teach routines that are used in recommended lessons, for example, making and checking words, matching words, sorting and locating words, using consonant clusters and short vowel sounds, and using onsets and rimes.

Throughout September and at the end of the month, observe children to determine whether they can engage in basic classroom routines and use the routines of the Buddy Study System. Check to see whether they can identify consonant clusters at the beginning and end of words, locate words in text by blending sounds and looking at first letters, use knowledge of vowel sounds to solve words in reading and spelling, and recognize simple compound words. Also, assess their acquisition of high frequency words; they should be constantly adding to the list of words they know.

Organization of Instruction: *Whole group for minilesson, learning routines, and sharing; individual work on applications with teacher support; partner work on Buddy Study System.*

Learning Contexts

Start the year by establishing a predictable schedule that includes three blocks of time: language and word study, reading workshop, and writing workshop. Read aloud every day in the language/word study block and begin to build children's knowledge of poems as well as many stories and informational texts that will build vocabulary. Build a sense of community by teaching them to care for the room and use the routines in an orderly way. Keep a chart of children's first and last names handy so that you can make connections with your word study lessons.

New Routines to Teach

- Routines for sitting, moving, listening, getting a turn to speak, joining in on reading, listening to you read aloud, and participating in the minilesson.
- Routines for getting, using, and putting away materials.
- Names of class activities, for example, "community meeting time," or "Buddy Study System."
- The regular daily schedule.
- Word sort with consonant clusters.
- Saying and blending sounds.
- Locating words using sound-to-letter correspondence.
- Using onsets and rimes (on cards) to make words.
- Making and writing high frequency words and words with patterns.
- Making and taking apart simple compound words.
- Using the Consonant Cluster Linking Chart.
- Using Make-Say-Check-Mix Sheets.
- Using List Sheets—Compound Words.
- Routines for the Buddy Study System (five days).
- Routines for independent work in reading and writing.

Suggested Lessons

LS 1	Recognizing Beginning Consonant Clusters with *r* (Make-Say-Check-Mix)
LS 2	Identifying Words with Short Vowel Sounds (Making Words)
SP 1	Learning a Variety of Word Patterns (Making Words)
HF 1	Learning High Frequency Words 1 (Make-Say-Check-Mix)
WS 1	Recognizing Compound Words (Making Words)
WS 2	Making Compound Words (Word Match)
WSA 1	Buddy Study 1 (Choose, Write, Build, Mix, Fix, Mix)
WSA 2	Buddy Study 2 (Look, Say, Cover, Write, Check)
WSA 3	Buddy Study 3 (Buddy Check)
WSA 4	Buddy Study 4 (Making Connections)
WSA 5	Buddy Study 5 (Buddy Test)

Assessment — Children Can:

- Listen, share, and work productively in community meeting time and group share.
- Work independently and with a partner to perform applications.
- Identify consonant clusters in words, both those with one sound (digraphs) and those with two sounds (blends) at the beginning of words.
- Identify the number of syllables in words.
- Sort words by syllables.
- Blend sounds and locate words using sound-to-letter relationships.
- Make and write high frequency words and consistently add to their repertoire of high frequency words; in a testing situation can write the words they have studied.
- Independently perform routines for the Buddy Study System.

October

By October, you will have established the basic classroom routines as well as the word study structure of: (1) lesson; (2) application; and (3) group share. Demonstrate and remind them over several weeks of lessons. No time will be lost because at the same time, you will be delivering the lessons on principles that students need to learn.

Lessons in October include using larger chunks of written language such as consonant clusters, long and short vowel sounds, and onsets and rimes. Continue to work with students on adding high frequency words to their repertoires and explore principles related to word structure, including syllables and inflectional endings. Word solving actions involve children in breaking down words into syllables and connecting words to solve them.

New routines to teach include using forms such as the Four-Way Sort Sheet (see *Teaching Resources*), the Make-Say-Check-Mix Sheet (see *Teaching Resources*), the List Sheet, and the Word Pairs Sheet, as well as playing Lotto and Concentration. Be sure that children know how to perform the tasks that you are sending with them to do at home; if possible, have a meeting with parents to demonstrate how to work with children on word study at home. If you plan to have a weekly or monthly newsletter, alert parents that they will see brief suggestions to help their children with phonics and spelling.

By the end of October, you will want to assess children's ability to blend sounds and use consonant clusters at the beginning of words and to use patterns such as the CVVC structure. You should expect children to have added to their repertoire of high frequency words and to make connections between words by how they start and end. Learning about word structure involves adding the ending *ed* and recognizing and using syllables and vowels.

For assessment, be sure that children can identify and use consonant clusters at the beginning of words, make words with the CVVC construction, are making progress with high frequency words, work easily with *ed* endings. A basic understanding for word solvers is recognizing that words have syllables and that there is a vowel in each syllable; check to be sure that your students can clap syllables and know that each syllable has a vowel. Also, notice whether they are recognizing patterns.

Organization of Instruction: *Whole group for minilesson and sharing; independent work in application activities with teacher support; partner work in Buddy Study System.*

Learning Contexts

You may need to repeat lessons for the Buddy Study routines several times, using new content; or, you may simply need to remind them of the routines. Continue building children's literacy experiences in enjoyable ways through reading aloud and enjoying poetry as well as engaging daily in reading and writing continuous texts. Be sure that basic classroom routines are well established before beginning small-group instruction or expecting children to engage in application activities independently. Whenever you introduce a new routine or application activity, have all children do it simultaneously, or, you may demonstrate in a "fishbowl." Establish responsibility for taking home materials and present your word study program at a parent meeting. Set up a word wall to which you can add examples from lessons.

New Routines to Teach

- Using the Three-Way and Four-Way Sort Sheets and Cards.
- Using the Making Words Sheet.
- Lotto—high frequency words.
- Using onset and rime cards to make words.
- Concentration with long and short vowel sounds as well as synonyms.
- Make-Say-Check-Mix Sheets.
- Word sorting—beginning consonant clusters, vowels, onsets and rimes, and phonograms.
- Using List Sheets—syllables and double consonants.
- Recognizing syllables and dividing words made with magnetic letters.
- Consonant Cluster Linking Chart.
- Follow the Path.
- Word Study Notebook.
- Word Grid—syllables.
- List Sheets—adding *ed*.
- Follow the Path/Syllable Race.
- Word Pairs Sheet.

Suggested Lessons

LS 3	Identifying Words with Long Vowel Sounds (Making Words)
LS 4	Identifying Long and Short Vowel Sounds in Words (Vowel Concentration)
LS 5	Recognizing Beginning Consonant Clusters with *s* (Make-Say-Check-Mix)
SP 2	Learning Onsets and Rimes: *-ack, -ick* (Word Sort)
HF 2	Learning High Frequency Words 2 (Lotto)
WM 1	Recognizing and Using Synonyms (Concentration)
WS 3	Forming Possessives (Making Sentences)
WS 4	Recognizing Syllables in Words with Double Consonants (Word Puzzles)
WS 5	Forming the Past Tense by Adding *ed* 1 (Say and Write)
WS 6	Forming the Past Tense by Adding *ed* 2 (Three-Way Sort)
WS 7	Recognizing Syllables in Words (Syllable Sort)
WSA 6	Recognizing and Using Syllables (Syllable Race)
WSA 7	Making Connections Between Words That Start the Same (Making Connections)

Assessment — Children Can:

- Demonstrate increased knowledge of high frequency words.
- Recognize beginning consonant clusters (blending *r* and *s*) and use this information while reading continuous text.
- Represent beginning consonant clusters (blending) in words that they write.
- Recognize long and short vowel sounds in words.
- Recognize *ed* endings in reading and add *ed* to make past tense in writing.
- Make connections between and among words by their beginning sounds and letters.
- Recognize syllables in words and use them in reading and writing.
- Recognize simple synonyms.

Month-by-Month Planning Guide – November

November lessons expand children's knowledge of word parts and patterns. They will be working with word patterns, double vowels, vowels with *r*, onsets and rimes, and syllables. At the same time, they should be adding to the high frequency words they know. With each lesson, add examples to the word wall; you will also want to display the charts you make in lessons so that children can refer to them.

Continue developing children's language resources through reading aloud to them and discussing stories. Across all components of the framework, make connections with word study lessons. If children are becoming very independent with application activities, they can rotate to the word study center (or do them at their desks or tables) during the reading workshop, leaving you more time to work with guided reading groups. October, November, and December are traditionally festive months but, without detracting from children's enjoyment, keep the focus on interesting content areas and avoid spending too much time on holidays as the curriculum. If child are working well in word study, introduce the Word Study Notebook. Have children use the notebook only at your direction. They can begin by recording weekly tests in the notebook.

Monitor children's work in the Buddy Study System. It is important for them to become expert and efficient in using these study strategies so that they can perform them quickly with their attention on features of words. If the routines of word study (lesson, application, and sharing) are not in place, reexamine your schedule and make sure that it is predictable and manageable. Also, look at the way materials are organized and be sure that tasks are clear for children. Avoid teaching new routines until children are very comfortable with the ones they know.

Continue sending home word study materials and publish a weekly or monthly newsletter that focuses on classroom news, children's writing, poetry, and other areas but also includes one or two suggestions for working on word study at home. New routines to teach include playing Follow the Path with high frequency words, Concentration with antonyms, and Lotto with syllables. You'll also be teaching children how to do a multiple sort, that is, a set of words that can be sorted more than one way.

Organization of Instruction: *Whole group for minilesson and sharing; independent work in application activities with teacher support; partner work in Buddy Study System.*

Learning Contexts

Continue developing children's knowledge of language through reading aloud children's literature and engaging them in all components of the framework. If the routines of word study are not well established (lesson, application, and sharing as well as the Buddy Study System), work more with children to be sure that they understand tasks and can work independently. If children are working independently in word study, they can complete the application activity during reading time, along with additional reading and writing activities, giving you the opportunity to work with at least three reading groups per day. With each new word study lesson you teach, add one or two examples to the word wall. If a small group of second graders are having difficulty writing, work with them in a small group, combining shared, interactive, and independent writing.

New Routines to Teach

- Using the List Sheet for words with silent *e*.
- Follow the Path—high frequency words.
- Using a Word Study Notebook.
- Using the Three-Way Sort Card.
- Using the Two-Way Sort Sheets.
- Using the Three-Way Sort Sheets.
- Word Grid game.
- Using Two-Way Sort Cards.
- Using Three-Way Rhyme Sheets.
- Using Word Grids.
- Concentration for antonyms.
- Lotto—syllables and phonograms.
- Sorting words using consonants, vowels with *r*.
- Using Two-Column Sheet.
- Word Grid—words that end the same.

Suggested Lessons

- **LS 6** Recognizing Beginning Consonant Clusters (Closed Word Sort)
- **LS 7** Recognizing Words with Vowels and *r* (Word Grid Game)
- **LS 8** Identifying the *y* Sound in Words (Two-Way Sort)
- **LS 9** Identifying Words with the *oo* Vowel Team (Two-Way Sort)
- **SP 3** Learning the Silent *e* Pattern (Making Word Pairs)
- **SP 4** Learning Onsets and Rimes: *-ame, -ate, -ake* (Three-Way Word Sort)
- **SP 5** Learning Onsets and Rimes: *-ice, -ide, -ine* (Three-Way Rhyme Sort)
- **HF 3** Learning High Frequency Words 3 (Follow the Path)
- **WM 2** Recognizing and Using Antonyms (Concentration)
- **WS 8** Identifying Syllables in Words (Syllable Lotto)
- **WS 9** Forming Plurals with *s* and *es* (Say and Sort)
- **WSA 8** Making Connections Between Words That End the Same (Make and Write)

Assessment — Children Can:

- Recognize the role of the vowel before the letter *r* and represent it in spelling.
- Notice the combination of vowel + *r* while solving words in reading.
- Place words in categories by looking at the onset (first part) or the rime (last part).
- Accurately spell some words with the CVC*e* pattern.
- Demonstrate an increase in known high frequency words.
- Make connections among words that end the same.
- Successfully form plurals using *s* and *es*.
- Identify syllables in a word.
- Identify words with the vowel team *oo* and the *y* sound.
- Recognize and use simple antonyms.

December

Incorporate in an integrated way all components of the language/literacy framework. By December, children should be proficient in the routines of the word study component and the Buddy Study System. You'll be selecting one lesson per week to use on day one of the system; children choose their spelling words from this lesson. You may want to teach a few other lessons during the week, but children will not use the words from these lessons for the Buddy Study System. Children can continue to use the Word Study Notebook for assigned word study activities such as charts, sorts, and other activities linked to lessons.

New routines to teach include using games such as Go Fish, Follow the Path, Lotto, and Concentration for different purposes. Continue adding words to the word wall; you may want to assess children's knowledge of high frequency words. Remove words that all the children know so that you will have room for more exemplar words. Help children learn to use both the word wall and the word study charts as resources when writing.

Identify children who are having difficulty in applying word study principles in reading and writing. These students will need word work in guided reading; make strong and explicit connections to word study principles. Also, you may want to place them in a small group and work for a brief period on interactive and/or independent writing, reminding them of what they have learned about words. Assess children's ability to connect words and place them in categories by rimes. Notice children's ability to write and read words with endings you have taught, as well as their accurate reading and writing of high frequency words.

Organization of Instruction: *Whole group for minilesson and sharing; independent work in application activities with teacher support; partner work in Buddy Study System; small groups for guided reading and interactive writing (for children who need more support).*

Learning Contexts

Continue implementing all elements of the language/literacy framework, including phonics lessons, application, and sharing. Remember to make connections between word study and other framework components, such as read-aloud. After the Buddy Study System is established, you will be providing one core lesson on day one each week. Select lessons that center on the most important principles for children to learn and draw spelling words from. You then can select other lessons as needed to use on other days. Identify children who are having difficulty applying word study principles in reading and writing. For those students, be sure to include word work in guided reading and work with them in a small group using interactive writing. Continue adding examples to the word wall; you may want to remove high frequency words that children know very well. During the reading workshop, begin to gradually increase the time children spend reading independently. Help children use references as tools: lesson charts and word wall.

New Routines to Teach

- Using the List Sheet for onsets and rimes and double letters.
- Go Fish—ending consonants.
- Follow the Path using double consonants in the middle of words and double vowels.
- Matching words using medial sounds.
- Lotto using phonograms, onsets and rimes, synonyms and antonyms, and contractions.
- Concentration using high frequency words and contractions.
- Using the Two-Column Sheet for contractions.
- Using the Three-Way Sort Sheet for contractions.
- Word Ladders—using word parts.

Suggested Lessons:

LS 10	Recognizing Ending Consonant Clusters (Go Fish)
LS 11	Noticing Double Consonants in the Middle of Words (Follow the Path)
LS 12	Identifying Medial Consonant Sounds and Letters (Matching Words)
SP 6	Learning Onsets and Rimes: *-obe, -oke, -ore, -ope* (Making Words)
SP 7	Learning Onsets and Rimes: *-ing, -ink* (Lotto)
SP 8	Learning Patterns with Double Letters (Making Words)
SP 9	Learning Patterns with *ee* Double Vowels (Follow the Path)
HF 4	Learning High Frequency Words 4 (Concentration)
WM 3	Exploring Synonyms and Antonyms (Lotto)
WS 10	Understanding Contractions of *am, is,* and *will* Phrases (Contraction Lotto)
WS 11	Forming Contractions of *not* and *are* Phrases (Contraction Concentration)
WSA 9	Making Connections Between Words with the Same Pattern (Pattern Highlight)

Assessment — Children Can:

- Connect words and place them in categories by looking at rimes *(-obe, -oke, -ore, -ope).*
- Read and write words with double letters and double vowels *(ee)*
- Demonstrate expansion of known high frequency words.
- Demonstrate ability to make connections among words that have the same patterns.
- Recognize and use simple antonyms and synonyms.
- Read and write contractions of *is, will, are, not* phrases.

Month-by-Month Planning Guide – January

Continue using all elements of the language/literacy framework and making explicit links to word study lessons when appropriate, gradually increasing the time children spend on reading (as opposed to center activities). Children can use the Word Study Notebook, starting from the back, to maintain a list or words to learn, or, this list may be in the Writing Workshop Folder. Provide explicit instructions to children on how to write in the notebook and to keep it in a special place.

Routines to teach include playing Concentration with words that have consonants that have two sounds and using several sheets: (1) Two-Way Sort Cards and Sheets for vowel combinations and for plural pairs; (2) Three-Way Sort Sheets for high frequency words; (3) Two-Way Sort Sheets and Cards; and (4) Three-Column Sheets for comparatives.

At midyear, you may want to do a more systematic assessment of children's knowledge of letters, sounds, and words. Assess children's knowledge of high frequency words at midyear. You may want to use the 150 words for Grade 2, highlighting those they know. Children can choose words from this list for use in the Buddy Study System. Additionally, assess children's ability to write and read words with consonant clusters and digraphs at beginnings and ends of words. Observe reading to determine children's ability to take words apart to solve them using letter clusters and onsets and rimes. Assess children's ability to represent ending consonant clusters and to flexibly use consonant digraphs, read words with double vowel patterns, write words with the *oo* vowel pattern, and recognize and use simple contractions. They should also be able to spell some words in past tense and add *-er* to words.

Organization of Instruction: *Whole group for minilesson and sharing; independent work in application activities with teacher support; partner work in Buddy Study System; small groups for guided reading and interactive writing (for children who need more support).*

Learning Contexts

Continue using all elements of the language/literacy framework, being sure to make word study connections across all three blocks of instruction, gradually increasing the time children spend reading longer texts. Carefully choose the core lesson for day one of the Buddy Study System; children will be choosing spelling words that exemplify this principle. As needed, use other lessons later in the week, but children will not be using these words for the Buddy Study System. Observe children carefully in reading, taking notes of their behavior to document application of word study principles to decoding words in continuous text. Look at their writing produces for evidence that children are using word study principles to produce accurate spellings. Do some systematic, mid-year assessment to identify children who need extra help on principles.

New Routines to Teach

- List Sheet for words that add *-er* and double the consonant.
- Using Two-Way Sort Cards and Sheets for consonants with two sounds and *oo* double vowels.
- Concentration using words with consonants having two sounds and plurals.
- Using the Three-Way Sort Sheet—high frequency words, phonograms, and past tense.
- Using the Three-Column Sheets to sort comparisons with *-er* and *-est* and suffixes ending in *y*.
- Using the List Sheet.
- Making Word Ladders.
- Blind Sort—consonant digraphs.
- Two-Way Closed Sort—consonant with two sounds.
- Using Word Study Notebooks.
- Word Grid Game.
- Using the Four-Box Sheet—comparatives with *-er* and *-est*.
- Word Race—using what is known.

Suggested Lessons

LS 13 Summarizing Consonant Digraphs (Blind Sort)
LS 14 Recognizing consonants with Two Sounds: *c, g,* and *th* (Two-Way Closed Sort)
LS 15 Summarizing Consonants with Two Sounds: *c, g,* and *th* (Concentration)
SP 10 Learning Patterns with *oo* Double Vowels (Say and Sort)
HF 5 Learning High Frequency Words 5 (Word Sort)
WS 12 Summarizing Contractions *(am, is, will, are, not, have, had)*
WS 13 Forming Comparisons with *-er, -est* (Word Pictures)
WS 14 Forming Past Tense: Double the Consonant and Add *ed* (Making Words)
WS 15 Adding *-er* and Doubling the Consonant (Making Words)
WSA 10 Using Word Parts to Solve Words (Word Ladders)
WSA 11 Using What Is Known to Solve Words (Word Race)
WSA 12 Using Letter Clusters to Solve Words (Word Grid Game)

Assessment — Children Can:

- Demonstrate expansion of known high frequency words.
- Recognize in reading and spell words with all common consonant digraphs.
- Know and identify consonants that are associated with more than one sound and give examples or locate words for each sound.
- Recognize words with double vowels *(oo).*
- Form past tense by adding *ed.*
- Add inflectional endings to words.
- Add *-er, -est* endings to show comparatives.
- Represent consonant clusters at the ends of words when writing *(-st, -mp, -nd, -nk, -nt).*

February

Based on January assessment, work in small groups with children who are having difficulty with word study principles. Your assessment may reveal the need to repeat some lessons before moving on to new ones. Continue using the Word Study Notebook as a vehicle for teaching children how to keep records, write simple rules, complete assignments, make lists, and use writing to support and organize their thinking. You may want to create at least three sections in the notebook, for example: (1) Tests; (2) Lessons; (3) Words to Learn.

Lessons in February bring together and systematize children's knowledge of phonograms and simple homophones. They continue to expand their knowledge of high frequency words and also learn more about solving words while reading by working with a range of suffixes. The emphasis in lessons is making children flexible as word solvers.

Routines to teach include Follow the Path and Lotto, as well as making a Word Search. Children will also be using Three-Way Sort Sheets, Word Ladders, and Word Pairs Sheets.

Assessment focuses on observing how children work flexibly with beginning and ending sounds to match or categorize letters and also to notice them in reading as part of word solving. In their writing, observe to see that they represent the wide range of phonograms that have been taught as well as consonant clusters and vowel combinations, and in reading, observe word solving to assure that children use what they know to take words apart. If they are having difficulty, provide explicit directions and demonstrations and link to word study lessons.

Organization of Instruction: *Whole group for minilesson and sharing; independent work in application activities with teacher support; partner work in Buddy Study System; small groups for guided reading and interactive writing (for children who need more support).*

Learning Contexts

Continue to assess children's knowledge by observing them in application activities and sharing and also to note their ability to apply principles in reading and writing. Work with small groups as needed to reinforce principles and give some children more practice. Use the Word Study Notebook to record examples and principles from word study lesson as well as for taking the buddy test. Make strong connections between word study lessons and other components of the language/literacy framework.

New Routines to Teach

- Three-Way Sort Sheets to work with onsets and rimes.
- Follow the Path—onsets and rimes.
- Word Searches—high frequency words.
- Using Lined Four-Box Sheets with homophones.
- Word Grids—homophones.
- Using the Three-Column Sheets to work with suffixes.
- Using Two-Way and Three-Way Sort Cards and Sheets to work with past tense.
- Lotto using abbreviations.
- Using Word Ladder Sheets.
- Using Word Pairs Sheet.

Suggested Lessons

SP 11 Learning Onsets and Rimes: *-ail, -ain, -an* (Three-Way Word Sort)
SP 12 Learning Onsets and Rimes: *-ight* (Follow the Path)
HF 6 Learning High Frequency Words 6 (Word Search)
WM 4 Exploring Simple Homophones 1 (Sentence Pictures)
WM 5 Exploring Simple Homophones 2 (Word Grids)
WS 16 Adding Suffixes to Words Ending in *y* (Make and Write)
WS 17 Forming Past Tense: Summary for *ed* Words (Three-Way Sort)
WS 18 Forming New Words: Summary for Adding *s, ed,* and *ing* (Make and Write)
WS 19 Forming Plurals with Words Ending in *y* (Make and Write)
WS 20 Forming Abbreviations (Abbreviation Lotto)
WSA 13 Adding Letters to the Beginning and End of Words (Making New Words)

Assessment — Children Can:

- Demonstrate growth in knowledge of high frequency words.
- Demonstrate accurate use of homophones by selecting words to place in sentences.
- Represent a wide range of phonograms (all that have been taught) in spelling words.
- Use word parts (phonograms, consonant clusters, vowel combinations) to decode words in reading.
- Sort words by phonograms.
- Read and write words using the *-ight* phonogram.
- Recognize and use simple homophones.
- Recognize and create changes in spelling by adding *es* and *ed* to words.
- Use conventional plural forms for words that end in *y*.

Month-by-Month Planning Guide – March

Give attention to word study across instructional contexts, and hold children accountable for what they know about spelling and word solving. Increase the time that children sustain their reading of longer texts. Watch children carefully to determine whether they are able to read for longer periods of time, and adjust center requirements for individuals.

Lessons in March help children become flexible with their knowledge by sorting words in different ways, making connections between words, and making Word Ladders, which require problem solving. They will be learning more spelling patterns and homographs as well as using phonograms and extending their knowledge of suffixes.

Routines to teach include making Word Ladders with high frequency words and using Lotto with ending consonant clusters and Crazy Eights with vowel digraphs.

Observe children's reading behaviors to note whether they are noticing and using their knowledge of consonant clusters and vowel digraphs at beginnings and ends of words. You can also look at writing samples to notice whether children are representing homophones and homographs and using vowel digraphs, spelling patterns, and suffixes. Continue recording the high frequency words that children can write, and you may want to give a quick test asking children to read a list of words. This will give you an idea of children's flexibility in reading and writing these important words.

Organization of Instruction: *Whole group for minilesson and sharing; independent work in application activities with teacher support; partner work in Buddy Study System; small groups for guided reading and interactive writing (for children who need more support).*

Learning Contexts

Continue using all elements of the language/literacy framework and giving attention to word study across instructional contexts. In the reading workshop, increase children's time reading longer texts. Continue using the Word Study Notebook to help children record and organize examples of words as well as to take their tests and list "words to learn." Monitor children's efficiency and independence in using the Buddy Study System; the five-day sequence of learning activities should not take much time. Expand their ability to connect words in several different ways. Continue to send information to children's homes as well as short, interesting word study activities they can do at home.

New Routines to Teach

- Using the Four-Box Sheet—words with multiple meanings.
- Lotto—suffixes.
- Three-Way Sort Sheets for vowel combinations.
- Crazy Eights—vowel digraphs.
- Two-Way Sort Cards and Sheets for consonant clusters.
- Lotto using ending consonant clusters and homonyms.
- List Sheets—CVVC patterns.
- Using Spelling Patterns Sheets (summarize phonograms).
- Word Ladders using high frequency words.
- Four-Box Sheets using comparatives.
- Two-Column Sheets for working with plurals.
- Using the Word Study Notebook.
- Concentration—two-vowel pattern.
- Make-Say-Check-Mix Sheet—CVVC patterns.
- Go Fish using high frequency words.

Suggested Lessons

LS 16 Recognizing and Using *ai, ay, oa, ee, ea, ow* Vowel Combinations (Making Words)
LS 17 Identifying Words with *ai, ay, ee, ea, oa, ow* (Crazy Eights)
LS 18 Recognizing *st* Consonant Clusters in Words (Blind Sort)
LS 19 Recognizing *mp, nd, nk, nt* Ending Consonant Clusters (Lotto)
SP 13 Learning about CVVC Patterns (Making Words)
SP 14 Summarizing Phonograms (Building Words)
HF 7 Learning High Frequency Words 7 (Word Ladders)
WM 6 Exploring Simple Homographs (Sentence Pictures)
WS 21 Adding *-er* to Words Ending in *y* (Suffix Lotto)
WS 22 Forming Comparitives with *-er* and *-est* (Say and Sort)
WS 23 Forming Plurals for Words ending in *f* (Make and Write)
WSA 14 Removing Letters from the Beginning and End of Words (Word Pairs)

Assessment — Children Can:

- Use the Word Study Notebook as directed.
- Demonstrate increased knowledge of high frequency words.
- Accurately read homophones and homographs.
- Accurately represent ending consonant clusters when writing words *(mp, nd, nk, nt)*.
- Use knowledge of vowel digraphs in reading and writing.
- Use knowledge of consonant clusters in reading and writing words.
- Accurately read and spell words with the CVVC pattern.
- Use knowledge of spelling patterns in writing and reading.
- Demonstrate using connections between words to solve words in reading and writing.
- Read and write words with the *ed* suffix.
- Read and write plurals.
- Form comparisons with *-er, -est*.

April

In reading workshop, increase children's time reading longer texts and reduce time in work centers if you are using them. You may want to restructure independent work to include just one activity in addition to reading (and sometimes writing about reading). Over the five-day period, children could rotate to: (1) word study application—two or three days; (2) listening center; (3) poetry. You would be using the quieter centers and helping students sustain reading for longer periods of time, and students could also perform application activities for the lessons that you provide "outside" the Buddy Study System.

Continue to use the Word Study Notebook to help children organize their knowledge. This notebook is an important artifact. You can use it as an evaluation tool to assess children's progress in word study. In addition, the notebook provides a record for students of their own learning. It presents an organized picture of their productivity, a visible example of the results of their work. Through using this notebook, they will learn to self-evaluate and catalog their growing knowledge. They should gain a growing sense of their accomplishments.

Lessons in April continue to focus on patterns in words as well as noticing word parts. Children gradually expand their knowledge of double vowels *(ou, ow, aw)*. They also add to their knowledge of plurals by exploring those difficult words that change spelling. Routines to teach include Lotto with plurals, Dominoes with beginning and ending consonants, Crazy Eights with vowel combinations, and blind sorting with letters representing the sound of *a*. Children use several forms, including the the Four-Way Sort Sheet (see *Teaching Resources*). Observe children's reading and writing behavior to determine the extent to which they can read and write words with vowel combinations and understand words with multiple meanings.

Organization of Instruction: *Whole group for minilesson and sharing; independent work in application activities with teacher support; partner work in Buddy Study System; small groups for guided reading and interactive writing (for children who need more support).*

Learning Contexts

Increase children's time reading longer texts and begin to structure the reading workshop so that children independently engage in reading plus a word study application activity or the listening center. Take an inventory of children's knowledge of letters, sounds, and words by looking at their Buddy Tests and Making Connections Sheets, looking at writing samples to check which concepts children control, and doing systematic observation of reading behaviors to note word-solving strategies. You may also want to check suggestions on individual lessons and do some very specific word study assessment such as having children read and write lists of words, locate particular kinds of words, write words in categories, or write examples of principles. This inventory will help you identify children who need extra help with some principles before moving to the next grade. Provide evidence to parents of children's growth in phonics and spelling.

New Routines to Teach

- Four-Way Sort Card and Sheet—ending consonant clusters.
- Lotto—plurals and homonyms.
- Four-Box Sheets.
- Dominoes—beginning and ending consonants.
- Word Ladders—beginning and ending consonants.
- Crazy Eights—vowel sounds (combinations).
- Blind sort—sound of *a*.
- Using Four-Way Sort Cards and Sheets—representing the sound of *a* and ending consonant clusters.
- Two-Sided Spelling Patterns Sheets.
- Word Search—spelling patterns representing *a*.
- Word Search—high frequency words.
- Word Study Notebooks.

Suggested Lessons

LS 20 Recognizing Beginning and Ending Consonant Clusters (Dominoes)
LS 21 Recognizing *ou, ow,* and *aw* Vowel Sounds (Crazy Eights)
LS 22 Learning the Sound of *a* as in *Cake* 1: *a-e, ay, ai* (Blind Sort)
SP 15 Summarizing Spelling Patterns with *a* (Building Words)
SP 16 Recognizing Patterns with Ending Consonant Clusters (Say and Sort)
HF 8 Learning High Frequency Words 8 (Go Fish)
WM 7 Learning about Words with Multiple Meanings (Sentence Pictures)
WS 24 Changing Spelling to Form the Plural (Lotto)
WS 25 Making Plural Forms: Summary (Sort and Write)
WSA 15 Connecting Words That Sound the Same but Look Different (Homonym Lotto)

Assessment — Children Can:

- Demonstrate increased knowledge of high frequency words.
- Demonstrate flexible use of word parts to decode words in write and spell words.
- Break words into syllables and identify vowel sounds within them by reading.
- Accurately represent words with vowel combinations and double vowels in spelling.
- Recognize and match plural and singular forms for words that change their spelling.
- Accurately read and write plural forms.
- Read and write a range of words in which the sound of *a* is represented with different letters and letter clusters.
- Understand words with multiple meanings.

Month-by-Month Planning Guide – May/June

In most schools, June means the end of a productive learning period. Continue the routines of instruction as close as possible to the last day of school. The more predictability children experience, the more they will sustain productive behaviors. Organize the reading workshop so that you provide a minilesson on reading followed by children's independent reading. By now, almost all children should be reading during the entire period. Note children who need extra help and, in collaboration with colleagues, make decisions about instruction and extra help during the following year.

Lessons in May and June extend children's knowledge of plurals, suffixes, and compound words. They explore the many different ways vowels can be represented as they examine the letters representing the sounds of *a*. Routines to teach include using several forms, including the List Sheet (for taking words apart) and the Word Grids (for high frequency words).

Work with children to self-evaluate their progress in learning about letters, sounds, and words. They can look at their highlighted lists of high frequency words and see how many they have learned. They can also examine their Word Study Notebooks and look at the body of work represented there. Send home with children their Word Study Notebooks.

Organization of Instruction: *Whole group for minilesson and sharing; independent work in application activities with teacher support; partner work in Buddy Study System; small groups for guided reading and interactive writing (for children who need more support).*

Learning Contexts	New Routines to Teach	Suggested Lessons	Assessment — Children Can:
Organize the reading workshop so that you provide a minilesson on reading followed by children's reading independently; they write in the Word Study Notebook each week in response to the minilesson. Test children on the 100 and 150 high frequency words for second grade and highlight the ones they know to send with the child to the next grade. A good way to make best use of the last weeks of school is to keep your core instruction going in as many ways as possible. Perform any final assessments for the year and summarize progress. If possible, send home reading and writing materials for children to use during the summer. Send home children's writing workshop folders and Word Study Notebooks.	▸ Using Two-Way Sort Sheets—open and closed syllables. ▸ Blind sort—sound of *a* as in *cake.* ▸ Using Four-Way Sort Sheets—sound of *a* as in *cake.* ▸ Go Fish—vowel combinations spelling patterns. ▸ Word Grids—high frequency words and two syllable words. ▸ Word Searches—high frequency words. ▸ List Sheets—taking words apart. and open and closed syllables. ▸ Word Searches—*a* pattern words. ▸ Lotto with vowel combinations. ▸ Concentration—homographs.	**LS 23** Learning the Sound of *a* as in *Cake* 2: *ea, ey, eigh, aigh* (Blind Sort) **SP 17** Learning about Vowel Combination Spelling Patterns (Go Fish) **HF 9** Learning High Frequency Words 9 (Word Search) **WS 26** Recognizing Closed Syllables (Taking Words Apart) **WS 27** Recognizing Open Syllables (Taking Words Apart) **WS 28** Recognizing Open and Closed Syllables (Say and Sort) **WSA 16** Connecting Words—Same Spelling, Different Meaning (Concentration)	▸ Demonstrate knowledge of 250+ high frequency words. ▸ Demonstrate ability to read and write words with vowel combinations that represent *a* as in *Cake.* ▸ Read and write words with vowel combination phonograms. ▸ Demonstrate expansion of knowledge of high frequency words. ▸ Use knowledge of syllabication to divide words. ▸ Recognize open and closed syllables.

The Word Study Continuum

Systematic Phonics and Spelling, Grades K–3

The Word Study Continuum is the key to the minilessons. Over the course of the school year, you will use it, in concert with the Month-by-Month Planning Guide, the Lesson Selection Map, and continuous assessment, to inform your work. The Continuum comprises nine Categories of Learning (six for second grade) your students need to develop over time; it is a comprehensive picture of linguistic knowledge. Although there are easier and more complex concepts within each category, we are not suggesting that there is a rigid sequence. Instead, we want to help children develop their abilities along a broad front, often using and learning about several different kinds of information simultaneously.

While instruction and assessment are embedded within classroom activities, both are systematic. Indeed, every aspect of the phonics minilessons is systematic, including the observation of children, collection of data on what children know about letters, sounds, and words, and the teacher's selection of lessons to fit the specific instructional needs of individual children. Teaching is efficient and systematic when lessons are carefully selected and sequenced to provide what children need to learn next.

The shaded area of the Continuum performs two important functions. First, it serves as a guide for introducing principles to children; second, it helps you understand what principles you can expect your students to fully control and when. You'll notice that the shaded areas cross grade levels. These shaded areas provide broad indicators of expected achievement; however, learning rate and time will vary with individual children as well as for different groups. In general, at grade level (the earliest period of time indicated by shading), you can begin to assess children's knowledge of a specific principle and refer to the principle during reading and writing activities. Additionally, you will select specific lessons that help them expand their knowledge of the chosen principle. At the latest time indicated by shading, take steps to ensure that children fully understand and can use the principle. You may need to increase time spent on lessons related to the principle or work with small groups of children who are still having difficulty.

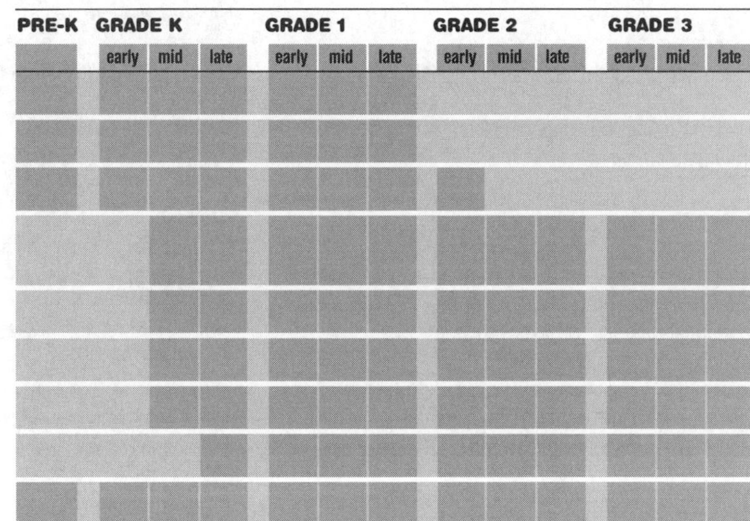

Early Literacy Concepts

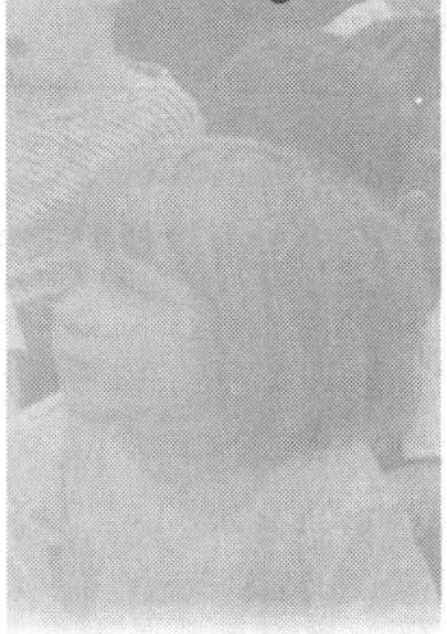

Learning about literacy begins long before children enter school. Many children hear stories read aloud and try out writing for themselves; through such experiences, they learn some basic concepts about written language. Nearly all children begin to notice print in the environment and develop ideas about the purposes of print. The child's name, for example, is a very important word. Kindergartners and first graders are still acquiring some of these basic concepts, and they need to generalize and systematize their knowledge. In the classroom, they learn a great deal through experiences such as shared and modeled reading and shared and interactive writing. Explicit teaching can help children learn much more about these early concepts, understand their importance, and develop ways of using them in reading and writing.

Early Literacy Concepts

PRINCIPLE	EXPLANATION OF PRINCIPLE (PRE-K · GRADE K early/mid/late · GRADE 1 early/mid/late · GRADE 2 early/mid/late · GRADE 3 early/mid/late)
Distinguishing between print and pictures	“We read the print to find out what the words say.”
Understanding the purpose of print in reading	“We look at the print to read the words in stories and other messages.”
Understanding the purpose of print in writing	“We write letters and words so readers will understand what we mean.”
Recognizing one's name	“Your name has letters in it.” “Your name starts with a letter that is always the same.” “Your name starts with a capital letter. The other letters are lowercase.” “Your name is always written the same way.” “You can find your name by looking for the first letter.”
Using letters in one's own name to represent it or “write” a message	“You can write the letters in your name.” “You can use the letters in your name along with other letters to write messages.”
Understanding the concept of “letter”	“A letter has a name and a shape.”
Understanding the concept of “word”	“A word is a group of sounds that mean something.” “A word in writing is a group of letters with space on either side.”
Using left-to-right directionality of print	“We read and write from left to right.”
Understanding the concepts of *first* and *last* in written language	“The first word in a sentence is on the left.” “The last word in a sentence is before the period or question mark.” “The first letter in a word is on the left.” “The last letter in a word is before the space.” “The first part of a page is at the top.” “The last part of a page is at the bottom.”
Understanding that one spoken word matches one group of letters	“We say one word for each word we see in writing.”
Using one's name to learn about words and make connections to words	“Your name is a word.” “You can connect your name with other words.”

PRE-K · GRADE K (early, mid, late) · GRADE 1 (early, mid, late) · GRADE 2 (early, mid, late) · GRADE 3 (early, mid, late)

Early Literacy Concepts, continued

Principle	Explanation of Principle
Locating the first and last letters of words in continuous text	"You can find a word by noticing how it looks." "You can find a word by looking for the first letter." "You can check a word by looking at the first and last letters."
Understanding the concept of a sentence	"A sentence is a group of words that makes sense."

Phonological Awareness

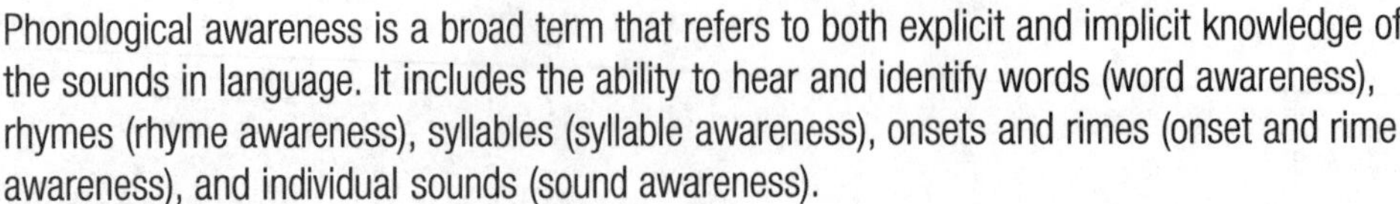

Phonological awareness is a broad term that refers to both explicit and implicit knowledge of the sounds in language. It includes the ability to hear and identify words (word awareness), rhymes (rhyme awareness), syllables (syllable awareness), onsets and rimes (onset and rime awareness), and individual sounds (sound awareness).

Phonemic awareness is one kind of phonological awareness. Phonemic awareness refers to the ability to identify, isolate, and manipulate the individual sounds *(phonemes)* in words. Principles categorized as phonemic awareness are labeled Phonemes [PA] in this Continuum.

Phonological awareness (and phonemic awareness) is taught orally or in connection with letters, when it is called *phonics.* Phonics instruction refers to teaching children to connect letters and sounds in words. While very early experiences focus on hearing and saying sounds in the absence of letters, most of the time you will want to teach children to hear sounds in connection with letters. Many of the lessons related to this section begin with oral activity but move toward connecting the sounds to letters. You will not want to teach all of the PA principles in this Continuum. It is more effective to teach children only two or three ways to manipulate phonemes in words so that they learn how words work.

Principles related to letter/sound relationships, or phonics, are included in the Letter/Sound Relationships category of this Continuum.

Phonological Awareness

PRE-K · GRADE K (early, mid, late) · GRADE 1 (early, mid, late) · GRADE 2 (early, mid, late) · GRADE 3 (early, mid, late)

	Principle	Explanation of Principle
Words	Hearing and recognizing word boundaries	**"You say words when you talk." "You can hear words in a sentence if you stop after each one. [*I - have - a - dog.*]"**
Words	Segmenting sentences into words	**"You can say each word in a sentence. [*I - like - to - go - shopping.*]"**
Rhyming Words	Hearing and saying rhyming words	**"Some words have end parts that sound alike. They *rhyme* [*new, blue*]." "You can hear the rhymes in poems and songs." "You can say words and hear how they rhyme."**
Rhyming Words	Hearing and connecting rhyming words	**"You can hear and connect words that rhyme [*fly, high, buy, sky*]."**
Rhyming Words	Hearing and generating rhyming words	**"You can make rhymes by thinking of words that end the same. [*I can fly in the ___.*]"**

PRE-K · GRADE K (early, mid, late) · GRADE 1 (early, mid, late) · GRADE 2 (early, mid, late) · GRADE 3 (early, mid, late)

Phonological Awareness, continued

	Principle	Explanation of Principle (PRE-K / GRADE K early, mid, late / GRADE 1 early, mid, late / GRADE 2 early, mid, late / GRADE 3 early, mid, late)
Syllables	Hearing and saying syllables	" You can hear and say the syllables in a word [*to-ma-to, tomato*]. " " Some words have one syllable [*cat*]. " " Some words have two syllables [*can-dy, candy*]. " " Some words have three or more syllables [*um-brel-la, umbrella*]. "
	Blending syllables	" You can blend syllables together [*pen-cil, pencil*]. "
Onsets and Rimes	Hearing and segmenting onsets and rimes	" You can hear and say the first and last parts of a word [*c-ar, car; pl-ay, play*]. "
	Blending onsets with rimes	" You can blend word parts together [*d-og, dog*]. "
Phonemes [PA]	Hearing and saying individual phonemes (sounds) in words	" You can say a word slowly. " " You can hear the sounds in a word [*m-a-k, make*]. "
	Segmenting words into phonemes	" You can say each sound in a word [*b-a-t*]. "
	Hearing and saying two or three phonemes in a word	" You can say a word slowly to hear all the sounds [*r-u-n*]. "
	Hearing and saying beginning phonemes in words	" You can hear the first sound in a word [*s-u-n*]. " " You can say a word to hear the first sound. "
	Hearing and saying ending phonemes in words	" You can hear the last sound in a word [*r-u-n*]. " " You can say a word to hear the last sound. "
	Hearing similar beginning phonemes in words	" Some words sound the same at the beginning [*run, race*]. " " You can connect words that sound the same at the beginning [*mother, mom, make*]. "
	Hearing similar ending phonemes in words	" Some words sound the same at the end [*win, fun*]. " " You can connect words that sound the same at the end [*get, sit, Matt*]. "
	Blending two or three phonemes in words	" You can blend sounds together to say a word [*d-o-g = dog*]. "
	Adding phonemes to the beginning of words	" You can add sounds to a word [*it + s = sit*]. " " You can add sounds to the beginning of a word [*rate + c = crate*]. "
	Manipulating phonemes at the beginning of words	" You can change the first sound in a word to make a new word [*not, hot*]. "
	Manipulating phonemes at the ending of words	" You can change the last sound in a word to make a new word [*his, him*]. "
	Hearing and saying middle phonemes in words	" You can hear and say the sound in the middle of a word [*s-u-n*]. "
	Hearing similar middle phonemes in words	" Some words sound the same in the middle [*cat, ran*]. " " You can match words that sound the same in the middle [*stop, hot, John*]. "
	Hearing four or more phonemes in a word	" You can say a word slowly to hear all the sounds [*s-p-e-n-d*]. "

early mid late early mid late early mid late early mid late
PRE-K GRADE K GRADE 1 GRADE 2 GRADE 3

Phonological Awareness, continued

PRINCIPLE	EXPLANATION OF PRINCIPLE
Phonemes [PA]	PRE-K · GRADE K (early, mid, late) · GRADE 1 (early, mid, late) · GRADE 2 (early, mid, late) · GRADE 3 (early, mid, late)
Hearing and identifying phonemes in a word in sequence	"You can say a word slowly to hear all the sounds, from first to last [/r/ *(first)*, /ʌ/ *(next)*, /n/ *(last)* = *run*]." "You can write the letter or letters for each sound."
Blending three or four phonemes in words	"You can blend sounds together to say a word [*n-e-s-t* = *nest*]."
Deleting phonemes in words	"You can say words without some of the sounds [*can* – *c* = *an; sand* – *s* = *and*]." "You can say a word without the first sound [*ch* – *air* = *air*]." "You can say a word without the last sound [*ant* – *t* = *an*]."
Adding phonemes to the end of words	"You can add sounds to the end of a word [*an* + *d* = *and; and* + *y* = *Andy*]."
Manipulating phonemes in the middle of words	"You can change the sounds in the middle of a word to make a new word [*hit, hot*]."
	PRE-K · GRADE K (early, mid, late) · GRADE 1 (early, mid, late) · GRADE 2 (early, mid, late) · GRADE 3 (early, mid, late)

Letter Knowledge

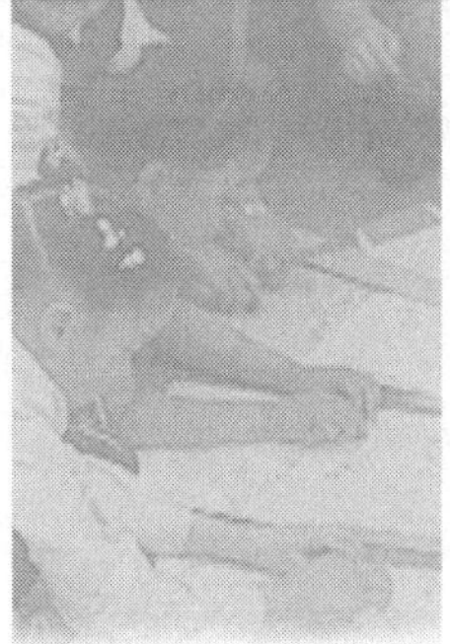

Letter knowledge refers to what children need to learn about the graphic characters that correspond with the sounds of language. A finite set of twenty-six letters, two forms of each, is related to all of the sounds of the English language (approximately forty-four phonemes). The sounds in the language change as dialect, articulation, and other speech factors vary. Children will also encounter alternative forms of some letters—for example, g, g; a, a; y, y—and will eventually learn to recognize letters in cursive writing. Children need to learn the names and purposes of letters, as well as the particular features of each. When children can identify letters by noticing the very small differences that make them unique, they can then associate letters and letter clusters with phonemes and parts of words. Knowing the letter names is useful information that helps children talk about letters and understand what others say about them. As writers, children need to be able to use efficient directional movements when making letters.

Letter Knowledge

Identifying Letters

Principle	Explanation of Principle (PRE-K; GRADE K early, mid, late; GRADE 1 early, mid, late; GRADE 2 early, mid, late; GRADE 3 early, mid, late)
Understanding the concept of a letter	"The alphabet has twenty-six letters." "A letter has a name and a shape."
Distinguishing letter forms	"Letters are different from each other." "You can notice the parts of letters." "Some letters have long sticks. Some letters have short sticks." "Some letters have curves, circles, tunnels, tails, crosses, dots, slants."
Producing letter names	"You can look at the shape of a letter and say its name."
Categorizing letters by features	"You can find parts of letters that look the same." "You can find the letters that have long sticks [short sticks, curves, circles, tunnels, tails, crosses, dots, slants]."
Understanding alphabetical order	"The letters in the alphabet are in a special order."
Recognizing uppercase and lowercase letters	"A letter has two forms. One form is uppercase (or capital) and the other is lowercase (or small) [*B, b*]." "Your name starts with an uppercase letter." "The other letters in your name are lowercase letters." "Some lowercase forms look like the uppercase forms [*W, w*] and some look different [*R, r*]."
Recognizing consonants and vowels	"Some letters are consonants [*b, c, d, f, g, h, j, k, l, m, n, p, q, r, s, t, v, w, x, y, z*]." "Some letters are vowels [*a, e, i, o, u,* and sometimes *y* and *w*]." "Every word has a vowel."
Understanding special uses of letters	"Your initials are the first letters of your first name and your last name." "You use capital letters to write your initials."

PRE-K GRADE K (early, mid, late) GRADE 1 (early, mid, late) GRADE 2 (early, mid, late) GRADE 3 (early, mid, late)

Letter Knowledge, continued

	Principle	Explanation of Principle
Recognizing Letters in Words and Sentences	Understanding that words are made up of letters	"Words have letters in them." "Your name has letters in it." "You can say the first letter of your name."
	Making connections between words by recognizing letters	"You can find words that have the same letters in them."
	Recognizing the sequence of letters in words	"Letters in a word are always in the same order." "The first letter is on the left." "You can find the first letter in a word."
	Recognizing letters in words	"You can find letters in words." "You can say the names of letters in words."
	Recognizing letters in continuous text	"You can find letters in sentences and stories."
	Making connections between words by recognizing letter placement	"You can find words that begin with the same letter." "You can find words that end with the same letter." "You can find words that have the same letter in the middle."
Forming Letters	Using efficient and consistent motions to form letters	"You can make the shape of a letter." "You can say words that help you learn how to make a letter." "You can check to see if your letter looks right."

PRE-K | GRADE K (early, mid, late) | GRADE 1 (early, mid, late) | GRADE 2 (early, mid, late) | GRADE 3 (early, mid, late)

Letter/Sound Relationships

The sounds of oral language are related in both simple and complex ways to the twenty-six letters of the alphabet. Learning the connections between letters and sounds is basic to understanding written language. Children first learn simple relationships that are regular in that one phoneme is connected to one grapheme, or letter. But sounds are also connected to letter clusters, which are groups of letters that appear often together (for example, *cr, str, st, bl, fr*), in which you hear each of the associated sounds of the letters; and consonant digraphs *(sh, ch)*, in which you hear only one sound. Vowels may also appear in combinations *(ea, oa)* in which you usually hear the first vowel *(ai)* or you hear a completely different sound *(ou)*. Children learn to look for and recognize these letter combinations as units, which makes their word solving more efficient. It is important to remember that children will be able to hear and connect the easy-to-identify consonants and vowels early and progress to the harder-to-hear and more difficult letter/sound relationships—for example, letter clusters with two and three letters and those that have more than one sound. You will want to connect initial letter sounds to the Alphabet Linking Chart (see *Teaching Resources*). It is not necessary to teach every letter as a separate lesson. When using the children's names to teach about words, substitute *name* for *word* when explaining the principle.

Letter/Sound Relationships

Consonants

PRINCIPLE	EXPLANATION OF PRINCIPLE (PRE-K; GRADE K early, mid, late; GRADE 1 early, mid, late; GRADE 2 early, mid, late; GRADE 3 early, mid, late)
Recognizing that letters represent consonant sounds	"You can match letters and sounds in words. For example: *b* is the letter that stands for the first sound in *bear*."
Recognizing and using beginning consonant sounds and the letters that represent them: *s, m, t, b, f, r, n, p, d, h, c, g, j, l, k, v, w, z, qu, y, x*	"You can hear the sound at the beginning of a word." "You can match letters and sounds at the beginning of a word." "When you see a letter at the beginning of a word, you can make its sound." "When you know the sound, you can find the letter." "You can find a word by saying it and thinking about the first sound."
Recognizing similar beginning consonant sounds and the letters that represent them	"Words can start with the same sound and letter [*box, big*]."
Recognizing and using ending consonant sounds and the letters that represent them: *b, m, t, d g, n, p, f, l, r, s, z, x, ss, ll, tt, ck*	"You can hear the sounds at the end of a word." "You can match letters and sounds at the end of a word." "When you see a letter at the end of a word, you can make its sound." "When you know the sound, you can find the letter." "You can find a word by saying it and thinking about the ending sound."
Recognizing similar ending consonant sounds and the letters that represent them	"Words can end with the same sound and letter [*duck, book*]."
Recognizing and using middle consonant sounds sometimes represented by double letters: *bb, dd, ll, mm, nn, pp, rr, tt, zz*	"You can hear consonant sounds in the middle of a word." "You can match letters and sounds in the middle of a word." "When you see letters in the middle of a word, you can make their sound." "When you know the sound in the middle of a word, you can find the letter." "Sometimes two consonant letters stand for the consonant sound in the middle of a word." "You can find words by saying the word and thinking about the sound in the middle."

	early	mid	late	early	mid	late	early	mid	late	early	mid	late
PRE-K	GRADE K			GRADE 1			GRADE 2			GRADE 3		

Letter/Sound Relationships, continued

Principle	Explanation of Principle
Consonants	
Recognizing and using consonant sounds represented by consonant digraphs: *sh, ch, th, ph* (at the beginning or end of a word), and *wh*	"Some clusters of consonants stand for one sound that is different from either of the letters. They are called consonant digraphs." "You can hear the sound of a consonant digraph at the beginning or end of a word." "You can match a consonant digraph at the beginning or end of a word with its sound." "You can find words by saying the word and thinking about the sound of the consonant digraph."
Recognizing and using letters that represent two or more consonant sounds at the beginning of a word: *c, g, th, ch*	"Some consonants make two or more different sounds [*car, city; get, gym; think, they; chair, chorus, chateau*]."
Recognizing and using consonant clusters that blend two or three consonant sounds (onsets): *bl, cl, fl, pl, pr, br, dr, gr, tr, cr, fr, gl, sl, sn, sp, st, sw, sc, sk, sm, scr, squ, str, thr, spr, spl, shr, sch, tw*	"Some consonants go together in clusters." "A group of two or three consonants is a consonant cluster." "You can hear each sound in a consonant cluster." "You can hear and connect consonant clusters at the beginning of words." "You can hear and connect consonant clusters at the end of words." "You can find a word by saying the word and thinking about the first (or ending) sounds." "Knowing a consonant cluster helps you read and write words."
Recognizing and using consonant letters that represent no sound: *lamb, light*	"Some words have consonant letters that are silent."
Recognizing and using letters that represent consonant clusters at the end of a word: *ct, ft, ld, lp, lt, mp, nd, nk, nt, pt, rd, rk, sk, sp, st*	"You can hear each sound in a consonant cluster at the end of a word." "You can hear and connect consonant clusters at the end of words." "You can find a word by saying it and thinking about the ending sounds." "Knowing an ending consonant cluster helps you read and write words."
Recognizing and using letters that represent consonant digraph sounds at the end of a word (making one sound): *sh, th, ch, ck, tch, dge, ng, ph, gh*	"You can hear the sound in a consonant digraph at the end of a word." "You can connect a consonant digraph at the end of a word with its sound." "You can find a word by saying it and thinking about the last sound (consonant digraph)."
Recognizing and using letters that represent less frequent consonant digraph sounds at the beginning of a word (making one sound): *gh, gn, kn, ph, wr*	"You can hear the sound of a consonant digraph at the beginning of a word." "You can connect a consonant digraph at the beginning of a word with its sound." "You can find a word by saying it and thinking about the first sound (consonant digraph)."
Vowels	
Understanding letters that represent consonant sounds or vowel sounds	"Some letters are consonants and some letters are vowels." "Every word has a vowel sound." "*A, e i, o,* and *u* are vowels (and sometimes *y* and *w*)."
Hearing and identifying short vowel sounds in words and the letters that represent them	"In some words, *a* sounds like the *a* in *apple* and *can.*" "In some words, *e* sounds like the *e* in *egg* and *net.*" "In some words, *i* sounds like the *i* in *igloo* and *sit.*" "In some words, *o* sounds like the *o* in *octopus* and *hot.*" "In some words, *u* sounds like the *u* in *umbrella* and *cup.*"
Recognizing and using short vowel sounds at the beginning of words: *at, apple*	"Some words have one vowel at the beginning [*apple, at, Andrew*]." "The sound of the vowel is *short.*"

PRE-K	GRADE K			GRADE 1			GRADE 2			GRADE 3		
	early	mid	late	early	mid	late	early	mid	late	early	mid	late

Letter/Sound Relationships, continued

Vowels

Principle	Explanation of Principle (PRE-K · GRADE K early mid late · GRADE 1 early mid late · GRADE 2 early mid late · GRADE 3 early mid late)
Recognizing and using short vowel sounds in the middle of words (CVC): *hat, bed*	"Some words have one vowel between two consonants [*hat, bed*] and the sound of the vowel is *short.*"
Hearing and identifying long vowel sounds in words and the letters that represent them	"In some words, *a* sounds like the *a* in *name* and *came.*" "In some words, e sounds like the *e* in *eat* and *seat.*" "In some words, *i* sounds like the *i* in *ice* and *kite.*" "In some words, *o* sounds like the *o* in *go* and *boat.*" "In some words, *u* sounds like the *u* in *use* and *cute.*"
Recognizing and using long vowel sounds in words	"You can hear and say the vowel in words like *make, pail, day.*" "You can hear and say the vowel in words like *eat, meat, see.*" "You can hear and say the vowel in words like *I, ice, ride.*" "You can hear and say the vowel in words like *go, grow, boat.*" "You can hear and say the vowel in words like *use, cute, huge.*"
Recognizing and using vowels in words with silent *e* (CVC*e*): *make, take, home* A: *make, ate, take, came, same, base* [Exceptions: *are, dance*] E: *Pete, breeze* [Exception: *edge*] I: *bite, bike, five, ice, slime, shine* [Exceptions: *mince, fringe*] O: *rode, hole, joke* [Exceptions: *come, some, goose*] U: *use, cube, cute, fume* [Exceptions: *judge, nurse*]	"Some words end in an *e* that is silent and the vowel usually has the long sound (sounds like its name)."
Contrasting long and short vowel sounds in words	"A vowel can have a sound like its name [*a* as in *make*], and this is called a long vowel sound." "A vowel can have a sound that is different from its name [*a* as in *apple*], and this is called a short vowel sound."
Recognizing and using *y* as a vowel sound: *happy, family, my, sky*	"*Y* is a letter that sometimes makes a vowel sound." "*Y* sounds like *e* on the end of words like *happy, funny, family.*" "*Y* sounds like *i* in words like *my, sky, by.*"
Recognizing and using other vowel sounds: *oo* as in *moon, look; oi* as in *oil; oy* as in *boy; ou* as in *house; ow* as in *cow; aw* as in *paw*	"Some letters go together and make other vowel sounds [*moon, look, oil, boy, house, cow, paw*]."
Recognizing and using letter combinations that represent long vowel sounds: *ai, ay, ee, ea, oa, ow, ie, ei*	"Some vowels go together in words and make one sound." "When there are two vowels [*ai, ay, ee, ea, oa, ow, ie, ei*], they usually make the sound of the name of the first vowel [*rain, day, meat, seat, snow*]."
Recognizing and using vowel sounds in open syllables: (CV): *ho-tel*	"Some syllables have a consonant followed by a vowel." "The sound of the vowel is long [*ho-tel, Pe-ter, lo-cal*]."
Recognizing and using vowel sounds in closed syllables: (CVC): *lem-on*	"Some syllables have a vowel that is surrounded by two consonants." "The sound of the vowel is short [*lem-on; cab-in*]."
Recognizing and using vowel sounds with *r*: *car, first, hurt, her, corn*	"When vowels are with *r* in words, you blend the vowel sound with *r* [*car, first, hurt, her, corn*]."

early mid late · early mid late · early mid late · early mid late
PRE-K GRADE K GRADE 1 GRADE 2 GRADE 3

LS Letter/Sound Relationships

Spelling Patterns

Phonograms are spelling patterns that represent the sounds of *rimes* (last parts of words). They are sometimes called *word families.* You will not need to teach children the technical word *phonogram,* although you may want to use *pattern* or *word part.* A phonogram is the same as a rime, or ending of a word or syllable. We have included a large list of phonograms that will be useful to primary-age children in reading or writing, but you will not need to teach every phonogram separately. Once children understand that there are patterns and learn how to look for patterns, they will quickly discover more for themselves.

Another way to look at phonograms is to examine the way simple words and syllables are put together. Here we include the consonant-vowel-consonant (CVC) pattern in which the vowel often has a short, or terse, sound; the consonant-vowel-consonant-silent *e* (CVC*e*) pattern in which the vowel usually has a long, or lax, sound; and the consonant-vowel-vowel-consonant (CVVC) pattern in which the vowel combination may have either one or two sounds.

Knowing spelling patterns helps children notice and use larger parts of words, thus making word solving faster and more efficient. Patterns are also helpful to children in writing words because they will quickly write down the patterns rather than laboriously work with individual sounds and letters. Finally, knowing to look for patterns and remembering them help children make the connections between words that make word solving easier. The thirty-seven most common phonograms are marked with an asterisk.

Spelling Patterns

PRINCIPLE	EXPLANATION OF PRINCIPLE
Recognizing that words have letter patterns that are connected to sounds (phonograms are spelling patterns)	"Some words have parts (patterns) that are the same." "You can find patterns (parts) that are the same in many words."
Recognizing and using the consonant-vowel-consonant (CVC) pattern	"Some words have a consonant, a vowel, and then another consonant. The vowel sounds like the *a* in *apple* [*e* in *egg, i* in *igloo, o* in *octopus, u* in *umbrella*]."
Recognizing and using simple phonograms with a VC pattern (easiest): *-ad, -ag, -am, -an*, -at*, -ed, -en, -et, -ig, -in*, -it*, -og, -op*, -ot*, -ut*	"You can look at the pattern (part) you know to help you read a word." "You can use the pattern (part) you know to help you write a word." "You can make new words by putting a letter or letter cluster before the word part or pattern."
Recognizing and using more difficult phonograms with a VC pattern: *-ab, -ap*, -ar, -aw*, -ay*, -eg, -em, -ib, -ip*, -ix, -ob, -od, -ow (blow), -ow (cow), -ug*, -um, -un*	"You can look at the pattern (part) you know to help you read a word." "You can use the pattern (part) you know to help you write a word." "You can make new words by putting a letter or letter cluster before the word part or pattern."
Recognizing and using phonograms with a vowel-consonant-silent *e* (VC*e*) pattern: *-ace, -ade, -age, -ake*, -ale*, -ame*, -ane, -ape, -ate*, -ice*, -ide*, -ike, -ile, -ime, -ine*, -ite, -ive, -obe, -oke*, -ope, -ore**	"Some words have a vowel, a consonant, and a silent *e*. The vowel sound is usually the name of the vowel [*a* in *make, e in Pete, i* in *ride, o* in *rode, u* in *cute*]."

Grade-level bands: PRE-K; GRADE K (early, mid, late); GRADE 1 (early, mid, late); GRADE 2 (early, mid, late); GRADE 3 (early, mid, late)

* Indicates most common phonograms.

Spelling Patterns, continued

PRE-K GRADE K GRADE 1 GRADE 2 GRADE 3
early mid late early mid late early mid late early mid late

Principle	Explanation of Principle
Recognizing and using phonograms that end with double letters (VCC): *-all, -ell*, -ill*, -oll, -uff*	**“Some words have double consonants at the end. The sound of the vowel is short.”**
Recognizing and using phonograms with double vowels (VVC): *-eek, -eel, -eem, -een, -eep, -eer, -eet, -ood, -ook, -ool, -oom, -oon*	**“Some words have double vowels followed by a consonant.”** **“Sometimes the vowel sounds like its name (long sound).”** **“Sometimes the vowel stands for other sounds.”**
Recognizing and using phonograms with ending consonant clusters (VCC): *-ack*, -act, -alk, -amp, -and, -ank*, -ant, -ard, -ark, -arm, -art, -ash*, -ask, -ath, -aw*, -eck, -elp, -elt, -end, -ent, -esh, -est*, -ick*, -ift, -igh, -ing*, -ink*, -ish, -ock*, -old, -ong, -uck*, -ump*, -ung, -unk*, -ush*	**“Some words have patterns that end with consonant clusters.”**
Recognizing and using phonograms with vowel combinations (VVC): *-aid, -ail*, -ain*, air, -ait, -aw, -ay*, -ea, -ead, -eak, -eam, -ean, -eap, -ear, -eat*, -oad, -oak*	**“Some words have two vowels together (vowel combinations).”** **“The vowel sound in the middle is usually the name of the first vowel.”**
Recognizing and using more difficult phonograms (VVCC, VVC*e*, VCC*e*, VCCC, VVCCC): *-aint, -aise, -ance, -anch, -arge, -aste, -atch, -each, -ealth, -east, -eath, -eave, -edge, -eech, -eeze, -eight, -ench, -ight*, -itch, -ooth, -ouch, -ound, -udge, -unch*	**“Some words have parts (patterns) that are the same.”** **“You can find patterns (parts) that are the same in many words.”** **“You can use the pattern you know to help you read (or write) a word.”**

early mid late early mid late early mid late early mid late
PRE-K GRADE K GRADE 1 GRADE 2 GRADE 3

High Frequency Words

A core of known high frequency words is a valuable resource as children build their reading and writing processes. Young children notice words that appear frequently in the simple texts they read; eventually, their recognition of these words becomes automatic. In this way, their reading becomes more efficient, enabling them to decode words using phonics as well as attend to comprehension. These words are powerful examples that help them grasp that a word is always written the same way. They can use known high frequency words to check on the accuracy of their reading and as resources for solving other words (for example, *this* starts like *the*). In general, children learn the simpler words earlier and in the process develop efficient systems for learning words. They continuously add to the core of high frequency words they know. Lessons on high frequency words help them look more carefully at words and develop more efficient systems for word recognition.

High Frequency Words

PRE-K | GRADE K (early, mid, late) | GRADE 1 (early, mid, late) | GRADE 2 (early, mid, late) | GRADE 3 (early, mid, late)

PRINCIPLE	EXPLANATION OF PRINCIPLE
Recognizing and using high frequency words with one or two letters	**“You see some words many times when you read: *I, is, in, at, my, we, to, me, am, an.*”** **“Some have only one letter: *I* and *a.*”** **“Some have two letters: *am, an, as, at, be, by, do, go, he, in, is, it, me, my, of, on, or, so, to, up, us, we.*”** **“Words you see a lot are important because they help you read and write.”**
Locating and reading high frequency words in continuous text	**“When you know a word, you can read it every time you see it.”** **“You can find a word by knowing how it looks.”**
Recognizing and using high frequency words with three or four letters	**“You see some words many times when you read.”** **“Some have three or four letters: *the, and, but, she, like, come, this.*”** **“Words you see a lot are important because they help you read and write.”**
Recognizing and using high frequency words with five or more letters	**“You see some words many times when you read.”** **“Some have five or more letters: *would, could, where, there, which.*”** **“Words you see a lot are important because they help you read and write.”**

PRE-K | GRADE K (early, mid, late) | GRADE 1 (early, mid, late) | GRADE 2 (early, mid, late) | GRADE 3 (early, mid, late)

Word Meaning

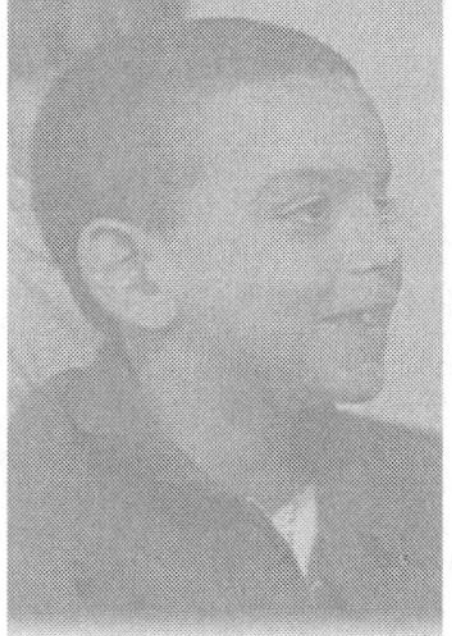

Children need to know the meaning of the words they are learning to read and write. It is important for them constantly to expand their vocabulary as well as develop a more complex understanding of words they already know. Word meaning is related to the development of vocabulary—labels, concept words, synonyms, antonyms, and homonyms. Concept words such as numbers and days of the week are often used in the texts they read, and they will want to use these words in their own writing. When children learn concept words (color words are another example), they can form categories that help in retrieving them when needed. In our complex language, meaning and spelling are intricately connected.

Often you must know the meaning of the word you want to spell or read before you can spell it accurately. In addition to lists of common concept words that children are often expected to know how to read and spell, we include synonyms, antonyms, and homonyms, which may be homographs (same spelling, different meaning and sometimes different pronunciation) or homophones (same sound, different spelling). Knowing synonyms and antonyms will help children build more powerful systems for connecting and categorizing words; it will also help them comprehend texts better and write in a more interesting way. Being able to distinguish between homographs and homophones assists in comprehension and helps spellers to avoid mistakes.

Word Meaning

Principle	Explanation of Principle
	PRE-K · GRADE K (early, mid, late) · GRADE 1 (early, mid, late) · GRADE 2 (early, mid, late) · GRADE 3 (early, mid, late)
Recognizing and learning concept words: color names, number words, days of the week, months of the year	**"A color (number, day, month) has a name."** **"Days of the week have names and are always in the same order."** **"Months of the year have names and are always in the same order."** **"You can read and write the names of colors (numbers, days, months)."** **"You can find the names of colors (numbers, days, months)."**
Recognizing and using words that are related	**"Some words go together because of what they mean: *mother–father; sister–brother;* clothing; animals; food."**
Recognizing and using synonyms (words that mean about the same)	**"Some words mean about the same and are called synonyms: *begin/start, close/shut, fix/mend, earth/world, happy/glad, high/tall, jump/leap, keep/save, large/big.*"**
Recognizing and using antonyms (words that mean the opposite)	**"Some words mean about the opposite and are called antonyms: *hot/cold, all/none, break/fix, little/big, long/short, sad/glad, stop/start.*"**
Recognizing and using homophones (same sound, different spelling and meaning). (It is not necessary to teach children the technical term *homophone.*)	**"Some words sound the same but look different and have different meanings: *to/too/two; there/their/they're; hare/hair; blue/blew.*"**
Recognizing and using homographs (same spelling, different meaning, and may have different pronunciation —heteronym). (It is not necessary to teach children the technical term *homograph* or *heteronym.*)	**"Some words look the same, have a different meaning, and may sound different: *bat/bat; well/well; read/read; wind/wind.*"**
Recognizing and using words with multiple meanings (a form of homograph)	**"Some words are spelled the same but have more than one meaning: *beat, run, play.*"**
	early, mid, late · PRE-K · GRADE K · GRADE 1 · GRADE 2 · GRADE 3

Word Structure

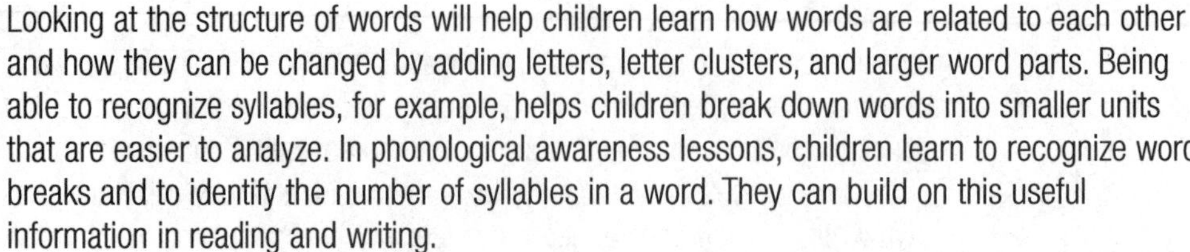

Looking at the structure of words will help children learn how words are related to each other and how they can be changed by adding letters, letter clusters, and larger word parts. Being able to recognize syllables, for example, helps children break down words into smaller units that are easier to analyze. In phonological awareness lessons, children learn to recognize word breaks and to identify the number of syllables in a word. They can build on this useful information in reading and writing.

Words often have affixes, parts added before or after a word to change its meaning. An affix can be a prefix or a suffix. The word to which affixes are added can be a *base* word or a *root* word. A base word is a complete word; a root word is a part with Greek or Latin origins (such as *phon* in *telephone*). It will not be necessary for young children to make this distinction when they are beginning to learn about simple affixes, but working with suffixes and prefixes will help children read and understand words that use them as well as use affixes accurately in writing.

Endings or word parts that are added to base words signal meaning. For example, they may signal relationships *(prettier, prettiest)* or time *(running, planted)*. Principles related to word structure include understanding the meaning and structure of compound words, contractions, plurals, and possessives as well as knowing how to make and use them accurately. We have also included the simple abbreviations that children often see in the books they read and want to use in their writing.

Word Structure

Syllables

Principle	Explanation of Principle (Pre-K · Grade K early/mid/late · Grade 1 early/mid/late · Grade 2 early/mid/late · Grade 3 early/mid/late)
Understanding the concept of syllable	"You can hear the syllables in words." "You can look at the syllables to read a word."
Recognizing and using one or two syllables in words	"You can look at the syllables in a word to read it [*horse, a-way, farm-er, morn-ing*]."
Understanding how vowels appear in syllables	"Every syllable of a word has a vowel."
Recognizing and using three or more syllables in words	"You can look at the syllables in a word to read it [*bi-cy-cle, to-geth-er, ev-er-y, won-der-ful, li-brar-y, com-put-er, au-to-mo-bile, a-quar-i-um, un-der-wat-er*]."
Recognizing and using syllables in words with double consonants	"Divide the syllables between the consonants when a word has two consonants in the middle [*run-ning, bet-ter*]."
Recognizing and using syllables ending in a vowel (open syllable)	"When a syllable ends with a vowel, the vowel sound is usually long [*ho-tel*]."
Recognizing and using syllables ending in a vowel and at least one consonant (closed syllable)	"When a syllable ends with a vowel and at least one consonant, the vowel sound is usually short [*lem-on*]."
Recognizing and using syllables with a vowel and silent *e*	"When a vowel and silent *e* are in a word, the pattern makes one syllable with a long vowel sound [*hope-ful*]."

Word Structure, continued

Principle	Explanation of Principle
Syllables	
Recognizing and using syllables with vowel combinations	“When vowel combinations are in words, they usually go together in the same syllable [*poi-son, cray-on, ex-plain*].”
Recognizing and using syllables with a vowel and *r*	“When a vowel is followed by *r*, the *r* and the vowel form a syllable [*corn-er, cir-cus*].”
Recognizing and using syllables made of a consonant and *le*	“When *le* is at the end of a word and preceded by a consonant, the consonant and *le* form a syllable [*ta-ble*].”
Compound Words	
Recognizing and understanding simple compound words: *cannot, inside, into, itself, maybe, myself, nobody, outside, something, sometimes, sunshine, today, upset, without, yourself*	“Some words are made up of two words put together and are called compound words.” “You can read compound words by looking at the two words in them.”
Recognizing and understanding more complex compound words: *airplane, airport, another, anyone, anybody, anything, everyone, homesick, indoor, jellyfish, skyscraper, toothbrush, underground, whenever*	“Some words are made up of two words put together and are called compound words.” “You can read compound words by looking at the two words in them.”
Contractions	
Understanding the concept of contractions	“A contraction is one word made from two words [*can + not = can't*]. A letter or letters are left out and an apostrophe is put in.” “A contraction is a short form of the two words.”
Recognizing and understanding contractions with am: *I'm*	“To make a contraction, put two words together and leave out a letter or letters. Write an apostrophe where letter(s) are left out. Here is a contraction made with *I + am: I'm*.”
Recognizing and understanding contractions with is: *here's, he's, it's, she's, that's, there's, what's, where's, who's*	“To make a contraction, put two words together and leave out a letter or letters. Write an apostrophe where the letter(s) are left out.” “Many contractions are made with is: *here + is = here's*.”
Recognizing and understanding contractions using will: *I'll, it'll, he'll, she'll, that'll, they'll, we'll, you'll*	“To make a contraction, put two words together and leave out a letter or letters. Write an apostrophe where the letter(s) are left out.” “Many contractions are made with will: *I + will = I'll*.”
Recognizing and understanding contractions with not: *aren't, can't, couldn't, didn't, doesn't, don't, hadn't, hasn't, haven't, isn't, mustn't, needn't, shouldn't, wouldn't*	“To make a contraction, put two words together and leave out a letter or letters. Write an apostrophe where the letter(s) are left out.” “Many contractions are made with not: *can + not = can't*.”
Recognizing and understanding contractions with are: *they're, we're, you're*	“To make a contraction, put two words together and leave out a letter or letters. Write an apostrophe where the letter(s) are left out.” “Many contractions are made with are: *they + are = they're*.”
Recognizing and understanding contractions with have: *could've, I've, might've, should've, they've, we've, would've, you've*	“To make a contraction, put two words together and leave out a letter or letters. Write an apostrophe where the letter(s) are left out.” “Many contractions are made with have: *should + have = should've*.”

PRE-K | GRADE K (early, mid, late) | GRADE 1 (early, mid, late) | GRADE 2 (early, mid, late) | GRADE 3 (early, mid, late)

Word Structure, continued

Principle	Explanation of Principle
Contractions	
Recognizing and understanding contractions with is or has: *he's, it's, she's, that's, there's, what's, where's, who's*	**"To make a contraction, put two words together and leave out a letter or letters. Write an apostrophe where the letter(s) are left out."** **"Many contractions are made with is and/or has: *he + is = he's* [*He's going to the zoo*]; *he + has = he's* [*He's finished his work*]."**
Recognizing and understanding contractions with would or had: *I'd, it'd, she'd, there'd, they'd, we'd, you'd*	**"To make a contraction, put two words together and leave out a letter or letters. Write an apostrophe where the letter(s) are left out."** **"Many contractions are made with would or had: *she + would = she'd; they + would = they'd.*"**
Recognizing and understanding contractions with us: *let's*	**"To make a contraction, put two words together and leave out a letter or letters. Write an apostrophe where the letter(s) are left out."** **"One contraction is made with us: *let + us = let's* [*Let's go*]."**
Plurals	
Understanding the concept of plural	**"Plural means more than one."**
Recognizing and using plurals that add *s: dogs, cats, apples, cans, desks, faces, trees, monkeys*	**"Add *s* to some words to show you mean more than one (make them plural)."** **"You can hear the *s* at the end."**
Recognizing and using plurals that add *es* when words end with *x, ch, sh, s, ss, tch, zz: boxes, peaches, branches, dishes, buses, kisses, patches, buzzes, quizzes*	**"Add *es* to words that end with *x, ch, sh, s, ss, tch,* or *zz* to make them plural."** **"The *s* at the end sounds like /z/."**
Recognizing and using plurals that change the spelling of the word: *child/children, foot/feet, goose/geese, man/men, mouse/mice, ox/oxen, woman/women*	**"Change the spelling of some words to make them plural."**
Recognizing and using plurals that add *s* to words that end in a vowel and *y: boys, days, keys, plays, valleys*	**"Add *s* to words that end in a vowel and *y* to make them plural."**
Recognizing and using plurals that add *ies* to words that end in a consonant and *y: babies, candies, cities, countries, families, flies, ladies, ponies, skies, stories*	**"Change the *y* to *i* and add *es* to words that end in a consonant and *y* to make them plural."**
Recognizing and using plurals that change *f* to *v* and add *es* for words that end with *f, fe,* or *lf: wolves, hooves, scarves, lives, wives, selves, shelves*	**"Change *f* to *v* and add *es* to words that end with *f, fe,* or *lf* to make them plural."**
Recognizing and using plurals for words that end in a consonant and *o* by adding *es: zeroes, heroes, potatoes, volcanoes*	**"Add *es* to words that end in a consonant and *o* to make them plural."**
Recognizing and using plurals for words that end in a vowel and *o* by adding *s: radios, rodeos, kangaroos*	**"Add *s* to words that end in a vowel and *o* to make them plural."**
Recognizing and using plurals that are the same word for singular and plural: *deer, lamb, sheep, moose*	**"Some words are spelled the same in both the singular and plural forms."**

Grade scale: PRE-K | GRADE K (early, mid, late) | GRADE 1 (early, mid, late) | GRADE 2 (early, mid, late) | GRADE 3 (early, mid, late)

Word Structure, continued

Verb Endings

PRINCIPLE	EXPLANATION OF PRINCIPLE
Recognizing and using endings that add *s* to a verb to make it agree with the subject: *skate/skates; run/runs*	"Add *s* to the end of a word to make it sound right in a sentence." "She can *run.*" "She *runs.*" "She can *skate.*" "She *skates.*"
Recognizing and using endings that add *ing* to a verb to denote the present participle: *play/playing; send/sending*	"Add *ing* to a base word to show you are doing something now." "I can *read.*" "I am *reading.*" "She can *jump.*" "She is *jumping.*"
Recognizing and using endings that add *ed* to a verb to make it past tense: *walk/walked; play/played; want/wanted*	"Add *ed* to the end of a word to show that you did something in the past." "I can *play* a game today." "I *played* a game yesterday." "I *want* to play." "I *wanted* to play."
Recognizing and using endings that add a *d* to a verb ending in silent *e* to make it past tense: *like/liked*	"Add *d* to words ending in silent *e* to make the *ed* ending and show it was in the past." "I *like* vanilla ice cream." "I *liked* vanilla ice cream, but I don't anymore."
Recognizing and using endings that add *ing* to words that end in a single vowel and consonant to denote the present participle: *run/running; bat/batting; sit/sitting*	"Double the consonant and add *ing* to words ending in a single vowel and consonant." "I can *run.*" "I am *running.*"
Recognizing and using endings that add *ing* to words ending in silent *e* to denote the present participle: *come/coming; write/writing; bite/biting*	"Drop the *e* and add *ing* to most words that end with silent *e.*" "Will she *come?*" "She is *coming.*" "I can *write.*" "I am *writing.*"
Recognizing and using endings that add *ing* to words that end in *y* to denote the present participle: *carry/carrying; marry/marrying*	"Add *ing* to words that end in *y.*" "I can *carry* the flag." "I am *carrying* the flag."
Recognizing that *ed* added to a word to make it past tense can sound several different ways	"When you add *ed* to a word, sometimes it sounds like /d/: *grabbed, played, yelled.*" "When you add *ed* to a word, sometimes it sounds like /ed/ (short *e* plus the /d/ sound): *added, landed, melted.*" "When you add *ed* to a word, sometimes it sounds like /t/: *dressed, liked, talked, laughed, walked.*" "Sometimes you change the *y* to *i* and add *ed* and the ending sounds like *d: cried, fried, carried.*"

PRE-K | GRADE K (early, mid, late) | GRADE 1 (early, mid, late) | GRADE 2 (early, mid, late) | GRADE 3 (early, mid, late)

Principle	Explanation of Principle
Verb Endings	
Recognizing and using endings that add *es* to a verb: *cry/cries; try/tries; carry/carries*	"You can add endings to a word to make it sound right in a sentence." "Change the *y* to *i* and add *es* to words that end in a consonant and *y*." "I can *carry* the flag." "She *carries* the flag."
Recognizing and using endings that add *es* or *ed* to verbs ending in a consonant and *y* to form present or past tense: *cry/cries/cried; try/tries/tried*	"You can add word parts to the end of a word to show you did something in the present or in the past." "Change the *y* to *i* and add *es* or *ed* to words that end in a consonant and *y*." "I can *try* to run fast." "He *tries* to run fast." "We *tried* to run fast in the race yesterday."
Recognizing and using endings that add *ed* to verbs ending in a single short vowel and consonant or a vowel and double consonant to make it past tense: *grab/grabbed; grill/grilled; yell/yelled*	"You add word parts to the endings of words to show you did something in the past." "Double the consonant before adding *ed* to words ending in a short vowel and one consonant. Add *ed* if the word ends with a vowel and a double consonant." "She can *yell* loud." "She *yelled*, 'Run!'" "Mom can *grill* the hot dogs." "Mom *grilled* the hot dogs." "*Grab* the end of the rope." "She *grabbed* the end of the rope."
Recognizing and using endings that add *-er* to a verb to make it a noun: *read/reader; play/player; jump/jumper*	"Add *-er* to a word to talk about a person who can do something." "John can *read*." "John is a *reader*."
Recognizing and using endings that add *-er* to a verb that ends with a short vowel and a consonant: *dig/digger; run/runner*	"Double the consonant and add *-er* to words ending in a short vowel and one consonant." "Sarah can *run*." "Sarah is a *runner*."
Recognizing and using endings that add *r* to a verb that ends in silent *e*: *bake/baker; hike/hiker*	"Add *r* to words that end in silent *e* to make the *er* ending." "I like to hike." "I am a *hiker*."
Recognizing and using endings that add *-er* to a verb that ends in *y*: *carry/carrier*	"Change the *y* to *i* and add *-er* to words that end in *y*." "He can *carry* the mail." "He is a mail *carrier*."

PRE-K | GRADE K (early, mid, late) | GRADE 1 (early, mid, late) | GRADE 2 (early, mid, late) | GRADE 3 (early, mid, late)

Word Structure, continued

	Principle	Explanation of Principle
Adjectives—Comparatives and Superlatives	Recognizing and using endings that show comparison (*-er, -est*): *cold/colder; hard/harder; dark/darker; fast/faster; tall/taller; rich/richest; thin/thinner/thinnest*	"Add ***-er*** or ***-est*** to show how one thing compares with another." "John can run ***fast,*** but Monica can run ***faster.***" "Carrie is the ***fastest*** runner in the class."
	Recognizing and using endings that show comparison for words ending in *e: pale/paler/palest; ripe/riper/ripest; cute/cuter/cutest*	"Add ***-r*** or ***-st*** to words that end in silent ***e*** to make the ***-er*** or ***-est*** ending." "Jolisa has a ***cute*** puppy." "Matthew has a ***cuter*** puppy." "Jaqual has the ***cutest*** puppy."
	Recognizing and using endings that show comparison for words ending in a short vowel and a consonant	"Double the consonant and add ***-er*** or ***-est*** to words that end in a short vowel and one consonant." "The red box is big." "The blue box is bigger." "The green box is biggest."
	Recognizing and using endings that show comparison for words ending in *y: scary/scarier/scariest; funny/funnier/funniest*	"Change ***y*** to ***i*** and add ***-er*** or ***-est*** to words that end in ***y.***" "Ciera told a ***funny*** story." "Kyle's story was ***funnier*** than Ciera's." "Amanda told the ***funniest*** story of all."
Prefixes	Recognizing and using common prefixes (*re* meaning *again*): *make/remake; tie/retie*	"Add a word part or prefix to the beginning of a word to change its meaning." "Add ***re*** to mean ***do again.***" "I ***made*** the bed and took a nap. I had to ***remake*** the bed."
	Recognizing and using common prefixes (*un* meaning *not* or *the opposite of*): *do/undo; tie/untie; known/unknown; believable/unbelievable*	"Add a word part or prefix to the beginning of a word to change its meaning." "Add ***un*** to the beginning of a word to mean ***not*** or ***the opposite of.***" "I don't ***believe*** it. That is ***unbelievable.***" "I ***tied*** my shoes and then they came ***untied.***"
	Recognizing and using more complex prefixes (*im, in, il, dis* [meaning *not*]): *possible/impossible; valid/invalid; like/dislike*	"Add a word part or prefix to the beginning of a word to change its meaning." "Add ***im, in, il,*** or ***dis*** to the beginning of words to mean ***not.***" "That is not ***possible.*** It is ***impossible.***" "We cannot ***cure*** the disease. It is ***incurable.***" "It is not ***legal.*** It is ***illegal.***" "I do not ***like*** broccoli. I ***dislike*** broccoli."
Possessives	Recognizing and using possessives that add an apostrophe and an *s* to a singular noun: *dog/dog's; woman/woman's, girl/girl's, boy/boy's*	"A person, animal, place, or thing can own something. To show ownership, you add ***'s*** to a word." "The collar belongs to the ***dog.*** It is the ***dog's*** collar." "The ball belongs to the ***girl.*** It is the ***girl's*** ball." "The ***book*** has a cover. It is the ***book's*** cover."
	Recognizing and using possessives for words that end in *s: dogs' dishes, pigs' houses, Marcus' papers, Charles' lunch box*	"If a word already ends in s, just add an apostrophe to show ownership." "Those balls belong to the ***boys.*** They are the ***boys'*** balls." "Here is ***Marcus'*** lunch box. It belongs to ***Marcus.***" "The ***girls*** are getting the jump ropes. The ropes belong to the ***girls.*** They are the ***girls'*** jump ropes."
Abbreviations	Recognizing and using common abbreviations: Mrs., Ms., Mr., Dr., St., Ave., Rd., months of the year, days of the week	"Some words are made shorter by using some of the letters and a period. They are called abbreviations."

PRE-K | GRADE K (early, mid, late) | GRADE 1 (early, mid, late) | GRADE 2 (early, mid, late) | GRADE 3 (early, mid, late)

WS Word Structure

Word-Solving Actions

Word-solving actions are the strategic moves readers and writers make when they use their knowledge of the language system to solve words. These strategies are "in-the-head" actions that are invisible, although we can infer them from some overt behavior. The principles listed in this section represent children's ability to *use* the principles in all previous sections of the Continuum.

All lessons related to the Continuum provide opportunities for children to apply principles in active ways; for example, through sorting, building, locating, reading, or writing. Lessons related to word-solving actions demonstrate to children how they can problem-solve by working on words in isolation or while reading or writing continuous text. The more children can integrate these strategies into their reading and writing systems, the more flexible they will become in solving words. The reader/writer may use knowledge of letter/sound relationships, for example, either to solve an unfamiliar word or to check that the reading is accurate. Rapid, automatic word solving is a basic component of fluency and important for comprehension because it frees children's attention to focus on the meaning and language of the text.

Word-Solving Actions

PRE-K | GRADE K (early, mid, late) | GRADE 1 (early, mid, late) | GRADE 2 (early, mid, late) | GRADE 3 (early, mid, late)

Using What Is Known to Solve Words

PRINCIPLE	EXPLANATION OF PRINCIPLE
Recognizing and locating words (names)	"You can find your name by looking for the letters in it."
Making connections between names and other words	"You can find the letters that are in your name in other words." "You can connect your name with other names [*Mark, Maria*]." "You can connect your name with other words [*Mark, make*]."
Using the letters in names to read and write words: *Chuck, chair*	"You can connect your name with the words you want to spell or read."
Using known words to monitor reading and spelling	"You can use words you know to check on your reading."
Using first and last names to read and write words	"You can think of the first and last names you know to help you read and spell words [*Angela, Andy*]."
Recognizing and spelling known words quickly	"You can read or write a word quickly when you know how it looks [*the*]." "When you know how to read some words quickly, it helps you read fast." "When you know how to write some words quickly, it helps you write fast."
Using letter/sound knowledge to monitor reading and spelling accuracy	"You can use what you know about letters and sounds to check on your reading (and writing)."
Using parts of known words that are like other words: *my/sky; tree/try; she/shut*	"You can use parts of words you know to read or write new words."
Using what you know about a word to solve an unknown word: *her, mother*	"You can use what you know about words to read new words."

PRE-K | GRADE K (early, mid, late) | GRADE 1 (early, mid, late) | GRADE 2 (early, mid, late) | GRADE 3 (early, mid, late)

Word-Solving Actions, continued

Taking Words Apart to Solve Them

Principle	Explanation of Principle
Saying words slowly to hear sounds in sequence	"You can say words slowly to hear the sounds." "You can hear the sounds at the beginning, middle, or end of a word." "You can write the letters for the sounds you can hear." "You can say words slowly to hear the sounds from left to right."
Changing beginning letters to make new words: *sit/hit; day/play*	"You can change the first letter or letters of a word to make a new word."
Listening for sounds to write letters in words	"You can say words slowly to hear the sounds." "Hearing and saying the sounds help you write words."
Changing ending letters to make new words: *car/can/cat*	"You can change the last letter or letters of a word to make a new word."
Changing middle letters to make new words: *hit/hot; sheet/shirt*	"You can change the middle letter or letters of a word to make a new word."
Using letter/sound analysis from left to right to read a word	"You can read words by looking at the letters and thinking about the sounds from left to right."
Learning to notice the letter sequence to spell a word accurately	"You can make a word several times to learn the sequence of letters."
Studying features of words to remember the spelling	"You can look at a word, say it, cover it, write it, and check it to help you learn to spell it correctly."
Noticing and correcting spelling errors	"You can write a word, look at it, and try again to make it 'look right.'" "You can notice and think about the parts of words that are tricky for you." "You can write words to see if you know them."
Noticing and using word parts (onsets and rimes) to read a word: *br-ing*	"You can use word parts to solve a word." "You can look at the first and last parts of a word to read it."
Changing the onset or rime to make a new word: *bring/thing; bring/brown*	"You can change the first part or the last part to make a new word."
Adding letters to the beginning or end of a word to make a new word: *in/win; bat/bats; the/then*	"You can add letters to the beginning of a word to make a new word." "You can add letters to the end of a word to make a new word."
Adding letter clusters to the beginning or end of a word to make a new word: *an/plan; cat/catch*	"You can add letter clusters to the beginning or end of a word to make a new word."
Removing letters or letter clusters from the beginning of words: *sit/it; stand/and; his/is*	"You can take away letters from the beginning of a word to make a new word."
Removing letters from the end of a word to make a new word: *and/an; Andy/and; kite/kit*	"You can take away letters from the end of a word to make a new word."

PRE-K | GRADE K (early, mid, late) | GRADE 1 (early, mid, late) | GRADE 2 (early, mid, late) | GRADE 3 (early, mid, late)

Word-Solving Actions, continued

PRE-K | GRADE K (early, mid, late) | GRADE 1 (early, mid, late) | GRADE 2 (early, mid, late) | GRADE 3 (early, mid, late)

Principle	Explanation of Principle
Taking Words Apart to Solve Them	
Recognizing and using word parts (onsets, rimes) to read a word: *br-ing, cl-ap*	"You can notice and use word parts to read (or write) a new word." "You can look at the first part and last part to read a word."
Taking apart compound words or joining words to make compound words: *into, sidewalk, sideways*	"You can read compound words by finding the two smaller words." "You can write compound words by joining two smaller words."
Removing letter clusters from the end of a word to make a new word: *catch/cat*	"You can take away letter clusters from the end of a word to make a new word."
Removing the ending from a base word to make a new word: *sit/sits/sitting; big/bigger/biggest*	"You can take off the ending to help you read a word."
Breaking down a longer word into syllables in order to decode manageable units: *for-got-ten*	"You can divide a word into syllables to read it."
Making Connections Between and Among Words to Solve Them	
Connecting words that mean the same or almost the same: *wet/damp*	"You think about the words that mean almost the same."
Connecting words that start the same: *tree/tray*	"You can connect the beginning of a word with a word you know."
Connecting words that end the same: *candy/happy*	"You can connect the ending of the word with a word you know."
Connecting words that have the same pattern: *light/night; running/sitting*	"You can connect words that have the same letter patterns."
Connecting words that sound the same but look different and have different meanings: *blew/blue*	"You can read words by noticing that they sound the same but look different and have different meanings."
Connecting words that rhyme: *fair/chair*	"You can think about words that rhyme."
Connecting words that look the same but sometimes sound different and have different meanings: *read/read*	"You can read words by remembering that some words look the same but sometimes sound different and have different meanings."
Connecting and comparing word patterns that look the same but sound different: *dear/bear*	"You can read words by remembering that some words have parts or patterns that look the same but sound different."
Connecting and comparing word patterns that sound the same but look different: *said/bed*	"You can read words by remembering that some words have parts or patterns that sound the same but look different."

PRE-K | GRADE K (early, mid, late) | GRADE 1 (early, mid, late) | GRADE 2 (early, mid, late) | GRADE 3 (early, mid, late)

Letter/Sound Relationships

The sounds of oral language are related in both simple and complex ways to the twenty-six letters of the alphabet. Learning the connections between letters and sounds is basic to understanding written language. Children first learn simple relationships that are regular in that one phoneme is connected to one grapheme, or letter. But sounds are also connected to letter clusters, which are groups of letters that appear often together (for example, *cr, str, ch, st, bl, fr*), in which you hear each of the associated sounds of the letters; and to consonant digraphs *(sh, ch),* in which you hear only one sound. Vowels may also appear in combinations *(ea, oa),* in which you usually hear the first vowel *(ai)* or you hear a completely different sound *(ou).* Children learn to look for and recognize these letter combinations as units, which makes their word solving more efficient. It is important to remember that children will be able to hear and connect the easy-to-identify consonants and vowels early and progress to the harder-to-hear and more difficult letter/sound relationships—for example, letter clusters with two and three letters and those that have more than one sound. You will want to connect initial letter sounds to the Alphabet Linking Chart (see *Teaching Resources*). If children need support with two or three initial consonants, connect initial consonant clusters and digraphs to the Consonant Cluster Linking Chart (see *Teaching Resources*). It is not necessary to teach every letter as a separate lesson. When using the children's names to teach about words, substitute *name* for *word* when explaining the principle.

Connect to Assessment

See related LS Assessment Tasks in the Assessment Guide in *Teaching Resources:*

- Hearing and Representing Beginning and Ending Sounds in Words
- Matching Beginning Consonant Cluster Sounds with Letters
- Matching Ending Consonant Cluster Sounds with Letters
- Matching Beginning Consonant Digraph Sounds with Letters
- Matching Ending Consonant Digraph Sounds with Letters
- Matching Short Vowel Sounds with Letters
- Matching Long Vowel Sounds with Letters
- Matching Long and Short Vowel Sounds with Letters
- Reading and Writing Words with Simple Vowel Clusters

Develop Your Professional Understanding

See *Word Matters: Teaching Phonics and Spelling in the Reading/Writing Classroom* by G.S. Pinnell and I.C. Fountas. 1998. Portsmouth, New Hampshire: Heinemann.

Related pages: 46–48, 71–73, 90–93, 123, 141.

1 Recognizing Beginning Consonant Clusters with r

Make-Say-Check-Mix

Consider Your Children

If the children already understand the concept of consonant clusters and have begun to recognize them as units, this lesson will serve as a review of clusters that include the letter *r*. It may be a little harder for children to identify the *tr* words, which some may confuse with *ch*. You may not need to spend much time on clusters if children demonstrate that they fully control this principle.

Working with English Language Learners

Be sure that English language learners understand and can read the words you are using on the chart. You may want to quickly check their word knowledge before having them sort words, and discard words that are meaningless. Also, call the children's attention to consonant clusters during shared reading and interactive writing. Have them say words slowly to identify the first two sounds. Remember that speakers of some languages find English *r* quite difficult to say, so accept approximate pronunciations and help children use visual features of words.

You Need

- Chart paper.
- Markers.
- Magnetic letters.
- Small magnetic whiteboard or cookie sheet.

From *Teaching Resources:*

- Lesson LS 1 Word Cards.
- Consonant Cluster Linking Chart.
- Make-Say-Check-Mix Sheets.

Understand the Principle

The first part of many words consists of a consonant cluster in which both sounds are heard. It is important for children to begin to think of these consonant clusters (or *blends*) as units because they will then be able to solve words more efficiently when they read and write. They will also be able to write letter clusters quickly and automatically.

Explain the Principle

“You can hear each sound in a consonant cluster.”

“You can hear and connect consonant clusters at the beginning of words.”

“You can find a word by saying the word and thinking about the first sounds.”

“Knowing a consonant cluster helps you read and write words.”

plan

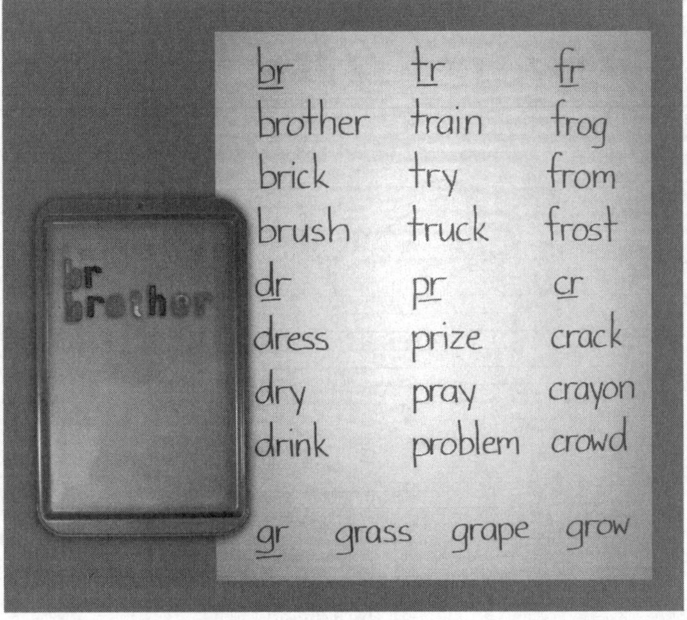

Explain the Principle

“ You can hear each sound in a consonant cluster. ”

“ You can hear and connect consonant clusters at the beginning of words. ”

“ You can find a word by saying the word and thinking about the first sounds. ”

“ Knowing a consonant cluster helps you read and write words. ”

① Tell the children that they are going to be learning more about consonant clusters (consonant blends).

② Suggested language: “You know that there are some consonants that go together in many words and that they are called *consonant clusters*. When you say a word with a consonant cluster, you hear both sounds, but they are smoothly blended together.”

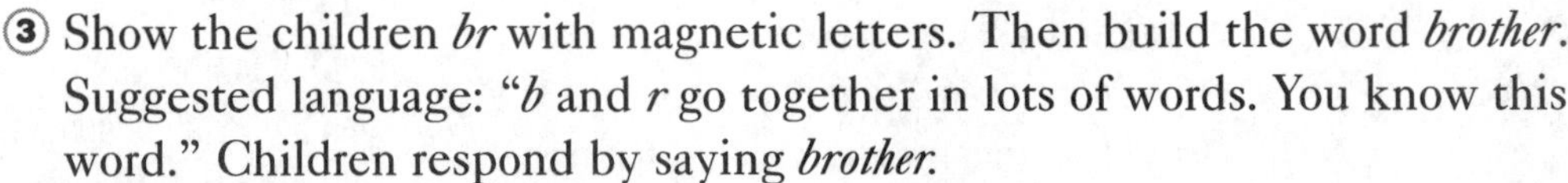

③ Show the children *br* with magnetic letters. Then build the word *brother*. Suggested language: “*b* and *r* go together in lots of words. You know this word.” Children respond by saying *brother*.

④ Suggested language: “You can hear the *b* and the *r*, can’t you. The *br* is the first part of the word *brother*.” Separate the *br* from *other* to show that *b* and *r* go together.

⑤ Ask children to suggest more words that begin with *br*.

⑥ Continue working with words that begin with *tr, fr, gr, dr, pr,* and *cr* until you have several examples for each on the chart. Use the magnetic letters on a cookie sheet or a magnetic whiteboard to emphasize the consonant blend.

⑦ After the chart is finished, say words in random order and ask the children to quickly locate them.

⑧ Show the children how to use the Make-Say-Check-Mix Sheet to make words that begin with letter clusters containing *r*.

⑨ Finally, read the boxes with *r* clusters on the Consonant Cluster Linking Chart to the group, and then have them read it with you a few times to develop fluency and flexibility.

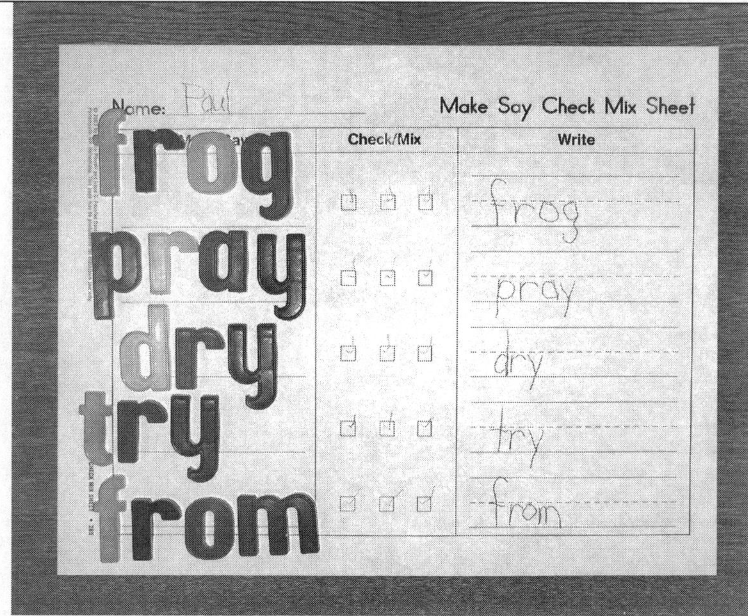

make
say
check
mix (3x)
write

- Distribute the Make-Say-Check-Mix Sheets.
- Have the children use word cards and magnetic letters to make a word that begins with a consonant cluster with *r*, say it, check it, and make a check mark in the box. Then ask them to mix up the letters, make the word again, say it and check the box. Have them do this a third time. Then they write the word. After making all the words, they read the Consonant Cluster Linking Chart to a partner.

In groups of four, have the children, in turn, read all the words on their Make-Say-Check-Mix Sheets. Read the words on the chart again with the whole class.

Link

Interactive Read-Aloud: Read aloud books that emphasize repetition of consonant blends. (See *Teaching Resources,* Alliteration Bibliography.) Examples are:

- ***Rosie's Roses*** by Pamela Duncan Edwards
- ***Clara Caterpillar*** by Pamela Duncan Edwards

Shared Reading: Point out words beginning with letter clusters in texts that children are reading, such as "The Goat," "The Bear," and "The Months of the Year" (see *Sing a Song of Poetry*). Have them highlight the letter cluster with transparent tape or a marker.

Guided Reading: Help children solve words by noticing beginning consonant clusters and starting the word. During the text introduction or after reading, have children locate words that include an *r* cluster.

Interactive Writing: When children want to write a word beginning with an *r* cluster, have them say the word slowly to identify the cluster and then write the letters together quickly. Point out that knowing the consonant cluster helps them write better.

Independent Writing: When conferring with children, ask them to point out words with *r* letter clusters that they have written.

Expand the Learning

Read the Consonant Cluster Linking Chart in reverse order or point to random boxes for reading.

Repeat the lesson with *bl, cl, fl, gl, pl,* and *sl* clusters. Use the word cards for Lesson LS 5 for *s* clusters and the Word Card Template to create cards for other consonant clusters.

Make a chart comparing *r* and *s* clusters. Children will discover that *s* is always first while *r* is always second in the cluster.

Connect with Home

Give children word cards for the words on the chart. Have them cut off the beginning letter clusters and take the divided cards home so that they can put words together and read them to family members.

assess

- Check individually whether the children can quickly locate *r* clusters on the chart.
- Check the children's ability to represent *r* clusters by dictating a list of ten or so words, some that have *r* clusters and some that don't.

2 Identifying Words with Short Vowel Sounds

Making Words

Consider Your Children

Because the sound of a vowel is influenced by the surrounding letters, children learn vowel sounds most easily within phonogram patterns. If your children have little familiarity or experience with vowels, you will want to select only one or two vowels to work with at a time, as in this lesson. You can then repeat the lesson with the other vowel letters.

Working with English Language Learners

Pronunciation of vowel sounds varies a great deal according to the speaker's native language as well as the geographic part of the United States (or other area) from which she comes. It is difficult for children to identify vowel sounds, and that is especially true for English language learners, who may not expect the range of sounds connected to each vowel in English. Provide opportunities for English language learners to say the words themselves and check their pronunciation, and use pictures that are meaningful to them.

You Need

- Chart paper.
- Markers.

From *Teaching Resources:*

- List Sheets.
- Category Word Cards, Onsets and Rimes.

Understand the Principle

Children need to be able to hear the vowel sounds in words and connect them to the letters that represent them. In many regular words, the short vowel sounds are represented by the single vowels *a, e, i, o, u.* The sounds of short *a, o,* and *u* tend to be easier for children to identify.

Explain the Principle

" In some words, *a* sounds like the *a* in *apple* and *can.* "

" In some words, *e* sounds like the *e* in *egg* and *net.* "

" In some words, *i* sounds like the *i* in *igloo* and *sit.* "

" In some words, *o* sounds like the *o* in *octopus* and *hot.* "

" In some words, *u* sounds like the *u* in *umbrella* and *cup.* "

plan

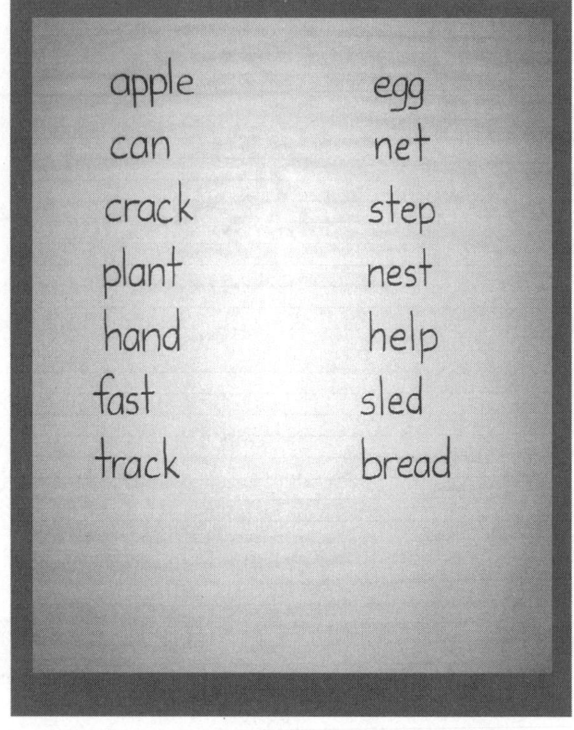

apple
egg
can
net
crack
step
plant
nest
hand
help
fast
sled
track
bread

Explain the Principle

"**In some words, *a* sounds like the *a* in *apple* and *can.***"

"**In some words, *e* sounds like the *e* in *egg* and *net.***"

"**In some words, *i* sounds like the *i* in *igloo* and *sit.***"

"**In some words, *o* sounds like the *o* in *octopus* and *hot.***"

"**In some words, *u* sounds like the *u* in *umbrella* and *cup.***"

① Explain to the children that you are going to teach them how to listen for and recognize the vowel sounds in words.

② Place the word *apple* at the top of a chart and list the words *can, crack, plant, hand, fast, track* below it. Read the words. Suggested language: "Listen to the vowel sound you hear in apple. Now listen to *can, crack, plant, hand, fast, track*. You can hear the same vowel sound."

③ Then place the word *egg* at the top of another column on the chart. List the words *net, step, nest, help, sled, bread* below it. Suggested language: "Listen to the vowel sound you hear in *egg* and *net*. You can hear the same sound in *step, nest, help, sled, bread*."

④ If children have had quite a bit of experience with vowels and control these first two vowels pretty well, continue with *i* as in *igloo* and *sit, o* as in *octopus* and *hot,* and *u* as in *umbrella* and *cup*.

⑤ Explain to the children that today they are going to make words in which they can hear short vowel sounds. Show the onset and rime cards and make two or three words: *n-est, p-ack, b-ell, c-atch*. Tell the children they will make twenty words with the cards, write them on the List Sheet, and read them to a partner.

sh ed | sm ell | t est | br ead | n eck | s and | tr ack | bl ack | t ack | r at

t ell | p ack | n est | f ed | b ell | l eg | c atch | b ack | l ast | h and

Name: Angela

1. hand
2. shed
3. last
4. back
5. tell
6. bell
7. leg
8. nest
9. fed
10. black
11. track
12. rat
13. test
14. smell

make
write
read

- ▸ Have the children make twenty words using the onset and rime cards, focusing on rimes that have short *a* and short *e* sounds. They write their words on a List Sheet and then read them to a partner.

Invite the children to turn to a different partner and read their lists.

Add one or two words to each column of the chart.

* The blends (first 1/2 of words) are in LS 3 *

Link

Interactive Read-Aloud: Read aloud books that include many words with short vowel patterns, such as

- ***I'm Gonna Like Me*** by Jamie Lee Curtis
- ***The Lorax*** by Dr. Seuss

Shared Reading: After reading and enjoying poems such as "Miss Mary Mack" or "Away Down East" (see *Sing a Song of Poetry*), give the key words *apple* and *egg* and have the children highlight a word with the same vowel sound. You might also give the key words *igloo, octopus,* and *umbrella,* if you have covered those vowel sounds.

Guided Reading: During word work, write several words containing short vowels on the whiteboard and encourage quick recognition. Erase the word quickly and write a new one to build speed.

Interactive Writing: Help the children notice short vowel sounds in words they are writing with you.

Independent Writing: Point out words with short vowel sounds as you confer briefly with writers. Help them notice patterns.

Expand the Learning

Repeat the lesson with short *i, o,* and *u.*

Repeat the lesson and include all five short vowel sounds.

Connect with Home

Ask the children to look around their homes or neighborhoods and list five words that have short vowel sounds and name things they can see. Have them share these words in class as you list them in columns according to the vowel sound on the class chart.

assess

- Observe the children's ability to read words with short vowel patterns.
- Notice how children write words with short vowel patterns.
- Dictate five or six words with short vowel sounds and assess the patterns and sounds the children control.

3 Identifying Words with Long Vowel Sounds

Making Words

Consider Your Children

In this lesson, children work with spelling patterns that represent long vowel sounds. They should have previous experience with short vowel patterns and CVC*e* patterns that represent long vowel sounds. If your children have very limited knowledge of long vowel sounds, work with only one or two sounds at a time. Since the long vowel sounds can be represented by many different letter patterns, start with easier patterns before moving to more complex ones.

Working with English Language Learners

Be sure that English language learners work with simple examples they understand. Go over the words you will use several times and let them repeat them. It may help to link the sound with the name of the letter of the alphabet.

You Need

- Pocket chart.

From *Teaching Resources:*

- Pocket Chart Card Template.
- Category Word Cards, Onsets and Rimes.
- List Sheets.

Understand the Principle

Children tend to be able to hear and identify long vowel sounds more easily than short vowel sounds because the vowel sound is the same as the name of the letter and is less subject to dialect variations. However, the sound of the long vowels can be represented by many different letter patterns.

Explain the Principle

“In some words, *a* sounds like the *a* in *name* and *came.*”

“In some words, *e* sounds like the *e* in *eat* and *seat.*”

“In some words, *i* sounds like the *i* in *ice* and *kite.*”

“In some words, *o* sounds like the *o* in *go* and *boat.*”

“In some words, *u* sounds like the *u* in *use* and *cute.*”

plan

Explain the Principle

"In some words, *a* sounds like the *a* in *name* and *came.*"

"In some words, *e* sounds like the *e* in *eat* and *seat.*"

"In some words, *i* sounds like the *i* in *ice* and *kite.*"

"In some words, *o* sounds like the *o* in *go* and *boat.*"

"In some words, *u* sounds like the *u* in *use* and *cute.*"

① Tell the children that you are going to teach them more about the vowel sounds and letters in words. Begin with a pocket chart that has the word cards *name, seat, kite, boat,* and *cute* at the top of five columns.

② Ask the children to listen to the vowel sound they hear as you read each word and then have them say each word with you.

③ Give several children a word card (for example, *gave, gate, meat, seal, line, like, vote, coat, huge*). In turn, have each child come to the front of the group, hold the card up, and read it. Then have the group tell him where to place it—for example, *line* would go under *kite.* Repeat until all the word cards are placed in the correct columns.

④ Once the word cards are all sorted, invite the class to read each column as you point to the words. Invite the children to tell what they notice about the words. Help them see that the long vowel sounds sound like their names and can be represented by more than one letter.

⑤ Explain that today they will use the onset and rime cards to make twenty words with long vowel sounds.

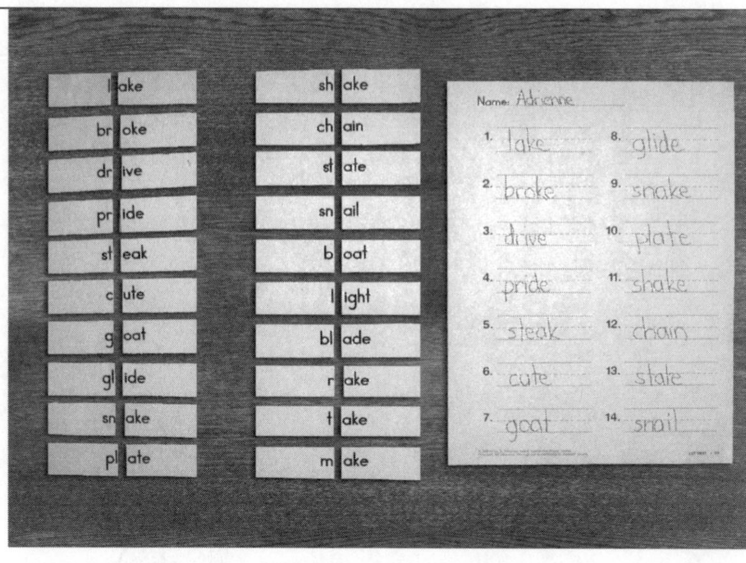

make
write
read
tell

- Have the children use the onset and rime cards to make twenty words containing the long vowel sound.
- Then ask them to write their words with long vowel sounds on a List Sheet and read them to a partner, telling them the name of the vowel heard.

With the children, add one new word to each column on the chart.

Invite the children to share any discoveries they made about the words.

Link

Interactive Read-Aloud: Read aloud books with long vowel patterns. Rhyme books (see *Teaching Resources*, Rhymes Bibliography) are excellent choices. Examples are:

- ***Street Rhymes Around the World*** by Jane Yolen
- ***Fix It Duck*** by Jez Alborough

Shared Reading: Engage the children in reading a variety of poems such as "A Caterpillar Crawled" or "I Live in the City" (see *Sing a Song of Poetry*). After enjoying the poem, say one of the key words—*name, seat, kite, boat,* or *cute*—and have the children locate and highlight one or two words that have the same vowel sound.

Guided Reading: During word work, write a few words with long vowel sounds on the whiteboard, encouraging the children to identify them quickly.

Interactive Writing: Help the children notice words with long vowel sounds. Point out the spelling patterns.

Independent Writing: As the children edit their writing, encourage them to attend to the long vowel spelling patterns.

assess

- Dictate four or five words with long vowel patterns to determine whether the children control particular vowel patterns.
- Observe the children's speed and accuracy in decoding words with long vowel patterns.

Expand the Learning

Have children play Follow the Path (see *Teaching Resources*) on game boards that feature words with long vowels. Create different levels of the game by making boards incorporating easier or more difficult long vowel patterns.

Connect with Home

Give the children two sheets of long vowel words (use the Word Card Template in *Teaching Resources*) to cut, sort, and read with family members.

Generative Lesson

early
mid
late

4 Identifying Long and Short Vowel Sounds in Words

Vowel Concentration

Consider Your Children

Your children will need to have worked with short and long vowel sounds (see Lessons LS 2 and LS 3) prior to this lesson. Here, they apply their short and long vowel knowledge by creating pairs of words, one with a short vowel sound and one with a long vowel sound. Select easier patterns for this lesson first, and repeat later with more challenging patterns.

Working with English Language Learners

This lesson and the Concentration game that is part of it will help English language learners become more flexible in using their knowledge of vowel sounds in words. However, you will want to be sure that they have a large repertoire of English words and that they have worked in a supported way with long and short vowels before expecting them to play the game. Observe children sorting words to determine how well they can distinguish between long and short vowels. Remove words that are too difficult.

You Need

- Chart paper.
- Markers.

From *Teaching Resources:*

- Concentration Game Cards made from Lesson LS 4 Word Cards and Deck Card Template.
- Directions for Concentration.

Understand the Principle

Vowel sounds are often difficult for children because of differences in dialect and because they can be represented by many different spelling patterns. Long vowel sounds are easier to hear because they sound like the vowel name. Short *a, e,* and *i* are the most challenging short vowel sounds.

Explain the Principle

"A vowel can have a sound like its name [*a* as in *make*], and this is called a long vowel sound."

"A vowel can have a sound that is different from its name [*a* as in *apple*], and this is called a short vowel sound."

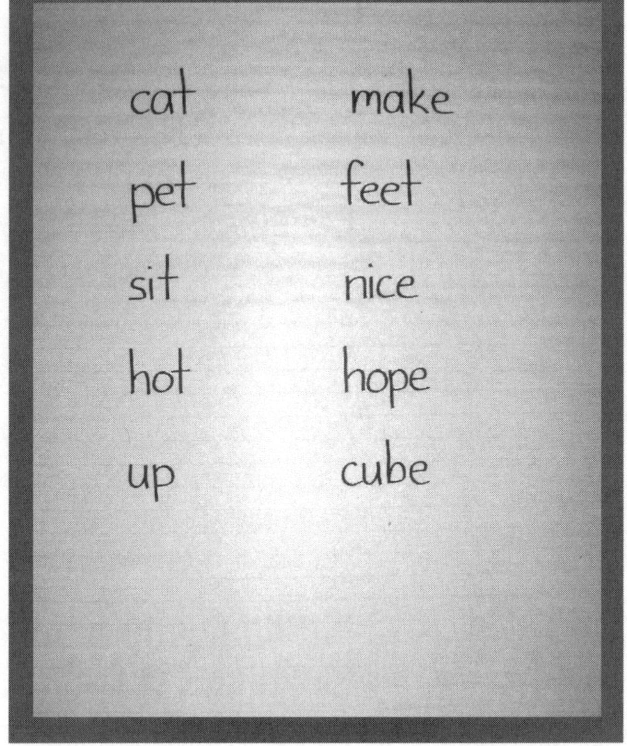

cat
make
pet
feet
sit
nice
hot
hope
up
cube

teach

Explain the Principle

“A vowel can have a sound like its name [*a* as in *make*], and this is called a long vowel sound.”

“A vowel can have a sound that is different from its name [*a* as in *apple*], and this is called a short vowel sound.”

① Tell the children that today they are going to learn more about vowel sounds in words.

② Suggested language: “When a vowel has a sound like its name *(make, meat, nine, hope, cute)*, it is called a long vowel sound. When a vowel has a sound that is different from its name *(apple, egg, igloo, octopus, umbrella)*, it is called a short vowel sound.”

③ Invite the children to say a word with a long and short vowel sound for each of the vowel letters. List their suggestions on the chart until you have two pairs of words for each vowel.

④ Explain that today they are going to play Vowel Concentration. They will turn a deck card over, read it, tell the vowel sound and whether it is long or short, turn over another card, read it, and tell the vowel sound and whether it is long or short. If the two cards include the same vowel and one is long and one is short, they have a pair and can keep the pair. The person with the most pairs at the end wins the game.

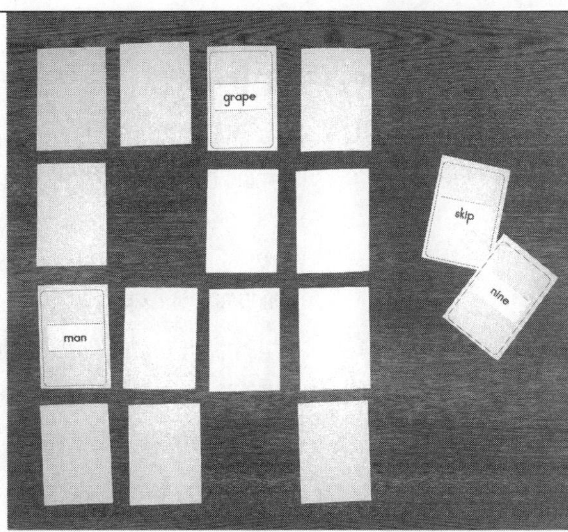

turn
read
say vowel
say long/short
turn
read
say vowel
say long/short
match pair

- Have the children play Vowel Concentration, making word pairs containing the same vowel, one with a long sound and one with a short sound.

Have a few children share a pair of words they made. Add some of these words to the chart.

Link

Interactive Read-Aloud: Read aloud rhyming books so the children can attend to the long and short vowel sounds they hear in words. (See *Teaching Resources,* Rhymes Bibliography.) Examples are:

- ***Alphabet Under Construction*** by Denise Fleming
- ***The Best Place to Read*** by Debbie Bertram

Shared Reading: Select poems such as "Jack Sprat," "Two Times Table," or "Over the River" (see *Sing a Song of Poetry*). Have children say a word with a long or short vowel sound and find one in the poem with the same vowel sound.

Guided Reading: During word work, have the children read two or three words with a long or short vowel pattern as you make them with magnetic letters or write them on a whiteboard.

Interactive Writing: As you compose and construct texts together, point out long and short vowel patterns.

Independent Writing: Help children notice vowel patterns as they write.

assess

- Observe the long and short vowel patterns children use in their writing.
- Make notes about the children's ability to take words apart as they read texts.
- Note the vowel patterns that are easy or more challenging for the children.

Expand the Learning

Have the children play Vowel Concentration, matching words with the same vowel sound.

Connect with Home

Send home a deck of Vowel Concentration cards for children to play the game with family members.

5 Recognizing Beginning Consonant Clusters with s

Make-Say-Check-Mix

Consider Your Children

This lesson will be effective if the children know the consonant sounds as well as some words that begin with consonant blends. If your children have learned a great deal about consonant blends in first grade, you may not want to use this lesson (work with two or three cluster families or present a summary just to remind your children of the concept). This lesson will be very helpful for children who have little letter/sound knowledge.

Working with English Language Learners

Use pictures or actions to be sure that English language learners know the meaning of the words you are using to illustrate the principle. Give them many opportunities to say the words and listen for the two sounds. Accept approximate pronunciations, and help children make connections between their own pronunciations and the letters. If the *s* family is particularly hard for children to say because of language differences, start with some other group.

You Need

- Chart paper.
- Markers.
- Magnetic letters.
- Small magnetic whiteboard or cookie sheet.

From *Teaching Resources:*

- Lesson LS 5 Word Cards.
- Consonant Cluster Linking Chart.
- Make-Say-Check-Mix Sheets.

Understand the Principle

Consonant clusters in which both sounds are heard but are smoothly blended are often called *blends.* Children need to learn how to blend together more than one consonant sound. Eventually, children will recognize the frequently occurring consonant clusters as units, making their decoding much more efficient.

Explain the Principle

“You can hear each sound in a consonant cluster.”

“You can hear and connect consonant clusters at the beginning of words.”

“You can find a word by saying the word and thinking about the first sounds.”

plan

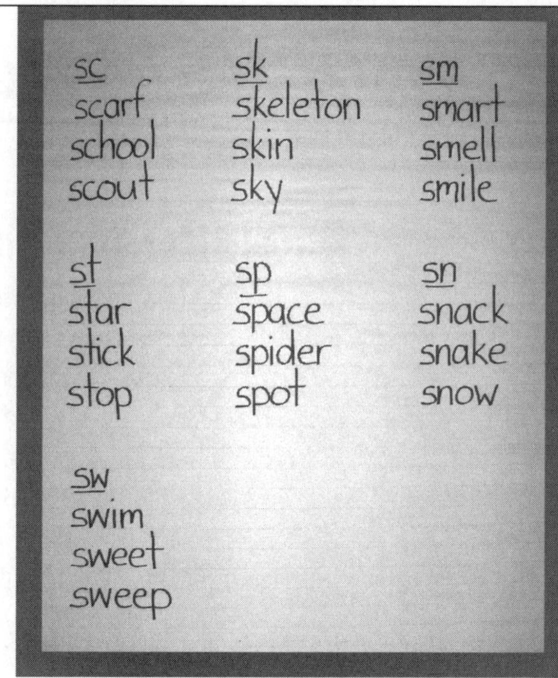

teach

Explain the Principle

“You can hear each sound in a consonant cluster.”

“You can hear and connect consonant clusters at the beginning of words.”

“You can find a word by saying the word and thinking about the first sounds.”

① Tell the children that they are going to be learning about consonant clusters (consonant blends).

② Suggested language: “You know the sounds of all the consonants. There are some consonants that go together in many words; they are called *consonant clusters.*”

③ Show the children *sc* in magnetic letters. Then build the word *scale.* Suggested language: “*s* and *c* go together in lots of words. This word is *scale.* You weigh things on a *scale.*”

④ Have the children say the word; point out that you can hear the *s* and the *c* even though they are blended together. Move *sc* and *ale* apart to show that *s* and *c* go together, and then make the word solid again. Suggested language: “The *sc* is the first part of the word, and the *ale* is the last part.”

⑤ Ask the children to suggest more words that begin with *sc* and write them on a chart. Children may suggest words like *skin,* which have the same sound. If they do, compliment them on the way they are listening for sounds and put these words in the next column on the chart. Point out that *s* and *k* also go together in many other words and that the sound is the same as *sc.*

⑥ Continue working with words for *sm, st, sp, sn,* and *sw* until you have several examples for each on the chart. Use the magnetic letters on the cookie sheet to emphasize the consonant blend.

⑦ After the chart is finished, say words in random order and ask the children to quickly locate them.

⑧ Show the children how to use the Make-Say-Check-Mix Sheet to make words that begin with *s* consonant clusters.

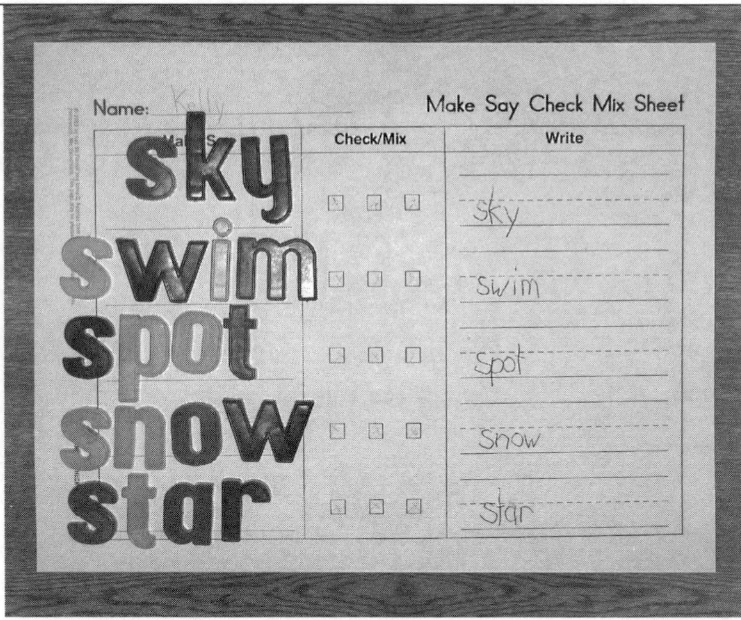

apply

make
say
check
mix (3x)
write
read

- Distribute the Make-Say-Check-Mix Sheets.
- Have the children use word cards and magnetic letters to make a word that begins with an *s* consonant cluster, say it, check it, and make a check mark in the box. Then ask them to mix up the letters, make the word again, say it, and check the box. Have them do this a third time. Then they write the word. Then they read their words to a partner.
- Finally, they point to and read the Consonant Cluster Linking Chart to their partner.

share

In groups of four, have the children, in turn, read all the words on their Make-Say-Check-Mix Sheets to a different partner. Read the chart again with the whole class.

* Give the children five of your pocket word cards per pair to use on the Make Say Check Sheet.

Link

Interactive Read-Aloud: Read aloud books that emphasize repetition of consonant blends. (See *Teaching Resources,* Alliteration Bibliography.) Examples are:

- ***Oliver's Vegetables*** by Vivian French
- ***Night Becomes Day*** by Richard McGuire

Shared Reading: Point out words beginning with letter clusters with *s* in texts that the children are reading. Some examples are "Good Morning, Merry Sunshine," "The Months of the Year," and "December Leaves" (see *Sing a Song of Poetry*). Have them use a masking card to locate these words.

Guided Reading: Help the children solve words by noticing beginning consonant clusters with *s* and starting to say the word. At the end of the lesson, quickly write words with *s* clusters for the children to solve.

Interactive Writing: When the children want to write a word beginning with an *s* cluster, have them use the chart to think about how to start it. You may want to add words that come up in interactive writing to the chart.

Independent Writing: Encourage children to write words with *s* clusters quickly. Expect the first two letters to be accurate but not necessarily the entire word.

assess

- Check individually to see whether children can quickly locate *s* clusters on the chart.
- Dictate three to five words with *s* clusters to see how many children can write them.

Expand the Learning

Review other consonant clusters (*r* and *l*) by repeating the lesson. You will not need to have a lesson for every type of letter cluster, but you may want to summarize each one on a chart to which children can refer. Use the word cards for LS 1 for *r* consonant clusters. Use the Word Card Template to make cards for other consonant clusters.

Repeat the lesson with three-letter clusters: *scr, str, spr.*

Connect with Home

Give children word cards for the words on the chart. Have them cut off the beginning letter cluster and take the divided cards home so that they can put words together and read them to family members.

6 Recognizing Beginning Consonant Clusters

Closed Word Sort

Consider Your Children

This lesson is best used when the children can easily relate letters and sounds, know most consonant sounds and consonant clusters with two letters, have worked with common phonograms, and understand the substitution principle (that is, that you can change a word by changing the beginning letter/sound). The children should also have a core of known words that they can use as examples.

Working with English Language Learners

Be sure that English language learners know the words you are using as examples and the words they will sort. Do a quick check with the children and discard any words that are too difficult. Use pictures or actions to help them understand the meaning of the words. If necessary, work with a small group on the word sorting task the first time they do it.

You Need

- Chart paper.
- Markers.
- Word Study Notebooks.

From *Teaching Resources:*

- Consonant Cluster Linking Chart.
- Lesson LS 6 Word Cards.
- Three-Way Sort Cards.

Understand the Principle

The more children can notice larger chunks of written language—for example, letter clusters—the more efficient their decoding will be. They will soon build categories of words with the same clusters, which they will recognize quickly, freeing attention for thinking about the meaning as they read text.

Explain the Principle

“Some consonants go together in clusters.”

“A group of two or three consonants is a consonant cluster.”

“You can hear each sound in a consonant cluster.”

sing	sting	string
by	bring	scream
so	cry	stripe
may	fly	street
back	stop	stray
pay	crack	spray
	black	scrape
	play	
	stay	

teach

Explain the Principle

"Some consonants go together in clusters."

"A group of two or three consonants is a consonant cluster."

"You can hear each sound in a consonant cluster."

① Tell the children that you are going to help them notice something about the beginning of words.

② On the easel, have three columns with one word in the first column—*sing.*

③ Suggested language: "You know the word *sing.* The first sound in *sing* is. . . . [Children respond.] Now, I'm going to write another word. [Write *sting* in the second column.] This word is *sting.* Can you hear the sounds of the first two letters? [Children respond by naming the letters.] Sometimes there are two consonants at the beginning of a word. You can hear both the *s* and the *t.*"

④ "Now, I'm going to write another word. It is *string.* [Say *string* slowly and have students say the word.] What sounds can you hear?"

⑤ Children will respond that they hear *s, t,* and *r.* Write *string* in the third column and ask the children to check the word to see if they were right.

⑥ Go over one or two more examples of words beginning with single consonants, two-consonant clusters, and three-consonant clusters. Use the words on the chart in the example or select other words your students know.

⑦ Then say several more words that have a consonant cluster at the beginning (with either one, two, or three consonants). Ask students to tell you the column in which to write them.

⑧ Ask students to identify consonants that you often see together at the beginning of a word: *pl, pr, br, st, tr, str, scr,* etc. Don't try to make an exhaustive list, but start students on the way to being aware that there are common letter patterns. They will notice that most of the words with three consonants at the beginning start with *s.*

⑨ Suggested language: "We often see two or three consonants together at the beginning of a word. When two or three consonants are together at the beginning of a word, you can usually hear the sound of each letter." This

statement repeats the principle, but it is not necessary to write it on the chart. The main goal of this lesson is to build students' knowledge of categories of examples.

10 Tell the children they will be sorting words, first into single-consonant, two-consonant cluster, and three-consonant cluster beginning categories. When they finish sorting, they are to write two examples of each category in their Word Study Notebook.

take
read
sort
write
read

- Have students use Three-Way Sort Cards to sort word cards into the three categories. Then ask them to write examples of each type of word in three columns in their Word Study Notebooks. Then have them read the Consonant Cluster Linking Chart to a partner.

Ask the children to share the words they wrote in their notebooks and identify the consonant clusters they found. Ask them to discuss what they found out about consonant clusters. Comments like these indicate that students are going further in their exploration of words and application of the principle:

> "You see *p* and *l* together a lot."
>
> "Words that have three consonants at the beginning usually start with *s*."

Link

Interactive Read-Aloud: Read aloud books that feature many words beginning with consonant clusters (see *Teaching Resources,* Alliteration Bibliography). Examples of appropriate books are:

- ***The Little Skyscraper*** by Scott Santoro
- ***On the Wing*** by Douglas Florian

Shared Reading: When reading poems together such as "A Lady Went A-marketing" or "The Littlest Worm" (see *Sing a Song of Poetry*), mask several words that begin with consonant clusters. Stop before each masked word so that students can predict the beginning letter or letters.

Guided Reading: During word work, make words with consonant clusters. Point out words in the text that begin with consonant clusters.

Interactive Writing: Call attention to words with consonant clusters. Encourage children who need more help understanding the concept to come up to the easel and write the consonant cluster letters.

Independent Writing: During conferences, call attention to words with consonant clusters that the children have spelled correctly. Have the children correct words beginning with the consonant clusters they know but have not spelled conventionally.

assess

- Notice whether children are using consonant clusters rather than single letters while solving words in reading.
- Conduct a quick check by asking children to write five to ten words with consonant clusters you have taught. Check to see whether clusters are represented.

Expand the Learning

Expand the sorting activity to include more words, including some that have consonant clusters in the middle (see *Teaching Resources,* Word Card Template). Children can sort word cards by where the consonant cluster appears in the word (beginning, middle).

Repeat the lesson with other words containing two- and three-consonant clusters.

Connect with Home

At a meeting or in a newsletter, teach family members to play a game with their children using words containing consonant clusters that they see at home or around the neighborhood. The adult says the word and the child identifies the letters.

Recognizing Words with Vowels and r

Word Grid Game

Consider Your Children

This lesson is best used when the children know the common letters and associated sounds and have worked with some phonograms. They should be familiar with easy examples of words that have vowels influenced by *r*, such as *her, bird, car, mother, father, sister, for, fur.* In this lesson the children consider the principle in relation to five different vowels. If your students are less experienced, build the chart slowly over several days or a couple of weeks, considering only two new word structures at a time. Start with the easy words that children know best.

Working with English Language Learners

Depending on their first languages, it may be quite difficult for English language learners to pronounce words that have vowels with *r.* Accept approximate pronunciations and draw the children's attention to the visual features of words. The important understanding here is that the vowel in a word with *r* doesn't have the same sound as other vowels in medial position. Have the children concentrate on the *r* sound, but also be sure they realize that there must be a vowel in every syllable. Then help them form categories of words for the different vowels.

You Need

- Chart paper.
- Markers.
- Die or block with *ar, ir, or, er, ur,* and *free* on the sides (one for each group).

From *Teaching Resources:*

- Directions for Word Grid Game.
- Word Grid Sheets made from Lesson LS 7 Word Cards and Word Grid Template.

Understand the Principle

When young children first begin to write, they often use the letter *r* to represent the sounds spelled as *ar, er, ir, or,* and *ur.* For a child who knows the letter name *r,* that makes sense. As they grow more proficient, child spellers need to know that when a vowel is followed by *r,* it often sounds different from that same vowel in other positions; they need to think about the letter cluster, which includes a vowel along with the letter *r.* This cluster may appear in the middle, at the beginning, or at the end of words, and there is always a vowel with the *r.* To decide which vowel to use, children need to think about the sound but also about how the word looks.

Explain the Principle

" When vowels are with *r* in words, you blend the vowel sound with *r [car, her, fir, corn, hurt].* "

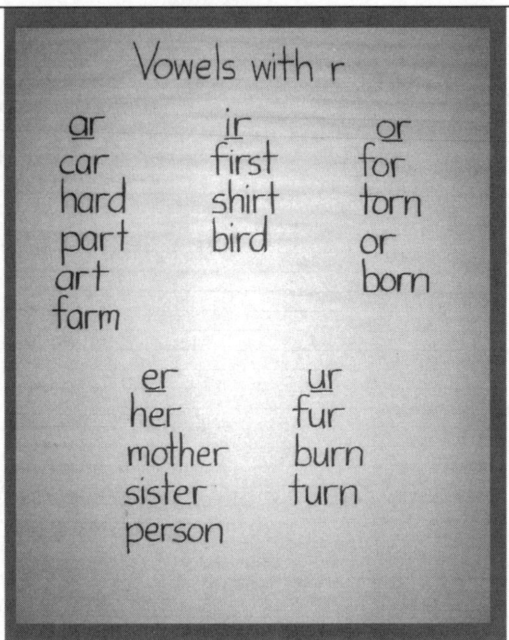

teach

Explain the Principle

“ When vowels are with *r* in words, you blend the vowel sound with *r [car, her, fir, corn, hurt]*. ”

① Working at the easel, tell the children that you are going to be talking about vowels and the letter *r* in words. Write *car* on the chart.

② Suggested language: “Here is a word you know. [Children respond.] Yes, it’s *car*. What part of the word says *ar*? [Children respond.]”

③ Write *ar* at the top of the column and ask the children to generate some other examples of words they know that have *ar*. You can use the word wall as a resource. If the children offer examples of words that have other vowels, recognize that they are getting the idea and start another column. Suggested language: “*First* does have a vowel with an *r*, but it’s not *ar*. I’ll write it. [Demonstrate, starting another column.] What is the vowel before the *r*? [Children respond.] So I will put *first* in another column with *ir* at the top.”

④ Go back to generate more examples for *ar*, but then move to another category.

⑤ Explain that sometimes it is hard to hear the difference in vowel sounds when they are right before *r*. Introduce the *or* column to the children by writing the word *for*. Suggested language: “Here is another word you know that has a vowel with *r*. Say *for*. [Children respond.] Now say *car*. [Children respond.] Can you hear a little bit of difference?”

⑥ Discuss the difference with the children, but caution that you can’t always hear the difference when there is a vowel with *r*. Sometimes you have to think about how the word looks or connect it with other words.

⑦ Place *or* at the top of the column and generate examples that have *or*.

⑧ Continue to generate examples for each column, adding *er* and *ur*. (You may want to continue this lesson over two or more days.)

9. Summarize the lesson by stating the principle orally. Suggested language: "So today you see that you blend the vowel sound with *r* in some words."

10. Show the children how to play the Word Grid game. The first player rolls a die, looks for a word on his grid that contains the same word part shown on the die, reads the word aloud, and crosses the word out on the sheet. Then the next player takes a turn.

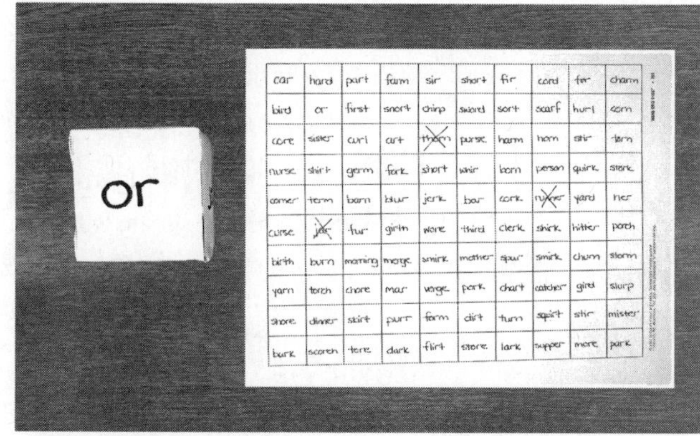

roll
find
read
cross out

- In pairs or threes, the children play the Word Grid game.

Have the children share a word from the grid to add to the class chart. Add one or two examples for each category to the word wall (or highlight words that are already there).

Ask children what they noticed about words. Encourage comments like these:

> "*ar* can be at the beginning of the word or after the first letter or at the end."
>
> "*Torn* and *born* rhyme."
>
> "You can make *car* into *cart* by adding a *t* at the end—like *go-cart.*"
>
> "There's an *er* in Peter's name."

Link

Interactive Read-Aloud: Read aloud books that have many words containing *r*-influenced vowels, such as

- ***The Emperor's Old Clothes*** by Kathryn Lasky
- ***The Butter Battle Book*** by Dr. Seuss

Shared Reading: Call attention to words with vowels and *r* in poems such as "The Chickens," "The Caterpillar," and "Mary Wore Her Red Dress" (see *Sing a Song of Poetry*). Cover the "vowel and *r*" part of the word and ask children to predict the letters.

Guided Reading: During word work, have the children use magnetic letters to make and mix several words that have a vowel and *r*.

Interactive Writing: When writing words that contain vowels with *r*, call attention to the letter cluster and connect it to the chart and the examples on the word wall.

Independent Writing: Encourage the children to make connections to known words with vowels and *r* when writing longer words. Add interesting words to the chart.

assess

- Notice whether children can quickly locate words with vowels and *r* in guided and shared reading.
- Examine students' writing to determine whether they are including a vowel before *r* in appropriate words and whether they are using vowels with *r* with increasing accuracy.
- A week or two later, give a quick test to see whether children are spelling most words with *r*-controlled vowels accurately.

Expand the Learning

Repeat the lesson with more complex examples of words containing vowels and *r*—for example, *birthday, partner, article, corner.*

Connect with Home

Give children a sheet of words (LS 7 Word Cards) that contain a vowel and *r*. Have them cut the words apart, sort them according to vowel, and read them to a family member.

8 Identifying the y Sound in Words

Two-Way Sort

Consider Your Children

The children should have worked with long and short vowel sounds. They will likely be familiar with words ending in *y* but may not have noticed the conditions in which it sounds like a long vowel.

Working with English Language Learners

English language learners need many experiences with words ending with *y* before you use this lesson. Be sure they have encountered and read (or written) words such as *funny* and *sky* many times so that they will be able to contrast the *y* sounds. Observe them as they sort the words to be sure they are saying the words out loud.

You Need

- Pocket chart.

From *Teaching Resources:*

- Pocket Chart Card Template.
- Lesson LS 8 Word Cards.
- Two-Way Sort Sheets.

Understand the Principle

The letter *y* can function as a consonant or vowel, depending on its placement and the letters it is next to. At the end of a word, it sounds like long *i* about 50 percent of the time and like long *e* about 50 percent of the time (usually at the end of words with more than one syllable). It is the single vowel sound in one-syllable words.

Explain the Principle

" *Y* is a letter that sometimes makes a vowel sound. "

" *Y* sounds like *e* on the end of words like *happy, funny, family.* "

" *Y* sounds like *i* in words like *my, sky, by.* "

plan

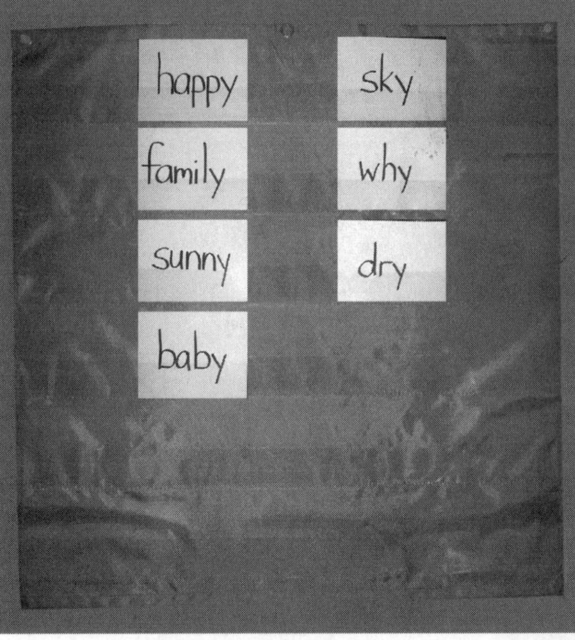

Explain the Principle

"Y **is a letter that sometimes makes a vowel sound."**

"*Y* sounds like *e* on the end of words like *happy, funny, family.*"

"*Y* sounds like *i* in words like *my, sky, by.*"

① Explain to the children that they are going to learn about how the letter *y* can stand for two different vowel sounds.

② Ask the children to read the words you have displayed, in random order, on the pocket chart: *happy, family, sunny, baby, sky, why, dry.*

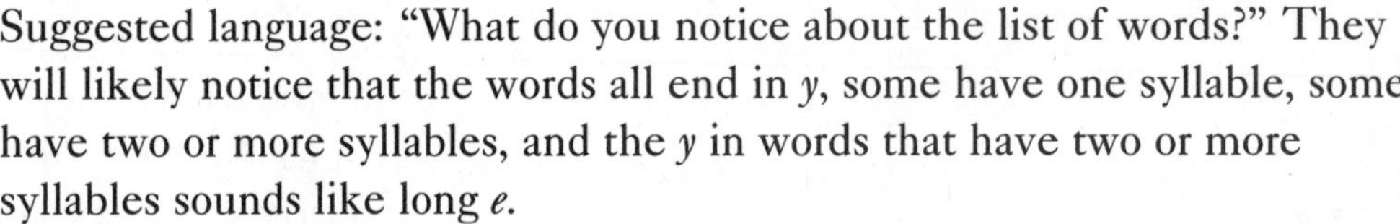

Suggested language: "What do you notice about the list of words?" They will likely notice that the words all end in *y*, some have one syllable, some have two or more syllables, and the *y* in words that have two or more syllables sounds like long *e*.

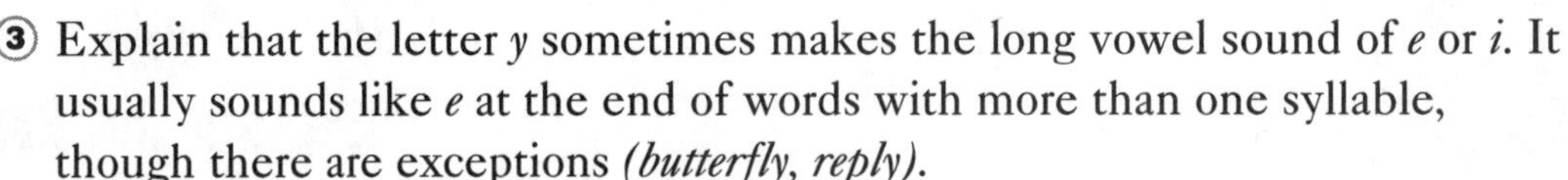

③ Explain that the letter *y* sometimes makes the long vowel sound of *e* or *i*. It usually sounds like *e* at the end of words with more than one syllable, though there are exceptions *(butterfly, reply).*

④ Ask the children to sort the cards in two columns so they can see the two different vowel sound patterns.

⑤ Tell them that today they are going to read and sort words that have *y* as a vowel sound. They will write the key words (*sky* and *sunny*) at the top of the sheet, take and read a word card, and write the word on the sheet under the word that has the same vowel sound.

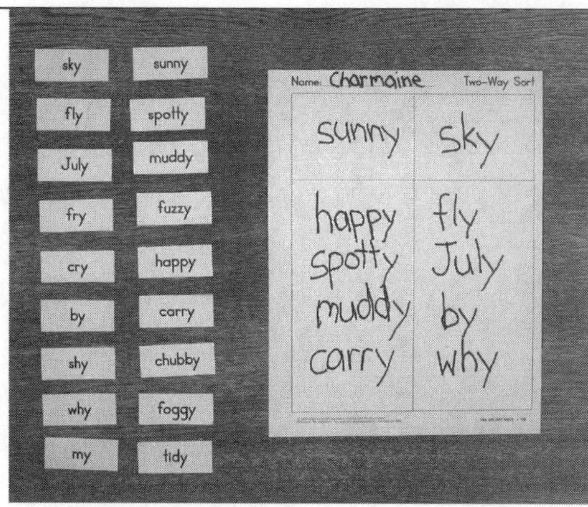

take
read
sort
write

- Using *sky* and *sunny* as key words, have the children use a Two-Way Sort Sheet and word cards to read, sort, and write words that contain a *y* that functions as a vowel.

Invite the children to suggest two or three more words to add to each column of the chart.

Link

Interactive Read-Aloud: Read aloud books that feature many words with *y* with the long vowel sound of *e* or *i*. Examples are:

- ***A Porcupine Named Fluffy*** by Helen Lester
- ***There Was an Old Lady Who Swallowed a Fly*** by Simms Taback

Shared Reading: Use poems that feature words that end in *y*, such as "Fuzzy Little Caterpillar," "The Secret," and "Caterpillar" (see *Sing a Song of Poetry*).

Guided Reading: During word work, write a few words with *y* on a whiteboard and have the children tell the sound it makes.

Interactive Writing: As the children write words on a group chart, ask them to notice the sound of *y* in words that have a *y* at the end.

Independent Writing: When conferring with writers, point out words that have a *y* at the end.

assess

- Dictate four or five words that end in *y* to assess children's control of words with *y* as a vowel.
- In reading, notice how efficient the children are in recognizing or taking apart words that have *y* at the end.

Expand the Learning

Construct a Follow the Path game (see *Teaching Resources*) with words that have *y* at the end.

Connect with Home

Send home a sheet of words ending in *y* for children to sort and read with family members.

9 Identifying Words with the oo Vowel Team

Two-Way Sort

Consider Your Children

Your children need to have good control of long and short vowel sounds and consonant clusters and digraphs before you present this lesson. They will also need many experiences with words ending with *y*. In this lesson, they learn that pairs of vowels such as *oo* can represent two unique vowel sounds.

Working with English Language Learners

Be sure that English language learners have encountered and read (or written) words such as *too* and *good* many times so that they will be able to contrast the *oo* sounds. Observe them as they sort the words to be sure they are saying the words out loud.

You Need

- Pocket chart.
- Word Study Notebooks.

From *Teaching Resources:*

- Pocket Chart Card Template.
- Two-Way Sort Cards.
- Lesson LS 9 Word Cards.

Understand the Principle

The vowel pair *oo* represents two unique vowel sounds. In some words it represents a longer sound, as in *moon;* in others it represents a shorter sound, as in *book.* Children need to learn that they should consider both sounds when trying to solve an unknown word.

Explain the Principle

"Some letters go together and make other vowel sounds: *moon, look.*"

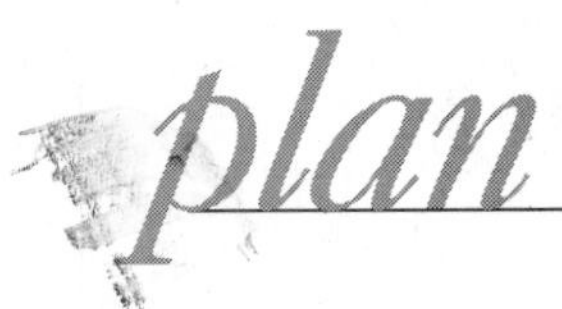

plan

Explain the Principle

"Some letters go together and make other vowel sounds: *moon, look.*"

① Explain to the children that they are going to learn more about vowel sounds.

② Have the words, in random order, *zoo, goose, book, wood, moon, look* on cards in a pocket chart.

③ Ask the children to read them with you. Suggested language: "What do you notice about these words?" Children will notice that they all have *oo* and that the *oo* makes two different sounds, as in *moon* and *look.*

④ Place *moon* and *look* as key words at the top of the chart and have the children place the words with the matching *oo* sound below each key word.

⑤ Show three or four more words *(tooth, took, room, good)* and have the children place them under the correct key word.

⑥ Tell the children, "Some letters go together and make other vowel sounds."

⑦ Explain that they are going to read, sort, and write words with *oo.*

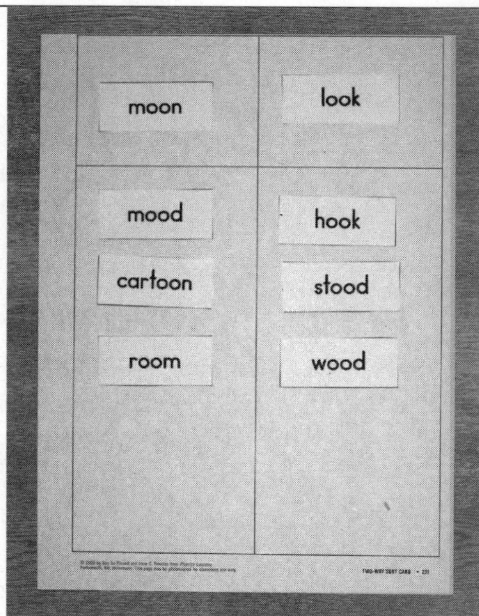

take
read
place
write

- Have the children place *moon* and *look* at the top of a Two-Way Sort Card. Ask them to take a word card, read it, and place it under the correct word. When they finish sorting the words, ask them to write the words in two columns in their Word Study Notebooks.

Invite the children to share three or four more words as you add the words to the chart.

Link

Interactive Read-Aloud: Read aloud a variety of books that have words with *oo,* such as

- ***Zoom Boom*** by Margie Palatini
- ***The Salamander Room*** by Ann Mazer

Shared Reading: Read many poems that include words containing vowel teams, such as "Buffalo Gals" and "Mr. Nobody" (see *Sing a Song of Poetry*). Have the children mark *oo* words with highlighter tape.

Guided Reading: If children come to an unknown word with *oo,* help them relate it to a word they know. For example, say, "That's like *look*" or "That's like *moon.*" During word work, make a few *oo* words with magnetic letters.

Interactive Writing: Point out the *oo* vowel team in words the children are writing in group texts.

Independent Writing: As you confer with the children, help them notice words that are like *look* or *moon.*

assess

- Observe the children's use of *oo* as they read or write.
- Dictate four or five words with the *oo* vowel team to learn whether the children control them.

Expand the Learning

Have the children play Follow the Path (see *Teaching Resources*) on game boards with *oo* words on the spaces.

Connect with Home

Send home a sheet of *oo* words for the children to cut apart and sort with family members.

Recognizing Ending Consonant Clusters

10

Go Fish

Consider Your Children

Your children should have a great deal of experience with beginning consonant clusters and good control of them before you present this lesson. They should also have experience with short and long vowel sounds and know many high frequency words. (They will also be working with ending consonant clusters in spelling pattern [phonogram] lessons.)

Working with English Language Learners

Pronounce the words for English language learners while at the same time helping them notice the cluster at the end of the word. Make explicit connections to the same cluster at the beginning of words that they know well. Sometimes ending sounds of words are difficult for English language learners to hear and imitate. Give them many opportunities to say the words and to play the game with support.

You Need

- Chart paper.
- Markers.

From *Teaching Resources:*

- Directions for Go Fish.
- Go Fish Game Cards made from Lesson LS 10 Word Cards and Deck Card Template.

Understand the Principle

When children understand that they can hear each consonant sound in an initial consonant cluster, they will be able to apply the same understanding to clusters of consonants at the end of words. It is important to help the children articulate the endings of the words carefully so they can record the correct letters.

Explain the Principle

“You can hear each sound in a consonant cluster at the end of a word.”

“You can hear and connect consonant clusters at the end of words.”

“You can find a word by saying it and thinking about the ending sounds.”

“Knowing an ending consonant cluster helps you read and write words.”

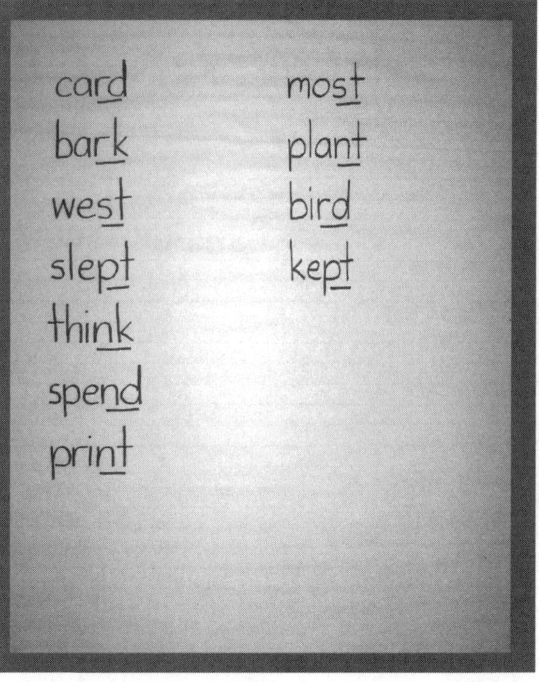

Explain the Principle

" You can hear each sound in a consonant cluster at the end of a word. "

" You can hear and connect consonant clusters at the end of words. "

" You can find a word by saying it and thinking about the ending sounds. "

" Knowing an ending consonant cluster helps you read and write words. "

① Explain to the children that you are going to help them notice the consonant clusters at the end of words.

② Have the children read the following words that you have written on a chart: *card, bark, west, slept, think, spend, print.*

③ Invite one child at a time to underline the consonant letters that they can hear at the end of each word. Suggested language: "You can hear each sound in a consonant cluster at the end of a word."

④ Demonstrate writing the words *most, plant, bird,* and *kept,* showing how you can hear each consonant sound for the two letters at the end of the word.

⑤ Explain to the children that today they are going to play Go Fish with words that have two consonants at the end. Give each player six cards. Players take turns saying a word they have on a card and asking if any other players have a card with a word that ends with the same consonant cluster. If another player has one, the first player takes that card and makes a pair on the table. If no one has a match, the player takes a card from the deck. The first player to run out of cards wins the game.

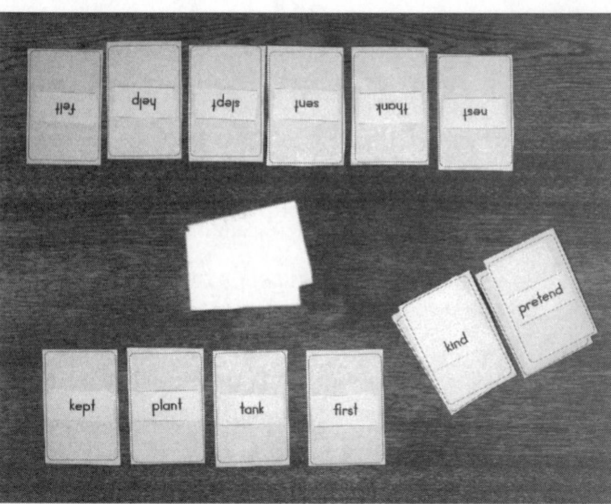

ask
match

- Have the children play Go Fish in pairs or small groups.

Have the children suggest three or four more words to add to the chart.

Link

Interactive Read-Aloud: Read aloud books that have many words with ending consonant clusters, such as

- ***Angelina on Stage*** by Katherine Holabird
- ***Big Time Ollie*** by William Joyce

Shared Reading: Select a variety of poems such as "There Was an Old Man with a Beard" or "A Thunderstorm" (see *Sing a Song of Poetry*) with words that have ending consonant clusters. Have children find and highlight these words in the text.

Guided Reading: During word work, have the children use magnetic letters to make a few words that end with consonant clusters. As the children are solving new words when reading the text, prompt them to read the last part of the word and notice the cluster.

Interactive Writing: When children are writing new words, have them say the word slowly, listening for and recording each sound in the consonant cluster at the end.

Independent Writing: As children try to write words with ending consonant clusters, get them to articulate each sound at the end and then check the letters.

Expand the Learning

Repeat the lesson using different words ending with consonant clusters or words ending with consonant digraphs (for example, *crash, much*). Use the Word Card Template (see *Teaching Resources*) to make word cards for the additional words you've chosen.

Give the children one word with each ending cluster and have them use magnetic letters to make another word with the same ending cluster.

Connect with Home

Give the children a Word Search (see the directions in *Teaching Resources*) containing twenty words that have ending consonant clusters, and ask them to find and circle the words at home with family members.

assess

- Observe the children reading words with ending clusters and notice the patterns they recognize quickly and easily.
- Dictate six to ten words that end with consonant clusters to determine which ones children control.

Generative Lesson

early
mid
late

11 Noticing Double Consonants in the Middle of Words

Follow the Path

Consider Your Children

In this lesson, the children work with two-syllable words that have a double consonant pattern in the middle. They should know consonants and short vowel sounds well and have worked with two-syllable words.

Working with English Language Learners

Observe English language learners carefully to determine their knowledge of consonants and their ability to identify them at the beginning and end of words. It will be easy for them to spot the double letters when they look at words, but they should also understand the meaning of these words. It will help them to notice some of the word endings that are common to words that have double middle consonants.

You Need

- Chart paper.
- Markers.

From *Teaching Resources:*

- Directions for Follow the Path.
- Follow the Path Game Cards made from Lesson LS 11 Word Cards and Deck Card Template.

Understand the Principle

Children find it useful to notice letter patterns in words. Some words have two syllables and contain the double letters *bb, dd, ll, mm, nn, pp, rr, tt,* or *zz.* The first syllable usually is a short vowel sound, and there is a second vowel sound in the second syllable. Children must learn to listen for and recognize both word parts.

Explain the Principle

“Sometimes two consonant letters stand for the consonant sound in the middle of a word.”

“You can find words by saying the word and thinking about the sound in the middle.”

plan

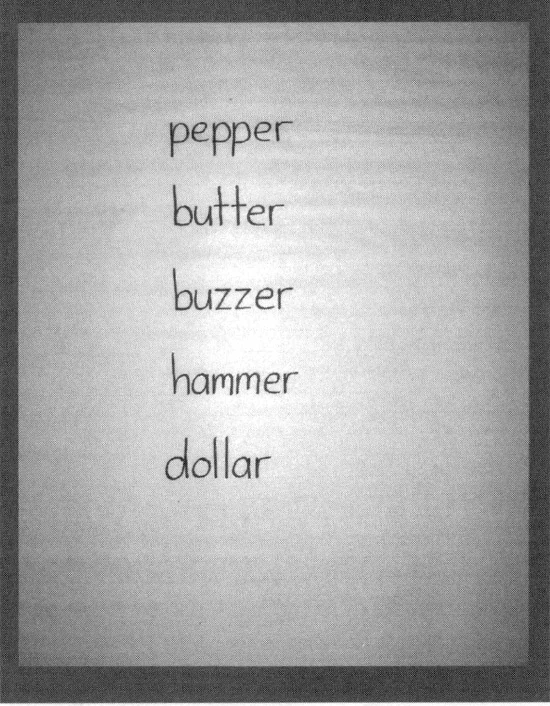

Explain the Principle

" Sometimes two consonant letters stand for the consonant sound in the middle of a word. "

" You can find words by saying the word and thinking about the sound in the middle. "

1. Tell the children that they are going to learn more about consonants in words.
2. Place four or five words with double consonants in the middle on a chart.
3. Suggested language: "Listen to me read these words—*pepper, butter, buzzer, hammer, dollar*. What do you notice about the words?"
4. Have the children say each word and listen for the middle sound. Children will likely notice that the words have double consonants in the middle and that they all have two syllables. They may notice that the first vowel is "short" in sound.
5. Point out, "Sometimes two consonant letters stand for the consonant sound in the middle of a word. You can find words by saying the word and thinking about the sound in the middle."
6. Invite the children to think of other words with two consonants in the middle and add the words to the chart.
7. Tell the children today they are going to play Follow the Path. They throw a pair of dice, move that number of spaces, read the word in the new space, tell the two consonants in the middle, and use it in a sentence. They go back to the space they were on if they can't read the word correctly and use it in a sentence. An alternative is to create a deck of game cards and a blank game board. Children throw the dice, take a card, read it, tell the two consonants in the middle, and use it in a sentence. Then they move the number of spaces.

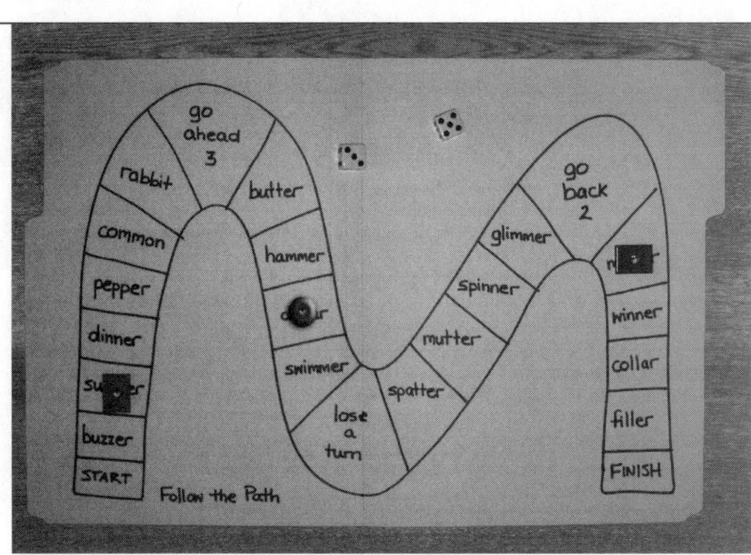

throw dice
take card
read and tell
say sentence
move

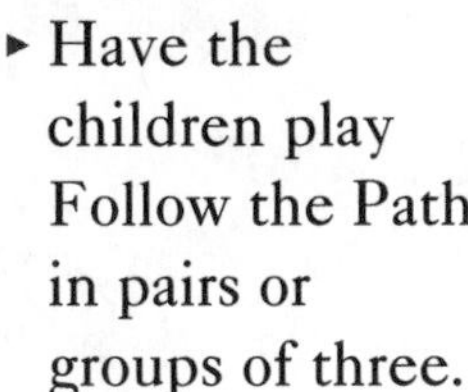

- Have the children play Follow the Path in pairs or groups of three.

Invite the children to tell a few more words with the double letter pattern to add to the class chart.

Review the principle and remind the children to notice words with double consonants.

Link

Interactive Read-Aloud: Read aloud books with a variety of words that have double consonants, such as

- ***Little Quack*** by Lauren Thompson
- ***Sally Goes to the Mountains*** by Stephen Huneck

Shared Reading: Use texts such as "What is Pink?," "Jelly on the Plate," "Donkey, Donkey," and "Little Arabella Miller" (see *Sing a Song of Poetry*) that feature words with double consonants. Have children mark the double consonants with highlighter tape.

Guided Reading: During word work, use magnetic letters to make a few words with double consonants for the children to read.

Interactive Writing: As you and the children construct words with double consonants in the middle, point out the pattern.

Independent Writing: As you confer with writers, point out words that have double consonants in the middle.

assess

- Dictate four or five words with double consonants in the middle.
- Observe how the children take apart words that have double consonants while they are reading.

Expand the Learning

Have children match pairs of words with the same double consonants in the middle.

Post a chart in the room and have the children add words with double consonants when they find them in books they read.

Connect with Home

Send Follow the Path home so that the children can play the game with family members.

Give the children a sheet of words (use the Word Card Template in *Teaching Resources*) with double consonants in the middle. Have them, with the help of family members, cut the words apart, sort them according to the double letters in the middle, and read them.

Identifying Medial Consonant Sounds and Letters

Matching Words

Consider Your Children

When the children can easily identify many consonant sounds and letter/sound relationships at the beginning and end of words, they can listen for sounds and look for letters within words. These sounds are not always strictly the middle letters, but they appear somewhere within the word. Start with simple examples that children will find easy to understand. It is a good idea to begin with words that they know how to read and write and then move on to words that they understand but do not fully control. Start by having children match words by medial sound. If that task is easy, quickly move to the second activity, specifying *how* words are connected by consonant sound and letter. If the task is difficult, divide this lesson into two. Stick with simple consonant sounds for this lesson, but acknowledge all the examples that children offer; later, you can work with consonant cluster sounds in medial position.

Working with English Language Learners

Pronounce words clearly and give English language learners many chances to say words slowly. Help as much as necessary in identifying sounds, and use simple examples. Children may have difficulty understanding when you switch from beginning to ending to medial sounds, so you may want to work only with medial sounds at first.

You Need

- Chart paper.
- Markers.

From *Teaching Resources:*

- Lesson LS 12 Word Cards.
- Pairs of word cards containing the same middle sound clipped together and the letter or letters representing the middle sound underlined in red. You can make deck cards (Deck Card Template) to make the pairs easier to read.

Understand the Principle

Children need to become flexible in making connections between words. In this lesson, they attend to consonant sounds in the middle of words and check the connections they make by looking at the letters. Attending to sounds and corresponding letters in several different positions will help them more fully represent sounds in spelling and also notice different parts of words while reading.

Explain the Principle

“You can hear consonant sounds in the middle of a word.”

“Sometimes two consonant letters stand for the consonant sound in the middle of a word.”

plan

lake fall
lunch sail

yellow reading funny
silly riddle Jenny
Billy meadow sunny
Tyler peanut
pillow
ceiling messy
Cassie
dresser
summer
swimmer

Explain the Principle

"You can hear consonant sounds in the middle of a word."

"Sometimes two consonant letters stand for the consonant sound in the middle of a word."

① Explain to the children that you are going to help them learn more about letters and sounds in words.

② Suggested language: "You have been learning to listen for sounds at the beginning and end of words and to connect them with letters. Say *lake* and *lunch*. How are these words alike? [Children respond.] Say *fall* and *sail*. How are these words alike?"

③ Write the words on a chart and let children notice that they start or end with *l*.

④ Suggested language: "You have been studying the beginning and ending sounds of words and the letters that you write for them. Today we are going to think about consonant sounds in the middle of words. Listen for a sound that is not at the begining or the end but somewhere within the word. Say *yellow* and *silly*." Children respond. If they have difficulty identifying the middle sound, have them say the words a couple of times; several will come up with *l*.

⑤ Suggested language: "That's right. We can hear the *l* sound in the middle of both of those words. Let's write them to check."

⑥ Write the words. The children will notice that there are two letter *l*s. Point out that often there is a double *l* in the middle or at the end of a word. Link the double *l*s to any appropriate children's names on the class name chart.

⑦ Suggest several more words: *Billy, Tyler, pillow, ceiling.* Each time, write them to check whether there is an *l*.

⑧ Repeat the process by matching other examples, varying the letter: *reading, riddle, meadow; funny, Jenny, sunny, peanut; messy, Cassie, dresser; summer, swimmer.*

⑨ The children may suggest words such as *Monday (nd)* or *sister (st)* for either medial sound. Accept what they offer, showing them that the sound of /n/, /d/, /s/, or /t/ is there along with another consonant sound; each sound is represented by a letter. In fact, they are noticing a consonant cluster in the middle of a word.

10 Tell the children that they will be matching words with consonant sounds. Working with a partner, they will first identify and then check the letters in the words. Go over the word cards so that you are sure children can read them. Tell them that if they have difficulty reading words, they should go on to the next pair.

read two words
say the middle sound and letters
check

▸ Working in pairs, one player draws a pair of matched cards and, without showing the words, reads them aloud to the other player, who identifies the consonant sound and letters in the middle. The first player lays the cards down, and both players check the medial sound. After they go through all the cards, each child writes one pair of words with matching middle sounds on a blank card to bring to group share.

Sit the children in a circle. Have each child, without showing the words, read the two words that he has written. The child then calls on someone to identify the middle sound and letters. The child who read the words then confirms or contests the answer. Continue until all children have had a turn.

If there is not enough time, choose four or five children to share.

Link

Interactive Read-Aloud: When you are reading aloud, select words that have the same medial sound (and letter or letters) and ask the children to compare them. Or read two words and ask the children if they are the same or different in the middle. Books that have rhyming multisyllable words may be especially helpful in helping the children consider the middle sounds. Examples are:

- ***Where, Where Is Swamp Bear?*** by Kathi Appelt
- ***The Sneetches*** by Dr. Seuss

Shared Reading: After enjoying a poem, chant, or song such as "The Greedy Man" or "Jelly on the Plate" (see *Sing a Song of Poetry*), have the children find words that have the same middle sounds and highlight them with a marker or transparent tape.

Guided Reading: When the children come to an unknown multisyllable word and they can identify the beginning sound, ask them to think beyond that to predict what letters they would expect to see later in the word.

Interactive Writing: When writing a new word, ask the children to predict the sounds in words, thinking about what they hear beyond the first letter.

Independent Writing: Prompt the children to say words and represent as many of the middle sounds as they can.

assess

- Examine the children's writing to notice the number of sounds that they represent in words.
- Ask the children to write four or five words and to write letters for as many sounds as they can. The spellings may not be accurate, but notice whether they are representing medial consonant sounds.
- Notice whether the children are going beyond the first letter in solving words in reading.

Expand the Learning

Have children play Concentration (see *Teaching Resources*), matching pairs of words with the same middle consonant sounds.

Connect with Home

Send home a sheet of word cards with matching medial sounds and letters. Children can cut them apart and match them at home.

Summarizing Consonant Digraphs

Blind Sort

Consider Your Children

This lesson assumes that the children have already worked on common digraphs and understand the concept that two consonants often appear together and are associated with one sound. If your children have not worked with digraphs, you may want to teach several lessons (for example, with *sh, ch, th,* and *wh*) before this one. If they learned a great deal about digraphs in Grade 1, this summary lesson will remind them of digraphs and help them systematize their knowledge so that it will be more accessible in word solving. If your class is quite advanced, you may want to include some more difficult words *(whether)*, words that are plural *(wishes)*, words that have digraphs in various positions *(other, weather)*, or words that mix blends and digraphs *(swish)*.

Working with English Language Learners

English language learners may find some digraphs difficult to pronounce, so accept approximations and help them connect their own ways of saying words with the visual information (the letter cluster in the word). As they expand their reading and writing in English, pronunciation will gradually improve; however, differences in speech patterns are not bad. They are, in fact, integral to our multicultural society and do not interfere with comprehension and skill. Use words in sentences so that children can understand their meaning as well as their function.

You Need

- Chart paper.
- Markers.

From *Teaching Resources:*

- Lesson LS 13 Word Cards.
- Pocket Chart Cards (Pocket Chart Card Template) for several words from Lesson LS 13 Word Cards, including all digraphs.
- Four-Way Sort Cards.

Understand the Principle

It is important for readers and spellers to see consonant clusters as chunks of information and to recognize and write them quickly as units. In this lesson, children systematize their knowledge of common consonant digraphs in words that begin or end with *sh, ch,* or *th* and that begin with *wh* so that they can easily notice them, making word solving more efficient. The consonant digraph *th* can stand for two different sounds *(the, think)*.

Explain the Principle

"Some clusters of consonants stand for one sound that is different from either of the letters. They are called consonant digraphs."

plan

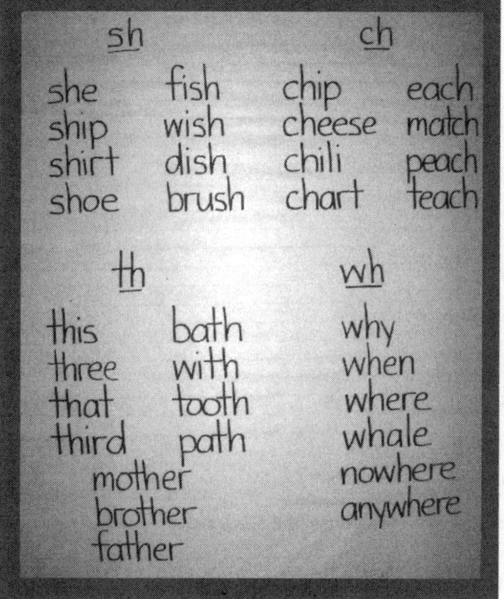

teach

Explain the Principle

“Some clusters of consonants stand for one sound that is different from either of the letters. They are called consonant digraphs.”

① Tell the children that you are going to help them think about what they know about letters in words.

② Suggested language: “You have been learning about consonant clusters. Do you know what we call consonant clusters that have only one sound?” Children respond with the name *digraphs*, or you can tell them. This technical term is useful only to help understand which category of sounds and letters you are referring to in lessons. Plenty of people are excellent readers and spellers without knowing the label, so don’t spend time helping the children apply such terms accurately or memorizing definitions. Just use the term naturally as it occurs. It *is* important for them to understand the principle.

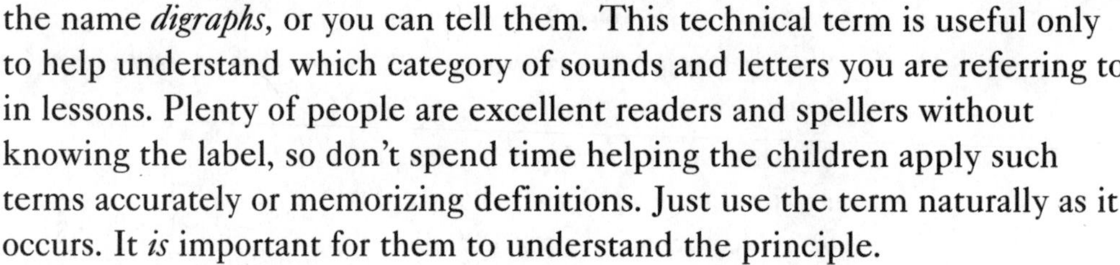

③ Show the children the word *she* on a card or write it at the top of the first column. Suggested language: “This word begins with a consonant digraph. What is it?” Children read the word and identify the *sh*. They then think of one or two other words that begin like *she*.

④ Prompt them to think of a word that ends with *sh*.

⑤ Move quickly to identifying key words for *ch*, *th*, and *wh*.

⑥ Show children a pile of cards with words on them. Quickly go through the cards and have children decide where to place them on the chart. Some words will have the digraph at the beginning and some will have it at the end. Underline the consonant digraph in the word each time. Or have one child hold up the cards one at a time and have other children suggest the key word under which to place it. Keep going until you get four or five words in each column.

⑦ If your children are more sophisticated, you can challenge them by including words such as *other, weather, teacher, nowhere, elsewhere, mother, brother.* They can discuss the idea that the word has the cluster in the middle. Pondering these examples will help children to become more flexible problem solvers.

8. Explain that children will be doing a blind sort, and demonstrate the process. Put the key words at the top of the four columns of the Four-Way Sort Sheet. One child reads a word to a partner without showing it. The partner must indicate in which column the word belongs without seeing the word. Both partners then check the word by looking at it on the card in relation to the key word. They place in a pile the words that they put in the wrong column and make those words with magnetic letters.

9. If the partner was correct about the column choice, then she places the word card in that column. If not, she places it in a pile and makes those words with magnetic letters.

listen
sort
check

▸ Have the children do a blind four-way word sort with a partner. Increase the number of words to make it more challenging.

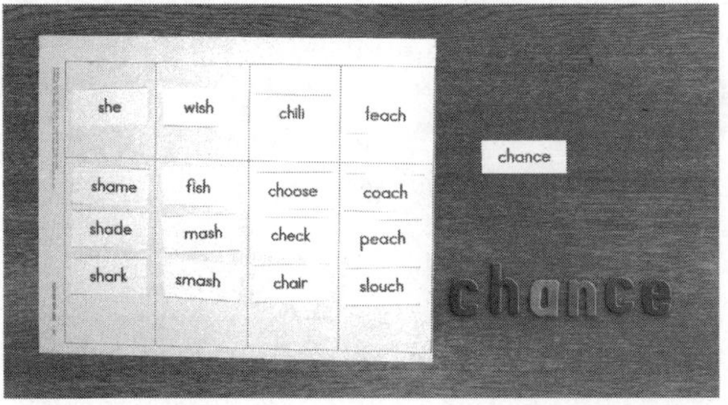

Have the children share their Four-Way Sort Sheets in groups of four. Any group of four may suggest new words for the class chart. End by asking children to talk about what they know about consonant digraphs. Watch for comments like these:

> "Consonant digraphs are clusters that have only one sound."
>
> "Consonant digraphs can be at the beginning or end of words."
>
> "*wh* can be in the middle of words."

Link

Interactive Read-Aloud: Read aloud books in which consonant digraph sounds are repeated. When you find examples of words that begin or end with these sounds, select one or two and have children say them and tell you how to write them on a small whiteboard. Examples of appropriate books are:

- ***Miss Spider's New Car*** by David Kirk
- ***The Little Old Lady Who Was Not Afraid of Anything*** by Linda Williams

Shared Reading: Point out words with consonant digraphs in poems such as "The Chickens" or "The Months of the Year" (see *Sing a Song of Poetry*). Have the children use highlighter marker or tape to emphasize the digraphs.

Guided Reading: After reading and discussing a text, have the children locate words that have consonant digraphs in them. During word work, write a few words that begin or end with consonant digraphs on a whiteboard and have the children read them quickly.

Interactive Writing: When the children want to write a word that has a consonant digraph in it, have a child write the digraph and you write in the rest of the word. After writing, have the children locate words with consonant digraphs, read them, and identify the digraph.

Independent Writing: Encourage the children to refer to the summary chart until they can write words with consonant digraphs independently.

assess

- Notice whether in their writing the children are representing consonant digraphs with the correct letters.
- Notice whether in their reading the children are able to begin consonant digraphs with the appropriate sounds.
- Have the children write a word that begins with each consonant digraph.
- Have children read and/or write a list of names that have consonant digraphs—for example, *Sharla, Shane, Chelsea, Chaka, Wheeler, Whitney, Theron, Thalia, Terish, Dash, Beach, Rich.* Note their representation of the digraph or their attempt to pronounce the word.

Expand the Learning

Practice and summarize the principle by playing the Word Grid game. Write six different consonant clusters on the die and a variety of words on the grid. (See Directions for Word Grid and the Word Grid Template in *Teaching Resources.*)

Have children play Lotto (see *Teaching Resources*) with words with beginning and/or ending consonant digraphs.

Use the Word Card Template *(Teaching Resources)* to include words that begin with *wr*—for example, *wrap, wreath, wrist.*

Connect with Home

Give children sheets of words that they have sorted. They can take them home, cut them apart, and sort them with a family member.

Give children cut-up words so that they can make new words by changing the consonant digraph or make word ladders. (See Directions for Word Ladders in *Teaching Resources.*)

14

Recognizing Consonants with Two Sounds: c, g, *and* th

Two-Way Closed Sort

Consider Your Children

Work with the two sounds of consonants using words that are very familiar to the children and that they understand. This lesson describes words with the two sounds of *c.* It can be repeated for *g* and then *th.* You may want to follow the lesson with the summary lesson on *c, g,* and *th,* Lesson LS 15.

Working with English Language Learners

Children who are just beginning to learn English may know some of the words used in this lesson but be unaware of spellings using *c* as in *city.* Help them make visual connections between these words and *c* as in *car* words so that they begin to develop a repertoire of examples. These connections will strengthen memory. It may be harder for children to say and identify the two sounds of *th,* so provide opportunities for practice and help them notice the use of air.

You Need

- Chart paper.
- Markers.

From *Teaching Resources:*

- Lesson LS 14 Word Cards.
- Two-Way Sort Cards.
- Two-Way Sort Sheets.

Understand the Principle

Realizing that *c* is connected to two different phonemes, depending on the word in which it appears, will help children pay greater attention to the visual patterns in words and become more sophisticated spellers. They will be able to make connections among these words that begin with the same letter but sound different at the beginning.

Explain the Principle

“Some consonants make two or more different sounds: *car, city, get, gym, think, they.*”

teach

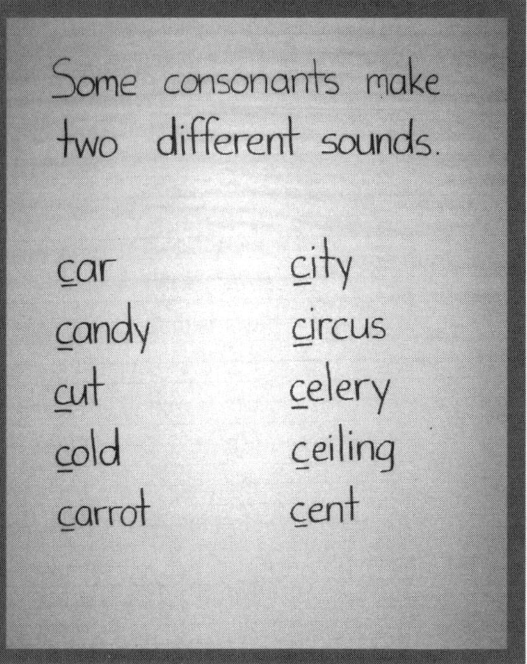

Explain the Principle

"Some consonants make two or more different sounds: *car, city, get gym, think, they.*"

1. Explain to the children that you are going to show them some new ways to think about letters and sounds.
2. Suggested language: "Listen to the first part of each of the words on our chart. [Read *car, candy, cut*]. What do you notice? [Children respond.] Yes, they all start with the same sound. It is a *c* and it sounds like /k/."
3. Invite the children to tell two or three more words like these words (for example, *cold, carrot*).
4. Read the second list (*city, circus, celery*) and help them notice that the initial *c* sounds like /s/.
5. Invite them to add one or two more similar words (for example, *ceiling, cent*).
6. At the top of the chart, write the principle: "Some consonants make two different sounds."
7. Explain to the children that today they are going to do a two-way sort with words that start with *c*. Tell them the two key words, *celery* and *car,* which they should place at the top of their Two-Way Sort Card.

read
sort
write
read

- Have children do a two-way sort with words that start with *c*. They place the key words *celery* and *car* at the top of the card. Then they read word cards and place those that start the same as each key word below each one. Then they write their sort in two columns on a Two-Way Sort Sheet or in their Word Study Notebooks. Finally they read the list to a partner.

Have each child say a word and tell whether it goes with *celery* or *car*. Have them read the Alphabet Linking Chart to develop automaticity in associating initial letters and sounds.

Link

Interactive Read-Aloud: Read aloud books that contain words that will reinforce the two sounds of *c,* such as

- ***Rotten Ralph*** by Jack Gantos
- ***City Chicken*** by Arthur Darros

Shared Reading: After reading and enjoying a text such as "The Centipede's Song" or "The City Mouse and the Garden Mouse" (see *Sing a Song of Poetry*), have children use a masking card or highlighter tape to locate words that start with *c.* Have children tell whether the *c* sounds like the *c* in *celery* or the *c* in *car.*

Guided Reading: After reading and discussing a text, put some words that start with *c* on a whiteboard for children to read quickly. When children come to a word in reading a text and try it with the wrong sound of *c,* prompt them by saying, "It starts like *car.*"

Interactive Writing: As children add words to the text, help them notice words that start with a *c* that sounds like /k/ or a *c* that sounds like /s/.

Independent Writing: Point out words that start with *c* and sound like *car* or *celery.*

assess

- Check children's understanding with a quick spelling test, not for a grade but to decide whether you want to do more lessons. Use a variety of words that begin with *c* and mix in other words, including some that start with *s.*

Expand the Learning

Repeat the lesson with the two sounds of *g,* as in *get* and *gym,* and the two sounds of *th,* as in *the* and *think.* (See Lesson LS 15 Word Cards.)

Connect with Home

Send home some sheets of words (use the Word Card Template in *Teaching Resources*) for children to sort and read to family members.

15

Summarizing Consonants with Two Sounds: c, g, *and* th

Concentration

Consider Your Children

This lesson will be more successful if the children have informally encountered and noticed words that have alternative consonant sounds. If your children have had a great deal of reading and writing experience in first grade, they will already implicitly know many examples. You can check quickly by having the children read a short list of words, listening to their pronunciation, and having them write some simple words. If they already understand the concept, this lesson will be quick and efficient and will help them organize their thinking.

Working with English Language Learners

The fact that many letters have more than one sound associated with them (and many sounds are related to more than one letter) increases the complexity of learning to read in English. Some English language learners may need to spend more time reading words in sentences and engaging in small-group interactive writing so that they can discuss the principle and participate in spelling words.

You Need

- Chart paper.
- Markers.
- Word Study Notebook.

From *Teaching Resources:*

- Alphabet Linking Chart.
- Directions for Concentration.
- Concentration Game Cards made from Lesson LS 15 and Lesson LS 14 Word Cards and Deck Card Template.

Understand the Principle

Becoming flexible readers and writers requires children to learn that letters and sounds do not necessarily have a one-to-one relationship. Sounds can be represented by several different letters, and letters can be related to more than one sound. Knowing this principle will help students develop broader understanding of letter/sound relationships and how they can be used to solve words. Also, they will think about these spellings when writing and be less likely to substitute *s* for *c* or *j* for *g*.

Explain the Principle

“Some consonants make two or more different sounds.”

plan

Explain the Principle

“Some consonants make two or more different sounds.”

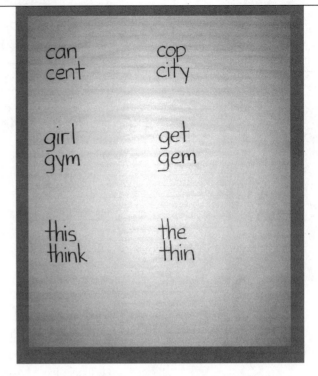

1. Explain to the children that they are going to be thinking about how words are the same and how they are different.

2. Have a blank chart with the following words placed in six columns: *can, cent; cop, city; girl, gym; get, gem; this, think; the, thin.*

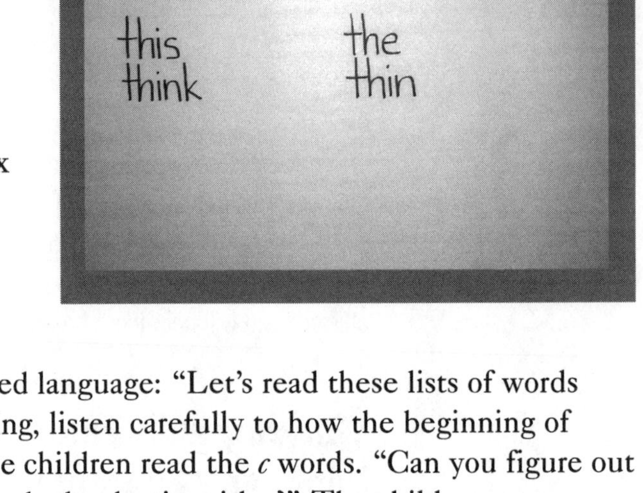

3. Start with the first two columns of *c* words. Suggested language: “Let’s read these lists of words together. While we are reading, listen carefully to how the beginning of each word sounds.” Have the children read the *c* words. “Can you figure out why there are two lists of words that begin with *c*?” The children may respond that the sound is different in the two lists.

4. Go over the *g* and *th* words in the same way.

5. Elicit responses from the group, providing guidance and suggesting specific language if necessary. Write the principle at the top of the chart in response to children’s thinking.

6. Have the children add examples to the list.

7. Read the Alphabet Linking Chart with the group to develop quick recognition of all initial sounds, including the two sounds *c* and *g*.

8. Explain that they will be playing the Concentration card game using words beginning with consonants that make two sounds. They will make pairs of words that have the same consonants but different sounds at the beginning.

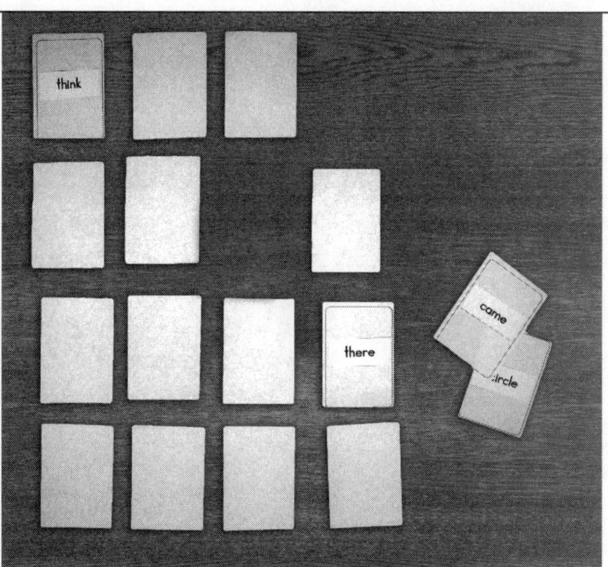

apply

turn
read
turn
read
match

- Have the children, in pairs, play Concentration using words beginning with consonants that make two sounds. Then have them write three words that start with each sound in their Word Study Notebooks.

When the whole group reconvenes, ask students to share some pairs of words that they matched while playing the game. Record their contributions by adding them to the chart. Then talk about any patterns children may notice. For example, they may notice that *ca* always has the /k/ sound. The principles the children come up with may not hold in every case. The important action is for them to search for patterns.

Link

Interactive Read-Aloud: Read aloud books that feature the two sounds of *c, g,* and *th,* such as

- ***Tiger and the Temper Tantrum*** by Vivian French
- ***Geoffrey Groundhog Predicts the Weather*** by Bruce Koscielniak

Shared Reading: In poems such as "The Donut Song" or "The Land of Counterpane" (see *Sing a Song of Poetry*), have the children notice and locate words beginning with the *c, g,* and *th* consonants. They will also be able to find these alternative sounds within words, such as *mother, father, circle, circus, cages.*

Guided Reading: During word work, use magnetic letters to make a few words that have consonants with two sounds.

Interactive Writing: When words with these consonants occur in interactive writing, point them out to the children and have them think carefully about the alternative sounds. Refer to the chart because it will help them think in an organized way about this category of letters.

Independent Writing: Call attention to the different sounds of *c, g,* and *th* while conferring with students as they write.

assess

- Notice whether the children are spelling words with *c, g,* and *th* conventionally in their writing.
- Give a quick spelling test to check on whether the children control some of these words.

Expand the Learning

Have the children play the Word Grid game (see *Teaching Resources*) with a die or block that has an example of the two *c* sounds, two *g* sounds, and two *th* sounds. They read the word on the die and find a word on their Word Grids that sounds the same.

Have children play Go Fish (see *Teaching Resources*) with word cards (pairs or sets of three) that contain the six different letter/sound combinations.

Invite the children to "Write Around the Room" (see *Teaching Resources*) to find words with *c, g,* or *th.*

Connect with Home

Invite family members and children to draw a picture that contains as many words as they can think of that have the different sounds of *c, g,* or *th.* An example might be a city scene with other *c* words such as *car.* Have the children bring in the pictures to share and ask other children to identify the *c, g,* or *th* words.

16 Recognizing and Using ai, ay, oa, ee, ea, ow Vowel Combinations

Making Words

Consider Your Children

Use this lesson after your children have worked with vowels and also understand that letters often appear together in words. They will already have worked with consonant clusters and with phonograms, so these vowel patterns will represent another kind of word part to notice. You may want to have the children write a few simple words with vowel patterns to get an idea whether they are aware that sometimes two vowels go together to make a sound.

Working with English Language Learners

It will be helpful to English language learners to see vowels as patterns in words that they know. These mostly regular vowel combinations will help them make word solving more efficient. Begin with simple words that have been part of their speaking, listening, and reading vocabularies for a while and work to systematize their knowledge. Comparisons of words they know will help them see these visual patterns more easily.

You Need

- Magnetic letters.
- Chart paper.
- Markers.

From *Teaching Resources:*

- Lesson LS 16 Word Cards.
- Three-Way Sort Sheets.

Understand the Principle

Sometimes these vowel combinations are called *vowel digraphs, vowel pairs,* or *vowel teams.* Many of these vowel combinations, especially *ai, ee,* and *ay,* are highly predictable in English and will help children increase their spelling accuracy. Once children understand that vowels often appear together and they know to look for these patterns, they can apply this information to reading text and spelling words.

Explain the Principle

“Some vowels go together in words and make one sound.”

“When there are two vowels, they usually make the sound of the name of the first vowel.”

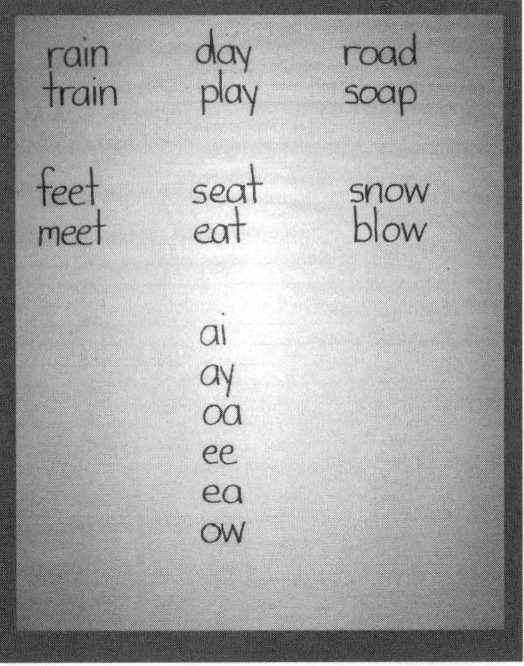

rain
train
day
play
road
soap
feet
meet
seat
eat
snow
blow
ai
ay
oa
ee
ea
ow

Explain the Principle

"Some vowels go together in words and make one sound."

"When there are two vowels, they usually make the sound of the name of the first vowel."

① Explain to the children that you are going to teach them something new about how vowels work.

② Read the first pair of words (*rain* and *train*) on the chart.

③ Ask them what they notice about the vowels. Children respond.

④ Remind them that *y* sometimes functions as a vowel, as in *day* and *play*. And make note of *w* in *snow*.

⑤ Ask what they notice.

⑥ Continue with *road* and *soap*, *feet* and *meet*, *seat* and *eat*, and *snow* and *blow*.

⑦ Help them conclude that in each word there are two letters together and they usually make the sound of the first vowel.

⑧ On an easel, place the vowel combinations *ai, ay, ea, ee, oa, ow*.

⑨ Explain that today they will make five words for each vowel combination with magnetic letters and word cards and list them on two Three-Way Sort Sheets.

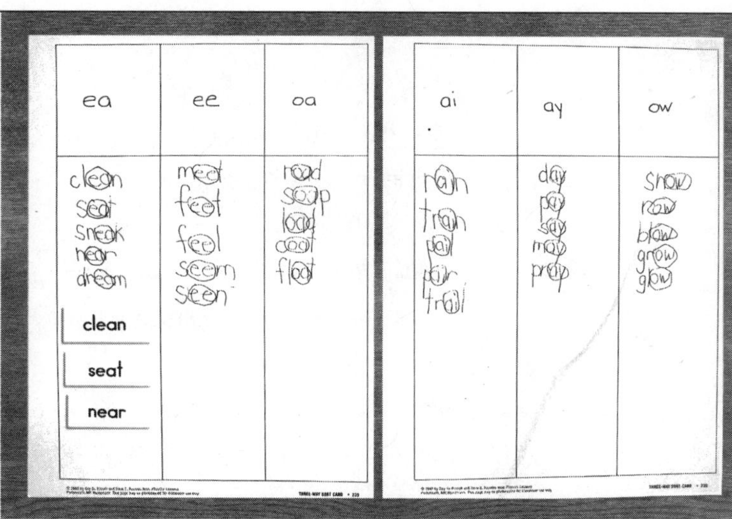

make
write
circle
read

▸ Have children use word cards and magnetic letters to identify and make five words containing the vowel combinations *ai, ay, ea, ee, oa*, and *ow*. Then ask them to write the words on two Three-Way Sort Sheets and circle the vowel combination. Finally, have them read their lists to a partner.

Have the children share one word in each category with a new partner.

Link

Interactive Read-Aloud: Read aloud books containing many words with vowel combinations, such as

- ***Felix Feels Better*** by Rosemary Wells
- ***Five Little Monkeys Sitting in a Tree*** by Eileen Christelow

Shared Reading: In poems you read together, such as "Where Go the Boats" and "The Months of the Year" (see *Sing a Song of Poetry*), revisit the text to locate and highlight words with vowel combinations.

Guided Reading: During word work, have the children use magnetic letters to make two or three words containing vowel combinations.

Interactive Writing: When children are contributing words, help them notice those with vowel combinations.

Independent Writing: Help writers look for words that are misspelled because one of a pair of vowels has been omitted.

assess

- Have children read a new passage that contains many high frequency words and some words with vowel digraphs. You may want to include a couple of names for them to decode. Their attempts will give you an idea how well they are applying the principle being taught in this lesson.

Expand the Learning

Have the children play the Word Grid game (see *Teaching Resources*) using a die containing the six vowel combinations dealt with in this lesson.

Repeat the lesson with other words that contain vowel combinations.

Use more complex vowel combination words that begin with consonant clusters or digraphs.

Connect with Home

Have children use magnetic letters to make six words, one with each vowel combination. Have them bring this list to school to share.

17 Identifying Words with ai, ay, ee, ea, oa, ow

Crazy Eights

Consider Your Children

Once children have learned to play this card game, they will be able to apply the routine with four of the six new patterns at a time. They should have good control of common long and short vowel patterns and initial consonant clusters and digraphs. They should also have a repertoire of known words with vowel patterns.

Working with English Language Learners

English language learners may need support in a small group to understand the rules of Crazy Eights and play it successfully. Quickly go over the words you use for examples to be sure they can read and understand them.

You Need

- Pocket chart.

From *Teaching Resources:*

- Pocket Chart Word Card Template, to create word cards for *rain, pail, day, pay, meet, feet, seat, beat, boat, soap, snow, row.*
- Directions for Crazy Eights.
- Crazy Eights Game Cards made from the previous lesson's word cards (Lessson LS 16) and Deck Card Template:

  13 cards of each of four selected vowel patterns.

  4 cards with a Crazy Eight on them.

Understand the Principle

Children need to learn that there are many common vowel patterns, or *vowel teams,* in words. These vowel patterns are best learned as part of phonograms or rimes.

Explain the Principle

“Some vowels go together in words and make one sound.”

“When there are two vowels *(ai, ay, ee, ea, oa, ow),* they usually make the sound of the name of the first vowel *(rain, day, meet, seat, snow).*”

plan

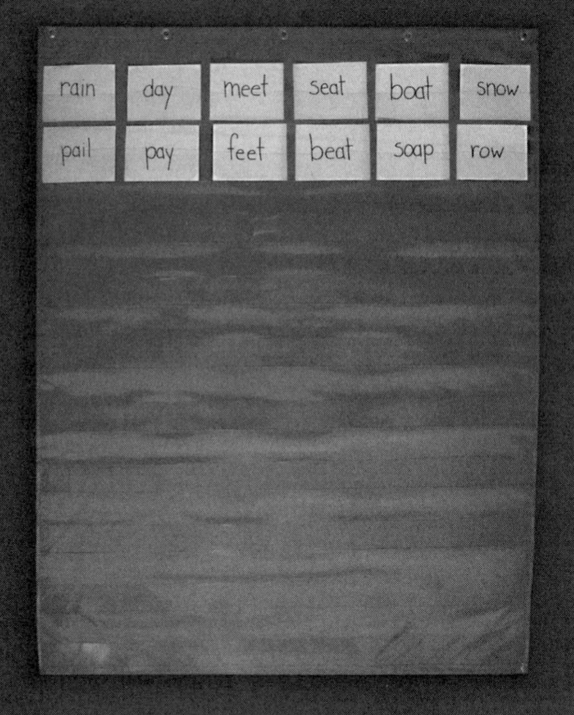

Explain the Principle

" Some vowels go together in words and make one sound. "

" When there are two vowels ***(ai, ay, ee, ea, oa, ow)***, they usually make the sound of the name of the first vowel ***(rain, day, meet, seat, snow)***. "

1. Explain to the children that you are going to tell them about more vowel patterns they will see in words.
2. Place in six columns the word cards for *rain* and *pail, day* and *pay, meet* and *feet, seat* and *beat, boat* and *soap*, and *snow* and *row.*
3. Read each word pair and ask the children to notice the vowel sound they hear and the two letters that make the sound.
4. Explain that some vowels go together in words and make one sound. They usually make the sound of the first vowel.
5. Invite the children to give one more example for each pattern. If they suggest a word that has a different pattern, write it off to the side and explain the pattern.
6. Tell the children they are going to play the Crazy Eights card game. Here's how it works. Give each player eight cards and place the remaining deck face down, with one card turned face up beside the deck. The first player reads the card that is face up, puts down a card with the same vowel sound, and reads it. The discarded card can match a word with the same vowel sound (an *ai* word can match an *ai* word or an *ay* word, and vice versa). If the player doesn't have a card that will match, he can discard a Crazy Eight card, which functions as a free card. Otherwise the player draws a card until he finds a match to put down. The first player to discard all cards wins the game.
7. Demonstrate and explain the game with two children until everyone understands how to play the game.

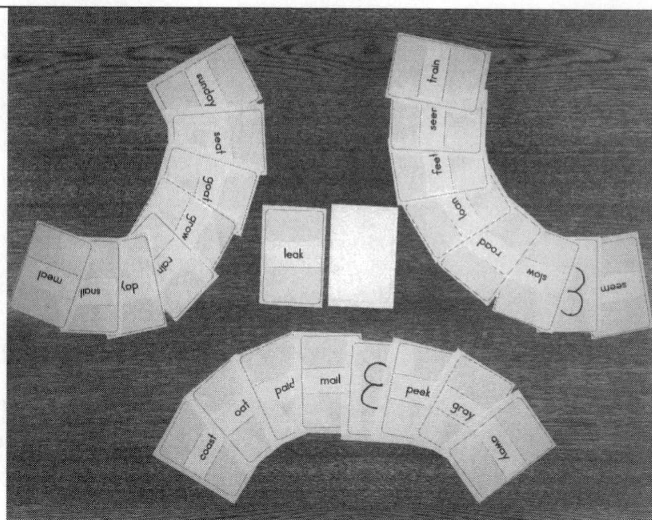

read card
match and put down

▸ Have the children play Crazy Eights in groups of three or four.

Have children suggest more examples of words with the sounds of *a* and *e*. Write the words on cards or a whiteboard, and have children place word cards or write words in the right categories. This chart can become a resource for spelling.

Link

Interactive Read-Aloud: Read aloud books that use words containing long vowel patterns, such as

- ***Madeline and the Bad Hat*** by Ludwig Bemelmans
- ***Horton Hatches the Egg*** by Dr. Seuss

Shared Reading: Select poems that contain some words with long vowel patterns, such as "Row, Row, Row Your Boat," "The Bear," "Slowly, Slowly," and "Sneeze on Monday" (see *Sing a Song of Poetry*). Have children locate and highlight two or three words containing a specific pattern.

Guided Reading: During word work, use magnetic letters to make three or four words with long vowel patterns. Have the children write some of these words.

Interactive Writing: When the children are constructing a word with a long vowel pattern, prompt them to think of another word with the same pattern: "Do you know a word like that?"

Independent Writing: Encourage the children to reread their writing and check for the correct spelling of the long vowel patterns in the editing process.

Expand the Learning

Repeat the lesson with a different deck of cards incorporating the two patterns not used in the first deck and eliminating two of the originally used patterns. (Each deck features only four patterns at a time.)

Connect with Home

Send home the deck of Crazy Eights cards so that the children can play the game with family members.

assess

- Dictate six to ten words with long vowel patterns and note how many of them the children control.
- Notice the children's use of long vowel patterns in their writing.

18 Recognizing st Consonant Clusters in Words

Blind Sort

Consider Your Children

This lesson will be of most benefit to your children if they understand the concept of consonant clusters in words and have worked with *st* and other combinations at the beginning of words. It will now be easy to notice this cluster at the end of words. This lesson introduces children to the idea that many consonant clusters appear at the end of words they know and will start them looking for such patterns. You will not need to teach a lesson on *every* consonant cluster.

Working with English Language Learners

English language learners will be able to hear both the /s/ and the /t/ in this consonant cluster. Help them feel the way their mouths work as they make the sounds and help them notice the visual features of words. Most of the words you'll use as examples cannot be connected to pictures, so work to explain to children words that are not in their oral vocabularies. If necessary, work with a small group, reducing the examples to those words that children understand, and have them write words, highlighting the *st* cluster.

You Need

- Magnetic letters.
- Small magnetic whiteboard or cookie sheet.

From *Teaching Resources:*

- Lesson LS 18 Word Cards.
- Two-Way Sort Cards.
- Two-Way Sort Sheets.

Understand the Principle

Recognizing consonant clusters at the beginning and end of words will help children pick up visual information more efficiently when they read and will lead them to be more careful in representing this information when spelling. Once they have learned to quickly identify these consonant clusters in beginning and ending positions, you can have them hunt for medial consonant clusters.

Explain the Principle

"You can hear and connect consonant clusters at the beginning of words."

"You can hear and connect consonant clusters at the end of words."

plan

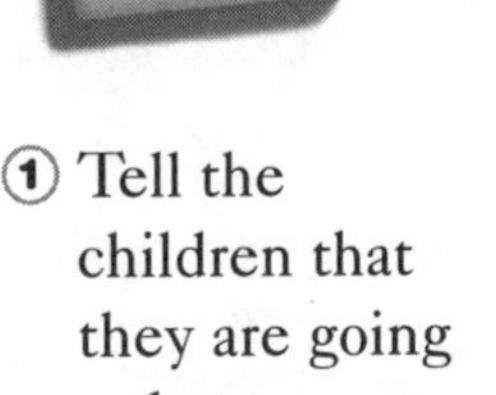

Explain the Principle

"You can hear and connect consonant clusters at the beginning of words."

"You can hear and connect consonant clusters at the end of words."

1. Tell the children that they are going to learn more about consonant clusters.
2. Suggested language: "You have been learning about consonant clusters at the beginning of words. Some words begin with *st*. Let's make some."
3. Have the children suggest words that begin with *st* while you make the words using magnetic letters.
4. Suggested language: "Those words begin with the letter cluster *st*. You also know some words that end with the letter cluster *st*. Here is one."
5. Make *fast* with magnetic letters and have the children read it. Then have the children suggest more words ending with *st*.
6. Explain that you can hear and connect consonant clusters at the beginning or ending of words.
7. Tell the children they will be sorting words that begin and end with *st*. Quickly go over the words they will be sorting to check their ability to read the words. Remove any that are too difficult.

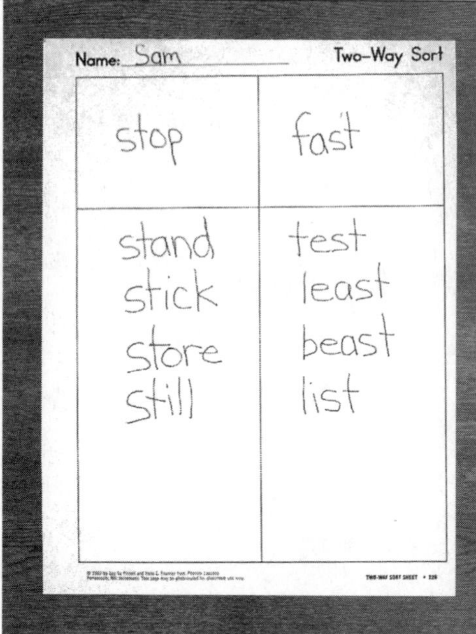

listen
sort
check
write

- Give the children the word cards and a Two-Way Sort Card with *stop* at the top of one column and *fast* at the top of the other column.
- Ask them to do a blind sort with a partner. One partner reads a word, and the other indicates which column it should be in. The first partner checks by looking at the word and showing it to the other child. If the word is sorted into the correct column, they place it there. If not, it goes to the bottom of the pile so that the partners can consider it again. After sorting the words, each child writes the two columns of words on a Two-Way Sort Sheet.

Have children read their *st* words to a new partner.

Read the chart to the whole class again to review the words.

Link

Interactive Read-Aloud: Read aloud books that emphasize beginning and ending consonant clusters, such as

- ***Bus Route to Boston*** by Maryann Cocca-Leffler
- ***A Pinky Is a Baby Mouse*** by Pam Ryan

Shared Reading: Have the children use highlighter tape, a highlighter marker, or a masking card to locate words that begin or end with *st.*

Guided Reading: At the end of the lesson, quickly review some words that begin or end with *st* in poems such as "The Boy Stood in the Supper-Room," "Star Light, Star Bright," or "Stepping Stones" (see *Sing a Song of Poetry*).

Interactive Writing: When the children want to write a word with *st* at the beginning or end, make connections with the chart. You may want them to write known words with *st* to get to words that they don't know.

Independent Writing: When the children want to write a word with *st,* have them say the word, write the letters, and then make connections with other words they know.

assess

- Have each child read a list of four or five words that begin or end with *st.*
- Dictate a short list of words that begin or end with the *st* cluster. Examine children's attempts to determine whether they are representing the pattern.

Expand the Learning

Expand the lesson to look at the same letter clusters in the middle of words, for example, *blister, yesterday, mister.* Use the Word Card Template *(Teaching Resources)* to create cards for the new words you choose.

Connect with Home

Give children word cards for the words on the chart (see Word Card Template in *Teaching Resources*) and others you have added. Have them sort the word cards at home with family members.

early
mid
late

Generative Lesson

19

Recognizing mp, nd, nk, nt *Ending Consonant Clusters*

Lotto

Consider Your Children

When your children understand the concept that some consonants appear together in words and have explored and sorted beginning consonant clusters, it will be easier for them to examine consonant clusters at the end of words. Chances are children already know the words you are using and have noticed through reading, writing, and phonogram study that consonants appear often together. You will not need a lesson and application activity on every ending consonant cluster, but it may be beneficial to focus on these useful word chunks for two or three lessons until the concept is fully established. Then you can gradually add ending consonant clusters to word sorts and games.

Working with English Language Learners

Nasal sounds such as *n* and *m* are especially hard to identify when they occur before another consonant and will pose particular challenges for English language learners. Say the word slowly and run a finger under it to help the children notice the ending sounds. We say both of these sounds, but the nasal consonant is so smoothly blended into the second consonant that the children will neglect it. Help them feel the sounds in their mouths and notice the visual features of words.

You Need

- Chart paper.
- Small index cards.
- Markers.

From *Teaching Resources:*

- Lesson LS 19 Word Cards.
- Lotto Game Cards.
- Directions for Lotto.

Understand the Principle

Patterns such as consonant clusters at the end of words will make processing more efficient in reading. In writing, you will find children quickly writing clusters once they know them. Once they have learned to quickly identify consonant clusters in beginning and ending positions, you can have them hunt for medial consonant clusters.

Explain the Principle

“You can hear and connect consonant clusters at the beginning of words.”

“You can hear and connect consonant clusters at the end of words.”

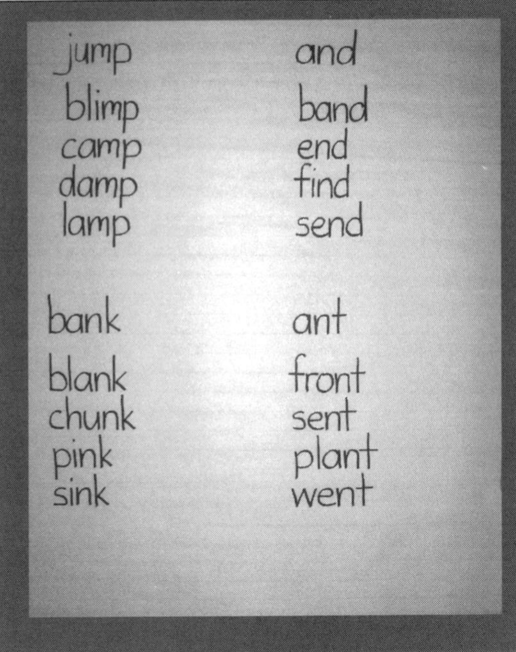

jump
blimp
camp
damp
lamp
and
band
end
find
send
bank
blank
chunk
pink
sink
ant
front
sent
plant
went

Explain the Principle

" **You can hear and connect consonant clusters at the beginning of words.** "

" **You can hear and connect consonant clusters at the end of words.** "

1. Tell the children that you are going to help them learn more about how words end.
2. Suggested language: "You have been learning about consonant clusters at the end of words. Today you are going to look at more of those kinds of words."
3. Show the children the word *jump*, and have them read it and identify the consonant cluster at the end. Then show them *and*, *bank*, and *ant*, and repeat the procedure.
4. Once the four key words have been placed on the chart (or in the pocket chart), read the other words one at a time. Have them listen to the words and tell you where to place or write them.
5. When you have finished, they will have sorted the words into four categories. Ask them to talk about what they notice about words. Model or observe for comments like these:

   "It's hard to hear the *n* in *bank*."

   "*Bank* is almost like *back*."

   "*Jumper* would have *mp* in the middle, not at the end."
6. Explain that you can connect consonant clusters at the beginning or end of words.
7. Tell the children that they are going to play Lotto with words that have ending consonant clusters. After playing the game, the children select and write three words with ending consonant clusters to bring to group share.

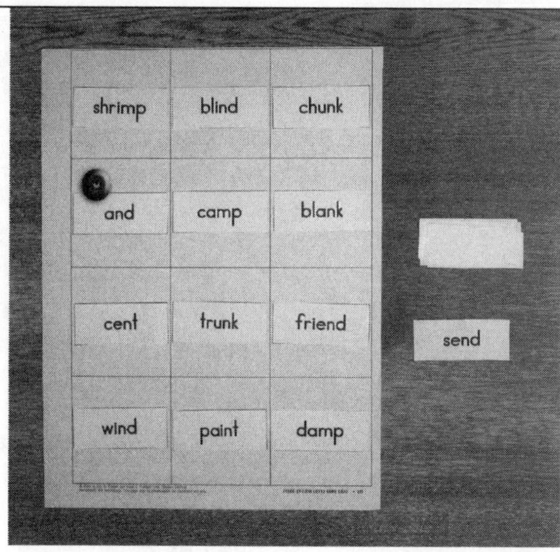

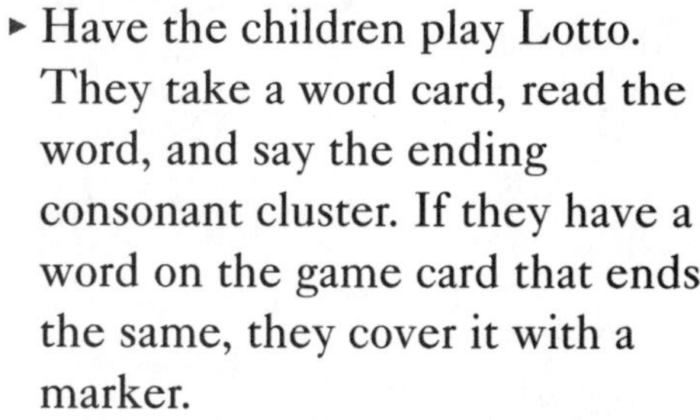

take
read
match
cover

- Have the children play Lotto. They take a word card, read the word, and say the ending consonant cluster. If they have a word on the game card that ends the same, they cover it with a marker.
- After they have played the game, ask the children to select and write three words with ending consonant clusters on an index card. Ask them to highlight the ending cluster and bring it to group share.

Have children, in turn, share one or two of their words and identify the consonant clusters. You might also ask them to locate the word on the chart or tell the category it belongs in.

Read the chart again with the whole class to review the principle.

Link

Interactive Read-Aloud: Read aloud books that have words containing ending consonant clusters. Many rhyme books (see *Teaching Resources,* Rhymes Bibliography) have words with ending consonant clusters. If you find an interesting word, add it to the chart. Examples of appropriate books are:

- ***A Place to Bloom*** by Lorianne Siomades
- ***Elephants on Board*** by Suse MacDonald

Shared Reading: Play a guessing game with a piece of text that children are familiar with; for example, "I see a word that ends in the consonant cluster *nt*." Some examples from *Sing a Song of Poetry* are "My Shadow" and "Two Little Feet."

Guided Reading: At the end of the lesson, quickly review some words with ending consonant clusters. As you write the words on a chart, have the children read them and suggest another word that ends the same.

Interactive Writing: Model using the chart to check on the spelling of a word with an ending consonant cluster.

Independent Writing: Encourage children to make connections between the words they want to write and the charts showing ending consonant clusters.

assess

- Observe the children as they play Lotto to determine their grasp of the principle. Pay particular attention to their solving of any new words you have added to the game.
- Dictate three to five words that have ending consonant clusters *(mp, nd, nk, nt)* to determine which ones are known.

Expand the Learning

Repeat the lesson with other groups of ending consonant clusters: *rd, rp, rt.* Use the Word Card Template (see *Teaching Resources*) to create cards for the new words you choose.

Expand the lesson to look at the same letter clusters in the middle of words, for example, *trumpet, winter, Andrew, mister, whistle.*

Connect with Home

Give children word cards for the words on the chart and others you have added. Have them sort the word cards at home with family members.

20

Recognizing Beginning and Ending Consonant Clusters

Consonant Cluster Dominoes

Consider Your Children

When your children have had experience identifying and using consonant clusters, both blends and digraphs, at the beginning and end of words, they need to be taught to apply these important concepts flexibly. They are ready to notice consonant clusters in any part of a word and to connect words using both beginnings and endings. This lesson summarizes the principle of consonant clusters and makes the important point that connections can be made between and among words. In this lesson the children learn how to notice beginning and ending consonant clusters (the ending clusters will be part of the rime).

Working with English Language Learners

English language learners may need more work with beginning or ending clusters before they are asked to switch back and forth between endings and beginnings. Work for flexibility as soon as you can, however, because they are likely to try to memorize examples rather than use the principle. Use a few examples the children really know and understand.

You Need

- Pocket chart.

From *Teaching Resources:*

- Pocket Chart Cards (Pocket Chart Card Template) for *crab, went, crush, brush, plan, burn, drink, plant, chart, sharp, friend, blind, send, print, black, slim, word, flower, stamp, blend, blast, from, work, bird.*
- Directions for Sound Dominoes.
- Lesson LS 20 Word Cards (Dominoes).
- Directions for Word Ladders.
- Word Ladders Template.

Understand the Principle

Once they know some consonant clusters, children will find it easier to notice them in words and connect the sounds and letters to solve words. Instead of a finite body of words as examples, they need to expand their use of the principle of consonant clusters so that they will automatically add it to their repertoires. They need to notice the clusters in the onset and also as part of the rime.

Explain the Principle

"You can hear each sound in a consonant cluster."

"You can hear and connect consonant clusters at the beginning of words."

"You can hear and connect consonant clusters at the end of words."

Explain the Principle

"You can hear each sound in a consonant cluster."

"You can hear and connect consonant clusters at the beginning of words."

"You can hear and connect consonant clusters at the end of words."

1. Explain to the children that you are going to summarize what they have learned about consonant clusters.
2. Suggested language: "You have been learning about consonant clusters in words. What do you know about consonant clusters?"
3. Lead a discussion in which students summarize what they know about consonant clusters. For example:

   "They appear often together in words."

   "Consonant clusters can be at the beginning or ending of words or in the middle."
4. Place a few word cards in the correct columns in the pocket chart. Suggested language: "On this chart I have some words. What do you notice about these words?" Students respond and may notice that many words have consonant clusters at both the beginning and the end.
5. Have children consider more word cards one at a time and then sort them into the three categories. In the first column, place words that have a consonant cluster *only* at the beginning; in the second column, place words that have a consonant cluster *only* at the end; in the last column, place words that have consonant clusters at both the beginning and the end.
6. After words are sorted, tell children that they will be playing Consonant Cluster Dominoes.

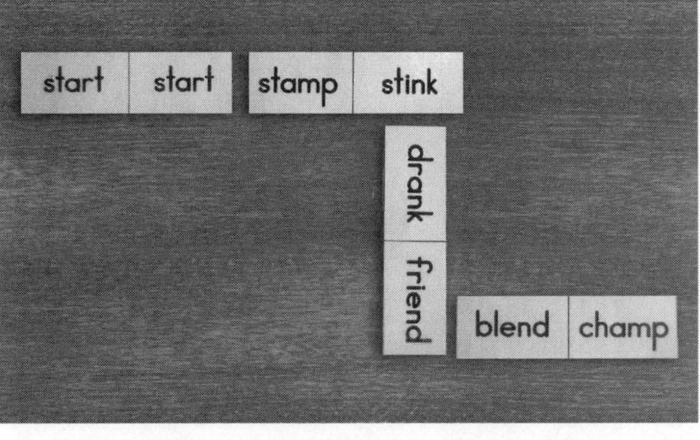

take
read
match

write
change
write

- Have the children play Consonant Cluster Dominoes. Each player takes five to ten dominoes, leaving a pile face down. The player with a "double" begins. If no one has a double, the child whose name comes first in the alphabet begins. Players can build on dominoes by matching either beginning or ending consonant clusters.When playing a domino, the student reads the word and then says what is being matched—the beginning or ending cluster. Some dominoes have words with only one cluster, and these may be built on *only* once. Exact words cannot be matched—only different words with the same consonant cluster. A player who cannot build draws until he can. The objective is to be the first player with no dominoes remaining. The Directions for Sound Dominoes describes two versions of the game. Choose the version more appropriate for your children.
- After the game, have children build word ladders using the word matches they made in the game.

Have children share their word ladders. You may want to add some of these words to the chart.

Link

Interactive Read-Aloud: Read aloud books that emphasize rhyming words (see *Teaching Resources,* Rhymes Bibliography), because many will have ending consonant clusters. If you find an interesting word, add it to the chart. Examples of appropriate books are:

- ***The Awful Aardvarks Shop for School*** by Reeve Lindbergh
- ***Madeline's Rescue*** by Ludwig Bemelmans

Shared Reading: Play a guessing game with a piece of text that children are familiar with; for example, "I see a word that ends in the consonant cluster *nt.*" Some examples from *Sing a Song of Poetry* are "The Months of the Year" and "Fuzzy Little Caterpillar."

Guided Reading: At the end of the lesson, quickly review some words with ending consonant clusters. As you write the words on a chart, have children read them and suggest another word that ends the same.

Interactive Writing: Model using the chart to check on the spelling of a word with an ending consonant cluster.

Independent Writing: Encourage children to make connections between the words they want to write and the charts showing ending consonant clusters.

Expand the Learning

Have children make Consonant Cluster Word Ladders (see *Teaching Resources*).

Connect with Home

Give children a sheet of Domino cards featuring consonant clusters. Have them play Consonant Cluster Dominoes at home with family members.

assess

- Observe children as they play Consonant Cluster Dominoes to determine their grasp of the principle. Pay particular attention to their solving of any new words you have added to the game.
- Give a child a list of three to five words with ending consonant clusters to read.

Recognizing ou, ow, and aw Vowel Sounds

Crazy Eights

Consider Your Children

Be sure your children have good control of long and short vowels and initial consonant clusters and digraphs. In this lesson, the children learn three vowel combinations as part of several different rime patterns. Your children should be well versed in some basic card games before learning this new game.

Working with English Language Learners

Help English language learners notice these patterns by linking them to very easy words that they know: *ow* as in *owl* or *cow*, for example. Use pictures to help the children make connections to these concepts so that the words are meaningful. Accept approximate pronunciations if the vowel sounds are hard for the children; pronounce them clearly yourself, and give them many chances to say them. Play the game in a small group to observe their performance.

You Need

- Pocket chart.

From *Teaching Resources:*

- Pocket Chart Card Template.
- Directions for Crazy Eights.
- Crazy Eights Game Cards made from Lesson LS 21 Word Cards and Deck Card Template:

13 words with *ou* as in *house.*

13 words with *ow* as in *cow.*

13 words with *aw* as in *saw.*

13 selected high frequency words of your choosing.

4 cards with a large Crazy Eight on them.

Understand the Principle

The letter combinations *ou, ow,* and *aw* represent vowel sounds: *aw* represents a sound similar to the short /o/ sound, and *ou* and *ow* make the same sound in many words. Children can learn these sounds easily when they are part of a phonogram or rime (for example, *-own, -owl, -out, -ouse, -aw, -awn*). (*Ou* has another sound in words such as *through*; *ow* has the long /o/ sound in words such as *know.*)

Explain the Principle

“Some letters go together and make other vowel sounds: *house, cow, paw.*”

plan

Explain the Principle

"Some letters go together and make other vowel sounds: *house, cow, paw.*"

1. Explain to the children that they are going to learn some new letter patterns.
2. Place the word cards *house, out; cow, town;* and *paw, saw* in three rows in a pocket chart.
3. Read the words. Suggested language: "*House, out.* What do you notice about the vowel sound in both words? What letters go together to make that sound?"
4. Repeat the process with *cow, town* and *paw, saw.*
5. Explain that some letters go together and make other vowel sounds. They will see the vowel combinations *ou, ow,* and *aw* in many words.
6. Select two or three other examples (for example, *count* and *fawn*) for the children to read and place in the correct row.
7. Tell the children they are going to play a card game called Crazy Eights. Here's how it works. Give each player eight cards, and place the remaining deck face down with one card turned face up beside it. The first player reads the face-up card and puts down a card with the same vowel sound and reads it. The discarded card can match one *aw* word with another *aw* word, an *ou* word with another *ou* word, or an *ow* word with another *ow* word; also, *ow* and *ou* cards can match if they have the same vowel sound. If the player doesn't have a card that will match, he can discard a Crazy Eight card or a high frequency word card. Both of these kinds of cards are "free" cards, but the player must be able to read the high frequency word in order to discard it. Otherwise the player draws a card from the deck and keeps taking a card until he finds a match to put down. The first player to discard all cards wins the game.
8. Demonstrate and explain the game with two children until everyone understands how to play the game.

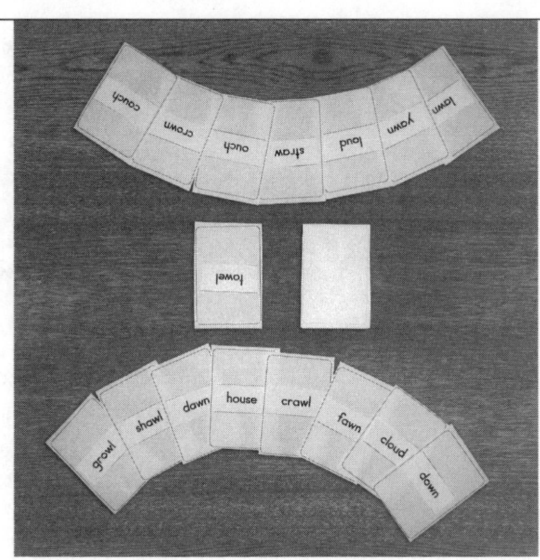

read card
match
put down

- Have the children play Crazy Eights in pairs or groups of three or four.
- After playing the game, each child records two words with the same vowel patterns on a card and brings it to sharing.

Have children share their vowel pairs. Introduce a few words you think they will not know (for example, *gown*, *shower*, *frown*, *growl*). Have them guess the spelling and then check it as you write it on a whiteboard. Or, write the word and have them read it.

Link

Interactive Read-Aloud: Read aloud books containing words that have *ou, ow,* and *aw* in them, such as

- ***Mr. Gumpy's Outing*** by John Burningham
- ***Tippy-Toe Chick, Go!*** by George Shannon

Shared Reading: After enjoying a poem such as "Bow Wow Says the Dog" (see *Sing a Song of Poetry*), have the children locate words with *ou, ow,* and *aw.*

Guided Reading: During word work, write a few words with *ou, ow,* or *aw* on the whiteboard to give the children practice recognizing them. Invite them to think of a few additional examples.

Interactive Writing: As the children attempt to write a word with an *ou, ow,* or *aw* vowel combination, prompt them to think of another word like it.

Independent Writing: During the editing process, have the children notice and check for the spelling of words with *ou, ow,* and *aw.*

assess

- Dictate four or five words with *ou, aw,* and *ow.* Observe the children's spelling of words with *ou, ow,* and *aw* to determine their ability to apply their knowledge.
- Notice how easily children recognize words with *ou, ow,* or *aw* as they read texts.

Expand the Learning

Have the children use the deck of Crazy Eights cards to play the game several more times.

Connect with Home

Send home the Crazy Eights deck for children to play the game with family members.

22 Learning the Sound of a as in Cake 1: a-e, ay, ai

Blind Sort

Consider Your Children

This lesson is appropriate when your children know and have worked with the five primary vowels and can identify the long and short sounds associated with them. They should have noticed that vowel sounds in words can be represented by many different patterns of letters and that vowels often appear in clusters, or combinations. They should be ready to generate examples and create categories of ways to represent a single sound. The *a-e* (point out that this is the same pattern as CVC*e*, with a silent *e*), *ay,* and *ai* patterns are the most common ways to represent the long sound of *a,* so begin with them. If your children are very sophisticated, you may want to combine this lesson with the next one.

Working with English Language Learners

The fact that different letter combinations can be used to represent the same sound in different words may at first be confusing to English language learners. They may become lost when they meet so many patterns. It will help them to start with a few simple examples of words they know and to build toward a summary chart more slowly. Meet with a small group and have them sort the words several times by visual features.

You Need

- Chart paper.
- Markers.

From *Teaching Resources:*

- Lesson LS 22 Word Cards.
- Four-Way Sort Cards.
- Four-Way Sort Sheets.

Understand the Principle

Dealing with the many ways of representing vowel sounds in words is tricky for spellers. Becoming familiar with these vowel combinations will help them make connections between words so that they can form categories. Having a systematic knowledge of vowel combinations and word patterns will help them get a good idea of the alternatives available for spelling a word, which will narrow the options and make it easier to decide among them. Knowing the range of combinations will also make decoding more efficient because children will see chunks of information rather than working letter by letter.

Explain the Principle

“You can hear and say the vowel in words like *make, pail, day.*”

plan

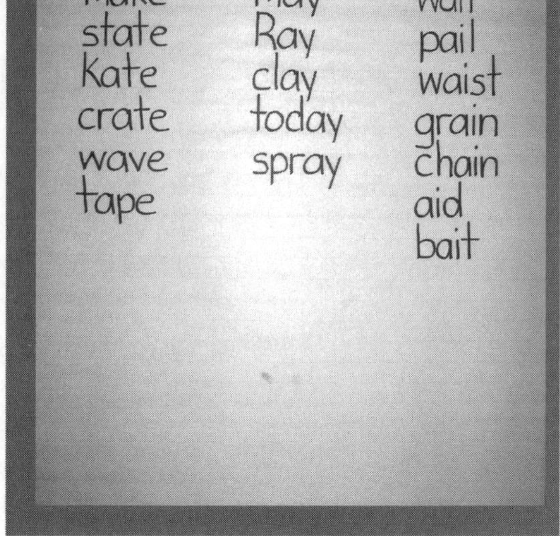

a-e
cake
make
state
Kate
crate
wave
tape
ay
day
may
Ray
clay
today
spray
ai
sail
wait
pail
waist
grain
chain
aid
bait

Explain the Principle

"You can hear and say the vowel in words like *make, pail, day.*"

① Explain to the children that you are going to help them notice more about vowel sounds and ways we write them.

② You may want to begin with a blank chart or with a few key words already written. Suggested language: "Today we are going to look at a lot of words that have the sound of *a* as in *cake*. I'll write that word. Who can think of more words that have the sound of *a* as in *cake*?"

③ The children may respond with words that rhyme with *cake* or other words. If they come up with *a*-consonant-*e* pattern words, write them in the first column. Suggest others yourself to be sure that the consonant is not always *k*.

④ As the children come up with more words, they will probably suggest words with spelling patterns different from *a*-consonant-*e*. As a new pattern is suggested, move to a new column, so that the words in each column show the same pattern.

⑤ When you have two or three examples in each column, ask the children to look again at the columns. Suggested language: "What do you notice about the way I have written your words on the chart?"

⑥ The children will respond that the letters in the words in each column have the same pattern. Suggested language: "In the first column, what letters represent the sound of *a*?" The children may say *a* or *ake*. Guide them to understand that the pattern is *a-e*. Encourage them to think of other words that have the pattern.

⑦ Tell them that you are going to write the pattern at the top of the column so that they can remember it when sorting words.

⑧ Repeat the process with the other two columns.

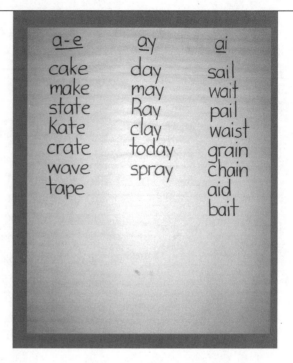

⑨ Tell the children they are going to be sorting words with the long sound of *a*. This will be a blind sort, in which they will read the word to a partner without showing it. The partner must decide and point to the column in which it belongs without seeing the word. Both partners can then check the word by looking at it in relation to the key word.

take
read
sort
check
write

- Have partners sort words in columns according to the spelling pattern.
- On a Four-Way Sort Sheet, have the children enter the key words at the top of the first three columns. Ask them to write the words containing each of the three vowel combinations in the appropriate column. The fourth column is for any words that don't contain one of these combinations. Have them place the words they put in the wrong column in a pile, and ask them to make those words with magnetic letters.

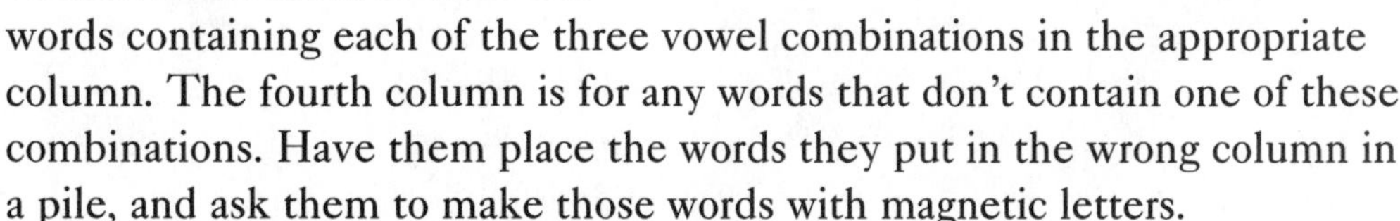

Ask the children to bring their Four-Way Sort Sheets to group share. Have them share their words in groups of four. Any group of four may suggest new words for the chart. End by asking children to talk about what they know about how to write the long sound of *a*. Watch for comments like these:

"You see *a* with other vowels a lot."

"The sound of *a* can be made different ways."

"When there is a vowel after the *a*, it usually has a long sound."

Link

Interactive Read-Aloud: Read aloud books that emphasize repetition of vowel sounds (see *Teaching Resources,* Rhymes Bibliography). As children notice rhymes with long *a,* add them to your chart. Examples of appropriate books are:

- ***Louella Mae, She's Run Away*** by Karen Alarcon
- ***Frog Went A-Courting*** by Dominic Catalano

Shared Reading: Point out words with the sound of *a* as in *cake* in poems such as "The Hobby Horse," "As I Was Going to Banbury Fair," and "Aiken Drum" (see *Sing a Song of Poetry*). Have the children use highlighter marker or tape to emphasize vowel digraphs.

Guided Reading: During word work, have the children quickly write words with these patterns and then check them against your writing of the same words on the whiteboard.

Interactive Writing: Encourage the children to think of the pattern first when writing a word that has the long *a* sound. Have them check it with the chart.

Independent Writing: Encourage the children to refer to the summary chart until they can write words with these patterns independently.

Expand the Learning

Have the children make word searches (see *Teaching Resources,* Directions for Word Searches) with words that have spelling patterns representing *a.*

Have the children look for words that have the sound of *a* as in *ate* but do not have patterns such as the ones you've studied.

Connect with Home

Give the children sheets of words (use the Word Card Template in *Teaching Resources*) that they have sorted. They can take them home, cut them apart, and sort them with a family member.

Have children take home word searches to complete with family members.

assess

- Notice whether the children, when they write, are representing vowel patterns with the correct letters.
- Notice whether the children, when they read, are able to solve new words that have different patterns representing *a.*
- Give the children a list of four or five words to read or write that have specific patterns representing *a.*

23 *Learning the Sound of* a *as in* Cake 2: ea, ey, eigh, aigh

Blind Sort

Consider Your Children

In this lesson, you will be expanding the chart previously made in Lesson LS 20. After your children have grasped the principle that *a* as in *cake* can be represented by several different spelling patterns and they understand and know the most common ones, you can move on to more complex and uncommon patterns. The children will become intrigued with discovering all the ways to represent this sound.

Working with English Language Learners

If English language learners are having trouble with the more common forms *(a-e, ay, ai)*, you may want to spend more time building and sorting words and omit the more difficult examples. Be sure to use examples of words they know and build slowly toward a summary chart. Meet with a small group, and have them sort the words several times by visual features. Have them pronounce the words, noticing the vowel sound.

You Need

- Chart paper.
- Markers.

From *Teaching Resources:*

- Word Cards from the previous lesson (Lesson LS 22).
- Four-Way Sort Sheets.

Understand the Principle

Exploring one sound and its many patterns will help readers and writers realize that there is not a one-to-one relationship between letters and sounds in English. This lesson will help children be more alert to patterns within words and search for the more complex way English letters and sounds are related. Be sure that you use words that the children understand.

Explain the Principle

“You can hear and say the vowel in words like *break, hey, eight,* and *straight.*”

plan

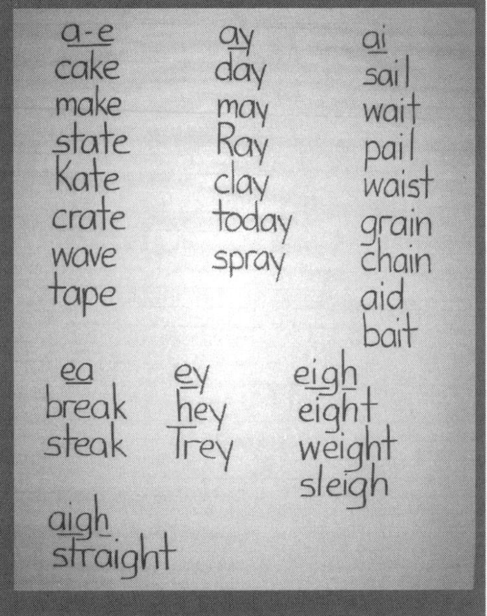

Explain the Principle

"*You can hear and say the vowel in words like* break, hey, eight, *and* straight."

① Tell the children that you are going to help them learn more spelling patterns that have the long vowel sound of *a*.

② Suggested language: "You have learned a lot about words that have the sound of *a* as in *cake*."

③ Ask the children to read the list from the previous lesson, or have them take turns quickly locating the words with their eyes when you say them. Review the patterns at the top of the columns.

④ Suggested language: "I have some more words to put on the chart. I'll say them and you will hear the sound of *a*, but it will be a different pattern. They will sound the same as a word already on the chart, but they will be spelled differently and mean something different. Say *break*. I don't want to *break* my leg."

⑤ The children repeat the word *break*. "I'll write the word." Write the word in the fourth (still blank) column. "Which two letters make the sound of *a* in this word?"

⑥ Have children discuss the *ea* digraph and how it makes the sound of *a*. Then repeat the procedure with *steak*. It will be hard for children to come up with words with the *ea* pattern, as there are very few.

⑦ Suggest other words and show children the patterns. You may want to show them *sleigh* or *neighbor* first for the *eigh* pattern and let them make the connection to the word *eight*.

⑧ Suggested language: "You have learned that when you are writing words with the sound of *a* as in *cake*, you need to think about what the pattern might be. Do you see any words on our chart that sound the same but look different and have different meanings?"

9 You may point out or children may suggest *pane, pain; stake, steak; brake, break; way, weigh;* or others. Write word pairs on the whiteboard and ask children to use them in a sentence. Stick to words they can understand.

10 Tell the children that today they will sort words with the sound of *a* as in *cake.* This will be a blind sort, in which they will read the word to a partner without showing it. The partner must decide and point to the column in which it belongs without seeing the word. Both partners can then check the word by looking at it in relation to the key word.

take
read
sort
check
write

- Have partners sort words in columns according to the spelling pattern. On a Four-Way Sort Sheet, have the children enter the key words at the top of the four columns. Ask them to write the words containing each of the four vowel combinations in the appropriate column. Have them place the words they put in the wrong column in a pile, and ask them to make those words with magnetic letters.

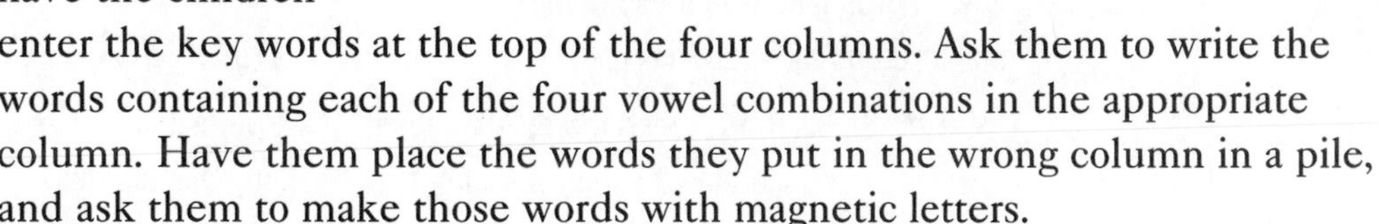

- Children may find other words on the word wall or in the dictionary to add to their sheets.

Ask the children to bring their Four-Way Sort Sheets to group share. Have them share their words in groups of four. Any group of four may suggest new words for the chart.

Link

Interactive Read-Aloud: Read aloud books that emphasize repetition of vowel sounds (see *Teaching Resources,* Rhymes Bibliography). When you find words that have the *a* sound, write them on a whiteboard and ask children to quickly identify the pattern. Examples of appropriate books are:

- ***Beautiful Blackbird*** by Ashley Bryan
- ***Magic Hat*** by Mem Fox

Shared Reading: Point out words with long *a* vowel patterns in poems such as "Rock-a-Bye Baby" and "One, Two, Buckle My Shoe" (see *Sing a Song of Poetry*). Have the children use highlighter marker or tape to call attention to words with the sound of long *a.*

Guided Reading: After reading and discussing a text, have the children locate words that contain patterns that represent the sound of *a* as in *cake.* During word work, write a few words that have these patterns and have the children read them quickly.

Interactive Writing: When the children want to write a word that has the long *a* sound, ask them to stop and think about the pattern they might need to use. Model referring to the chart.

Independent Writing: Encourage the children to refer to the chart to check their spelling of long *a* words.

assess

- Observe whether the children are using long *a* patterns successfully in their writing.
- Notice whether the children are spelling more long *a* pattern words correctly.
- Notice whether children, when reading, are able to figure out new words that have the long *a* vowel patterns.

Expand the Learning

Have children create a word search (see *Teaching Resources,* Directions for Word Searches) with the new *a* pattern words they have learned.

Continue to add words to the chart as children encounter unusual words in reading and writing. This summary chart should be displayed in the classroom for a significant length of time so that children can systematize their knowledge.

Have the children "write around the room," finding words containing five or six of the long *a* vowel combinations. (See *Teaching Resources* for the Write Around the Room directions and form.)

Connect with Home

Give children sheets of words containing the long *a* sound (use the Word Card Template in *Teaching Resources*). Ask them to take the sheets home, cut them apart, and sort the words with a family member.

Give children cut-up words containing long *a* spelling patterns so they can make new words by changing the initial consonant or consonant digraph or can make a word ladder (see the directions in *Teaching Resources*).

Spelling Patterns

Phonograms are spelling patterns that represent the sounds of *rimes* (last parts of a syllable in words). They are sometimes called *word families.* You will not need to teach children the technical word *phonogram,* although you may want to use *pattern* or *word part.* A phonogram is the same as a *rime,* or ending part of a syllable. We have included a large list of phonograms that will be useful to primary-age children in reading or writing, but you will not need to teach every phonogram separately. Once children understand that there are patterns and learn how to look for patterns, they will quickly discover more for themselves.

Another way to look at phonograms is to examine the way simple words and syllables are put together. Here we include the consonant-vowel-consonant (CVC) pattern, in which the vowel often has a short, or terse, sound; the consonant-vowel-consonant-silent *e* (CVC*e*) pattern, in which the vowel usually has a long, or lax, sound; and the consonant-vowel-vowel-consonant (CVVC) pattern, in which the vowel combination may have either one or two sounds.

Knowing spelling patterns helps children notice and use larger parts of words, thus making word solving faster and more efficient. Patterns are also helpful to children in writing words because they will quickly write down the patterns rather than laboriously work with individual sounds and letters. Finally, knowing to look for patterns and remember them helps children make the connections between words that make word solving easier. The thirty-seven most common phonograms are marked with an asterisk in the Continuum.

Connect to Assessment

See related SP Assessment Tasks in the Assessment Guide in *Teaching Resources:*

- Reading Words with Phonogram Patterns
- Writing Words with Phonogram Patterns
- Reading and Writing Names (Phonograms)

Develop Your Professional Understanding

See *Word Matters: Teaching Phonics and Spelling in the Reading/Writing Classroom* by G.S. Pinnell and I.C. Fountas. 1998. Portsmouth, New Hampshire: Heinemann.

Related pages: 65, 82, 95, 236.

1 Learning a Variety of Word Patterns

Making Words

Consider Your Children

This lesson will be appropriate for children who already know the simplest phonograms and have worked with CVC and CVC*e* patterns. You will want to teach a greater variety of VC patterns *(ab, ap, ed, eg, em, en, ib, ip, ix, ob, od, ug, um, un)* as well as phonograms with *w* and *y* (*y, aw, ay, ow* as in *blow* and *cow*). The *ap, ip, ug, aw,* and *ay* patterns are the most commonly used and form the basis for this lesson. You can use this lesson several times, focusing on phonograms that children need to learn. You will not need to teach all phonograms in formal lessons.

Working with English Language Learners

Making words is very helpful to English language learners because when they do so, they have the opportunity to notice the parts. Explicitly demonstrate making words. You may have children who have minimal English vocabularies. At first, limit this activity to words they know well and help them to make these words. Gradually increase the number of patterns with which they are working.

You Need

- Pocket chart.

From *Teaching Resources:*

- Pocket Chart Card Template.
- Category Word Cards, Onsets and Rimes (multiple copies).
- List Sheets.

Understand the Principle

Because it is very helpful for readers and writers to notice larger parts of words, the teaching of phonograms (spelling patterns, word families, or rimes) is important. Children also learn how vowel sounds vary, depending on the other letters in the sequence.

Explain the Principle

“You can look at the pattern (part) you know to help you read a word.”

“You can use the pattern (part) you know to help you write a word.”

plan

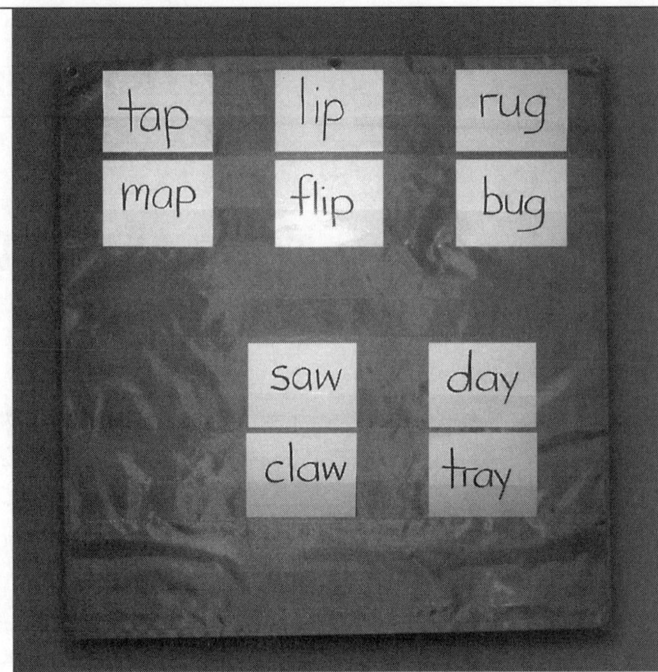

Explain the Principle

"You can look at the pattern (part) you know to help you read a word."

"You can use the pattern (part) you know to help you write a word."

① Explain to the children that you are going to show them more patterns they will see in words.

② Make the following words in the pocket chart or write them on a chart: *tap, lip, rug, saw, day.*

③ Invite the children to read each word with you. Suggested language: "In the word *tap*, the *t* is the first part and *ap* is the last part. Many words have the *ap* pattern. Can you think of another one?"

④ As the children tell another word, write it or make it below *tap.*

⑤ Repeat the process for each of the other words, creating several words containing each pattern.

⑥ Tell the children they are going to make words with word parts.

⑦ Show the children how to use onsets and rimes to make words; create one example for each pattern.

⑧ Also show them how to take an onset consisting of a two-consonant cluster, or digraph, and attach it in front of the last part (the rime) and make a word (for example, *fl* and *ag* make *flag*).

⑨ Tell the children they are going to make twenty different words using their set of five patterns *(ap, ip, ug, aw, ay).*

⑩ Then they will read the words and write them on a list sheet.

⑪ Remind the children to make four words for each pattern; emphasize that each word must be a real word.

apply

make
read
write
read

▸ Have the children make twenty words using the onset and rime cards. Ask them to read each word and write it on a List Sheet. Then have them read the complete list to a partner.

Have the children read their lists to a different partner.

Add one or two more words to the chart.

Place an example of each pattern on the word wall.

Link

Interactive Read-Aloud: Read aloud books with rhymes (see *Teaching Resources*, Rhymes Bibliography) so children can notice the sound and letter patterns. Examples are:

- ***Greetings, Sun*** by Phillis and David Gershator
- ***Earthsong*** by Sally Rogers

Shared Reading: Cover the last part of a few words with stick-on notes before reading a new poem such as "When I Was One" or "Snowman" (see *Sing a Song of Poetry*). Have the children predict the letters that are there before uncovering each letter of the word to confirm their predictions.

Guided Reading: During word work, make words with the *ap*, *ip*, *ug*, *aw*, and *ay* patterns. For each word, change the onset two or three times to make a new word.

Interactive Writing: Create some silly phrases such as *a lip to sip, a map to wrap, a claw to draw, a day in May.* Then have the children choose one to illustrate. They can write a few similar phrases of their own and add them to a bulletin board.

Independent Writing: Have the children reread their writing to see whether the words they know how to spell look right. Teach them to use the patterns they know and check the examples on the word wall.

assess

- Dictate a few words that contain each pattern, and evaluate the children's papers. Mix in a few high frequency words for an added challenge.
- Identify children who need more work in a small group.

Expand the Learning

Repeat the lesson with other VC spelling patterns (*ab, ed, eg, em, en, ib, ix, ob, od, um,* and *un*).

Have the children play Rhyming Lotto (see *Teaching Resources*, Games) with the variety of spelling patterns you have taught. This will give the children practice recognizing patterns quickly.

Have the children play the Word Grid game (see *Teaching Resources*, Games). Place six different spelling patterns on the six sides of the die or cube and words with the patterns in each box on the grid.

Connect with Home

Have the children use magnetic letters or letter cards (see *Teaching Resources*) to make and write five words with each pattern at home.

Alternatively, you can send home sheets of onsets and rimes for them to cut apart and then put together to make words. They can read the words they make to family members.

2 Learning Onsets and Rimes: -ack, -ick

Word Sort

Consider Your Children

Use this lesson when the children know a large number of high frequency words, most of the consonant letters and associated sounds, and some letter clusters. You will be teaching children two phonograms (*-ack* and *-ick*) that may be unfamiliar to them although they are likely to know some individual words (for example, *pack*) that have these word parts.

Working with English Language Learners

Check to be sure that English language learners can read the words you are using for the *-ack, -ick* sort, and talk with them about what the words mean. If they offer other examples, add them to the sort. Sorting will help these children look more closely at the patterns in words; it is a very engaging activity. You may want children to complete the sort twice by mixing up the words and sorting them more quickly the second time.

You Need

- Pocket chart.
- Whiteboard.

From *Teaching Resources:*

- Pocket Chart Card Template.
- Lesson SP 2 Word Cards.
- Three-Way Sort Sheets.

Understand the Principle

Noticing parts of words (the *onset,* or first part in a syllable, and the *rime,* the rest of the syllable) will make it easier for children to break words apart in order to analyze them. Working with the parts of words will help them realize the importance of looking at the entire word, not just the first letter.

Explain the Principle

“Some words have patterns that end with consonant letters.”

teach

Explain the Principle

"Some words have patterns that end with consonant letters."

① Tell the children that you are going to help them look at the parts of words.

② Write some words with the *-ack* and *-ick* pattern on a whiteboard.

③ Suggested language: "You know how to look at the first part of the word and the rest of the word. This word is *pack*. You may *pack* your lunch. What is the first part of *pack*? [Children respond.] The first part is *p*, and the rest of the word is *a-c-k*. If I change the first part of the word to a *b*, I have. . . ." Children respond, or you may tell them the word, *back*.

④ Suggested language: "We can make more words that end like *pack*." List more *-ack* words on the whiteboard.

⑤ Repeat the process with *-ick* words, beginning with the example that will be most familiar.

⑥ Then move to a pocket chart with word cards.

⑦ Demonstrate how to sort words by the first part (letter or letter cluster).

⑧ Continue sorting the words into columns by first letters: *b, p, ch, fl, qu, l,* and *r.*

⑨ Return all the word cards to the left-hand column. Suggested language: "Now sort the words by looking at the last part of the word. Think about the whole end part of the word, not just the last letter. What words end with the part *-ack*, like *sack*?"

⑩ Demonstrate sorting the words by the ending parts. This sort will require children to look carefully at the spelling patterns.

⑪ Tell children that they will be sorting the words first one way, then the other way. They will also have some words that don't fit the *-ack* or *-ick* pattern. They will then write several examples from their second sort on a list sheet and bring them to group share.

say
sort
read
write

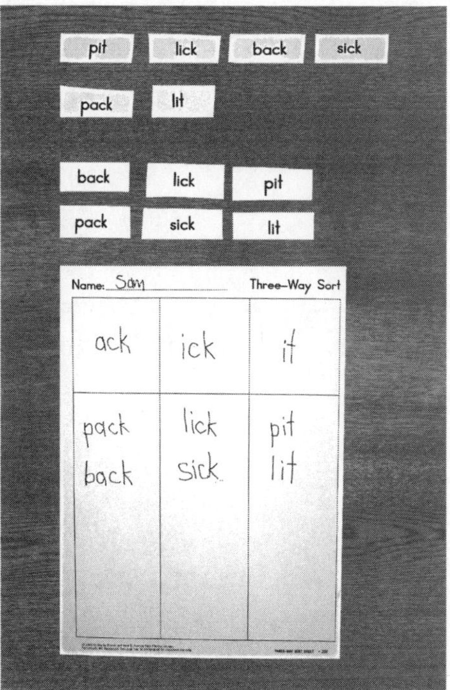

- Have the children say and sort the words by similar onsets and then by similar rimes (ending parts or phonograms). Have them read the sorted words to a partner. Then ask them to record at least two examples for each phonogram (*-ack*, *-ick*, and *-it*) on a Three-Way Sort Sheet and bring their lists to group share.

Ask children to talk about what they learned from sorting and recording words. Listen for comments like these:

> "Some words are alike at the end."
>
> "If you change the first part, you can make a new word."

Link

Interactive Read-Aloud: Read aloud books that have interesting word combinations in which onsets remain the same but the rimes change, and vice versa. (See *Teaching Resources,* Rhymes Bibliography.) Examples are:

- ***Motorcycle Song*** by Diane Siebert
- ***Bear Snores On*** by Karma Wilson

Shared Reading: Have the children use a masking card or transparent tape to highlight the first part or last part of words in texts they are reading such as "Miss Mary Mack" or "Spread It Thick" (see *Sing a Song of Poetry*).

Guided Reading: Cover up the first or last part of words with regular phonogram patterns and have the children solve them. Suggested language: "The first part of the word is _____. The last part is like [another word with the same phonogram]." Use the whiteboard to illustrate. For children who need more experience, make words with magnetic letters at the end of the lesson. Have them take the words apart to separate the first part and the rest of the word.

Interactive Writing: Have the children say the word they want to write, separating the first part and the rest of the word. Encourage them to make connections to words on the charts you have made.

Independent Writing: Encourage the children to think about the parts of words to help in writing them.

assess

- Notice whether children can sort words by the rime or phonogram.
- Give the children a sheet with two columns of words, and ask them to read the words and then draw lines to connect the ones that have rimes that sound alike.

Expand the Learning

Repeat the lesson with other phonograms. Use the Word Card Template (*Teaching Resources,* Templates) to make word cards for the additional phonograms. The Phonograms List in *Teaching Resources* contains an extensive list of phonograms and sample words.

Have children become fluent with phonogram patterns by writing words quickly.

Connect with Home

Have the children take home a sheet of word cards (Word Card Template, *Teaching Resources*) with the spelling patterns to sort at home.

3 Learning the Silent e Pattern

Making Word Pairs

Consider Your Children

This lesson introduces long vowel phonograms with a pattern of CVC*e*. Children generally find them easy to learn. Be sure the children have worked with long and short vowels and consonant clusters (including digraphs).

Working with English Language Learners

As English language learners become more familiar with the concept of word patterns and connect words and/or place them in categories, they will begin to use what they know about spelling patterns to figure out new words that they may know how to say but not how to read or write. Provide many repetitions of the words so that they can hear the patterns, and use pictures or actions to help them understand the meaning of words.

You Need

- Chart paper.
- Markers.
- Magnetic letters.

From *Teaching Resources:*

- Two-Column Sheets.
- Lesson SP 3 Word Cards.

Understand the Principle

The silent *e* is part of a very consistent spelling pattern. It can appear after a short vowel sound (*love,* for example), but it more often signals that the preceding vowel is long: *ate* (VC*e*), *make* (CVC*e*), *shape* (CCVC*e*), *stripe* (CCCVC*e*), *breathe* (CCVVCC*e*). Contrasting words without and with the final *e* helps children hear the difference *(at–ate).* (There are only a few examples with a preceding *e* or *u:* *pet–Pete* and *us–use.*)

Explain the Principle

“Some words have a vowel, a consonant, and a silent *e*. The vowel sound is usually the name of the vowel.”

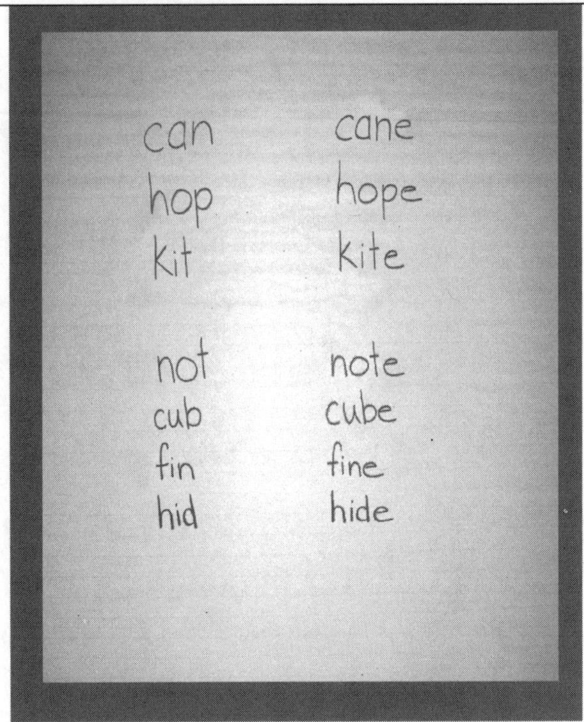

can cane
hop hope
kit kite
not note
cub cube
fin fine
hid hide

Explain the Principle

"Some words have a vowel, a consonant, and a silent *e*. The vowel sound is usually the name of the vowel."

1. Tell the children that you are going to show them a pattern they will see in many words.
2. Write *can, cane; hop, hope;* and *kit, kite* on the chart.
3. Ask the children what they notice about the letter patterns. They will likely say that the vowel sound changes when you add *e* to a word to make another word.
4. Now ask for more examples and add the pairs to the list—*not, note; cub, cube; fin, fine;* and *hid, hide*, for example.
5. Help the children generalize the principle from the examples, leading them to the understanding that with word patterns that consist of a consonant (or more than one consonant), a vowel, another consonant, and an *e,* the *e* is silent and the preceding vowel usually sounds like the name of the letter.
6. Explain to the children that today they are going to use word cards. They will read five words and then add a silent *e* to each one, making ten paired real words. They will write the pairs of words on a Two-Column Sheet or in the columns in a Word Study Notebook. Then they will use each pair of words in the same sentence—for example, *The* cute *little boy got a* cut *on his knee.*

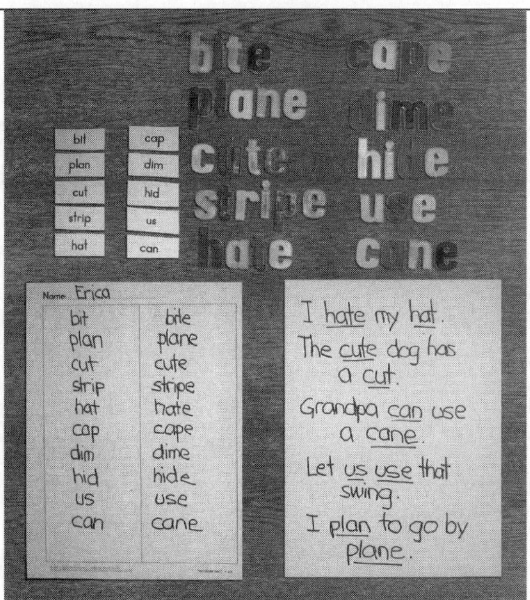

take
make
add
write

▸ Have the children take a word card, make the word with magnetic letters or letter cards, and add silent *e* to make another real word. Have them list ten word pairs on a Two-Column Sheet. Then ask them to write (on the back of the sheet) five sentences that include the word pairs, underlining the word pair in each sentence.

Have children read their sentences to a partner, or have each child read one sentence to the group.

Invite the class to give a few more word pairs for the chart.

Link

Interactive Read-Aloud: Read aloud books that include many words that end in silent *e*. Add two or three of these words to the group chart. Examples of appropriate books are:

- ***Jump Rope Magic*** by Afi-Odelia Scruggs
- ***Over the Green Hills*** by Rachel Isadora

Shared Reading: After enjoying a song or poem such as "Birds of a Feather" or "A Mouse in Her Room" (see *Sing a Song of Poetry*), have the children use a mask, flag, or highlighter tape to locate words ending in silent *e*.

Guided Reading: During word work, make three or four words, add silent *e*, and ask the children to read the words quickly. Then have the children make two or three words and do the same.

Interactive Writing: When the children are attempting to write a new word ending in a silent *e* pattern, help them notice how the *e* affects the sound of the preceding vowel.

Independent Writing: When conferring with individual writers, point out words ending in a silent *e* pattern.

Expand the Learning

Repeat the lesson using a variety of patterns with silent *e*, such as *-ade, -ace, -age, -ake**, *-ale, -ame, -one, -ape, -ate**, *-ide**, *-ile, -ime, -ine**, *-ite, -ive, -obe, -oke**, and *-ore.*

*These are the most common spelling patterns with silent *e*. Use the Word Card Template (*Teaching Resources,* Templates) to make word cards for the additional phonograms. The Phonograms List in *Teaching Resources* contains an extensive list of phonograms and sample words.

Have children play Concentration (see *Teaching Resources*) by matching word pairs linked by a silent *e (man, mane)*. Use the Lesson SP 3 Word Cards and the Deck Card Template *(Teaching Resources)* to make the deck of cards.

Connect with Home

Have children create five more sentences with word pairs *(kit, kite)* at home.

Alternatively, have the children, using magnetic letters or letter cards (see *Teaching Resources*), make ten words ending in silent *e* and bring a list of the words to school.

assess

- Observe the children's use of the silent *e* pattern when they write words.
- Dictate four or five words, some of which have the silent *e* pattern.

4 Learning Onsets and Rimes: -ame, -ate, -ake

Three-Way Word Sort

Consider Your Children

Use this lesson when your children know a large number of high frequency words, most of the consonant letters and associated sounds, and some letter clusters but still need to learn to look beyond the first letter when solving words while reading. You will be teaching the children three phonograms *(-ame, -ate, -ake)* that may be unfamiliar to them.

Working with English Language Learners

When teaching about phonograms, be careful that your English language learners don't rely solely on using onsets and rimes to solve words. They need to become flexible in how they look at words. Be sure that they sort words both ways, and also invite them to talk about what they are noticing. They should also be learning new high frequency words and using letter/sound relationships in different ways.

You Need

- Pocket chart.
- Chart paper.
- Markers.

From *Teaching Resources:*

- Pocket Chart Card Template.
- Three-Way Sort Sheets.
- Lesson SP 4 Word Cards.

Understand the Principle

Noticing parts of words (the *onset,* or first part, and the *rime,* the rest of the word) makes it easier for children to break words apart in order to analyze them. Working with the parts of words helps them realize the importance of looking at the entire word, not just the first letter. Connecting words that have the same rime or phonogram will help children learn to look for more recognizable chunks within a word.

Explain the Principle

" Some words have a vowel, a consonant, and a silent *e.* The vowel sound is usually the name of the vowel. "

plan

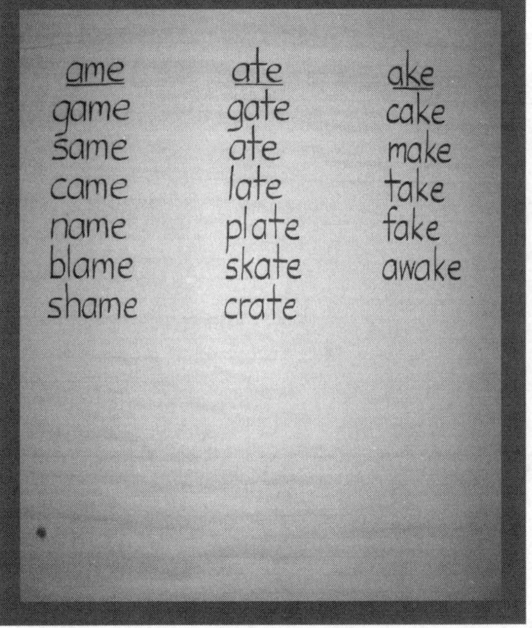

ame
game
same
came
name
blame
shame
ate
gate
ate
late
plate
skate
crate
ake
cake
make
take
fake
awake

Explain the Principle

"Some words have a vowel, a consonant, and a silent *e*. The vowel sound is usually the name of the vowel."

① Tell the children that they are going to learn more about spelling patterns.

② Suggested language: "You know how to look at the first part of the word and the rest of the word. This word is *game*. What is the first part of *game*? [Children respond.] The first part is *g*, and the rest of the word is *a-m-e*. If I change the first part of the word to *s*, I have. . . ." Children respond, or you may tell them the word *same*.

③ Ask the children for examples and/or show them more *-ame* words, and list them under *-ame*.

④ Repeat the process with *-ate* and *-ake* words, and have children read the lists.

⑤ Then direct the children's attention to the pocket chart with word cards on the left. "Today you are going to be sorting these words. Let's sort them by the first part of the word."

⑥ Demonstrate sorting the cards by first letter.

⑦ Then mix the words up again. Suggested language: "Now sort the words by looking at the rest of the word. Think about the whole end part of the word, not just the last letter. What word is like *came* after the first part?"

⑧ Demonstrate sorting the words by the three ending parts.

⑨ Tell the children that they will be sorting the words first by the way they start and then by their ending patterns. Then they will write down groups of words with a similar pattern.

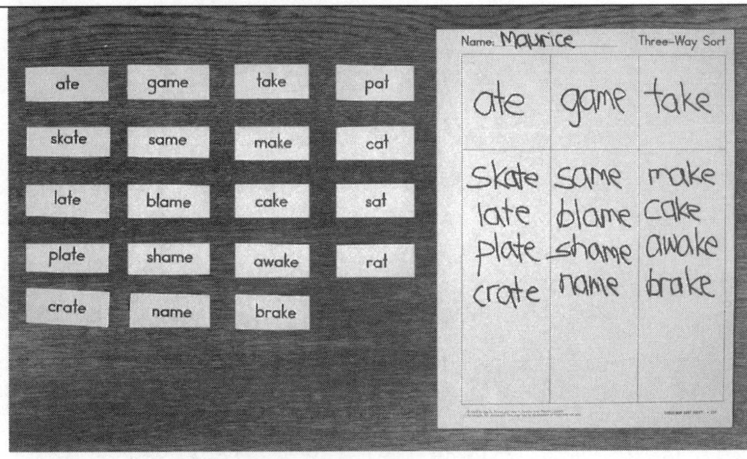

take
say
sort
read
write

▸ Have the children sort the words two ways. First, they sort the word cards by the way they start. Then they read their sorts to a partner. Next, they sort by ending pattern, and when they are finished with the second sort, then they record the three groups of words (based on ending patterns) on a Three-Way Sort Sheet.

Ask the children to talk about what they learned from sorting and writing these words. Look for comments like these, which indicate flexibility:

> "*Frame* is like *came* with *f* and *r* at the beginning."
>
> "If you change the *r* in *frame* to *l*, you get *flame*."

If they may think of an example that fits the pattern but is not a real word, recognize their thinking, but tell them that the word is not real.

Link

Interactive Read-Aloud: Read aloud books in which onsets remain the same but the rimes change, and vice versa. Examples are:

- ***Cousin Ruth's Tooth*** by Amy MacDonald
- ***Vroom Chugga Vroom Vroom*** by Anne Miranda

Shared Reading: After sharing a text in poems such as "Calico Pie" or "Bat, Bat" (see *Sing a Song of Poetry*), ask the children to use highlighter tape or a masking card to locate words with *-ame, -ate,* and *-ake.*

Guided Reading: Cover up the first or last part of words with *-ame, -ate,* and *-ake* phonograms and have the children solve them. During word work, have the children build words with *-ame, -ate,* and *-ake.*

Interactive Writing: Connect *-ame, -ate,* and *-ake* words the children want to write with words that have the same pattern.

Independent Writing: Encourage the children to think about the parts of *-ame, -ate,* and *-ake* words as a way to help them write the words.

Expand the Learning

Repeat the lesson with other phonograms. Use the Word Card Template (*Teaching Resources,* Templates) to make word cards for the additional phonograms. The Phonograms List in *Teaching Resources* contains an extensive list of phonograms and sample words.

Ask the children to write *-ame, -ate,* and *-ake* words quickly to help them become fluent with these patterns.

Connect with Home

Have children take *ame, -ate,* and *-ake* word cards (Word Card Template, *Teaching Resources*) home to sort with family members.

assess

- Notice whether the children can sort words by the *-ame, -ate,* and *-ake* rime or phonogram.
- Give the children two columns of *-ame, -ate,* and *-ake* words and ask them to draw lines between the ones that are alike.

5 Learning Onsets and Rimes: -ice, -ide, -ine

Three-Way Rhyme Sort

Consider Your Children

Use this lesson when the children know a large number of high frequency words, most of the consonant letters and associated sounds, and some letter clusters but still need to learn to look beyond the first letter when solving words while reading. You will be teaching children three phonograms *(-ice, -ide, -ine)* that may be unfamiliar to them. If children have trouble working with three phonograms, use only one or two.

Working with English Language Learners

By the time you use this lesson, English language learners should be very familiar with the concept of patterns in words and should be good at looking for and identifying them. If they are still having trouble connecting words by patterns, work with them on simpler patterns and use fewer examples. They may be able to connect words by looking at them but may be unable to read the words and may not know what they mean. In this case, the patterns are not really helping them. Discard words they find difficult, and use VC*e* words in sentences during shared reading.

You Need

- Chart paper.
- Markers.

From *Teaching Resources:*

- Three-Way Rhyme Sheets.
- Lesson SP 5 Word Cards.

Understand the Principle

Noticing parts of words (the *onset,* or first part, and the *rime,* the rest of the word) makes it easier for children to break words apart in order to analyze them. Working with the parts of words helps them realize the importance of looking at the entire word, not just the first letter. Some phonograms (rimes) have a VC*e* pattern.

Explain the Principle

"Some words have a vowel, a consonant, and a silent *e.* The vowel sound is usually the name of the vowel."

plan

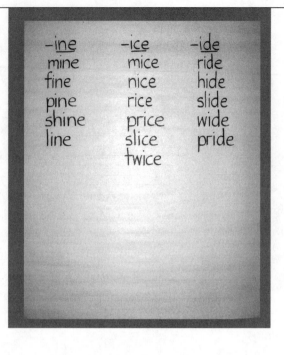

-ine	-ice	-ide
mine	mice	ride
fine	nice	hide
pine	rice	slide
shine	price	wide
line	slice	pride
	twice	

Explain the Principle

“Some words have a vowel, a consonant, and a silent *e*. The vowel sound is usually the name of the vowel.”

① Tell the children that they are going to learn more about spelling patterns.

② Write down examples on the chart. Suggested language: “You know how to look at the first part of the word and the rest of the word. This word is *mine*. What is the first part of *mine*? [Children respond.] The first part is *m*, and the rest of the word is *i-n-e*. If I change the first part of the word to *f*, I have. . . .” Children respond, or you may tell them the word *fine*.

③ Suggested language: “We can make more words that end like *mine* and *fine*.” Ask the children for examples and/or show them more *-ine* words. List them under *-ine* on the chart. Point out that the words have a CVC*e* pattern.

④ Repeat the process with the phonograms *-ice* and *-ide*, beginning with the examples that will be most familiar.

⑤ Have the children read the lists.

⑥ Tell the children they will be sorting these words by their spelling patterns and writing them on a Three-Way Rhyme Sheet.

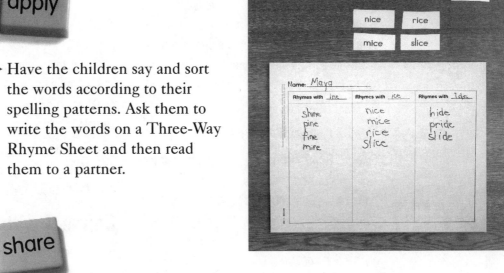

take
say
sort
write
read

▸ Have the children say and sort the words according to their spelling patterns. Ask them to write the words on a Three-Way Rhyme Sheet and then read them to a partner.

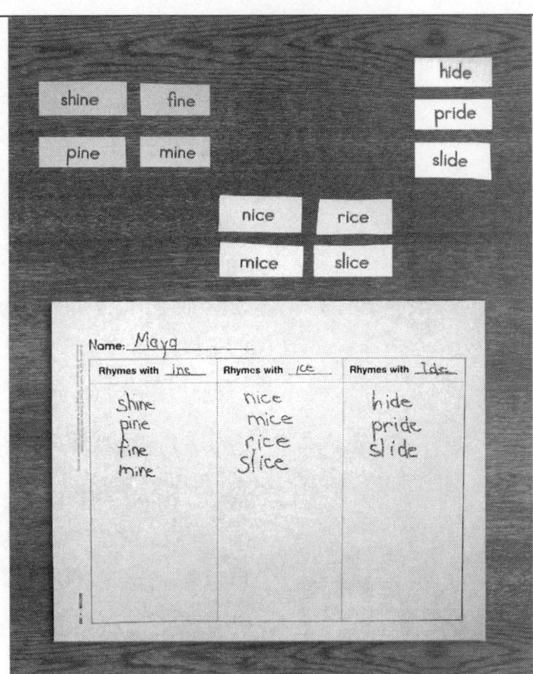

Ask the children to talk about what they learned from sorting and writing these words. Comments like these indicate the children are becoming more flexible with words:

"*Ice* is a word all by itself, but *ine* isn't a word."

"If you put *sp* at the beginning of *ice*, you get *spice*."

"Is *sine* like a sign on the door?"

Encourage the children to discuss the new examples they have discovered.

Link

Interactive Read-Aloud: Read aloud rhyming books (see *Teaching Resources,* Rhymes Bibliography) that have interesting word combinations in which the onsets remain the same but the rimes change, and vice versa. Examples are:

- ***Mice Twice*** by Joseph Low
- ***Barn Dance!*** by Bill Martin Jr.

Shared Reading: Ask the children to look for examples of *-ice, -ide,* and *-ine* spelling patterns in poems such as "There Was an Old Man from Dumbree" *(-ice),* "Stepping Stones" *(-ide),* and "Queen, Queen, Caroline" *(-ine)* (see *Sing a Song of Poetry*).

Guided Reading: Cover up the first or last part of words with *-ice, -ide,* and *-ine* phonograms and have the children solve them. During word work, make words with the *-ice, -ide,* and *-ine* patterns and change the onset. Invite the children to come up with additional examples for each.

Interactive Writing: Connect *-ice, -ide,* and *-ine* words the children want to write with the words that have the same spelling pattern.

Independent Writing: Encourage the children to think about *-ice, -ide,* and *-ine* spelling patterns as a way to help them write new words.

assess

- Notice whether children can sort words by the *-ice, -ide,* and *-ine* rime or phonogram.
- Give the children two columns of words containing *-ice, -ide,* and *-ine,* and ask them to draw lines between the ones that are alike.

Expand the Learning

Repeat the lesson with other phonograms that have ending consonant clusters of vowel combinations. Use the Word Card Template (*Teaching Resources,* Templates) to make word cards for the additional phonograms. The Phonograms List in *Teaching Resources* contains an extensive list of phonograms and sample words.

Ask the children to write some *-ice, -ide,* and *-ine* words quickly so that they will become fluent with these phonogram patterns.

Connect with Home

Have children take their Three-Way Rhyme Sheets home to read to family members.

6 Learning Onsets and Rimes: -obe, -oke, -ore, -ope

Making Words

Consider Your Children

Use this lesson when your children know a large number of high frequency words, most of the consonant letters and associated sounds, and some letter clusters but still need to learn to look beyond the first letter when solving words while reading. You will be teaching the children four VC*e* phonograms *(-obe, -oke, -ore, -ope)* that may be unfamiliar to them. If your children have trouble working with four phonograms, leave out *-ope.*

Working with English Language Learners

Your objective is to help English language learners detect patterns and at the same time connect patterns with word pronunciations and word meanings. Each student should have one good and very meaningful example to connect with a phonogram pattern. You may have to work individually with children to discover which words are most familiar to them.

You Need

- Chart paper.
- Markers.

From *Teaching Resources:*

- Category Word Cards, Onsets and Rimes.
- Spelling Patterns Sheets.

Understand the Principle

Noticing parts of words (the *onset,* or first part, and the *rime,* or phonogram, the rest of the word) makes it easier for children to break words apart in order to analyze them. Working with the parts of words helps them realize the importance of looking at the entire word, not just the first letter. The phonograms in this lesson have a vowel-consonant-silent *e* pattern.

Explain the Principle

“Some words have a vowel, a consonant, and a silent *e.* The vowel sound is usually the name of the vowel.”

plan

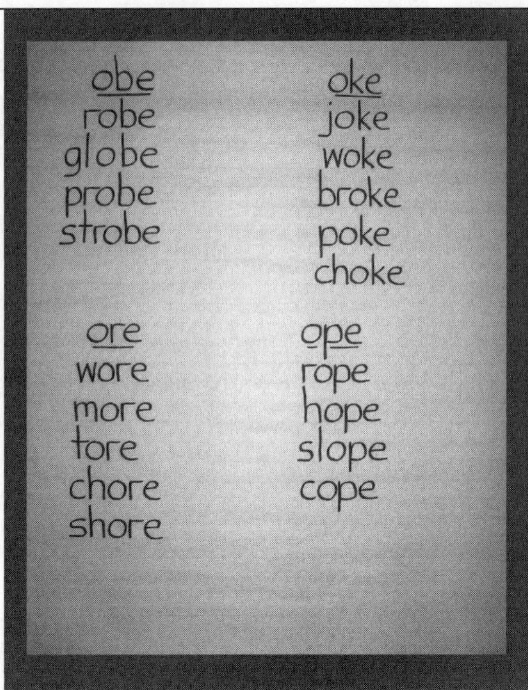

obe
robe
globe
probe
strobe
oke
joke
woke
broke
poke
choke
ore
wore
more
tore
chore
shore
ope
rope
hope
slope
cope

Explain the Principle

"Some words have a vowel, a consonant, and a silent *e*. The vowel sound is usually the name of the vowel."

① Tell the children that you are going to show them more about spelling patterns.

② Suggested language: "You know how to look at the parts of words and change the beginning to make a new word. This word is *robe*. If I change the *r* to *gl*, I have *globe*. You can see parts of the world on the globe." Ask the children to suggest other words that end like *globe*.

③ Repeat the process with other phonograms, beginning with examples that are most familiar to children. By this time, children should fully understand the concept of phonograms and should be able to think of examples quickly.

④ Have the children read the lists on the chart. Then point out that each phonogram has a VC*e* pattern.

⑤ Explain that the children will be making words with the VC*e* phonogram and then writing the words on a Spelling Patterns Sheet.

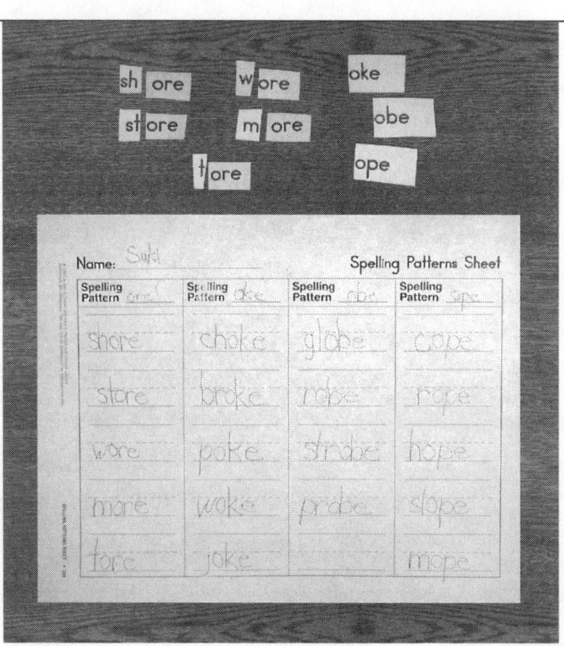

apply

take
make
read
write

- Have the children use the onset and rime cards to make five words for each of the following phonograms: *-obe, -oke, -ore, -ope.*
- Ask the children to write the words they made on a Spelling Patterns Sheet.

Play a game: "If you have a word that starts like *rat* and rhymes with *sock,* raise your hand." Children look at their examples and raise their hands if they have *rock.*

Link

Interactive Read-Aloud: Read aloud books that have interesting word combinations in which the onsets remain the same but the rimes change, and vice versa. Examples are:

- ***Moon Rope*** by Lois Ehlert
- ***Pigs Aplenty, Pigs Galore!*** by David McPhail

Shared Reading: Read poems with rhyming words; have children highlight the parts in the words that are alike.

Guided Reading: Cover up the first or last part of words with *-obe, -oke, -ore,* and *-ope* phonograms and have the children solve them. During word work, have the children build words with *-obe, -oke, -ore,* and *-ope.*

Interactive Writing: Connect *-obe, -oke, -ore,* and *-ope* words the children want to write with the word charts you have made.

Independent Writing: Encourage children to think about the parts of *-obe, -oke, -ore,* and *-ope* words as a way to help them write them.

assess

- Notice whether the children can sort words by a VC*e* rime or phonogram.
- Give the children two columns of words and ask them to draw lines between the ones that are alike.

Expand the Learning

Repeat the lesson with other phonograms.

Have the children quickly write words with VC*e* phonograms so that they will become fluent with these patterns.

Connect with Home

Have children take their Spelling Patterns Sheets home to read to family members.

Invite the children to find words containing the VC*e* spelling pattern with family members. Give them a Read and Write Around the Room Sheet (see *Teaching Resources*) and ask them to find five words each with *a, i, o,* and *e.*

7 Learning Onsets and Rimes: -ing, -ink

Lotto

Consider Your Children

Use this lesson when the children know some of the *-ing* or *-ink* words by sight and have also worked with phonograms and understand the principle of substituting letters to make new words. At the same time you are working with children on phonograms, you will want to be sure that they are constantly exposed to words that expand their repertoire of high frequency words and offer opportunities for looking at words in different ways. In this lesson, the *-ing* and *-ink* patterns end with a consonant cluster.

Working with English Language Learners

Many English language learners will know some words that have the *-ing* phonogram and may also be familiar with the *-ink* ending. Be sure that they continually hear books read aloud so that they will internalize the syntax of English, including these inflectional endings. It is very important for them to expand their listening and speaking vocabularies while at the same time learning about language patterns. Quickly check to be sure children know the words that you are using as examples in this lesson.

You Need

- Chart paper.
- Small index cards.
- Markers.

From *Teaching Resources:*

- Directions for Lotto.
- Lotto Game Cards.
- Lesson SP 7 Word Cards.

Understand the Principle

Noticing parts of words (the *onset,* or first part, and the *rime,* the rest of the word) makes it easier for children to break words apart in order to analyze them. Working with the parts of words helps them realize the importance of looking at the entire word and parts of words, not just the first letter.

Explain the Principle

"Some words have patterns (parts) that end with consonant clusters."

plan

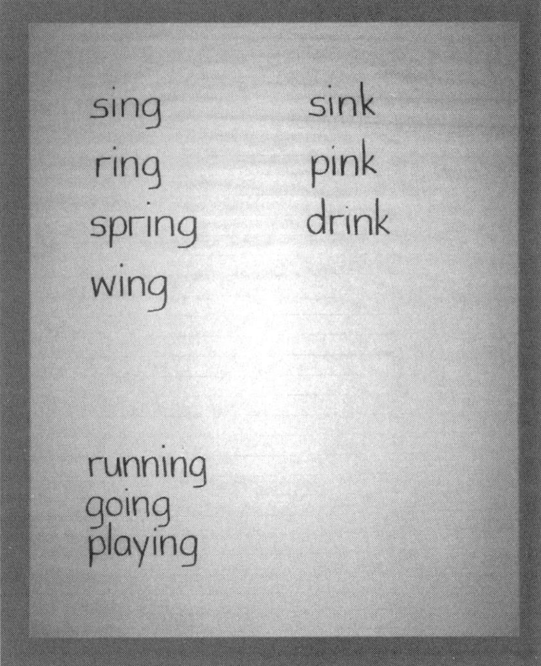

sing
ring
spring
wing
sink
pink
drink
running
going
playing

Explain the Principle

"Some words have patterns (parts) that end with consonant clusters."

① Explain to the children that you are going to show them some more spelling patterns.

② Suggested language: "You know how to look at the parts of words and change the beginning to make a new word. You know this word." Write *sing* on the chart, and ask children to read it and identify the first part and the rest of the word.

③ Suggested language: "I am going to change the first part of the word to an *r*. The new word is *ring*." Guide children to suggest other words.

④ Children may suggest other *-ing* words they know, such as *running* or *playing*. Compliment them on thinking about what they know and write them in a third column to show that they are more complex examples. Point out that we can add *-ing* as an ending to another word to show that someone is doing something. But we also use *-ing* to make words such as *sing*.

⑤ Repeat the process with the words based on the phonogram *-ink*.

⑥ Have the children read the list. Tell them they will be playing Lotto with *-ing* and *-ink* words.

apply

take
say
match
cover

▸ Have the children play Lotto with *-ink* and *-ing* words. You can also include a variety of words ending in other phonograms they know. To get a match, children match a word card to a square on their Lotto Game Card that has the same phonogram. The first to fill her Lotto Game Card wins. After playing Lotto with a partner, each child records two examples each of *-ink* and *-ing* words on an index card to bring to group share.

share

Have each child read an *-ing* and an *-ink* word.

Play a game: "I'm thinking of a word with *-ing* that has *r* at the beginning." Have children locate the word on the chart.

Link

Interactive Read-Aloud: Read aloud books that have interesting word combinations in which onsets remain the same but the rimes change, and vice versa. (See *Teaching Resources*, Rhymes Bibliography.) Examples are:

- ***The Rusty, Trusty Tractor*** by Joy Cowley
- ***Imagine*** by Alison Lester

Shared Reading: Read poems that have rhyming words in them, such as "The Swing" or "The Wind Doth Blow" *(-ing)* and "If All the World Were Apple Pie" or "Once I Saw a Bunny" *(-ink)* (see *Sing a Song of Poetry*), and have children match words that include the same phonogram.

Guided Reading: Cover up the first or last part of words with regular phonogram patterns and have the children solve them. During word work, have the children build words with *-ing* and *-ink*.

Interactive Writing: Connect words the children want to write with the word charts you have made.

Independent Writing: Encourage the children to think about the parts of words as a way to know how to write them.

assess

- Ask the children to read a list of *-ing* and *-ink* words in random order. Include a few tricky words such as *pinky* or *sinking.*

Expand the Learning

Ask the children to quickly write four or five words with *-ing* to help them become fluent with phonogram patterns.

Repeat the lesson with other phonogram patterns that end with consonant clusters: *-act, -alk, -amp, -and, -ank, -ant, -ard, -ark, -arm, -art, -ash, -ask, -eck, -elf, -end, -est, -ock, -uck, -unk.* Use the Word Card Template (*Teaching Resources*, Templates) to make word cards for the additional phonograms. The Phonograms List in *Teaching Resources* contains an extensive list of phonograms and sample words.

Connect with Home

Have children take home a set of Lotto word cards and two Lotto Game Cards so that they can play Lotto with family members.

8 Learning Patterns with Double Letters

Making Words

Consider Your Children

This lesson introduces the phonogram that includes short vowels followed by double consonants. Use it after lessons on the VC*e* pattern. The *-all, -ell,* and *-ill* patterns in the lesson are very common. The *-oll* pattern (*doll,* for example) is rare, but it can be connected with names such as Molly, Dolly, and Polly. (There is also a long *o* vowel–double consonant pattern—*roll.*)

Working with English Language Learners

The more English language learners become familiar with the patterns of written language, the easier it will be for them to learn new words. Once they develop the concept of looking for patterns, they will actively try to connect words. You may need to show them how to do this active searching by demonstrating it and taking special care to point out patterns such as double letters in guided reading, shared reading, and the interactive writing that you do with small groups. Be sure that the children are dealing with familiar words as examples of patterns.

You Need

- Magnetic letters (or letter cards).
- Chart paper.

From *Teaching Resources:*

- Lesson SP 8 Word Cards.
- List Sheets.

Understand the Principle

Patterns in words are very useful to readers and writers. When children learn to notice sequences of letters in words, they can write them or read them more quickly. Phonograms are the vowel-bearing unit of a syllable (often called a *rime*). The rimes in this lesson include a short vowel followed by double consonants. (There are always exceptions to these patterns—*pull, roll, full,* for example.)

Explain the Principle

“Some word patterns have double consonants at the end. The sound of the vowel is short.”

plan

teach

Explain the Principle

"Some word patterns have double consonants at the end. The sound of the vowel is short."

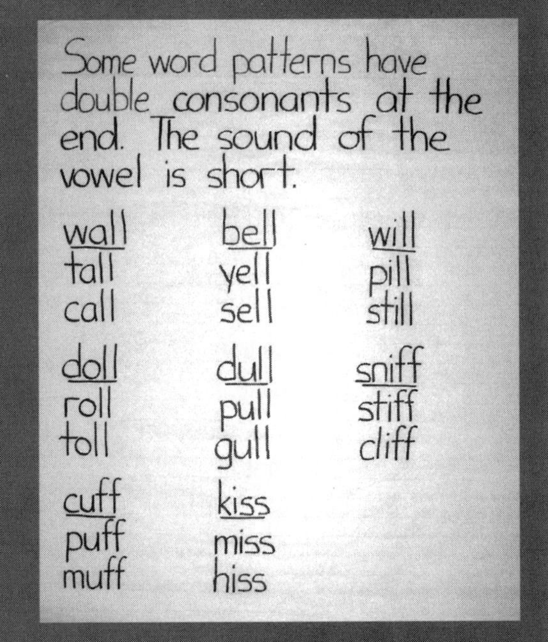

Some word patterns have double consonants at the end. The sound of the vowel is short.
wall bell will
tall yell pill
call sell still
doll dull sniff
roll pull stiff
toll gull cliff
cuff kiss
puff miss
muff hiss

1. Explain to the children that you are going to help them learn more about spelling patterns.
2. Write the key words *wall, bell, will, doll, dull, sniff, cuff,* and *kiss* at the top of the chart and read them to the children.
3. Show one word card at a time, and ask a child to read the word and decide which column is appropriate. Write the new words under the key words.
4. After two words have been placed in each column, have the children read each column with you.
5. Suggested language: "What do you notice about the last part or the pattern in each of these words?"
6. Help the children notice the spelling pattern (rime) in each and generalize that the words in each family end with a short vowel sound followed by double consonants. They will likely notice the vowel in all sounds like a short *o*.
7. Write the principle on a strip at the top of the chart.
8. Explain to the children that they are going to use magnetic letters to make words with several different spelling patterns. After they make the words, they are to write them on a list sheet. They will make, read, and write a total of twenty words using the *-all, -ell, -ill, -oll, -ull, -iff, -uff,* and *-iss* patterns.

⑨ Demonstrate how to take the first part of a word *(sp)* and the last part *(ell)* and make the word *spell.*

⑩ Remind them to make at least one word with each pattern.

⑪ Post the class chart in clear view for reference.

make
write
circle
read

- Using word cards and magnetic letters, have the children make words with the seven different patterns, at least two words for each pattern. Have them record two words for each pattern on a list sheet and circle any word that has the letter pattern but sounds different (*toll,* for example). Then ask them to read their lists to a partner.

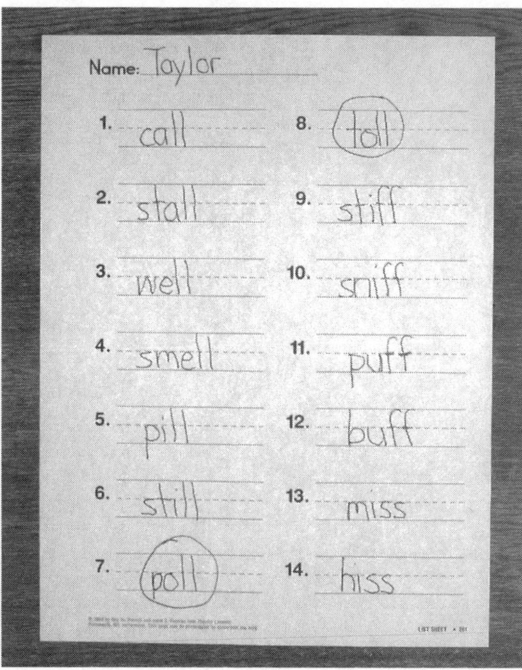

Have the children read their lists to a different partner.

Invite the children to give a few more words to add to the class chart.

Link

Interactive Read-Aloud: Read aloud books that include many words with patterns. Rhyming books are excellent choices (see *Teaching Resources*, Rhymes Bibilography). Examples are:

- ***Four and Twenty Dinosaurs*** by Bernard Most
- ***The Great Divide*** by Dayle Ann Dodds

Shared Reading: After reading and enjoying a poem such as "The Postman" or "My Father Is Extremely Tall" (see *Sing a Song of Poetry*), have the children locate words with a short vowel followed by double consonants.

Guided Reading: During word work, write five or six words with a short vowel followed by double consonants for the children to read quickly.

Interactive Writing: Encourage the children to think about the vowel and double consonant pattern when writing words. After writing a text together, point out the pattern in two or three words.

Independent Writing: Prompt the children to use a word they know with a short vowel followed by double consonants when attempting to write a new word (for example, *ball, bell*).

assess

- Notice the children's use of the vowel and double consonant pattern.
- Write five or six words with the pattern on index cards, and quickly determine the children's ability to read them.

Expand the Learning

Repeat the lesson and include words that have more than one syllable: *doorbell, eggshell, nutshell, retell, anthill, treadmill, windowsill, refill, windmill, baseball, basketball, football, meatball, eyeball, rainfall, snowball, snowfall, waterfall, pinball.* Children may realize that each of these words is made up of two smaller words. You can also use words with *-er (smaller).*

Have the children read charts and other writing around the room. Have them write words with the vowel and double consonant phonogram on a Word Around the Room Sheet (see *Teaching Resources*).

Connect with Home

Send home a sheet of word cards with the short vowel and double consonant pattern for children to sort and read to family members.

Show the children how to make a small word search with the pattern. (See *Teaching Resources,* Directions for Word Searches.) First, they select five or six words and write them across, down, and diagonally, one letter in each square. Then they fill in the other boxes with any letters. Finally, they have family members look for and circle the five or six words.

9 Learning Patterns with ee Double Vowels

Follow the Path

Consider Your Children

This lesson is best taught after the children control the CVC and CVC*e* patterns. Focus on the pattern *ee* in one-syllable words. It is important for students to learn to recognize the pattern but also to learn to analyze how each letter contributes to the sound of the word.

Working with English Language Learners

The *ee* pattern is easy for English language learners to identify in words. They may be able to connect the words visually, but they must also know what the words mean and connect the letter pattern with the sound it represents in order to pronounce the words. Begin with words that your English language learners know; go over all of the words before playing the game with them or expecting them to play the game.

You Need

- Chart paper.
- Markers.

From *Teaching Resources:*

- List Sheets.
- Directions for Follow the Path.
- Follow the Path Game Cards made from Lesson SP 9 Word Cards and Deck Card Template.

Understand the Principle

Phonograms or spelling patterns are also called *word families* or *rimes*. In a one-syllable word, the rime is the vowel and all the letters after it, while the onset is the consonant, consonant cluster, or digraph that comes before the rime. Double vowel phonograms are a common spelling pattern.

Explain the Principle

“Some words have double vowels followed by a consonant.”

“Sometimes the vowel sounds like its name (long sound).”

plan

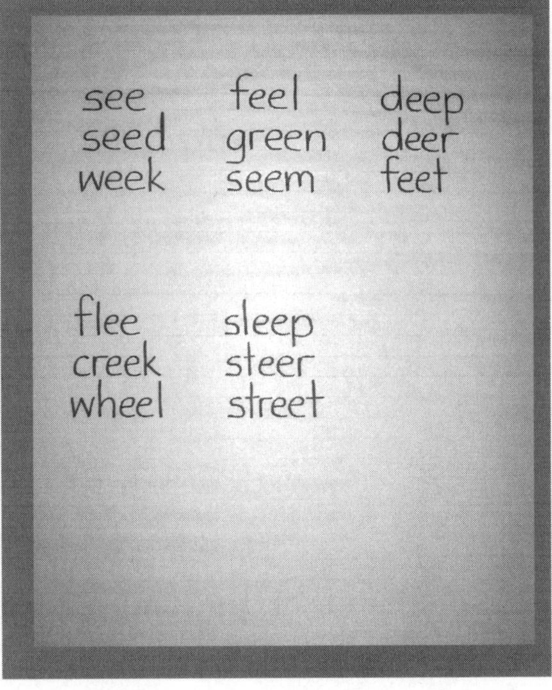

Explain the Principle

" **Some words have double vowels followed by a consonant.** "

" **Sometimes the vowel sounds like its name (long sound).** "

① Tell children that you'll be helping them notice more patterns in words.

② Write several words beginning with a consonant and *ee (see, seed, week, feel, green, seem, deep, deer, feet)* on a chart. Suggested language: "What do you notice about the letters? [Children respond.] Yes, each word starts with a consonant, has two vowels, and then usually has another consonant."

③ Now write words that start with a consonant cluster or digraph *(flee, creek, wheel, sleep, steer, street)*. Suggested language: "Now what do you notice about the words? [Children respond.] Yes, they start with a consonant cluster of two or three letters, such as *sleep* or *street,* or a consonant digraph, such as *wheel.*"

④ Explain that the long *e* vowel sound can be found in the spelling patterns *ee, eed, eek, eel, een, eem, eep, eer, eet.* Explain that sometimes they will also see the *ee* pattern in a word ending in *ch,* as in *beech* (a kind of tree).

⑤ Invite the children to give you one or two more words for each pattern. If the words they give you do not have the *ee* spelling, make or write them off to the side, explaining that there are other letter patterns that make the long *e* sound (*steam,* for example). They will be building a category of words in which two vowels appear together and sound like long *e;* they will divide this category further into words that have *ee* or *ea* (or even *ie*).

⑥ Explain to the children that they are going to play Follow the Path with words that have the *ee*-consonant (VVC) pattern.

⑦ Then they will write twenty words that have the *ee*-consonant pattern on a List Sheet.

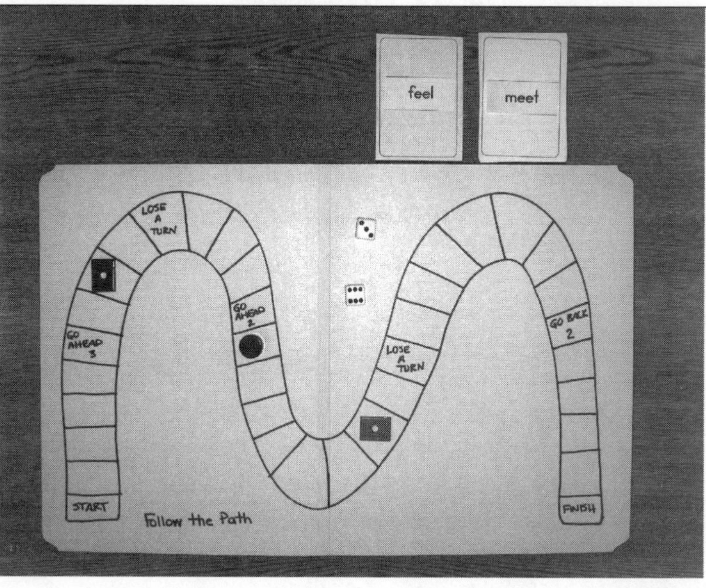

take
say
throw
move
write

▸ Have the children, in groups of two or three, play Follow the Path. Using a deck of cards with words that have the *ee*-consonant pattern, the children take a card, read it, throw the dice, and move the number of spaces indicated. The player to reach the end first wins the game. Then have the children, on a List Sheet, write twenty words that have the *ee*-consonant pattern.

Have the children suggest a few words to add to the *ee* chart.

(Note: If you used magnetic letters to teach the lesson, also make a written chart listing the principles and patterns for children's reference.)

Link

Interactive Read-Aloud: Read aloud books that have many examples of words with the *ee* phonogram, such as

- ***The Lotus Seed*** by Sherry Garland
- ***Fair-Weathered Friend*** by Udo Weigelt

Shared Reading: After reading and enjoying a poem or song such as "Denise Sees the Fleece," "The Cupboard," or "Buffalo Gals" (see *Sing a Song of Poetry*), have the children use a masking card or highlighter tape to locate words that have the *ee* pattern.

Guided Reading: During word work, write several words with the *ee* phonogram on a whiteboard. Change the first letter or letters or the last letter or letters to make new words: *feel–wheel, weep–sweep, weep–weed, deep–deed, screen–screech.*

Interactive Writing: When the children write new words, help them notice those that have phonogram patterns with *ee* and a consonant.

Independent Writing: Point out the *ee* pattern in words the children are writing. Help them see how a word they want to write has a pattern like another word they know.

Expand the Learning

Add the pattern *eeze*, as in *sneeze, breeze, freeze, squeeze, tweeze,* to show another variation.

As a challenge, repeat the lesson with *ee* words that have more than one syllable: *indeed, seaweed, succeed, cartwheel, between, eighteen, fifteen, thirteen, fourteen, sixteen, sunscreen, asleep, pioneer, volunteer, parakeet, bittersweet, freezer.*

Connect with Home

Send home a deck of word cards and a copy of Follow the Path so the children can play the game with family members.

assess

- Notice the children's use of patterns with *ee* and a consonant as they read and write.
- Dictate four or five words with the *ee*-consonant pattern.

10 Learning Patterns with oo Double Vowels

Say and Sort

Consider Your Children

In this lesson, your children learn to notice *oo* as a double vowel, usually preceded and followed by a consonant letter or letters. They learn that these phonograms can have two sounds (*good* and *food,* for example). (As always, there will be variants, such as *door.*) This lesson best follows lessons on CVC, VC*e,* and other easy common phonograms. It helps children attend to the sequence of letters in words and quickly recognize them.

Working with English Language Learners

English language learners need a large core of known words as well as systems for learning words. If they try to remember each word separately, they will not develop efficient word-solving systems. It is important for them to develop their ability to search for and find patterns. They may need many explicit demonstrations of patterns; while they can see the patterns, the words may not be meaningful and/or they may not know how to pronounce them. Say the words clearly and have students repeat them as many times as needed while you also write them on a small whiteboard. Be sure that students understand the meaning of the words you select as examples.

You Need

- Chart paper.
- Markers.
- Pocket chart.

From *Teaching Resources:*

- Pocket Chart Card Template.
- Lesson SP 10 Word Cards.
- Two-Way Sort Sheets.

Understand the Principle

Children need to be able to detect patterns in words. There are many common phonograms, or *rimes* (also called word families), that are helpful to children when they want to take a word apart in order to read or spell it. The double vowel *oo* is part of several common phonograms and makes several different sounds.

Explain the Principle

"Some words have double vowels followed by a consonant."

"Sometimes the vowel sounds like its name (long sound)."

"Sometimes the vowel stands for other sounds."

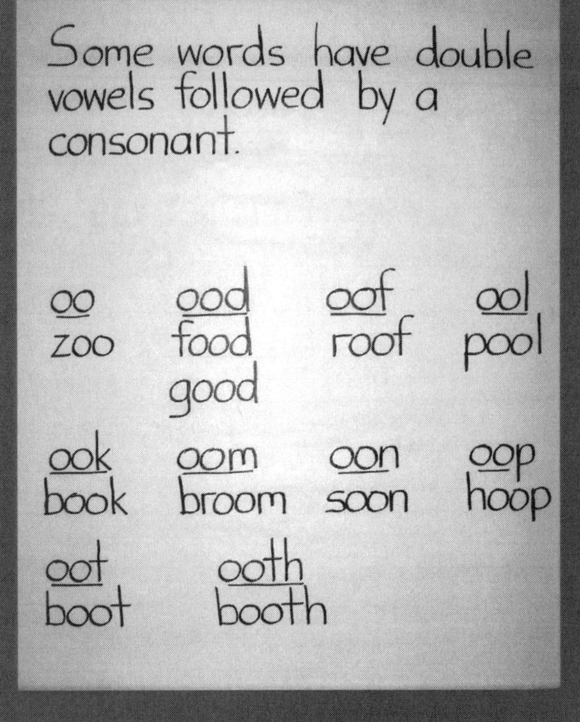

teach

Explain the Principle

" Some words have double vowels followed by a consonant. "

" Sometimes the vowel sounds like its name (long sound). "

" Sometimes the vowel stands for other sounds. "

① Tell the children that you are going to show them how to notice more patterns in words.

② Have examples already written on a chart (see photograph).

③ Invite the children to read the words on the chart with you.

④ Suggested language: "You can see that all the words on the chart have *oo* and a consonant or consonants before or after the two vowels. What do you notice about the sound of the vowels?"

⑤ Children will likely notice that the *oo* sound in *food* and *good* are different even though the letter patterns are the same. They may also notice that *book* has the same vowel sound as *good.*

⑥ Explain that *oo* followed by a consonant or consonants is a common pattern or letter sequence in many words. Sometimes the vowel sounds like the *oo* in *moon,* and other times it sounds like the *oo* in *look* or *good.* Write the principle on the top of the chart, and invite the children to give one or two more examples for each pattern.

⑦ Use a pocket chart and a set of large word cards that have the *oo* followed by consonant(s) pattern. Place the words *moon* and *look* at the top of two columns.

⑧ Show the children how to read and say each word and place it under one of the two key words, *moon* and *look.* Demonstrate with two or three examples.

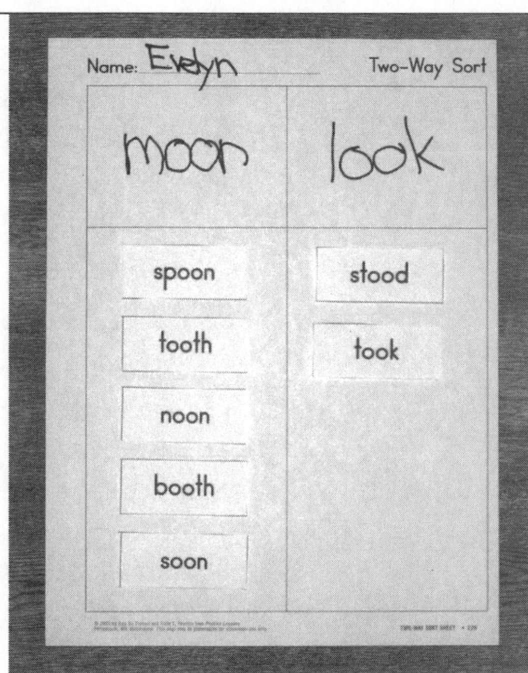

say
sort
glue/write
read

- Have the children write the key words *(moon, look)* at the top of a Two-Way Sort Sheet. Ask them to say and sort the words and then glue them or write them on the sheet. Then have them read each column to a partner.

Have the children read their two columns to a different partner.

Using the children's suggestions, add a few more examples to the class chart.

Link

Interactive Read-Aloud: Read aloud books that have a variety of phonogram patterns including *oo* and a consonant, such as

- ***Ook the Book*** by Lissa Rovetch
- ***Going to the Zoo*** by Tom Paxton

Shared Reading: Before reading a poem such as "Fuzzy Little Caterpillar," "Silly Simon," or "Mr. Nobody" (see *Sing a Song of Poetry*), use stick-on notes to cover a few words with the *oo* pattern. Ask the children to predict what the word will say based on the meaning and the structure. Uncover the word letter by letter as children tell what letters they expect to see.

Guided Reading: When the children come to a difficult *oo* word, encourage them to use patterns they know. Ask questions such as, "Do you see a part that you know?" and "What do you know that might help?"

Interactive Writing: Prompt the children to think of *oo* patterns they know when they try to write new words. If they need more support, tell them a word that is like it; for example, "That word has a pattern like *moon.*"

Independent Writing: Show the children how they can use the *oo* pattern by quickly having them write a word they know in the margin of the paper. Then point out the *oo* and consonant that is like the word they are trying to write.

assess

- Observe how the children use the *oo* pattern in words they try to read or write.
- Dictate a few words with the *oo* pattern for the children to write.

Expand the Learning

Add the *-oose* pattern to the chart using words such as *goose, loose,* and *moose;* add *-ooze* as in *snooze.*

Repeat the lesson with words that have more than one syllable: *bamboo, kangaroo, shampoo, tattoo, seafood, fireproof, soundproof, toadstool, classroom, bathroom, mushroom, bridegroom, cocoon, raccoon, macaroon.*

Connect with Home

Give the children a sheet of words (SP 10 Word Cards in *Teaching Resources*) with *oo* phonograms to say and sort at home.

Generative Lesson

early
mid
late

11 Learning Onsets and Rimes: -ail, -ain, -an

Three-Way Word Sort

Consider Your Children

Use this lesson when the children know a large number of high frequency words, most of the consonant letters and associated sounds, and some letter clusters but still need to learn to look beyond the first letter when solving words while reading. You will be teaching children two phonograms (*-ain* and *-ail*) that may be unfamiliar to them.

Working with English Language Learners

Sorting words in two ways will help English language learners become more flexible in looking at words and will strengthen their knowledge of patterns. If you are not sure these children can read the words they will be sorting, work with them in a small group and remove any words they cannot read and/or do not understand. You may want to use words in meaningful sentences to bolster their understanding.

You Need

- Chart paper.
- Markers.
- Pocket chart.

From *Teaching Resources:*

- Pocket Chart Card Template.
- Three-Way Sort Sheets.
- Three-Way Sort Cards.
- Lesson SP 11 Word Cards.

Understand the Principle

Noticing parts of words (the *onset,* or first part, and the *rime,* the rest of the word, which is also a phonogram) makes it easier for children to break words apart in order to analyze them. Working with these parts of words helps them realize the importance of looking at the entire word, not just the first letter. Words with single-letter onsets are easier to read than those with consonant cluster onsets.

Explain the Principle

"Some words have two vowels together."

"The vowel sound in the middle is usually the name of the first vowel."

SP 11 Spelling Patterns

plan

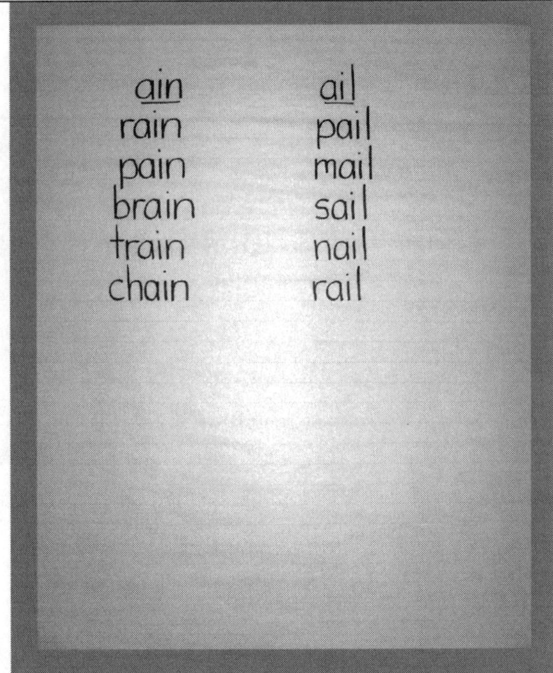

ain
rain
pain
brain
train
chain
ail
pail
mail
sail
nail
rail

Explain the Principle

“Some words have two vowels together.”

“The vowel sound in the middle is usually the name of the first vowel.”

1. Explain to the children that they are going to learn about spelling patterns.
2. Suggested language: “You know how to look at the first part of the word and the rest of the word. This word is *rain*. What is the first part of *rain*? [Children respond.] The first part is *r*, and the rest of the word is *a-i-n*. If I change the first part of the word to a *p*, I have. . . .” Children respond, or you may tell them the word *pain*.
3. Suggested language: “We can make more words that end like *rain* and *pain*.” Ask the children for examples and/or show them more *-ain* words. List them under *-ain* on the chart. Point out that *brain*, *train*, and *chain* begin with a consonant cluster.
4. Repeat the process with *-ail* words, beginning with the example that will be most familiar.
5. Have the children read both lists of words.
6. Then direct the children’s attention to a pocket chart that has the word cards for this lesson on the left side. “Today you are going to be sorting these words. Let’s sort them by the first part of the word.”
7. Take the word *rain* and place it on the right side of the pocket chart. Suggested language: “Which words begin like *rain*?” Have the children quickly find the *r* words and place them under *rain*.
8. Sort the rest of the words quickly by first letter.
9. Then mix the word cards up again. Suggested language: “Now sort the words by looking at the rest of the word. Think about the whole end part of the word, not just the last letter. What word is like *rain* after the first part?”

⑩ Demonstrate sorting the words by the rimes (ending parts, or phonograms). Including the easy phonogram *-an*, which the children already know, will require them to look carefully at the spelling patterns.

⑪ Tell the children they will be sorting the words first by the way they begin and a second time by the way they end.

take
say
sort
read
write

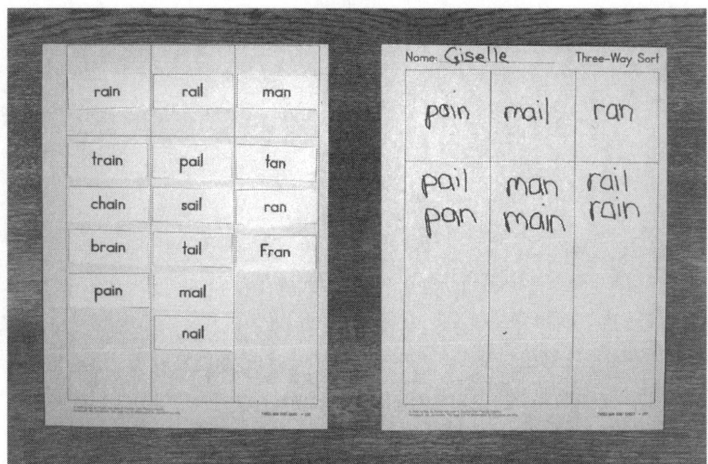

▸ Using a Three-Way Sort Card, children sort the words by the first letter and then by the ending spelling pattern. Then they read the words to a partner. Finally they list the words by the ending spelling pattern on a Three-Way Sort Sheet.

Ask the children to talk about what they learned from sorting and writing these words. Listen for comments like these:

"Lots of words have *ai* together."

"You can change the first part or the last part to make a new word."

Link

Interactive Read-Aloud: Read aloud books that have interesting word combinations in which onsets remain the same but the rimes change, and vice versa. Examples are:

- ***We All Sing with the Same Voice*** by J. Philip Miller
- ***Wherever Bears Be*** by Sue Ann Alderson

Shared Reading: Using a familiar text such as "The Goat" *(-ain)* and "Slowly, Slowly" *(-ail)* (see *Sing a Song of Poetry*), have the children point out words that have the *-ain* or *-ail* pattern.

Guided Reading: Cover up the first or last part of words with *-ain* and *-ail* phonograms, and have the children solve them. During word work, have the children build words that contain *-ain* and *-ail*.

Interactive Writing: Connect *-ain* and *-ail* words the children want to write with the word charts you have made. Point out the *-ain* and *-ail* spelling patterns.

Independent Writing: Encourage children to think about *-ain* and *-ail* patterns in words as a way to help them write the words.

Expand the Learning

Use the Word Card Template (*Teaching Resources,* Templates) to make word cards for the additional phonograms. The Phonograms List in *Teaching Resources* contains an extensive list of phonograms and sample words. Repeat the lesson with other phonograms.

Have the children write *-ain* and *-ail* words quickly in order to become fluent with these phonograms.

Connect with Home

Have children take a blank sort sheet and word cards home so they can sort the words with family members.

assess

- Notice whether the children can sort words by the *-ain* and *-ail* rime or phonogram.
- Give the children two columns of *-ain* and *-ail* words and ask them to draw lines between the ones that are alike.

12 Learning Onsets and Rimes: -ight

Follow the Path

Consider Your Children

Use this lesson when your children know some of the *-ight* words by sight and have also worked with phonograms and understand the principle of substituting letters to make new words. Observe whether they are having difficulty understanding *-ight* as a unit with the same sound as *i* in *mine.* Also be sure that the children are not becoming overdependent on phonogram patterns. You don't want to limit their decoding ability to patterns alone; make this technique one part of a flexible repertoire.

Working with English Language Learners

Struggling readers need many more encounters with words in order to learn them because they have not developed efficient decoding systems and do not easily detect patterns. This problem is greater when they are also working in a new language. Play the Follow the Path game with a small group to be sure that they recognize and understand the words in the game. Demonstrate how to record words.

You Need

- Chart paper.
- Markers.

From *Teaching Resources:*

- Directions for Follow the Path.
- Follow the Path Game Cards made from Lesson SP 12 Word Cards and Deck Card Template. You will need additional word cards to fill out the deck. You can use the SP 11 Word Cards or any other cards of your choosing.

Understand the Principle

Noticing parts of words (the *onset,* or first part, and the *rime,* the rest of the word) makes it easier for children to break words apart in order to analyze them. Working with the parts of words helps them realize the importance of looking at the entire word, not just the first letter. Learning patterns will help them decode by analogy; in other words, they can make connections between the parts of known words and the new words they are trying to solve.

Explain the Principle

“Some words have parts (patterns) that are the same.”

“You can find patterns (parts) that are the same in many words.”

“You can use the pattern you know to help you read (or write) a word.”

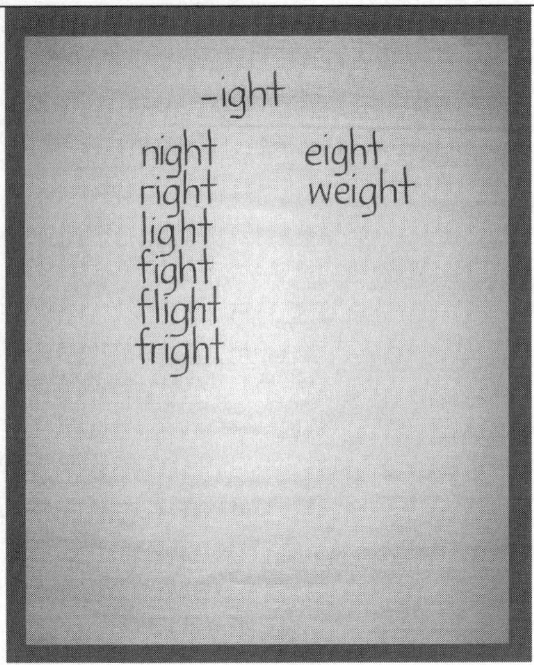

Explain the Principle

" Some words have parts (patterns) that are the same. "

" You can find patterns (parts) that are the same in many words. "

" You can use the pattern you know to help you read (or write) a word. "

① Tell the children that you'll be teaching them more about spelling patterns.

② Suggested language: "You know how to look at the parts of a word and change the beginning to make a new word. We're going to look at a very interesting word today. You know this word." Write *night* on the chart, and ask the children to read it and identify the first part and the rest of the word.

③ Suggested language: "I am going to change the first part of the word to an *r*. The new word is *right*."

④ Guide the children to suggest other words.

⑤ Children may know the word *eight* and bring it up as an example, or you may write it in a separate column. Suggested language: "You know the word *eight*. It is spelled like *night* at the end, but it sounds different, so I will put it over here. Here is another word like *eight*." Write *weight*. Other words, such as *freight*, are probably too difficult for children, but it is important to recognize the number word *eight* as an exception. Children will notice (or you point out) that there is an *e* before the *ight* in words like *weight*.

⑥ Have the children read the words on the list.

⑦ Tell the children they will be playing Follow the Path with words that have the *-ight* pattern as well as words with other patterns.

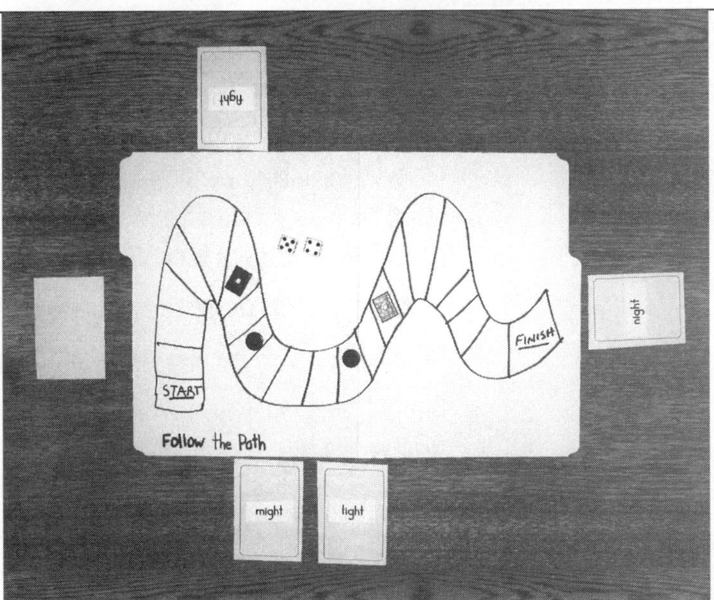

apply

take
say
throw
move

- Have children play Follow the Path using *-ight* word cards and word cards containing other patterns they know. They take a card and read it, and then they throw the dice to move their markers the indicated number of spaces.

Play a word game: "I'm thinking of a word with *-ight* that has *r* at the beginning." Have the children locate the word on the chart and hold up their examples.

Have children read their examples to a partner.

Link

Interactive Read-Aloud: Read aloud books that have interesting word combinations in which the onsets remain the same but the rimes change, and vice versa. Examples are:

- ***Madeline's Rescue*** by Ludwig Bemelmans
- ***Little Bunny on the Move*** by Peter McCarty

Shared Reading: Read poems such as "Jack-in-the-Box" or "Star Light, Star Bright" (see *Sing a Song of Poetry*) that have rhyming words in them, and have children use a masking card or highlighter tape to locate words that match.

Guided Reading: Cover up the first or last part of words with *-ight* phonograms, and have the children solve them. During word work, take words with the *-ight* pattern and add different beginnings. Invite the children to come up with others.

Interactive Writing: Connect *-ight* words the children want to write with words they know with that spelling pattern.

Independent Writing: Encourage the children to think about the *-ight* spelling pattern to help them write a new *-ight* word.

assess

- Ask children to read the *-ight* words in random order.
- Dictate three *-ight* words for the children to write.

Expand the Learning

Have the children write *-ight* words quickly so that they will become fluent with this phonogram pattern.

Help children notice the *-ite* pattern and how it sounds the same but looks different.

Connect with Home

Have children take the Follow the Path game and word cards home so they can play the game with family members.

Learning about CVVC Patterns

Making Words

Consider Your Children

In this lesson, children learn about the consonant-vowel-vowel-consonant pattern. This learning builds on children's understanding of consonant-vowel-consonant (CVC) and consonant-vowel-consonant-silent *e* (CVC*e*) patterns and phonogram patterns with double vowels (for example, the *ee* in *green* or the *oo* in *look*).

Working with English Language Learners

Working with word patterns helps English language learners internalize both the phonology and the sound-to-letter relationships in English words. A key idea is making connections among words, which will accelerate children's learning of English as well as their literacy development. Work with children to be sure they understand and can pronounce the words you are using as examples. Praise them for approximations; their pronunciation will gradually improve.

You Need

- Magnetic letters.

From *Teaching Resources:*

- List Sheets.

Understand the Principle

The letter patterns children notice are the basis for their learning other words. The spelling patterns in this lesson are long vowel phonograms containing two vowels, or a *vowel combination.* Some patterns are easier and more frequent (*ea* as in *steam*), and others are less frequent (*ue* as in *fuel*). And there will always be exceptions, such as *said.*

Explain the Principle

"Some words have two vowels together (vowel combinations)."

"The vowel sound in the middle is usually the name of the first vowel."

plan

teach

Explain the Principle

"Some words have two vowels together (vowel combinations)."

"The vowel sound in the middle is usually the name of the first vowel."

① Explain to children that they are going to learn some new spelling patterns.

② On an easel, make several words *(read, leaf; pail, rain; road, boat; fuel)* with magnetic letters (or write them on a chart), and read them aloud.

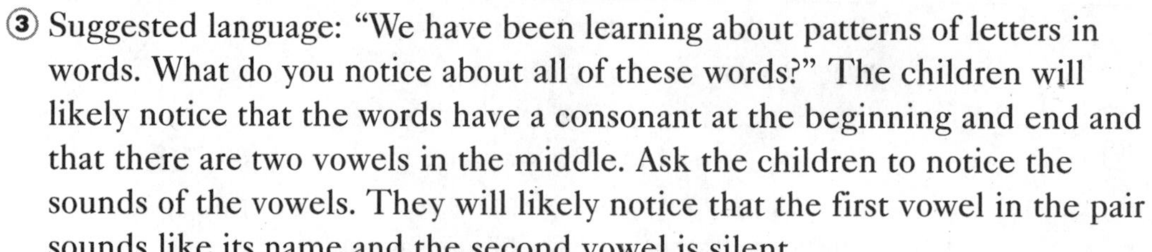

③ Suggested language: "We have been learning about patterns of letters in words. What do you notice about all of these words?" The children will likely notice that the words have a consonant at the beginning and end and that there are two vowels in the middle. Ask the children to notice the sounds of the vowels. They will likely notice that the first vowel in the pair sounds like its name and the second vowel is silent.

④ Help them conclude that some words have parts or patterns that are the same. Explain that you can find patterns or parts that are the same in many words and that you can use the patterns you know to help you read or write a word.

⑤ Explain to the children that some words have a CVVC pattern and that the vowel sound is usually the sound of the first vowel. Tell them there can be extra consonants in the beginning or end part of the word.

⑥ Explain to the children that today they are going to make and write five words with each of the CVVC patterns *(ai, ea, oa, ue)*. The *ue* pattern is more unusual, so they may make only two or three words with this pattern (for example, *glue, clue, fuel*). Demonstrate making the word *jeans*, with a *j* first, the *ea* next, and then *ns*.

⑦ Tell the children that they are to read the words they make and then write them on a List Sheet or in a Word Study Notebook.

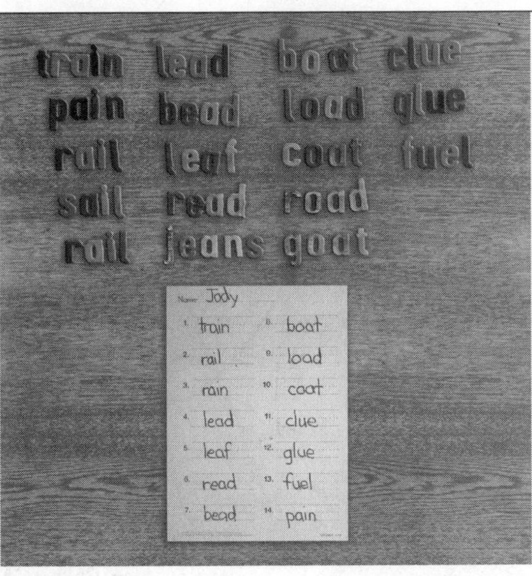

make
say
check
mix (3x)
write

▸ Using magnetic letters, have children make five words with each of the four spelling patterns (except *ue*). They make each word, say it, check it, mix it up, and then repeat the process until they've done this process three times for each word. Remind them that the words must be real words. Children then record their words on the List Sheet or in their Word Study Notebook.

Have the children, in turn, read one word for each pattern. Add a few words to the group chart.

Link

Interactive Read-Aloud: Read aloud rhyming books (see *Teaching Resources*, Rhymes Bibliography) so children can notice sound and letter patterns. Examples are:

- ***Clara Ann Cookie, Go to Bed!*** by Harriet Ziefert
- ***Come Meet Muffin*** by Joyce Carol Oates

Shared Reading: Use songs and poems that have several words containing CVVC phonogram patterns, such as "Row, Row, Row Your Boat" (see *Sing a Song of Poetry*). Have the children use a masking card, flag, or highlighter tape to locate words such as *boat, stream, dream, scream, rain, Spain.*

Guided Reading: When the children come to a difficult word with the CVVC pattern, prompt them with questions such as "Do you see a part you know?" or "Do you know a word like that?" During word work, make four or five words with the CVVC pattern and have children read them quickly.

Interactive Writing: When the children want to write a new word with the CVVC pattern, remind them to think of a word they know that is like it. Call attention to patterns in words whenever possible.

Independent Writing: As the children reread their writing, have them look for CVVC words that don't look right and think about CVVC patterns they know.

assess

- Look at the children's lists of words to find out whether they understand the principle.
- Work in small groups with children who are not able to make CVVC words or seem to be imitating others.

Expand the Learning

Repeat the lesson and mix in other vowel patterns—phonograms with silent e *(make)*, phonograms with double vowels *(queen)*. The Phonograms List in *Teaching Resources* contains an extensive list of phonograms and sample words.

Have the children make and write words with a consonant cluster or consonant digraph at the beginning and/or end *(wheat, scream, groan, coast, waist, drain, brain, braid, chain, faint, grain, paint, plain, snail, train, strain, beach, bleach, cheap, clean, cream, dream, each, leash, peach, pleat, sneak, speak, steal, steam, stream, teach, coach, cloak, croak, float, toast).*

Connect with Home

Give children a blank Make-Say-Check-Mix Sheet, and have them use magnetic letters or letter cards (see *Teaching Resources*) to make more words with CVVC patterns at home.

Send home a deck of Concentration cards (see *Teaching Resources*) and have the children play the game with family members, reading and matching pairs of words that have the same two-vowel pattern in the middle.

14 Summarizing Phonograms

Building Words

Consider Your Children

Use this lesson after your children have learned many spelling patterns and you want to help them review and practice recognizing them quickly. Select specific patterns your children need to work on.

Working with English Language Learners

Check to be sure that English language learners know, understand, and quickly recognize several good examples of words for each phonogram. Give them many opportunities to pronounce the words and make their own assessment of the differences and similarities between them.

You Need

- Chart paper.
- Markers.
- Magnetic letters or letter tiles.

From *Teaching Resources:*

- Spelling Patterns Sheets.

Understand the Principle

Good readers are familiar with spelling patterns and are able to spell the sounds they hear in words. A *rime* is a vowel and the letters that come after it in a syllable (*eet* in *feet,* for example). All syllables have a rime. Rimes are often called *spelling patterns, word families,* or *phonograms.* An *onset* is the consonant(s) that comes before the vowel in a syllable (*fr* in *frame,* for example). Not all syllables have an onset (*on,* for example). When children are able to notice and use the parts of words, they can recognize new words more quickly by using parts they know.

Explain the Principle

“You can look at (or use) the part you know to read (or write) a word.”

plan

Explain the Principle

"You can look at (or use) the part you know to read (or write) a word."

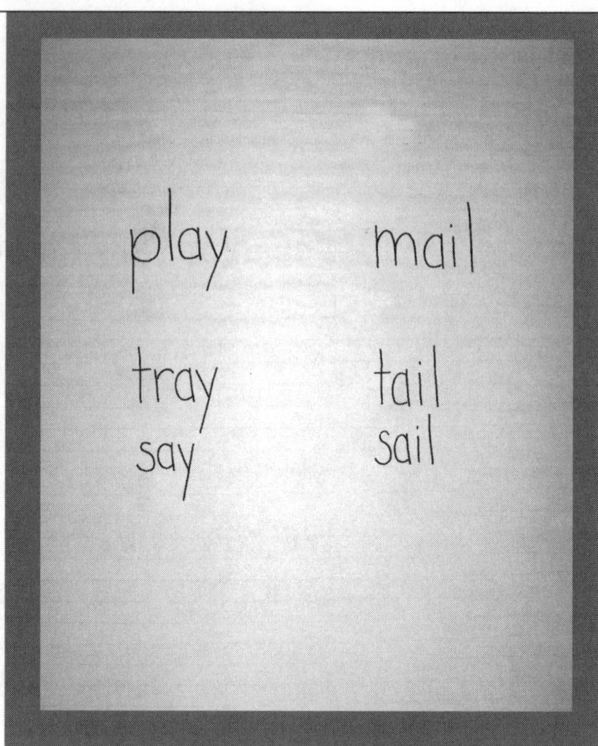

1. Explain to the children that you are going to help them think about the many different spelling patterns they know and how they can use them to read and write many different words.
2. Write a word at the top of a chart—*play*, for example. Cover the *pl* with your hand, and ask the children to write two words that end with the pattern *ay*.
3. Suggested language: "What is one word you wrote?" Invite the children to list additional words below *play* on the class chart.
4. Repeat the process with four or five other patterns. Then read the list with the children.
5. Explain to the children that you will post a list of four words. They will make the words with magnetic letters and write them at the top of their Spelling Patterns Sheets. They will then build five words with the same spelling pattern as each key word and write the words below the key words.

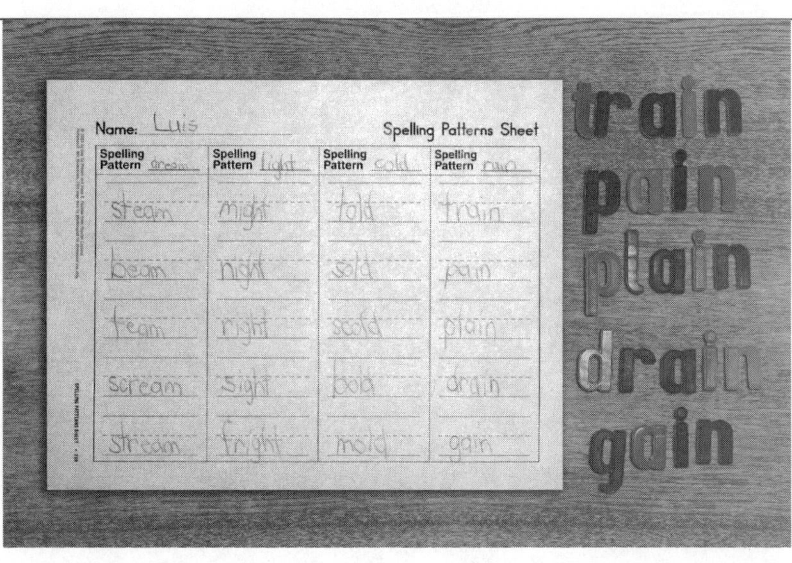

write
make
write
read

- Have the children write four particular words, such as *dream*, *light*, *cold*, and *rain*, in the key word boxes on a Spelling Patterns Sheet. Then, using magnetic letters, they are to make and write five more words with each spelling pattern. Finally, they read their words to a partner.

Have children read the four columns of words to a different partner.

Link

Interactive Read-Aloud: Read aloud many different rhyming books (see *Teaching Resources,* Rhymes Bibliography) so that children can notice sound and letter patterns. After reading, enjoying, and discussing a book, write one or two patterns on a chart and discuss them. Examples of appropriate books are:

- ***Monster Math*** by Anne Miranda
- ***Sailor Song*** by Nancy Jewell

Shared Reading: Using stick-on notes, cover the ending spelling patterns of four or five words in a poem such as "Owl" or "Pairs or Pears" (see *Sing a Song of Poetry*) you select. Read the poem with the children, and ask them to predict each covered word. Have them tell the letters they would see in the pattern as you expose the word.

Guided Reading: Following the lesson, have the children find two or three words with particular spelling patterns—for example, a word with the same pattern as *look.*

Interactive Writing: When the children are writing a new word, help them think of a similar pattern.

Independent Writing: Show the children how to edit for spelling by noticing patterns in words they know.

assess

- Ask the children to write four or five words with a particular spelling pattern. Have them write one more word with the same pattern.
- Observe the children's spelling of patterns in their daily writing.

Expand the Learning

Repeat the lesson with a variety of other phonograms, such as long vowel sound spelling patterns, short vowel sound spelling patterns, and double vowel spelling patterns. Use the Word Card Template (*Teaching Resources,* Templates) to make word cards for the additional phonograms. The Phonograms List in *Teaching Resources* contains an extensive list of phonograms and sample words.

Connect with Home

Give the children Spelling Patterns Sheets to take home (fill in the spelling pattern you want them to focus on), and have them write words that contain these spelling patterns with family members.

Generative Lesson

early
mid
late

15 Summarizing Spelling Patterns with a

Building Words

Consider Your Children

This lesson helps children systematize and generalize their knowledge of phonograms containing the sounds of long and short *a.* You may not have taught a minilesson on every one of these eight phonograms, but the children are likely to know them because they have explored the concept in many ways and worked with words informally. You can note patterns that your children find difficult and revisit them later. Once these patterns are learned, be sure to show the children how to use them in all the reading and writing they do. They may use the chart as a reference. (Prepare the chart ahead of time with the pattern heading and two or three examples for each.)

Working with English Language Learners

These patterns are a very useful resource for English language learners as they learn to read and write new words in English. Patterns help them take apart new words and pronounce them while also learning the meaning. Repeat the words many times. Asking the children to suggest their own examples for the chart will give you an idea of their thinking. Praise them for their attempts even if they are only partially correct.

You Need

- Chart paper.
- Markers.

From *Teaching Resources:*

- Category Word Cards, Onsets and Rimes.
- Spelling Patterns Sheets (two per child).

Understand the Principle

Children need to summarize their understanding of phonograms with a VC*e* pattern, ending consonant clusters, and vowel combinations so that they can become more flexible in using this knowledge. These phonograms appear frequently in English, and students must be able to recognize them quickly and automatically as they read and write.

Explain the Principle

“Some words have parts (patterns) that are the same at the end.”

“You can find parts that are the same in many words.”

plan

ake	ack	ail
take	sack	mail
rake	pack	pail
bake	rack	rail
ale	ank	ame
sale	tank	same
stale	bank	came
whale	thank	game
ask	ate	ash
task	late	cash
mask	state	mash
flask	hate	trash

Explain the Principle

“Some words have parts (patterns) that are the same at the end.”

“You can find parts that are the same in many words.”

① Tell the children that you are going to help them think about all the *a* spelling patterns they know.

② Suggested language: “You know a lot of the parts that we see in words. We’re going to review some of the patterns you know that include the letter *a*.”

③ Go over each column quickly; have children suggest one or two more examples for each, and write them on the chart.

④ Have children take turns choosing a pattern and reading quickly down the words in that column. If children’s names fit any of the patterns, add them to the chart.

⑤ Explain that today they are going to use onset and rime cards to make at least five words with each *a* pattern. They will write these words on a Spelling Patterns Sheet. Remind them that they should make words they can read and understand.

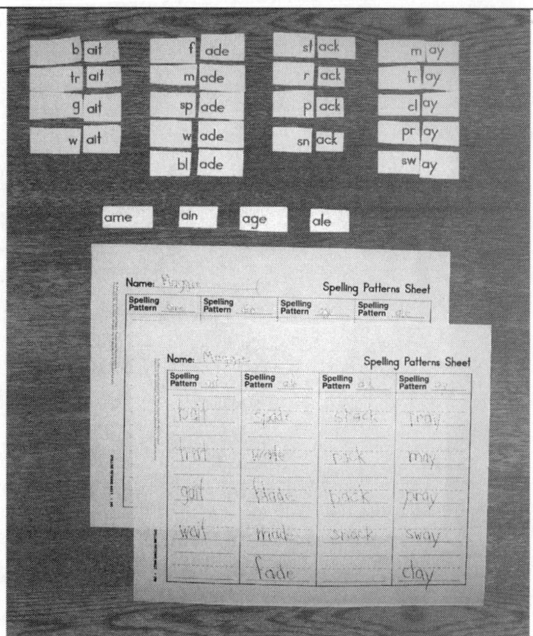

make
write
read

- Have the children use onset and rime word cards to make four or five words with each of the eight *a* patterns. As they make each word, they list it on the Spelling Patterns Sheet. Then they read the words in each box to a partner.

Bring children together to play a game. Have them use the examples they recorded to ask questions such as: "What is a word that starts with *m* and has *-ail* at the end?"

Link

Interactive Read-Aloud: Read aloud books that emphasize words with *a* spelling patterns. Examples are:

- ***Our Marching Band*** by Lloyd Moss
- ***Edwina the Emu*** by Sheena Knowles

Shared Reading: Have the children use highlighter tape or a masking card to quickly locate new words that contain any of the eight *a* phonogram patterns. See *Sing a Song of Poetry* for examples of text such as "They That Wash on Monday" or "Bat, Bat."

Guided Reading: Help the children use their knowledge of *a* phonogram patterns to solve words. Have children who need more work with words build phonogram patterns quickly. For example: "Make *cake.* Now make it say *take.* Make *ate.* Now make it say *rate.* Now make it say *rat* (by taking off the *e*)." Spend only a minute or two in this kind of activity. Keep it lively and quickly step in to demonstrate for children if they cannot perform the tasks. This activity is designed to help them become flexible in using their knowledge.

Interactive Writing: When appropriate, have the children use an *a* phonogram pattern they know to help them write a new word.

Independent Writing: Prompt the children to use *a* phonogram patterns to check on the spelling of words.

assess

- Have the children read words from the summary chart in random order.
- Have the children write words with an *a* phonogram pattern as you say them.

Expand the Learning

Use this same list of words for Follow the Path, Lotto, or Concentration (see *Teaching Resources*, Games).

Repeat the lesson using words with *-ice, -ick, -ide, -ight, -ill, -ine, -ink,* and *-ing.*

Repeat the lesson using words with *-ore, -ock, -oke, -uck, -ump,* and *-unk.*

Connect with Home

Reproduce a summary chart for each child to take home and read to family members.

16 Recognizing Patterns with Ending Consonant Clusters

Say and Sort

Consider Your Children

This lesson will give children a chance to act on and systematize their knowledge of word patterns by comparing them with one another. It should follow lessons introducing phonograms with other patterns, such as CVC, VC*e*, and VVC, as well as phonograms with double vowels ending with one consonant. The phonogram patterns in this lesson, which end with consonant clusters or digraphs (a form of consonant cluster), are more challenging. You may want to start with the more frequently used phonograms *-ack, -ank, -ash, -est, -ick, -ight, -ing, -ink, -ock, -uck, -ump,* and *-unk,* introducing three or four at a time so children can differentiate the patterns.

Working with English Language Learners

Working with the four phonograms *-ack, -ank, -ash,* and *-est* will allow you to select words that English language learners already have in their speaking or listening vocabularies. Be sure to take advantage of any names of class members that fit these patterns by including them as examples. Repeat the words many times, and work with English language learners in a small group the first time they say and sort words by pattern.

You Need

- Pocket chart.

From *Teaching Resources:*

- Pocket Chart Card Template.
- Lesson SP 16 Word Cards.
- Four-Way Sort Cards.
- Four-Way Sort Sheets.

Understand the Principle

A phonogram, or rime, is a vowel-bearing syllable pattern. The letters are in a particular sequence. Phonograms are usually combined with onsets (consonants, consonant clusters, or consonant digraphs). In a one-syllable word, the onset is the first part and the rime is the vowel and the letters that follow *(br–ead).* Phonograms can have short vowels *(pit),* long words with a silent *e (make),* long vowel combinations *(meat),* or other vowel sounds *(look).* The brain detects patterns; therefore, awareness of patterns helps readers and writers learn vowel sounds within words. Though phonograms are very useful for learning by analogy, children will also need to learn other decoding strategies (letter/sound relationships, high frequency words, word structure).

Explain the Principle

“Some words have patterns that end with consonant clusters.”

Explain the Principle

"Some words have patterns that end with consonant clusters."

1. Tell the children that you are going to help them learn more spelling patterns.
2. Use a pocket chart with the four patterns *-ack, -ank, -ash,* and *-est* at the top. Take a word card, have the children read it, and have a child place it under the correct pattern.
3. Continue until you have placed two or three words in each column.
4. Ask the children what they notice about the patterns. Suggested language: "What is the same about each pattern?" Children will notice that each ends with a consonant cluster or consonant digraph.
5. Explain to the children that today they are going to read and sort word cards into four columns. They are to place the words *back*, *bank*, *rash*, and *nest* at the top of a Four-Way Sort Card. They will then take each word card, read it, and place it in the correct column. After sorting all the cards, they will write the words on a Four-Way Sort Sheet (or in four columns in a Word Study Notebook).

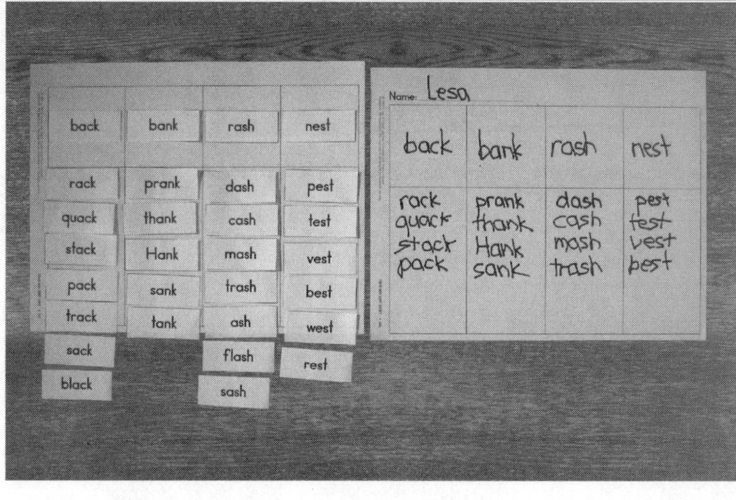

say
sort
write
read

- Have the children say and sort word cards on a Four-Way Sort Card. They write the words on a Four-Way Sort Sheet and read their lists to a partner.

Have the children suggest one or two new words to add to the class chart.

Link

Interactive Read-Aloud: Read aloud rhyming books that have a variety of phonogram patterns. After reading a book, call attention to a few of the patterns by making them with magnetic letters or writing them on a whiteboard. Examples of appropriate books are:

- ***Hippos Go Berserk*** by Sandra Boynton
- ***My Son John*** by Jim Aylesworth

Shared Reading: After enjoying a poem such as "The Chickens" or "December Leaves" (see *Sing a Song of Poetry*), ask the children to look for words that fit clues you give them. For example, "I am thinking of a word that ends like *black*."

Interactive Writing: As the children try to write a new word containing one of these phonograms, have them think of another word like it. You may want to show the relationship quickly on a whiteboard.

Independent Writing: Teach the children how to use phonograms they know to check the spelling of words they have written.

assess

- Have the children write eight words, two with each phonogram.
- Notice whether the children use these phonograms to solve words when they are reading.

Expand the Learning

Repeat the lesson with other phonograms that end with consonant clusters or consonant digraphs: *-alk, -amp, -and, -ant, -ard, -ark, -arm, -art, -ask, -ath, -eck, -elp, -end, -ent, -esh, -ift, -ight, -ing, -ink, -ish, -ock, -old, -ong, -uck, -ump, -ung, -unk, -ush.*

Use the Word Card Template (*Teaching Resources,* Templates) to make word cards for the additional phonograms. The Phonograms List in *Teaching Resources* contains an extensive list of phonograms and sample words.

Connect with Home

Give the children sheets of word cards (use Lesson SP 16 word cards) to cut apart, sort, and glue on paper at home. Also, give them copies of the Four-Way Sort Sheet (see *Teaching Resources,* Templates) and some key words to use when sorting.

17 Learning about Vowel Combination Spelling Patterns

Go Fish

Consider Your Children

This lesson is a more challenging one because it includes a variety of spelling patterns with two vowels (VVC) and includes words that begin with a single consonant, a consonant cluster, or a consonant digraph. You will also help the children notice that in some *ea* words, the vowel sounds like short *e*.

Working with English Language Learners

Vowel combinations are difficult for all learners and may be especially challenging to English language learners. It is worth spending time on these patterns because they occur in so many words and can help children accelerate their learning. Give explicit demonstrations and help children say the words. It may be necessary to use words in meaningful sentences. Work with your English language learners in a small group to play Go Fish so that you can monitor their understanding.

You Need

- Chart paper.
- Markers.

From *Teaching Resources:*

- Directions for Go Fish.
- Go Fish Game Cards made from Lesson SP 17 Word Cards and Deck Card Template.

Understand the Principle

Children need to learn how to notice letter sequences or phonograms because these patterns will help them solve new words when reading and writing. There are many regular sound and letter patterns that include two vowels together making one sound.

Explain the Principle

“Some words have two vowels together (vowel combinations).”

“The vowel sound in the middle is usually the name of the first vowel.”

hair	feed	tea
pain	street	bead
nail		speak
paid		team
		leap
toad	head	
soak	bread	
	sweat	

Explain the Principle

"Some words have two vowels together (vowel combinations)."

"The vowel sound in the middle is usually the name of the first vowel."

① Explain to the children that you are going to help them notice more patterns in words.

② Call on children to read each column of the chart.

③ Suggested language: "What do you notice about the words?" The children will probably notice the two vowels in each word.

④ You will need to explain that in some words *ea* sounds like short *e (bread, head).*

⑤ Invite the children to give one or two more words that fit each pattern. You may want to help them generalize the pattern and write it on the chart.

⑥ Explain to the children that they are going to play Go Fish in groups of three or four. Each player will have six cards. The first player asks the second for a particular type of card. For example, "Do you have a word with *-ait* like *bait*?" If the second player has a word with *-ait* (*wait,* for example), he gives it to the first player, who places the pair on the table. If he does not, he says, "Go fish," and the first player takes a card from the deck. The second player continues in like fashion. The first person to run out of cards wins the game.

read
ask
match

▸ Have children play Go Fish with words that include vowel combinations.

Invite the children to share a new word they learned that has a vowel combination.

Refer to or place a word with each of the vowel combination patterns on the word wall.

Link

Interactive Read-Aloud: Read aloud books with rhymes (see *Teaching Resources,* Rhymes Bibliography) so the children can learn more about letter and sound patterns. Examples of appropriate books are:

- ***Cloud Cuckoo Land (and Other Odd Spots)*** by Bernard Lodge
- ***Marsupial Sue*** by John Lithgow

Shared Reading: After enjoying a poem such as "Over in the Meadow" *(ea),* "Old Mother Hubbard" *(oa),* or "If All the World Were Apple Pie" *(ee),* have the children locate words with various vowel combinations.

Guided Reading: Demonstrate quickly for the children how to notice and use vowel combinations they know when they are trying to read a new word. For example, write *read* on a whiteboard and then the new word *beat,* showing how the middle is the same.

Interactive Writing: Use a whiteboard or MagnaDoodle to show children how to use a part of a word they know to write a new word—*boat, soap,* for example.

Independent Writing: When conferring with a child about editing, point out a vowel combination pattern and have the writer use it to correct the spelling of another word.

assess

- Observe the children's use of vowel combination phonograms as they read and write new words.
- Dictate ten words containing vowel combination phonograms.

Expand the Learning

Repeat the lesson using words with initial or ending consonant clusters, silent *e* patterns, or other phonogram patterns.

Have the children play Vowel Combination Lotto. They draw a card, read it, and match it with a game card word that has the same vowel combination and sound *(rain, maid),* covering the space with the card.

Use the Word Card Template (*Teaching Resources,* Templates) to make word cards for the additional phonograms. The Phonograms List in *Teaching Resources* contains an extensive list of phonograms and sample words.

Connect with Home

Send home a deck of Go Fish cards so the children can play the game with family members.

Send home sheets of onset and rime cards (see *Teaching Resources,* Word Card Template) for children to make words with phonogram patterns.

High Frequency Words

A core of known high frequency words is a valuable resource as children build their reading and writing processes. Young children notice words that appear frequently in the simple texts they read; eventually, their recognition of these words becomes automatic. In this way, their reading becomes more efficient, enabling them to decode words using phonics as well as attend to comprehension. These words are powerful examples that help them grasp that a word is always written the same way. They can use known high frequency words to check on the accuracy of their reading and as resources for solving other words (for example, *this* starts like *the*). In general, children learn the simpler and/or most frequently used words earlier and in the process develop efficient systems for learning words. They continuously add to the core of high frequency words they know. Lessons on high frequency words help them look more carefully at words and develop more efficient systems for word recognition.

Connect to Assessment

See related HF Assessment Tasks in the Assessment Guide in *Teaching Resources:*

- Reading High Frequency Words
- Writing High Frequency Words

Develop Your Professional Understanding

See *Word Matters: Teaching Phonics and Spelling in the Reading/Writing Classroom* by G.S. Pinnell and I.C. Fountas. 1998. Portsmouth, New Hampshire: Heinemann.

Related pages: 35–41, 44–46, 71–72, 88–90, 237–238.

Learning High Frequency Words 1

Make-Say-Check-Mix

Consider Your Children

Before using the lessons on high frequency words, determine how many of these words your children know. Have them individually read the list of 100 High Frequency Words (see *Teaching Resources,* Materials & Routines), or give a spelling test with the same words, working with small groups or the whole class. (Space this assessment over several days.) Also notice the substitutions children make, which tells you what they are noticing about letters and sounds as well as word parts. If most of your children know most of the 100 words, go on to the list of 150 High Frequency Words for Grade 2 (see *Teaching Resources*).

Working with English Language Learners

Be sure that English language learners understand the meaning of the words that you are using in these lessons. If possible, translate some words into their languages. Create some simple sentences using the words, and have the children read them together enough times to get a sense of how the word functions and what it means in context. For example: "*Cookie's Week* is a story *about* a cat." "I do not have *any* cookies." Accept approximate pronunciations, and pronounce the words clearly yourself, giving children many opportunities to repeat them both as single words and in sentences.

You Need

- Magnetic letters.
- Pocket chart.
- Whiteboard.

From *Teaching Resources:*

- Pocket Chart Card Template.
- Letter Cards (if you don't use magnetic letters).
- Category Word Cards, 100 High Frequency Word List. Choose fifteen to twenty words appropriate for your children.
- Make-Say-Check-Mix Sheets.

Understand the Principle

Recognizing high frequency words automatically while reading fosters fluency and allows children to concentrate on solving words they don't know and to think about the meaning of the text. The ability to write many high frequency words quickly makes it easier to pay attention to the message they are composing. Children can also connect unfamiliar words to high frequency words that look or sound the same.

Explain the Principle

"You see some words many times when you read."

"Some have three or more letters."

"Words you see a lot are important because they help you read and write."

plan

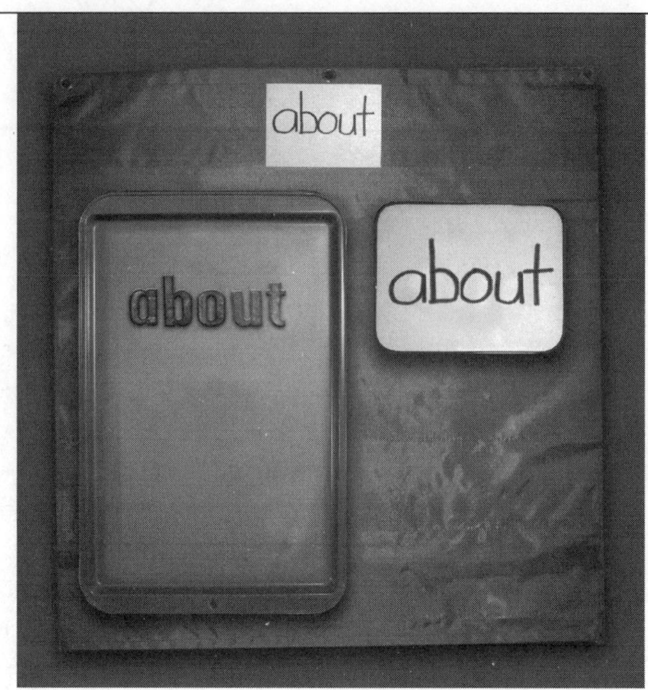

teach

Explain the Principle

“You see some words many times when you read.”

“Some have three or more letters.”

“Words you see a lot are important because they help you read and write.”

① Explain to the children that they are going to learn some important words that will help them read and write.

② Place a high frequency word card (*about,* for example) on the pocket chart, or write the word on a chart or the chalkboard.

③ Make the word with magnetic letters on a cookie sheet or magnetic board or with letter cards in the pocket chart. You may want to mix the letters up and make the word one or two more times, each time showing children how to check it letter by letter with the word on the card.

④ Ask children what they notice about the word. They may offer comments like these: “*About* has two parts.” “*About* has the word *out* in it.” “*About* starts like *around.*”

⑤ Then write the word quickly from beginning to end without stopping. Suggested language: “Once you have made a word and have looked carefully at all parts of it, you can write it quickly. After you write the word, check letter by letter to be sure you have spelled it correctly.”

⑥ Repeat for each high frequency word you have chosen for this lesson. Ask children to assist you on some of the steps.

⑦ Show the children a Make-Say-Check-Mix Sheet. Explain that they should take a word card, say it, make the word with magnetic letters, check it, place a check in the box, and then mix the letters. They make, say, and check it two more times. Each time, they should check letter by letter with the word on the card. Then they write the word quickly in the third column and check it with the card.

apply

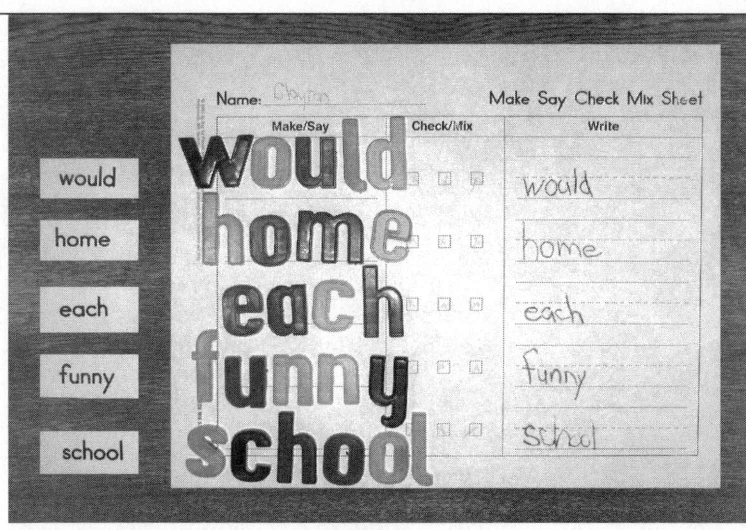

- take
- say
- make
- check
- mix (3x)
- write
- check

▸ Give the children copies of the Make-Say-Check-Mix Sheet and the word cards you have selected for this lesson. (Give more challenging words to the children who already know the easier ones.) They make, say, and check (mix) three times and then write the word in the third column and check it with the word card. Have the children work alone or with a partner. The partner can do the checking, or children can take turns making words and checking.

Have children read their words to a different partner.

You may want to invite two or three children to come to the board to make or write a word quickly.

Link

Interactive Read-Aloud: Read aloud books with large print (see *Teaching Resources,* Large Print Books Bibliography) and call the children's attention to some of the high frequency words. Examples of appropriate titles are:

- ***Big Bear Ball*** by Joanne Ryder
- ***Dim Sum for Everyone*** by Grace Li

Shared Reading: After reading poems together (see *Sing a Song of Poetry*), have the children use masking cards or highlighter tape to locate high frequency words they are studying. Emphasize finding the words quickly and saying them out loud.

Guided Reading: After reading and discussing a text, give the children three or four high frequency words to write quickly. Have them make three or four high frequency words with magnetic letters, mix them up, and make them again.

Interactive Writing: When the children want to write a high frequency word they have studied, have them think about how the word looks and then have one child write it quickly. Write the high frequency words children know well, and ask them to check the words with their eyes.

Independent Writing: Encourage the children to write high frequency words quickly rather than copying them from the word wall. Then they can use the word wall to check their spelling.

assess

- Notice how quickly the children recognize high frequency words while they are reading.
- Observe the extent to which the children can write high frequency words quickly and accurately.
- After the children have practiced making and writing twenty or twenty-five high frequency words, readminister the reading and/or writing test.

Expand the Learning

In each child's writing workshop folder, place a sheet of at least one hundred (or one hundred and fifty) high frequency words they should know by the end of the year (see *Teaching Resources,* Materials & Routines). Have the children highlight words that they know and help them choose the words they want to learn next.

Connect with Home

At a meeting or in a letter, explain to family members that children will be learning some words they will write and read often. Show them how to help children choose words, build them with letter cards, and then write them.

Print high frequency words each child needs to learn in the blank Word Grid Template (see *Teaching Resources*). Have the children take their personal word grids home and practice reading and writing the words and/or making them with magnetic letters or letter cards.

Generative Lesson

Learning High Frequency Words 2

Lotto

Consider Your Children

Work with words that most children in the class do not yet know. Choose words that appear frequently in the texts they read. If your children know only a few high frequency words, repeat Lesson HF 1 several times with many different words before using this lesson and those that follow.

Working with English Language Learners

Select words that English language learners understand. Accept approximate pronunciations, and give them many opportunities to say the words while looking at the spelling. Use words in sentences that the children can understand and repeat.

You Need

- Magnetic letters (or letter cards).
- Pocket chart.
- Whiteboard.

From *Teaching Resources:*

- Pocket Chart Card Template.
- Letter Cards (if you don't use magnetic letters).
- Directions for Lotto.
- Lotto Game Cards.
- Category Word Cards, High Frequency Words. Choose fifteen to twenty words appropriate for your children.

Understand the Principle

A continually growing repertoire of known high frequency words contributes to reading and writing fluency and helps children build systems for learning words quickly. Knowing a large number of high frequency words helps children monitor their reading and check their spelling. In this and other high frequency word lessons, you are teaching children ways to study words.

Explain the Principle

“You see some words many times when you read.”

“Some have three or more letters.”

“Words you see a lot are important because they help you read and write.”

Explain the Principle

"You see some words many times when you read."

"Some have three or more letters."

"Words you see a lot are important because they help you read and write."

① Tell the children that they are going to learn some important words that will help them read and write.

② Place a high frequency word card (*become*, for example) on the pocket chart, or write the word on a chart or the chalkboard.

③ Make the word with magnetic letters on a cookie sheet or magnetic board or with letter cards in the pocket chart. You may want to mix the letters up and make the word one or two more times, each time showing children how to check it letter by letter with the word on the card.

④ Ask the children what they notice about the word. They may offer comments like these: "*Become* starts like *because*." "It has six letters." "You don't hear the *e* at the end."

⑤ Then write the word quickly from beginning to end without stopping. Suggested language: "Now I'm going to write this word quickly because I know it and I don't even have to think about it. [Demonstrate.] When you know a word, you can write it, but if you are not sure, it's a good idea to check it." Demonstrate checking the word letter by letter.

⑥ Repeat for each high frequency word you have selected for this lesson. Ask children to assist you on some of the steps.

⑦ Tell children that they are going to play Lotto with words that they can read and write quickly.

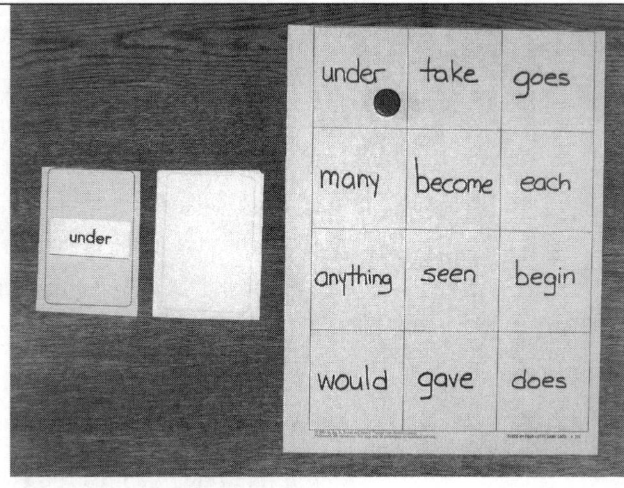

take
say
match

- Have the children play High Frequency Lotto in groups of three or four. Include in the game the high frequency words they have studied. At the end of the game, have each child write five words used in the game without looking at the word cards and then check the words.

Have the children share what they have noticed about the words in the game. Comments like these show the kinds of things they are learning about words:

"*Because, between*, and *become* all have *be* at the beginning."

"*Every* and *any* end with the same letter."

"If you take away the *m* from *must* and make it a *d*, it's *dust*."

Link

Interactive Read-Aloud: Read aloud books that show how high frequency words function in sentences. Take two or three high frequency words the children are studying and write them on a whiteboard. Examples of appropriate titles are:

- ***Fire Fighters*** by Norma Simon
- ***Four in All*** by Nina Payne

Shared Reading: After reading poems together (see *Sing a Song of Poetry*), have the children use masking cards or highlighter tape to locate high frequency words they are studying. Emphasize finding the words quickly and saying them out loud. Give the children a photocopy of the poem to read. Have them highlight the high frequency words.

Guided Reading: When introducing texts in guided reading, have the children turn to a particular page and locate two or three high frequency words.

Interactive Writing: Most of the time you will write the high frequency words yourself rather than have the children do it. Draw attention to new high frequency words they have been studying.

Independent Writing: Remind the children that they know how to write many common words and check their spelling.

assess

- Notice how quickly the children recognize high frequency words when they are reading.
- Observe the extent to which the children can write high frequency words quickly and accurately.

Expand the Learning

Repeat the lesson with other high frequency words.

Help the children learn all the high frequency words on the lists (see *Teaching Resources*, Materials & Routines) in their writing workshop folders.

Connect with Home

Have the children take home individual word grids (see *Teaching Resources*, Directions for Word Grid Game and Word Grid Template) of high frequency words and practice reading and writing the words.

Learning High Frequency Words 3

Follow the Path

Consider Your Children

Your objective is to help children develop ways of learning words quickly and remembering them. Select words that most children in the class do not yet know. If your children know only a few high frequency words, choose simpler words than the examples here. If your children have difficulty recognizing word cards, continue using the building and writing technique in Lesson HF 1.

Working with English Language Learners

Be sure your English language learners understand the meaning of the words you use in the lesson. Use the words in sentences they can understand, and provide many opportunities for them to repeat the sentences as well as the words.

You Need

- Chart paper.
- Markers.

From *Teaching Resources:*

- Pocket Chard Card Template.
- Directions for Follow the Path.
- Category Word Cards, High Frequency Words. Choose fifteen to twenty words appropriate for your children.

Understand the Principle

Readers and writers are always learning more high frequency words. Many are learned incidentally, but paying direct attention to how to look at them and remember them helps children realize the importance of learning words and develop more efficient systems for doing so. Having a large repertoire of high frequency words supports fluent, meaningful reading and writing. The words are important because they can be used to learn other words that have similar parts.

Explain the Principle

“You see some words many times when you read.”

“Some have three or more letters.”

“Words you see a lot are important because they help you read and write.”

plan

anything
game
give
goes
home
know
live
many
paper
party
school
shoes
some
something
teach
under
over

Explain the Principle

"You see some words many times when you read."

"Some have three or more letters."

"Words you see a lot are important because they help you read and write."

① Tell the children that they are going to learn some important words.

② Suggested language: "You know that there are some words that you see many times when you read. Knowing these words will help you read and write."

③ Show the word cards for this lesson one at a time, saying the word and asking the children what they notice about it. They may offer comments like these: "*Know* is like *no,* but it means a different thing and starts with a silent *k.*" "*Live* is like *love* but with an *i.*" "*Many* is *man* with a *y* like *funny.*"

④ Write each word clearly on a piece of chart paper so that every child can see it.

⑤ When you have briefly discussed each word, mix up the pile of word cards. Hold up one word card at a time, and have the children quickly match the word to one you have written on the chart. Emphasize speed.

⑥ After all words have been matched, mix them up again. Go through the word cards quickly, asking children to say them in unison. Or call on one child and quickly show a word card for her to say. If she does not know the word, quickly tell it to her; then show her the same word card again and ask her to say the word.

⑦ Tell the children that they are going to play Follow the Path with high frequency words. They will throw a die, move that number of spaces, and read the word on the space.

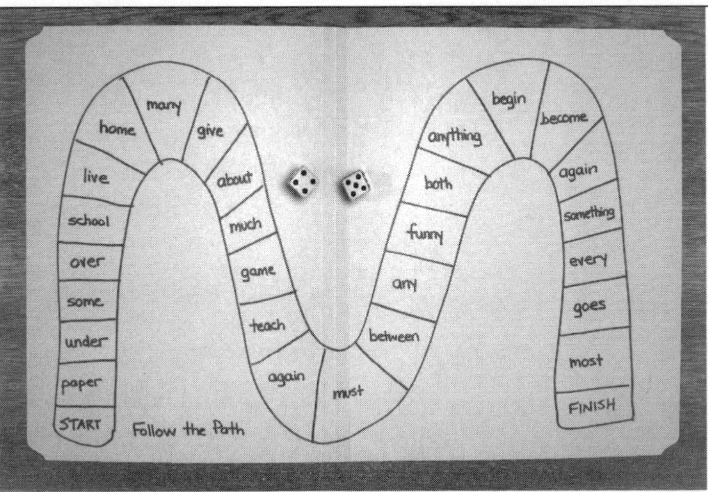

throw
move
read

- Have children play Follow the Path with high frequency words.

Invite several children to share what they noticed with the whole group, or repeat the comments yourself.

Link

Interactive Read-Aloud: Read aloud simple and engaging stories, and point out high frequency words. Examples of appropriate titles are:

- ***The Little French Whistle*** by Carole Schaefer
- ***What Baby Wants*** by Phyllis Root

Shared Reading: Ask children to quickly match high frequency word cards with the words in the text.

Guided Reading: After reading and discussing a text, give the children three or four high frequency words to write quickly.

Interactive Writing: When newly learned high frequency words arise, point out that these are words the children have studied and know how to read and write.

Independent Writing: Encourage the children to write high frequency words quickly rather than copying them from somewhere. Then they can use the word wall or some other reference to check the spelling.

assess

- Notice how quickly the children recognize high frequency words when they are reading.
- Observe the extent to which the children can write high frequency words quickly and accurately.
- Give quick tests of ten to fifteen high frequency words.

Expand the Learning

Repeat the game with a different variety of high frequency words.

Alternatively, make the game with blank spaces and word cards. The children throw a die, take a card, read it, and then move the correct number of spaces.

Help the children learn all the high frequency words on the lists (see *Teaching Resources,* Materials & Routines) in their writing workshop folders.

Connect with Home

Have the children take home their individual word grids (see *Teaching Resources,* Templates) of high frequency words to read quickly to family members.

Learning High Frequency Words 4

Concentration

Consider Your Children

Check your children's progress in learning the one hundred and fifty high frequency words for second grade. Help the children who are having difficulty make the words with magnetic letters (see Lesson HF 1). Use the children's lists of known/still-to-be-learned lists of high frequency words to suggest words to study for a few days or for the week.

Working with English Language Learners

To participate in the Buddy Study System (see Lessons WSA 1 through 5), English language learners will need to use words in comprehensible sentences, and they may need demonstrations and extra practice. If necessary, go over the high frequency words in this lesson. Help the English language learners understand the meaning of the words by using them in sentences. Then ask the children to compose sentences with each of the words. Write sentences on a chart and have them quickly locate words.

You Need

- Pocket Chart.

From *Teaching Resources:*

- Pocket Chart Card Template.
- Directions for Concentration.
- Concentration Game Cards made from High Frequency Word Cards (see Category Word Cards) and Deck Card Template. Choose a variety of words appropriate for your children.

Understand the Principle

Second graders need to begin to take charge of expanding their reading and writing vocabularies. Knowing most or all of the high frequency words they meet in the texts they read will greatly improve their reading accuracy and fluency, allowing them to pay more attention to the text meaning. As children become better at noticing and studying words, lessons and application activities will go more quickly. Children will not just be learning individual words but will develop efficient systems for learning words incidentally.

Explain the Principle

“You see some words many times when you read.”

“Some have three or more letters.”

“Words you see a lot are important because they help you read and write.”

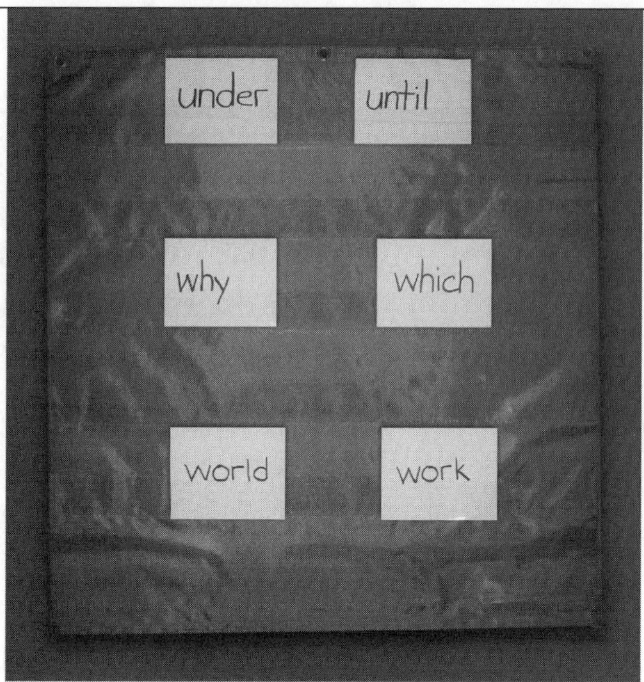

Explain the Principle

"You see some words many times when you read."

"Some have three or more letters."

"Words you see a lot are important because they help you read and write."

① Tell the children that they are going to learn some more high frequency words.

② Suggested language: "We are going to work more today on words that we see often in reading and also that we want to use in writing."

③ Prepare the word cards for this lesson in pairs or groups that have the same beginning letter. Show the children the words in each group and ask them to say them after you. Then ask them what they notice. Demonstrate comments like these: "*Under* and *until* have the same two letters at the beginning—*u-n*." "*Why* and *which* both start with *wh*, which has two letters that represent one sound." "*World* and *work* start with *w*, and the next two letters are *o-r*."

④ Have the children, in circles of four, go over the word cards. One child holds up the word cards one after the other as the others take turns saying the word. Then the next child takes the pile of word cards, and the process is repeated. Going over the cards repeatedly like this should take only a few minutes and will give each child three opportunities to see and say the words.

⑤ Tell the children they are going to play High Frequency Word Concentration. Go over the rules and play a demonstration round if necessary.

⑥ Tell the children that after they play the game, they should choose two words that are alike in some way and write them on a piece of paper to bring to group share.

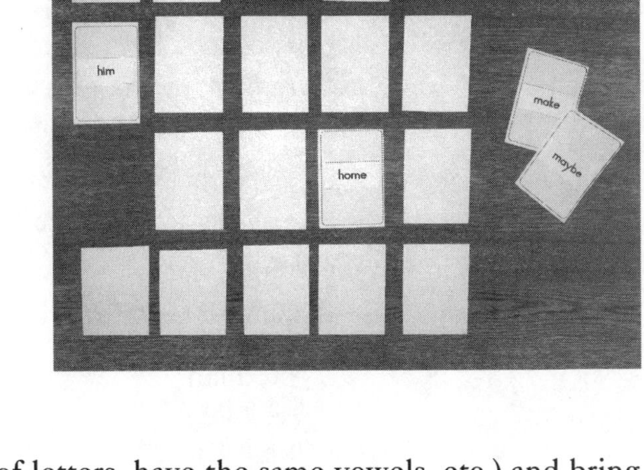

turn
say
turn
say
match

▸ Have the children play High Frequency Word Concentration. Ask each child to choose two words that have similar characteristics (start the same, have the same ending part, have the same number of letters, have the same vowels, etc.) and bring to group share.

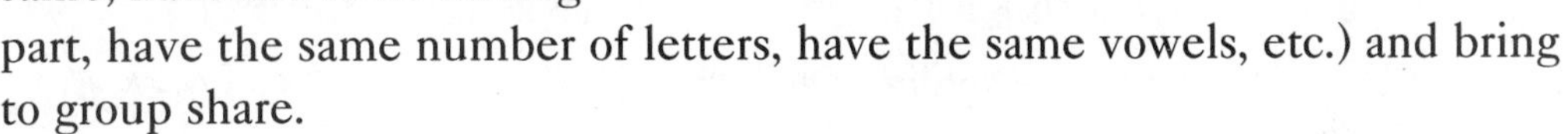

Have the children share the two words they chose and tell how they are alike.

As children provide examples, write the pairs of words on chart paper and underline or circle the parts that are alike. (This shouldn't take too long because many children will have the same pairs.)

Link

Interactive Read-Aloud: Read aloud books that will increase children's listening vocabularies and help them internalize the syntax of written language. Examples of appropriate books are:

- ***George Hogglesberry, Grade School Mouse*** by Sarah Wilson
- ***I Love You the Purplest*** by Barbara Joose

Shared Reading: After reading a poem or informational chart together, make a game of locating high frequency words: "I'm thinking of a word that begins with *be* and ends with a silent *e*."

Guided Reading: Following the lesson, invite the children to give the clues to each other. Have the children read high frequency words as you write them quickly on the whiteboard.

Interactive Writing: When newly learned high frequency words arise, point out that these are words the children have studied and know how to read and write.

Independent Writing: Encourage the children to write high frequency words quickly without looking at references. Have them use their word lists to check their spelling.

Expand the Learning

Have the children play the game with other pairs of high frequency words.

Help the children learn all the high frequency words on the lists (see *Teaching Resources,* Materials & Routines) in their writing workshop folders.

Combine all the high frequency words children have studied and work with small groups to teach them how to sort them several ways (see *Teaching Resources,* Materials & Routines Overview).

Connect with Home

Send home a deck of Concentration cards so the children can play the game with family members.

assess

- Notice how quickly the children recognize high frequency words when they are reading.
- Observe the extent to which the children can write high frequency words quickly and accurately.
- Give regular tests to see which words the children have learned. Have them highlight the words they know on the word lists in their folders.

Learning High Frequency Words 5

Word Sort

Consider Your Children

Use this lesson after your children know enough high frequency words to be able to sort them. They should be able to recognize these words quickly and make connections between them. You'll be using an open sort, so be sure they have had some previous experience in easy closed sorts (see *Teaching Resources,* Materials & Routines Overview).

Working with English Language Learners

Go over the words with your English language learners and show them how to sort them. Have them read words in the categories they are sorting. Reading these words repeatedly will help them form the categories.

You Need

- Pocket chart.

From *Teaching Resources:*

- Pocket Chart Card Template.
- Three-Way Sort Sheet.
- Category Word Cards, High Frequency Words. Choose a variety of words appropriate for your children.

Understand the Principle

Making connections among words helps children internalize the characteristics of language in a much more meaningful way than learning words in isolation. Even high frequency words are easier if children apply the principles and patterns for solving words that they are learning in other lessons.

Explain the Principle

“You see some words many times when you read.”

“Some have three or more letters.”

“Words you see a lot are important because they help you read and write.”

plan

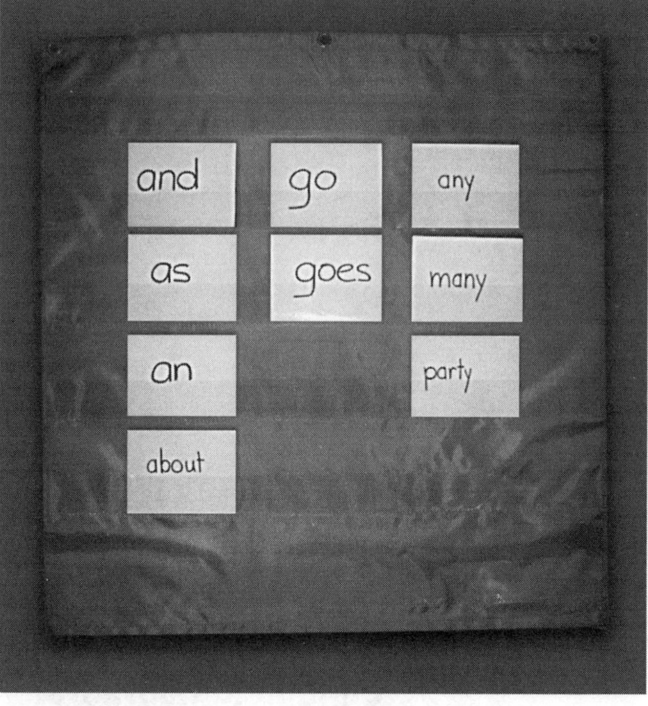

teach

Explain the Principle

"You see some words many times when you read."

"Some have three or more letters."

"Words you see a lot are important because they help you read and write."

① Let the children know that they are going to learn more about high frequency words.

② Suggested language: "You know a lot of words and you also know how to sort words. Today we are going to sort some of the words you know. What are the different ways you can sort words?"

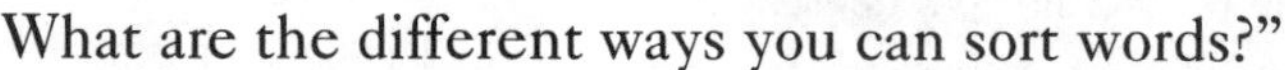

③ Children will respond by suggesting first letter, last letter, first or last sound, middle letter, number of letters, number of vowels or consonants. If your children haven't done a lot of sorting, you may need to show them several ways of sorting and ask them what is alike about the words in each category.

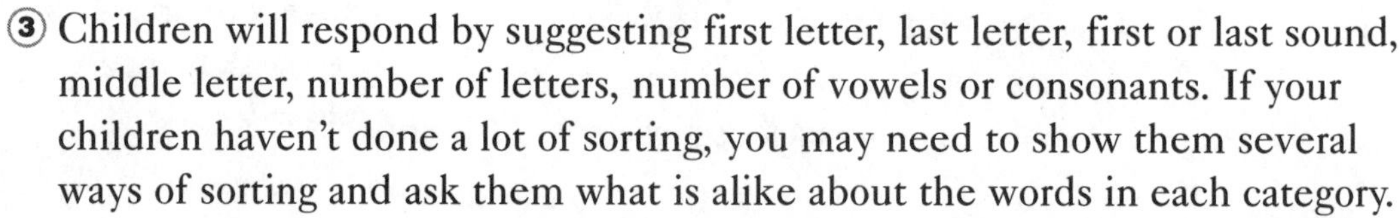

④ Demonstrate sorting the word cards for this lesson by specifying a category (beginning sound, number of letters, ending letter, double letters) and then searching for words that fit. You can sort the words on the floor or in the pocket chart, but be sure that all children can see. After the words have been sorted, take each category and ask the children to talk about what they notice. Model comments like this: "All these words start with *a*." "*Any* sounds like the *a* in *an* and *as*." "These words sound like the *a* in *about.*" "These words start with *g* like the *g* in *go*." "These words end with *y* like the *y* in *Andy*."

⑤ Show the children how to choose one category of words and list the words in that category.

⑥ Then, ask them to write down what they noticed about the words and bring the list to group share.

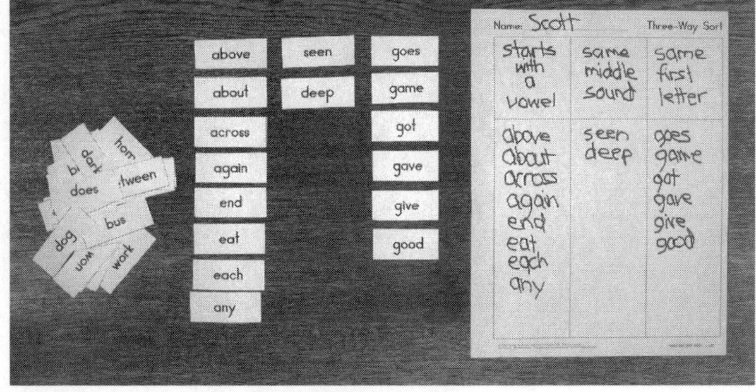

choose category
write category
find words
write words
read

▸ Have the children choose three sorting categories and write them at the top of a Three-Way Sort Sheet. Ask them to find the words that fit each category and list them on the sheet. Then have them read their lists to a partner.

Have the children share and discuss their lists of words with a different partner.

Talk about any new ways the children have found to sort the words.

Link

Interactive Read-Aloud: Read aloud stories that feature many high frequency words. Examples are:

- ***Dandelion*** by Don Freeman
- ***How Do Dinosaurs Get Well Soon?*** by Jane Yolen

Shared Reading: After reading a poem or informational chart together, make a game of locating words: "I'm thinking of a word that begins with *a* and ends with two consonants." Continue with several examples and then have the children turn to a partner and play the game with each other.

Guided Reading: After reading a text, have the children sort high frequency word cards by some connecting feature. (Children who have difficulty sorting will benefit from performing this quick exercise for a few minutes every day.)

Interactive Writing: When the children have written a new high frequency word, ask them to quickly find words that start like the word, end like the word, or have some other feature in common.

Independent Writing: Encourage the children to use known words as resources in writing new words.

assess

- Notice the children's flexibility in sorting and connecting high frequency words.
- Observe the extent to which the children make successful attempts at spelling new high frequency words.
- Go over a series of high frequency word cards with each child.

Expand the Learning

Use the "making connections" part of Buddy Study to help the children become more flexible in connecting words.

Combine all the high frequency words children have studied and teach small groups how to sort them several ways (see *Teaching Resources,* Materials & Routines Overview).

Use the "Words Around the Room Sheet" (see *Teaching Resources*) to create categories of high frequency words they can look for—for example, words that start with *th,* words with four letters, words with long vowel sounds, words with two vowels together, etc.

Connect with Home

Send home a Word Grid and a stack of high frequency word cards so the children can play the Word Grid game with family members (see *Teaching Resources*).

Learning High Frequency Words 6

Word Search

Consider Your Children

After your children know a large number of high frequency words, they will enjoy doing word searches and creating them for their friends to solve. The words are embedded (horizontally, vertically, or diagonally) in a rectangular grid of letters with no spaces between any of the letters. At first, use words your children know well. Be sure your children can locate words as a series of letters before expecting them to do word searches.

Working with English Language Learners

Be sure your English language learners know the words you select. You may need to demonstrate solving and making word searches several times in a small group before they grasp the procedure.

You Need

- An enlarged example of a word search grid containing the words *so, moon, am, made, knew, see, does, name, every, end,* and *yes.*

From *Teaching Resources:*

- Directions for Word Searches.
- Word Search Template.
- High Frequency Word List. (Choose a variety of words appropriate for your children.)

Understand the Principle

Being able to recognize common words rapidly and automatically helps children read fluently and accurately and allows them to focus on meaning. Being able to scan seemingly random print and spot words embedded in it sharpens their awareness of words.

Explain the Principle

“ You see some words many times when you read. ”

“ Words you see a lot are important because they help you read and write. ”

plan

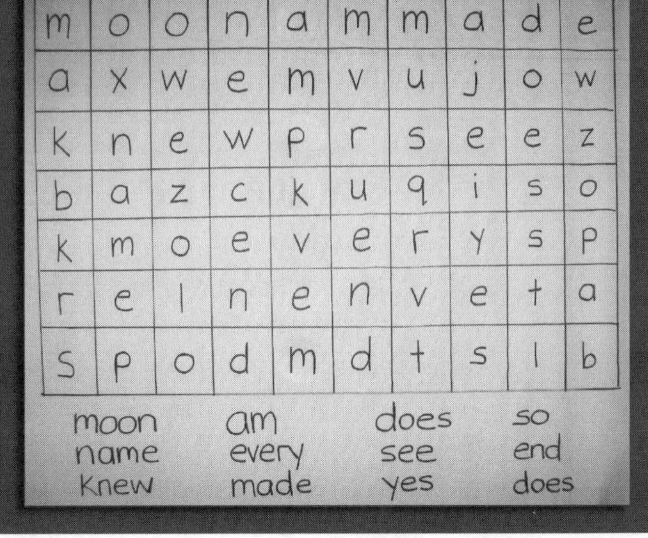

Explain the Principle

“You see some words many times when you read.”

“Words you see a lot are important because they help you read and write.”

① Tell the children that they are going to learn more about reading and writing high frequency words.

② Select a variety of high frequency words most of the children need to learn to read and write. Show each word with magnetic letters, mix them, and invite a child to make the word. Repeat the process several times.

③ Suggested language: “You know how to find words on charts and in the books you read. Today you are going to do a word search, which is a little like a mystery. I've made one for you, and I'll show you how to search for and find words on it.”

④ Show children your enlarged version of the word search. Suggested language: “I'm looking for a word I know. I see *moon*. I'm going to circle *moon* and write it in one of the spaces in the table below.” Demonstrate.

⑤ “I see another word I know. I see *knew*.” Circle *knew* and point out that the word is written from top to bottom. If necessary, write *knew* quickly on the whiteboard both top to bottom and left to right so that the children see the word clearly. Write the word *knew* in the table below the grid.

⑥ Have the children help you search for the remaining words. At first, you may need to tell them the word you want them to look for. Have children come up to the chart to circle words and write them in the table.

⑦ Suggested language: “Now I'm going to show you how to make a word search for your friends.” Display an enlarged blank word search grid.

⑧ Ask the children to suggest high frequency words for the word search, list them on the bottom of the form, and then place the letters that form the words in consecutive spaces on the grid. Make some words across and some words down. When the grid contains ten or so randomly written words, stop.

⑨ Have children read the words. Suggested language: "Those words are easy to find, aren't they? Now we'll put in some other letters to make them harder to find. We'll put in any letters we want." Have the children suggest alphabet letters, and fill in all of the empty spaces. Quickly demonstrate finding and searching for the words.

⑩ Give the children a blank Word Search Template; tell them to make a word search and then ask another student to solve the search.

list words
write words
fill in letters

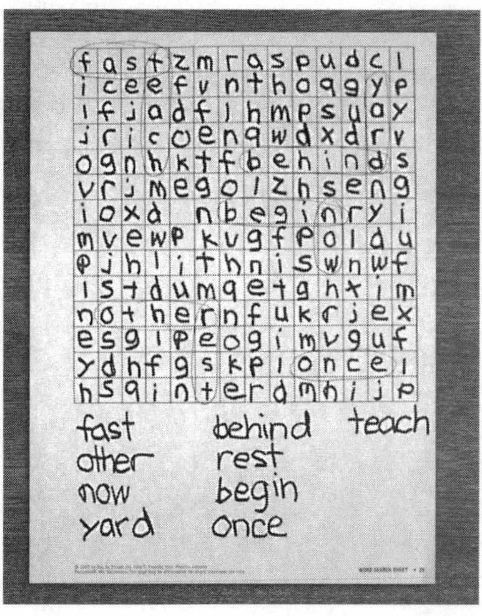

- Have the children make word searches, using their high frequency word lists as resources. (You may want a few extra simple word searches ready in case some children did not finish or found the task too difficult.) Have the children, in pairs, trade word searches and solve them by circling words and writing them below. Then the partners trade back, check the searches, and tell each other any words missed.

Invite children to talk about what they noticed about the words in the word searches they completed.

Link

Interactive Read-Aloud: Read aloud stories such as

- ***The Old Woman Who Named Things*** by Cynthia Rylant
- ***Where Did Bunny Go?*** by Nancy Tafuri

Shared Reading: Before reading a new poem together (see *Sing a Song of Poetry*), have the children quickly locate both known and new words after first saying them and predicting the first letter or other letters.

Guided Reading: After reading a text, have the children quickly write a few high frequency words. Choose words they need to learn to write rapidly and automatically.

Interactive Writing: Give children small whiteboards or stenographers' notebooks, and have them practice quickly writing high frequency words that you are writing on the chart.

Independent Writing: While conferring about a piece of writing, have the children point out words that they have recently learned and can now write without looking at a model.

Expand the Learning

Have children make several more word searches. Encourage them to use longer words.

After they can easily solve horizontal and vertical word searches, increase the difficulty by showing them how to include words written diagonally.

Connect with Home

Send home a newsletter or memo telling family members how to make word searches. Give children a list of words they are studying and blank Word Search Templates to take home and make more word searches with family members.

assess

- Notice the children's ability to find words in word searches.
- Give a quick spelling test to small groups and notice not only the children's accuracy but the speed at which they write words.

Learning High Frequency Words 7

Word Ladders

Consider Your Children

Use this lesson when your children have worked with high frequency words in a number of ways and know a hundred or more of them. Previous experience in sorting words will help children become very flexible as they work with words. Creating word ladders is a way to exercise that power in an interesting way. If children have difficulty with the task, show them shorter ladders, perhaps only four or five words, and limit the choice of words until they catch on.

Working with English Language Learners

Be sure that English language learners know the words you are using and can use them in sentences with your support. You may want to work with them in a small group to demonstrate making word ladders. Make the word ladders as simple as necessary to help the children learn the technique. If they need more support, place a variety of word cards, including some very simple high frequency words that they know, on the table. Make the task even easier by having each child work with prepared word cards that make a simple ladder.

You Need

- Pocket chart.
- Markers.

From *Teaching Resources:*

- Pocket Chart Card Template.
- Category Word Cards, High Frequency Words. Choose a variety of words appropriate for your children.
- Word Ladder Sheets.

Understand the Principle

Children need to constantly expand their vocabularies and become flexible in working with the body of words they know. The more they notice word parts, connect words, and sort them into categories, the easier it will be for them to learn more words and to recognize words rapidly and automatically while reading.

Explain the Principle

“You see some words many times when you read.”

“Words you see a lot are important because they help you read and write.”

plan

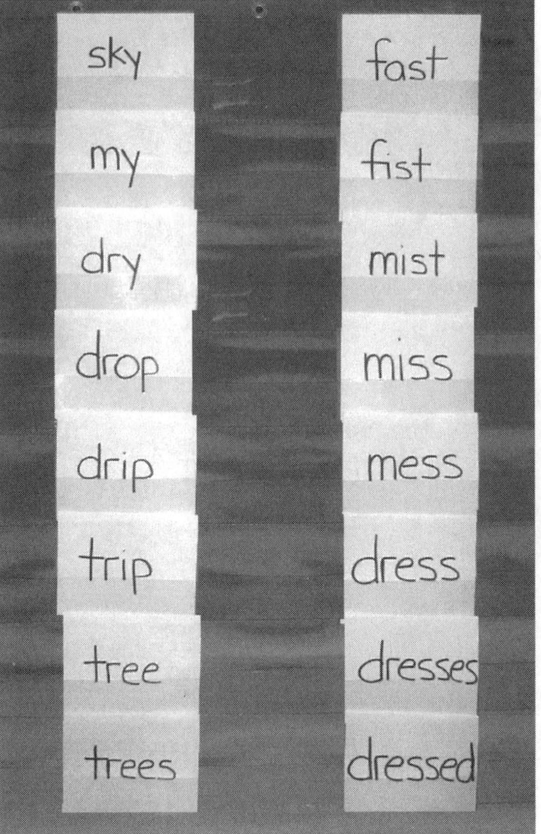

Explain the Principle

"You see some words many times when you read."

"Words you see a lot are important because they help you read and write."

① Tell the children that they will be working again with high frequency words.

② Suggested language: "You know many words that we see a lot while reading and often use when we are writing. Today you are going to make word ladders to help you think about the letters in some of these words."

③ Place a selection of word cards for this lesson on the right side of a pocket chart (or write them on the right side of a chart). Demonstrate forming the first word ladder by talking out loud while you search for and place words in descending order in a column on the left.

④ Suggested language: "I'm going to start with the word *sky*. For my next word, I want to make a new word by changing (or adding or taking away) one or two letters. So I'll pick *my*. [Place *my* under *sky*.] Now I'm going to look for another word that changes, adds, or takes away just one or two letters. I'll put *dry* under *my*. I changed two letters."

⑤ Demonstrate thinking aloud about what letters are different in each successive word. Make it clear that sometimes you have to back up and change your mind about the next word you use. If you think the task will be hard for your children, use only four or five words in your ladder.

⑥ After demonstrating making the first word ladder, show the children how to write the word ladder on the Word Ladder Template and then read the words.

⑦ Then have the children help you make another word ladder. (It may vary slightly from the one in the illustration because several variations are possible. Write the words from the second word ladder on the Word Ladder Template.

8 If the children suggest words that are not on the word cards you have provided, use them if they fit. The word cards make it easier for children to think of options, but eventually they will be able to make their own word ladders without cards.

9 Tell the children that they will be making word ladders and then writing them on a Word Ladder Template.

write
change
write
read

- Have the children make word ladders using high frequency words. You can ask them to use a specific number of steps or simply ask them to make ladders as long as they can. Ask them to write four of these ladders on the Word Ladder Template or on a separate sheet of paper if the ladders are long.

Have the children share and compare their word ladders with a partner.

Have several children read their word ladders while you write them. Ask the rest of the class to check whether only one or two letters have changed.

Link

Interactive Read-Aloud: Read aloud stories that emphasize connections among words (for example, words that start alike or end alike). Examples are:

- ***Jack's Garden*** by Henry Cole
- ***A-Tisket A-Tasket*** by Ella Fitzgerald

Shared Reading: After reading a poem or informational chart together, make a game of locating specific words: "I'm thinking of a word that begins like *fast* and ends like *star*."

Guided Reading: After the lesson, make two or three ladders with magnetic letters. Children who have difficulty making connections between words can make word ladders together on paper.

Interactive Writing: Help the children spell new words by taking familiar words and changing letters. Model thinking of a word you know that starts the same and another that ends the same or is the same in the middle.

Independent Writing: Encourage the children to think of the high frequency words they know as resources when they are trying to write new words.

Expand the Learning

Have the children make more of their own word ladders using their lists of known words as well as the word wall and charts in the room.

Increase the level of difficulty by allowing only a single letter change.

Connect with Home

Send home a blank Word Ladder Template and have the children make five word ladders with family members and bring at least one to school to share.

assess

- Notice whether the children can make connections between words in order to solve them as they read.
- Notice whether the children are using known words to help them spell new words.
- Give a spelling test that includes some words children have not studied. Notice their attempts: are they using word parts to help them?

Learning High Frequency Words 8

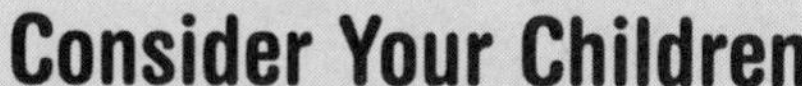

Go Fish

Consider Your Children

You needn't necessarily use the words in the illustration for this lesson. Refer to 150 High Frequency Words (see *Teaching Resources,* Materials & Routines) and select words that your children don't yet know (or words they "almost" know).

Working with English Language Learners

Be sure that most of the words you have your English language learners use for Go Fish are very familiar to them. Play the game with them and discard words that are too difficult, substituting others that they understand. You may need to use words they *know* in sentences to help them understand.

You Need

- Magnetic letters.

From *Teaching Resources:*

- Category Word Cards, High Frequency Words. Choose a variety of words appropriate for your children.
- Directions for Go Fish.
- Go Fish Game Cards made from High Frequency Word Cards and Deck Card Template.

Understand the Principle

Children need to develop growing control of words that appear frequently in the language. If children can learn to recognize or write them, they can attend to solving other words.

Explain the Principle

“You see some words many times when you read.”

“Some have three or four letters.”

“Some have five or more letters.”

“Words you see a lot are important because they help you read and write.”

plan

Explain the Principle

"You see some words many times when you read."

"Some have three or four letters."

"Some have five or more letters."

"Words you see a lot are important because they help you read and write."

① Explain to the children that they are going to learn more high frequency words.

② Make the words *come, there, which, where, would,* and *could* one at a time with magnetic letters. Make the word, mix the letters, and make it again. Talk aloud about what you are noticing, such as the silent *e* in *come* or *there,* the *wh* at the beginning of *which* and *where,* and the *ould* that sounds like *ood* as in *wood.*

③ Use each word in a sentence when you make it.

④ Remind the children they will need to study and remember the sequence of letters.

⑤ Explain that today they are going to make and mix each of these six words with magnetic letters three times to practice the letter sequence.

⑥ Then they will play Go Fish in groups of three or four.

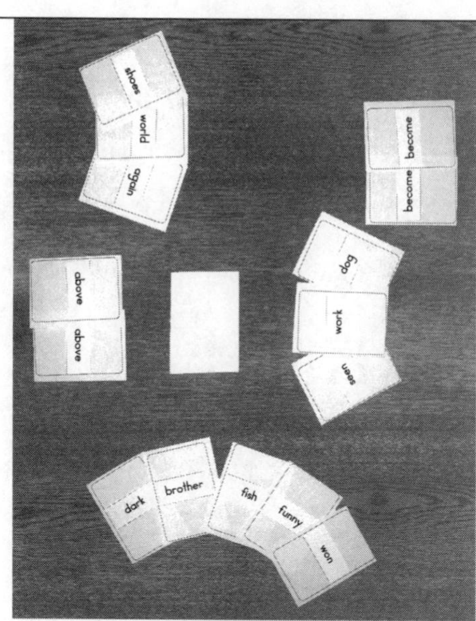

make
mix 3x

ask
match or take

- Using magnetic letters, have children make and mix each of the words used in the lesson three times.
- Then have the children play Go Fish with pairs of high frequency words. Each player takes a turn asking for a word. For example, "Do you have *could*?" A player who is holding the word *could* in her hand gives the card to the first player, who makes a pair on the table. If no one has *could*, the players say Go Fish, and the first player takes a card. The first player to get rid of all her cards wins the game. They can play the game more than once as time allows.

Invite a few children to come to the magnetic board one at a time to make a few selected high frequency words.

Ask them to discuss the part or parts of the words they want to remember. This action will build a habit of noticing and remembering tricky parts of high frequency words.

Link

Interactive Read-Aloud: Read aloud a few large print books that are appropriate for the age group so the children can see the high frequency words. (See *Teaching Resources*, Large Print Books Bibliography.) Appropriate titles are:

- ***Sally Goes to the Beach*** by Stephen Huneck
- ***Splash*** by Ann Jonas

Shared Reading: Use the overhead projector to display poems, or give children photocopies (see *Sing a Song of Poetry*). After enjoying the poem together, have the children highlight or underline particular high frequency words.

Guided Reading: During word work, use the whiteboard to write a few high frequency words for children to recognize quickly. Link the words to help them notice similar parts: *the, there, them, they; who, which, when, where; come, some.*

Interactive Writing: Encourage the children to write high frequency words quickly, without stopping. This will help them develop automatic recognition and flexibility.

Independent Writing: Hold writers accountable for correctly spelling the high frequency words they know. As they edit, have them check their spelling of high frequency words. Use the list of One Hundred and Fifty High Frequency Words as an individual ongoing record for each child. Highlight the words each child has learned how to spell.

assess

- As you look at the children's writing, list high frequency words they need to learn how to spell and notice those they can spell correctly.
- As the children read, observe the high frequency words they can read quickly. Use your observations to select words for future lessons.

Expand the Learning

Repeat the lesson with other high frequency words.

Connect with Home

Send home a card deck made with high frequency word cards so the children can play Go Fish with family members.

Learning High Frequency Words 9

Word Search

Consider Your Children

Give a high frequency pretest over several days (see the One Hundred and Fifty High Frequency Words in *Teaching Resources*); select words for this lesson that most children need to learn. Work with an easier selection of words before choosing more difficult ones.

Working with English Language Learners

It helps English language learners to overlearn some high frequency words, meaning that they know and automatically recognize them. This core contains words that they understand and can recognize and write very easily. The known words also become important anchors to help them monitor their reading accuracy. Fast, automatic word recognition increases fluency in reading and writing and frees attention for thinking about meaning.

You Need

- Magnetic letters.

From *Teaching Resources:*

- Word Search made using the Word Search Template and High Frequency Word Lists as a reference.
- Directions for Word Searches.

Understand the Principle

Knowing high frequency words is an important factor in reading fluency; for example, *150 high frequency words account for approximately 50 percent of the words in print.* Children need many lessons focused on teaching and reinforcing high frequency words, so that they build their reading and writing vocabularies. Many high frequency words have word parts that are similar to other words children are trying to learn.

Explain the Principle

“You see some words many times when you read.”

“Some have three or four letters.”

“Some have five or more letters.”

“Words you see a lot are important because they help you read and write.”

plan

Explain the Principle

“You see some words many times when you read.”

“Some have three or four letters.”

“Some have five or more letters.”

“Words you see a lot are important because they help you read and write.”

1. Tell the children that you are going to work together to learn more high frequency words.
2. Select words that many children are finding challenging.
3. Select a word such as *there.* Make it with magnetic letters, talking aloud about its features or what you want to remember about the letter sequence. Use the word in a sentence. Mix the letters and make it again. You may want to invite a child to the board to make the word quickly.
4. Continue with six or seven more words.
5. Tell the children that they are going to search for high frequency words.
6. Show an example of a word search in which words, written horizontally, vertically, or diagonally, are hidden in a rectangular array of letters. As the children find each word, they circle it and check it on the list. Then they make each word three times, mixing up the letters every time to learn its letter sequence.

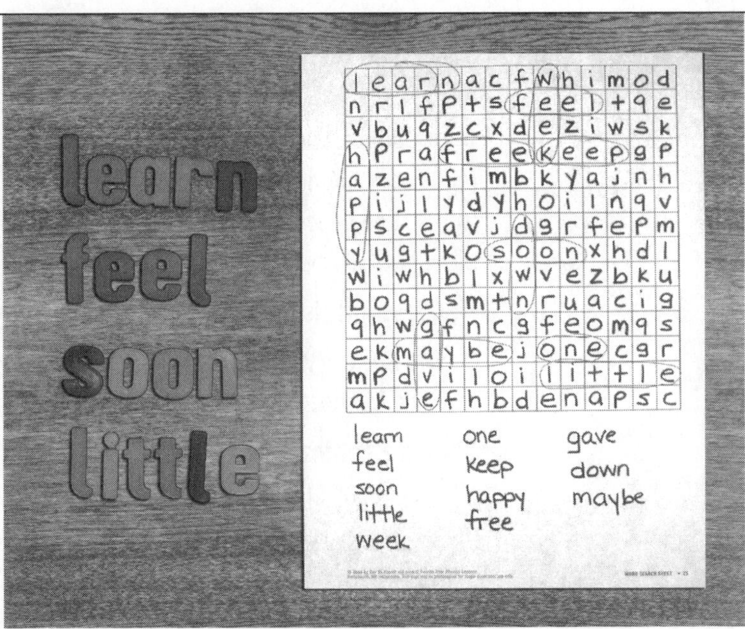

read
find
circle
check
make and mix (3x)

▸ Have the children solve a word search in which eleven or twelve high frequency words (listed underneath the grid) are hidden. Ask them to read the word on the list, find it in the grid, circle it, and check it. Then ask them to make each word three times with magnetic letters.

Invite the children to come to the board to make each word quickly with magnetic letters.

Have the children share what they want to remember about each word.

Link

Interactive Read-Aloud: Read aloud large print books that feature many high frequency words. (See *Teaching Resources*, Large Print Bibliography.) Appropriate titles are:

- ***Circus*** by Lois Ehlert
- ***The Book of Mean People*** by Toni and Slade Morrison

Shared Reading: Place a poem (see *Sing a Song of Poetry*) that includes many high frequency words on a chart (or project it on a transparency). Have the children highlight or underline particular high frequency words.

Guided Reading: During word work, write high frequency words on a whiteboard and encourage quick recognition.

Interactive Writing: Invite the children to write the high frequency words quickly in texts you are constructing together. Point out parts of words that are tricky.

Independent Writing: Hold the children accountable for correct spelling of the high frequency words they have learned.

assess

- Have the children keep a list of high frequency words in their writing folders. Have them check or highlight words they have learned to write.
- Observe the children's speed on recognizing high frequency words as they read.

Expand the Learning

Repeat the lesson with other high frequency words.

Once the children have solved several word searches, teach them how to make one for their classmates to solve (see Lesson HF 6).

Connect with Home

Send home a high frequency word search for children to complete with family members.

Word Meaning

Children need to know the meaning of the words they are learning to read and write. It is important for them to expand their vocabularies constantly as well as develop a more complex understanding of words they already know. Word meaning is related to the development of vocabulary—labels, synonyms, antonyms, and homonyms. A great deal of vocabulary expansion will be accomplished as you read aloud to children and as they read for themselves. Discussing the meaning of words they encounter in texts will be very helpful to them. In our complex language, meaning and spelling are intricately connected.

Often you must know the meaning of the word you want to spell or read before you can spell it accurately. In addition to lists of common concept words that children are often expected to know how to read and spell, we include synonyms, antonyms, and homonyms, which may be homographs (same spelling, different meaning, and sometimes different pronunciation) or homophones (same sound but different spelling). Knowing synonyms and antonyms will help children build more powerful systems for connecting and categorizing words; it will also help them comprehend texts better and write in a more interesting way. Being able to distinguish between homographs and homophones assists in comprehension and helps spellers to avoid mistakes.

Connect to Assessment

See related WM Assessment Tasks in the Assessment Guide in *Teaching Resources:*

- Reading Concept Words
- Understanding Concept Words
- Using Concept Words
- Understanding Synonyms
- Understanding Antonyms
- Understanding Homophones

Develop Your Professional Understanding

See *Word Matters: Teaching Phonics and Spelling in the Reading/Writing Classroom* by G.S. Pinnell and I.C. Fountas. 1998. Portsmouth, New Hampshire: Heinemann.

Related pages: 78–81, 88–89, 199–205.

1 Recognizing and Using Synonyms

Concentration

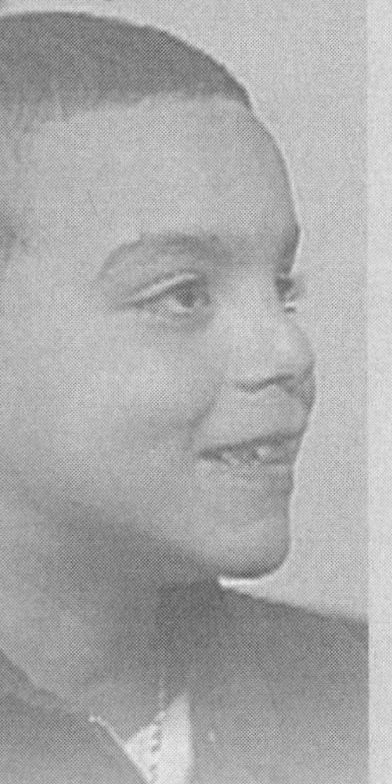

Consider Your Children

Use this lesson after your children have encountered synonyms in reading and writing and have discussed them informally. For example, you may have read aloud a selection and explained a word by using a word that means the same (is a synonym). Or you may have asked children to choose between two synonyms as they composed pieces in interactive writing. As always, the children need to be working with words they understand and can read.

Working with English Language Learners

Grasping the idea of synonyms helps English language learners expand their knowledge of English: when they truly understand one word, it is easier to learn others that mean about the same. At the same time, using words interchangeably increases the complexity of the language for beginners. Explicitly connecting synonyms helps them realize how the language is organized. Repeat the concept as often as necessary, and work with a small group of children if needed to help them match word cards and repeat the words in sentences.

You Need

- Chart paper.
- Markers.

From *Teaching Resources:*

- Concentration Game Cards made from Lesson WM 1 Word Cards and Deck Card Template.
- Directions for Concentration.

Understand the Principle

Increasing children's awareness of synonyms expands their speaking and reading vocabularies and prompts them to search for and notice words that mean about the same. When they increase the variety of words they use, their writing also becomes more interesting.

Explain the Principle

“Some words mean about the same and are called synonyms.”

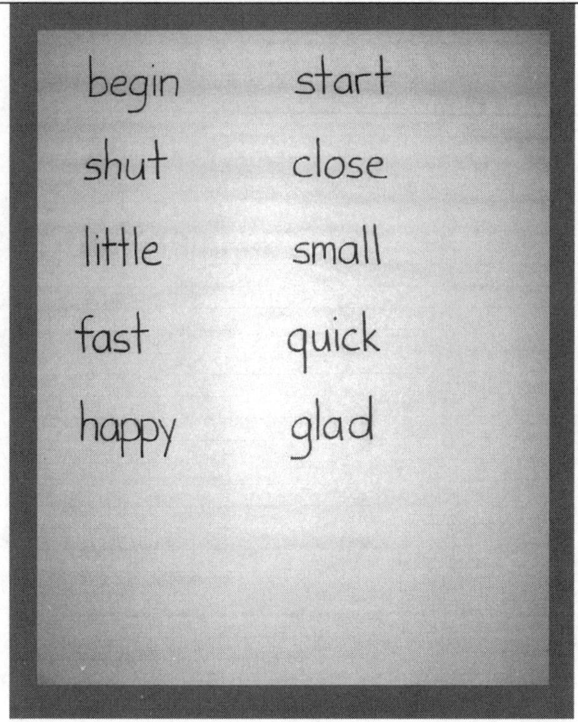

Explain the Principle

"Some words mean about the same and are called synonyms."

① Explain to the children that they are going to be learning about words that mean the same or almost the same thing. If the children have previously learned about antonyms, remind them that they already know some pairs of words that mean the opposite, such as *yes* and *no* or *day* and *night.*

② Present five pairs of synonyms selected from the word cards provided for this lesson. Be sure the children can read the words. Use easy examples.

③ Suggested language: "This word is *begin*. Now, what is this word [*start*]? [Children respond.] What do you notice about these words?" Children may say that they mean the same thing. If they focus on letters, recognize their thinking but guide them to talk about the meaning.

④ Suggested language: "Words that mean about the same thing are called *synonyms*. Say *synonym*." Have children clap and say the word *synonym* several times. Accept approximate pronunciations. (It will take many repetitions before students know and remember this technical word. It is more important for them to internalize the concept than to memorize the label. Once they do know the label it will be helpful in expanding their repertoire of synonyms.)

⑤ Present and discuss the other pairs of words, writing them on the chart or matching them in the pocket chart. Use some of the words in sentences, asking children whether they mean about the same thing.

⑥ Tell the children they will be playing Concentration with synonyms.

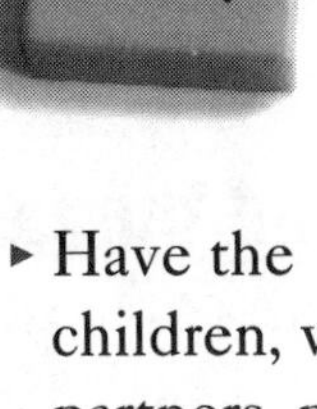

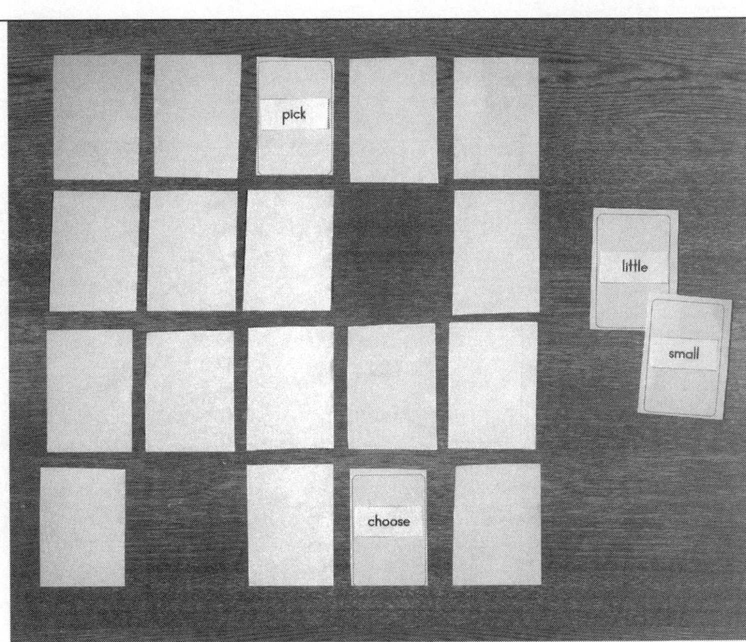

turn
turn
match

▸ Have the children, with partners, play Synonym Concentration. Unless your children are very proficient readers and already know some synonyms, limit the game to the words you have presented in the lesson when they first begin to play. Then lay all the cards face down on the table. In turn, they flip one card over, read it, and then turn over another and see whether it means about the same thing (is a synonym). The player with the most pairs wins. After the game, have each child write two pairs of synonyms on a piece of paper.

Have the children discuss their pairs of synonyms.

Add some of these synonyms to the class chart.

Link

Interactive Read-Aloud: Read aloud books that will increase the children's knowledge of synonyms. Examples are:

- ***A Huge Hog Is a Big Pig*** by Francis McCall and Patricia Keeler
- ***Amos and Boris*** by William Steig

Shared Reading: Have the children tape a synonym over one or two words in a poem or other text and then read the text with the new words. In "Two Little Feet" *small* is a synonym for all nine *little*s. However, "Cradle Song" is a bit more challenging in that *small* is not a synonym for all ten uses of *little.* (See *Sing a Song of Poetry* for other examples.)

Guided Reading: Using sentences in a story, have children generate synonyms for selected words. Reread the sentence with the suggested synonym and have children confirm it makes sense and is a synonym.

Interactive Writing: When the children are composing a text, encourage them to give synonyms for words that would make the text more interesting. Add to the list of synonyms on the board or chart so that children can use them in their own writing.

Independent Writing: As you confer with children, help them see places where they can cross out a word and put in a more interesting synonym.

assess

- Observe the children as they play Concentration and identify those who need more work in a small group.
- After the children are familiar with a number of synonyms, have them make a "synonym book" with words that mean about the same on left and right pages. They can write the words and illustrate them. Have them read the book to you, identifying the synonyms.

Expand the Learning

Repeat the lesson with additional synonyms.

Set up a synonym board and invite the children to put pairs of similar words on it, along with illustrations.

Connect with Home

Send home pairs of synonym word cards for children to match at home or to play Synonym Concentration with family members.

2 Recognizing and Using Antonyms

Concentration

Consider Your Children

Use this lesson after your children have encountered antonyms in reading and writing and have discussed them informally. For example, you may have read aloud a selection and explained a word by saying it means the opposite of another word (the two words are antonyms). Or the children may have used contrasting words such as *wet* and *dry* in interactive writing. As always, the children need to be working with words they understand and can read.

Working with English Language Learners

Learning words that have opposite meanings helps English language learners describe and understand contrasts. Start with very simple words that they understand, such as *yes* and *no*. Work with the children in a small group and create sentences that will help them better understand what the words mean. Use concrete objects or pictures if needed.

You Need

- Chart paper.
- Markers.

From *Teaching Resources:*

- Directions for Concentration.
- Concentration Game Cards made from Lesson WM 2 Word Cards and Deck Card Template.

Understand the Principle

Increasing children's awareness of antonyms helps them understand the meaning of words in sentences and expands their vocabularies. Once they understand the concept of antonyms, they can begin to add to that category of words. They will gradually expand their knowledge of opposite terms.

Explain the Principle

"Some words mean about the opposite and are called antonyms."

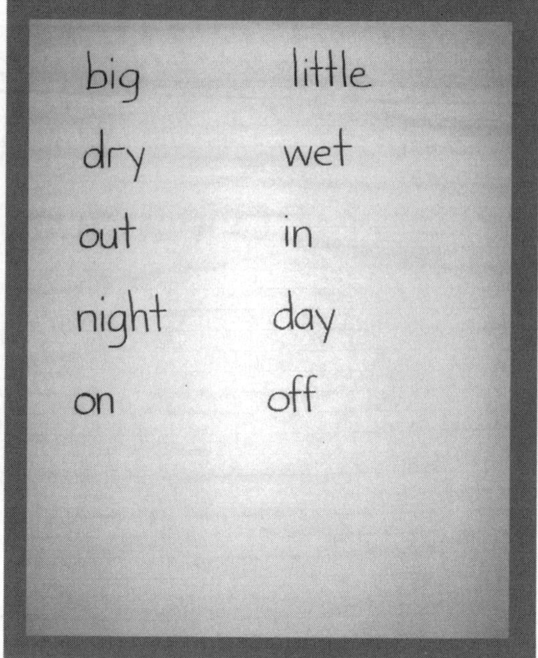

big
little
dry
wet
out
in
night
day
on
off

Explain the Principle

“Some words mean about the opposite and are called antonyms.”

① Let the children know that they are going to learn more about words that mean the opposite. If children have previously learned about synonyms, remind them that they already know some words that mean about the same thing, such as *happy, glad* or *little, small.*

② Present five pairs of antonyms selected from the word cards provided for this lesson. Be sure the children can read the words. Use easy examples.

③ Suggested language: “These two words are *big* and *little.* What can you tell me about these words?” Children respond that the words mean the opposite. Illustrate this simple contrast by asking the children to use the words in sentences.

④ Suggested language: “Words that mean the opposite or just about the opposite are called *antonyms.* Say *antonym.*” Have the children clap and say the word *antonym* several times. Accept approximate pronunciations. (It will take many repetitions before students know and remember this technical word. They will eventually learn the label as they examine and talk about more examples. You can point out that the first part of the word is like *anti* [or against] and the last part means *name.*)

⑤ Present and discuss the remaining pairs of opposite words, writing them on the chart or matching them in the pocket chart. Use some of them in sentences, asking children whether the pairs are antonyms.

⑥ Tell children that they will be playing Concentration with antonyms.

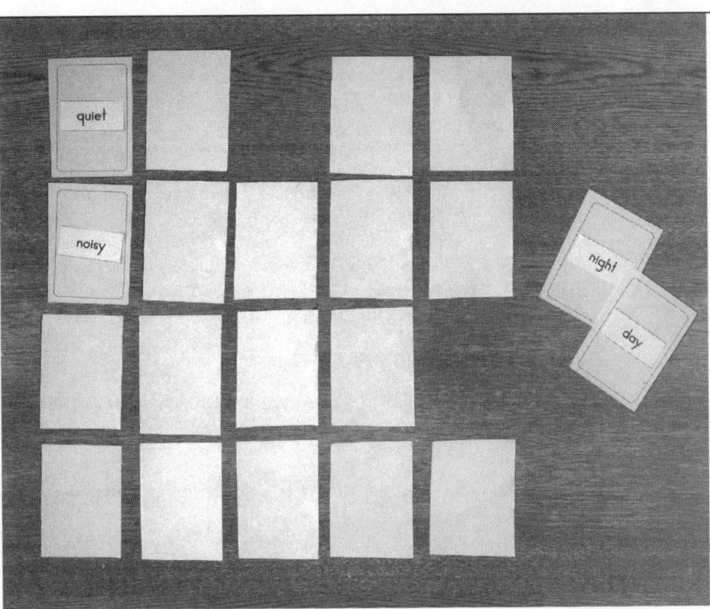

turn
turn
match

▸ Have the children, with partners, play Concentration. Limit the game at first to the words you have presented in the lesson, especially if children are dealing with the concept of antonyms for the first time. They lay all the cards face down on the table. In turn, they flip one card over, read it, and then turn over another and see whether it means the opposite (is an anotonym). The player with the most pairs wins. After the game, have each child write two pairs of antonyms on a piece of paper.

Have the children discuss their pairs of antonyms.

Add some of these antonyms to the class chart.

Link

Interactive Read-Aloud: Read aloud books that feature antonyms, and help children notice how antonyms are used to describe contrasts. Examples of appropriate books are:

- ***America: My Land, Your Land, Our Land*** by W. Nikola-Lisa
- ***Elephant Elephant: A Book of Opposites*** by Francissco Pittau

Shared Reading: Read together poems such as "The Zigzag Boy and Girl," "Little Arabella Miller," or "Out and In" (see *Sing a Song of Poetry*) that feature antonyms. Place stick-on notes with antonyms over words in a sentence or poem, and ask the children to read them and discuss how the meaning changes.

Guided Reading: When introducing or discussing a story, point out antonyms or ask the children to search for them. Emphasize antonyms during word work.

Interactive Writing: Help the children notice the antonyms they use in interactive writing, or have them find an antonym for a word on the class chart.

Independent Writing: Help the children use antonyms in their own writing.

assess

- Observe the children as they play Concentration and identify those who need more work in a small group.
- After the children are familiar with a number of antonyms, have them make an "antonym book" with words that mean the opposite on the left and right pages. They can write the words and illustrate them. Have them read the book to you, identifying the antonyms.

Expand the Learning

Repeat the lesson with additional antonyms.

Set up an antonym board and invite the children to put pairs of opposite words on it, along with illustrations.

Connect with Home

Send home pairs of antonym word cards for the children to match at home or to play Antonym Concentration with family members.

Exploring Synonyms and Antonyms

3

Lotto

Consider Your Children

This lesson requires your children to switch back and forth between thinking about words that mean the same and that mean the opposite. Before using this lesson, be sure that both concepts are firmly established and that the children are familiar with at least ten examples of both synonyms and antonyms.

Working with English Language Learners

Be sure your English language learners know the meaning of the synonyms and antonyms used in the lesson and in the Lotto game. Verify their knowledge by working with them in a small group and having them match pairs and talk about them. For example: "*Big* and *huge* mean almost the same. *Big* and *little* mean the opposite."

You Need

- The synonym and antonym charts made in Lessons WM 1 and 2.
- Shared reading charts (see *Sing a Song of Poetry*).

From *Teaching Resources:*

- Word Cards from the previous two lessons (Lesson WM 1 and Lesson WM 2).
- Directions for Lotto.
- Lotto Game Boards.

Understand the Principle

Children need to become flexible with the concepts of "the same" and "the opposite" in order to develop categories of these words as they read. Being able to think of good synonyms will help them make connections among words and also make their writing more interesting; knowing the meaning of antonyms will help their comprehension.

Explain the Principle

" Some words mean about the same and are called synonyms. "

" Some words mean about the opposite and are called antonyms. "

plan

teach

Pease Porridge

Pease porridge hot.
Pease porridge cold.
Pease porridge in the pot.
Nine days old.
Some like it hot.
Some like it cold.
Some like it in the pot.
Nine days old.

Jack Sprat

Jack sprat could eat no fat.
His wife could eat no lean.
So between them both you see,
They licked the platter clean.

Explain the Principle

"Some words mean about the same and are called synonyms."

"Some words mean about the opposite and are called antonyms."

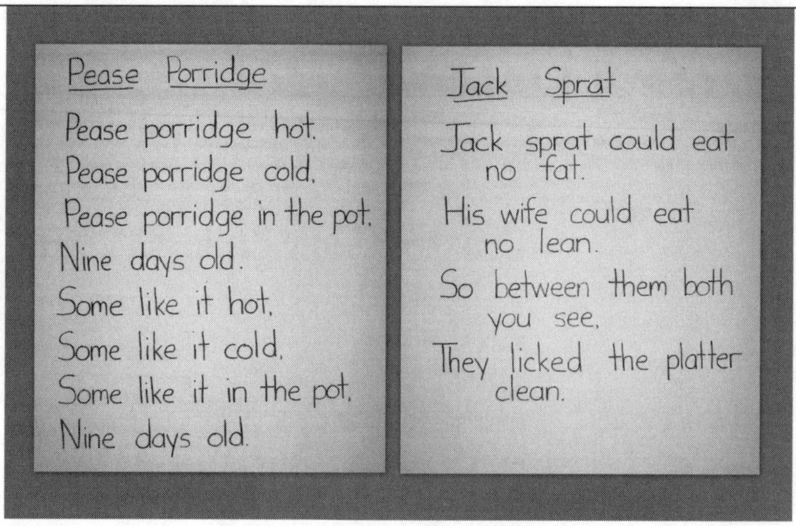

① Tell the children that they are going to be working more with synonyms and antonyms.

② Suggested language: "You have been learning about *synonyms*, words that mean about the same. You have also been learning about *antonyms*, words that mean about the opposite. Today you are going to be looking for both synonyms and antonyms."

③ Ask the children to give some examples for each concept.

④ Have the children quickly read a familiar rhyme together, one they have previously read several times. (There are two examples in the illustration, but you can use any rhyme you like.)

⑤ Play a game with the children, switching back and forth between synonyms and antonyms. Suggested language: "You know the poem 'Pease Porridge.' I'm going to give you a clue to find a word. I'm thinking of a word that means the opposite of *hot*. [Children respond *cold*.] I'm thinking of a word that means almost the same as *pan*. [Children respond *pot*.]"

⑥ Continue playing the game with "Jack Sprat" and other rhymes.

⑦ Then ask the children to suggest substitutions (opposite or the same) for words in the rhymes, and have them read the revised versions together. These "adaptations" are amusing and will sharpen the children's awareness of word meaning.

⑧ Tell the children that they are going to play Lotto with synonyms and antonyms.

take
say
match
cover

- Have the children, in small groups, play Lotto with synonyms and antonyms. A match can be a word that is either the same or the opposite of the card drawn. Whoever covers all the words first is the winner. Repeat as necessary. Be sure the children understand that they are to say whether the match is a synonym or an antonym.

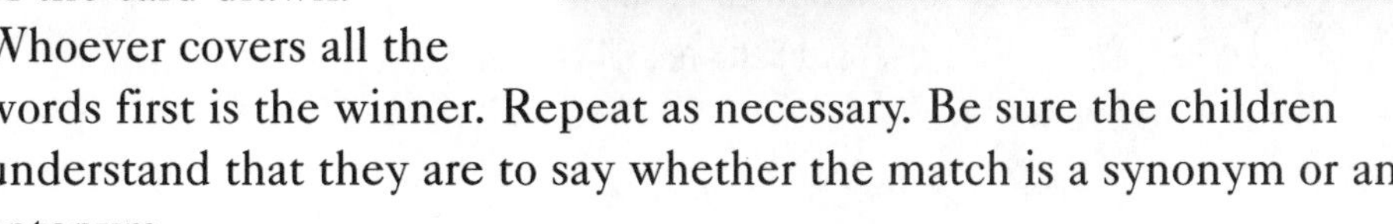

Invite children to talk about what they have noticed about words. Have them each tell a pair of synonyms and antonyms.

Link

Interactive Read-Aloud: Read books that include lots of synonyms and antonyms. Examples are:

- ***Too Big, Too Small, Just Right*** by Frances Minters
- ***To and Fro, Fast and Slow*** by Durga Bernhard

Shared Reading: Have the children tape a synonym or antonym over one or two words in a poem or other text such as "I Raised a Great Hullaballoo" or "A Lady Went A-marketing" (see *Sing a Song of Poetry*) and read it with the new word(s).

Guided Reading: During word work, spend a minute or two showing the children pairs of words and asking them to say whether they mean about the same or about the opposite.

Interactive Writing: When the children are composing a text, encourage them to give synonyms for words that would make the text more interesting. Use the list of synonyms as a resource.

Independent Writing: As you confer with the children, help them see places where they can cross out a word and put in a more interesting synonym.

assess

- Observe the children as they play Lotto to determine how quickly and easily they find synonyms and antonyms.
- Give the children a list of word pairs. Have them quickly read the pairs and circle either the synonyms or the antonyms.
- Have the children take the Lotto Word Cards and match them as either synonyms or antonyms.

Expand the Learning

Repeat the lesson with other rhymes or stories that you have used in shared reading.

Have the children play Follow the Path (see *Teaching Resources,* Games), telling a synonym or an antonym for the word in the space on which they land.

Connect with Home

Send Lotto Game Cards and Lotto word cards home so that the children can play the game with family members.

4 Exploring Simple Homophones 1

Sentence Pictures

Consider Your Children

Use this lesson after your children know the conventional spelling of many high frequency words and phonograms. Their independent writing should reflect a great deal of conventional spelling and good attempts at unfamiliar words but may be prone to homophone substitutions (using *to* for *two* or *too,* for example). Use sentences (ones that all the children can repeat and understand) to help them develop a contextual meaning for each of the words.

Working with English Language Learners

Homophones in oral language can be very confusing to English language learners. Noticing the differences in spelling will help them make distinctions among these words that sound the same but have different meanings. Help these children compose sentences with homophones during interactive writing, but don't attempt too many pairs at once. Repeated readings of these sentences give these children anchors to help them differentiate the meanings.

You Need

- Chart paper.
- Markers.

From *Teaching Resources:*

- Lesson WM 4 Word Cards (a set for every child).
- Lined Four-Box Sheets.

Understand the Principle

Children need to understand that words can *sound* the same but look different and have different meanings. Once they grasp this important principle, they can begin to develop examples and form categories for these *homophones* (a subset of *homonyms*). When they encounter one of these words, they will know they have to think carefully about meaning and spelling.

Explain the Principle

" Some words sound the same but look different and have different meanings. "

plan

teach

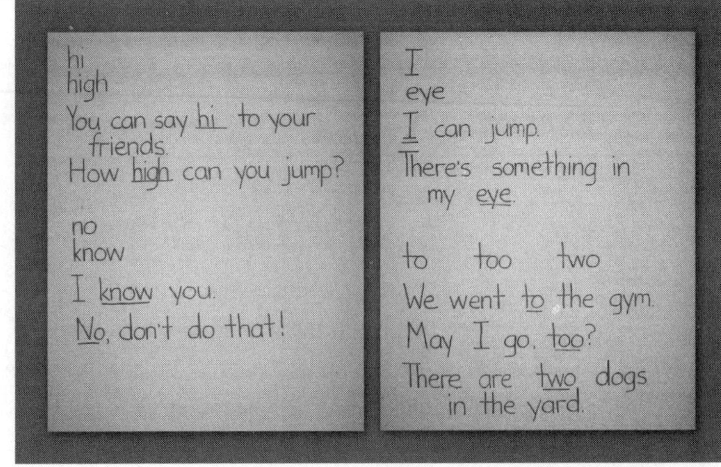

Explain the Principle

"Some words sound the same but look different and have different meanings."

① Tell the children that you are going to teach them something interesting about words.

② Start with a blank chart, writing the examples as you go.

③ Suggested language: "We are going to be looking at some words today that you all know. [Hold up or write *hi.*] You know this word, don't you? It's what you say to your friends when you come to school in the morning. It means *hello*."

④ Have the children read the word, and then explain that there is another word that sounds just the same but is spelled differently. Hold up the word *high,* and have children read it and suggest a sentence.

⑤ Children may respond by talking about a *high* hill, a *high* chair, or a kite being *high* in the sky. "That kind of *high* is spelled like this." You are not yet using the sentences, but you are familiarizing children with the homophones so they will find it easy to place them in the sentences later.

⑥ Repeat with *no, know; I, eye;* and *to, too, two.*

⑦ Then read (or add) the sentences below each group of words. Ask the children to identify the word that fits in the sentence and to explain if necessary. Write the appropriate word in the sentence.

⑧ Suggested language: "What do you notice about these words?" Children may respond with comments like these:

"They sound the same when you say them."

"They are spelled different."

"They mean different things when you say them in sentences."

9 After the children have discussed the words, guide them to articulate the principle: "Some words sound the same but look different and have different meanings."

10 Suggested language: "You have learned something important about words." Have children repeat the principle. They may spontaneously think of other homophones.

11 Tell the children they will be matching homophones and writing them in their own sentences.

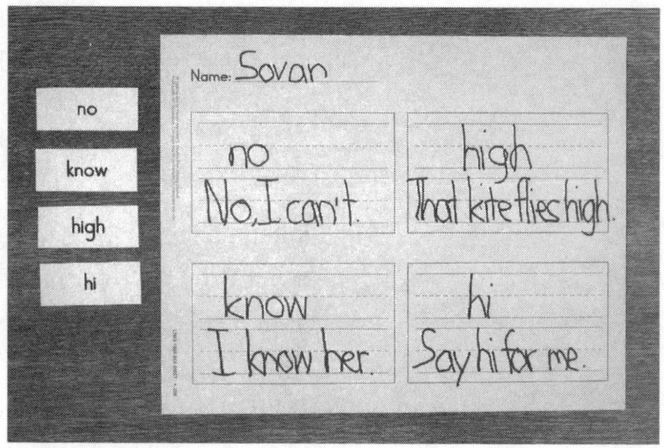

match cards
say words
write sentences

- Have the children match two pairs of Homophone word cards and say the words. Then they write four sentences using these four words on a Lined Four-Box Sheet (one sentence in each box). If time allows, children can choose one pair of sentences to illustrate on another piece of paper.

Have the children choose one pair of sentences to read to a partner.

Link

Interactive Read-Aloud: Read aloud books that increase children's awareness of homophones in an enjoyable way, and introduce more sophisticated homophones such as *moose* and *mousse.* Examples of appropriate books are:

- ***Like Likes Like*** by Chris Raschka
- ***A Chocolate Moose for Dinner*** by Fred Gwynne

Shared Reading: Read together poems that incorporate homophones, such as "A Sailor Went to Sea," "New Sights," "Taking Off," or "Whether the Weather" (see *Sing a Song of Poetry*). Have the children use highlighter tape to match homophones.

Guided Reading: When introducing or discussing a text, point out homophones, and have the children locate them and read them in the sentence.

Interactive Writing: As you work with small groups, point out homophones and ask the children to choose the correct spellings.

Independent Writing: When you confer with the children, help them distinguish between homophones and remind them of the sentences used in the lesson.

assess

- Notice whether the children can accurately use homophones in sentences.
- Observe the children's reading and writing to see whether they are using homophones correctly.

Expand the Learning

Encourage the children to compose more sentences using different homophones.

Give them more sentences and have them insert the correct homophones.

Connect with Home

Send home sets of Homophone word cards for children to match and read to family members.

They can also use these cards to play Concentration at home.

5 Exploring Simple Homophones 2

Word Grids

Consider Your Children

For this lesson, your children should have a beginning understanding of the concept of homophones and should be familiar with some examples. They should also understand the concepts of synonyms and antonyms. As always, they should be working with words that they understand and can read.

Working with English Language Learners

Help your English language learners by reading and rereading the sentences in a shared way. Have them locate and match homophones and talk about and even act out their meanings. Repeated readings of these sentences give these children anchors to help them differentiate the meanings.

You Need

- Chart paper.
- Markers.

From *Teaching Resources:*

- Word Cards from previous lessons (Lessons WM 1, WM 2, WM 4) for reference.
- Directions for Word Grids.
- Word Grids (write pairs of synonyms, antonyms, and homophones in the spaces on the Word Grid Template before photocopying).

Understand the Principle

Children need to understand the concept of homophones and have a sense of which words have alternative spellings. This awareness helps them establish a category of homophones and think carefully about meaning and spelling when they encounter them in reading or want to write them.

Explain the Principle

“Some words sound the same but look different and have different meanings.”

plan

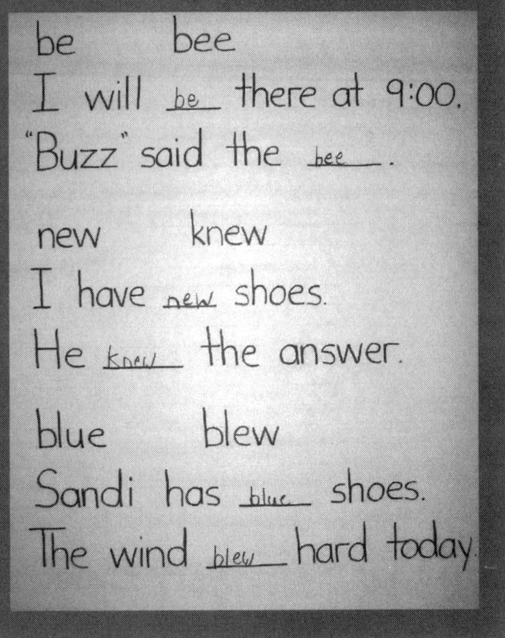

be bee
I will be there at 9:00.
"Buzz" said the bee.
new knew
I have new shoes.
He knew the answer.
blue blew
Sandi has blue shoes.
The wind blew hard today.

Explain the Principle

"Some words sound the same but look different and have different meanings."

① Let the children know that they will be working with more homophones.

② Suggested language: "You have been learning about words that sound the same but look different and have different meanings. Today we are going to look at more of those words. Some of these are words you know, but you may not have thought about them as homophones."

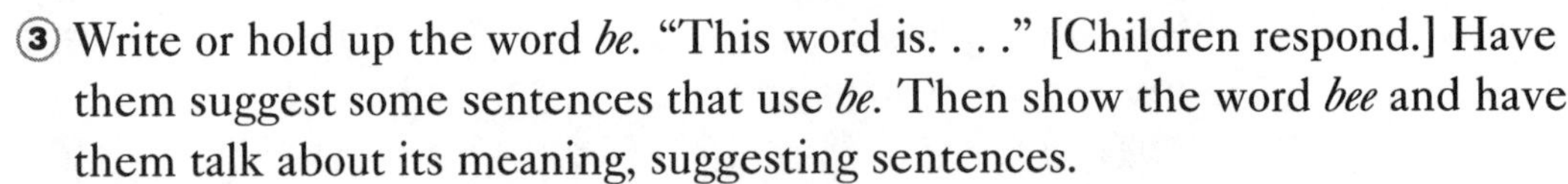

③ Write or hold up the word *be*. "This word is. . . ." [Children respond.] Have them suggest some sentences that use *be*. Then show the word *bee* and have them talk about its meaning, suggesting sentences.

④ Suggested language: "What word, *be* or *bee*, would you use in this sentence: *I will be there at 9:00*." [Children respond.] Write the word in the blank, or have a child come up and write it (or place the word card in the blank).

⑤ Do the same for the other sentence with *bee*. Obviously, once the first word is used correctly, the second one will be easy. Talk about the meaning of both words and how they fit in the sentences. To make the activity more challenging, create 3 or 4 sentences for each pair.

⑥ Discuss the meaning of the words *new* and *knew*, and then read both sentences, asking children to predict which word fits in each one.

⑦ Write the words in the sentences and ask children to confirm their predictions.

⑧ Follow the same procedure for *blue, blew* and *hour, our* (remembering that in some parts of the United States, the pronunciation of *our* sounds more like *are*).

⑨ After children have all discussed the words, guide them to compose the principle: "Some words sound the same but look different and have different meanings."

⑩ Suggested language: "You have learned something important about words." Have children repeat the principle. They may spontaneously think of other homophones.

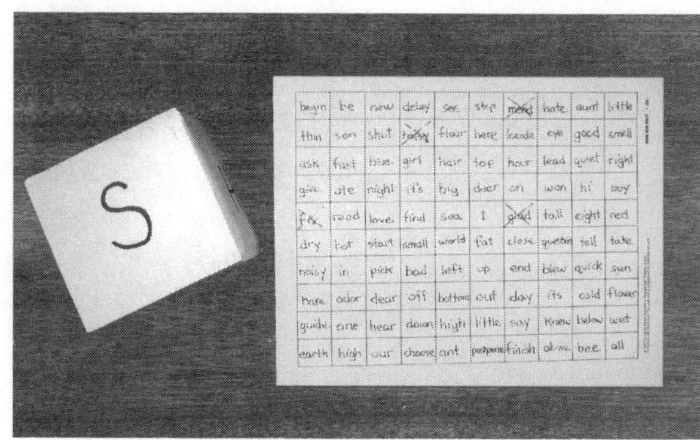

roll
find
say
cross out

▸ Have the children, in groups of two, three, or four, play the Word Grid game. They take turns rolling a die. If it says *S*, the child looks for two synonyms on his Word Grid and says them. If the group agrees they are synonyms, he crosses them out. (If the die says *A*, the child looks for antonyms; if it says *H*, he looks for homophones.)

Have the children, with a partner, choose and read one pair of words and tell whether they are synonyms, antonyms, or homophones. You could connect *phone* to the telephone and tell children that when they see *phon* in a word, it usually has something to do with sound or hearing sound.

Ask the children to talk about what they have noticed about homophones. They may respond with comments like these:

> "They sound the same when you say them."
>
> "They are spelled different."
>
> "They can have different numbers of letters."
>
> "They mean different things when you say them in sentences."

Link

Interactive Read-Aloud: Read aloud books that use more sophisticated homophones, such as

- ***A Little Pigeon Toad*** by Fred Gwynne
- ***Hey! Hay!*** by Marvin Terban

Shared Reading: Place stick-on notes over homophones in texts you read together. Ask children to choose the spelling of the word after they think about its meaning (you may write the options on a whiteboard). Good examples are "A Lobster Knows" *(knows/nose, way, to, seas, no, or)* and "Pairs or Pears" *(pairs/pears; knights, high, by, there)* (see *Sing a Song of Poetry*).

Guided Reading: When introducing or discussing a text, point out homophones, and have the children locate them and read them in a sentence.

Interactive Writing: Show the children how to refer to the class homophone chart to check the correct spelling.

Independent Writing: Notice the children's errors in substituting homophones in their writing. Ask them to check the class chart to help them decide which spelling is accurate.

Expand the Learning

Repeat the lesson with additional homophones.

Have the children "write around the room" (see *Teaching Resources,* Games) using the categories synonyms, antonyms, and homophones.

Add other categories such as contractions, compound words, words ending in silent *e,* and words beginning with consonant clusters.

Connect with Home

Send home a Word Grid game for children to play with family members.

assess

- Give the children a series of sentences, perhaps five or six, that include both spellings of a pair of homophones. Have them quickly write or circle the correct one.
- Work in a small group with children who make many errors.

6 Exploring Simple Homographs

Sentence Pictures

Consider Your Children

To understand homographs, your children should have a great deal of experience reading words in context. Awareness of the syntax of written language, built through hearing it read aloud, will help them figure out homographs. Be sure these experiences are in place before working with homographs in isolation. Even adults often need to correct their pronunciation of homographs, so don't expect immediate accuracy. The important thing is for students to understand the principle and notice homographs in sentences. The chart illustrated in the lesson has words that most second graders will have in their speaking vocabularies. Select words that are appropriate for your students, and start with a chart on which only the sentence pairs are prewritten, with the words highlighted or underlined.

Working with English Language Learners

The more English language learners understand about English syntax, the easier it will be for them to understand the different meanings and pronunciations of homographs. Take extra time for repeated oral rereadings of enjoyable texts so that they not only hear but say and internalize the syntactic patterns. Talk with them about the meaning of words, and use many examples whenever you can. You may want to present only two or three homographs that the children really understand rather than using the entire list illustrated in the lesson.

You Need

- Chart paper.
- Markers.

From *Teaching Resources:*

- Lesson WM 6 Word Cards.
- Four-Box Sheets (two per child).

Understand the Principle

Homographs are a subset of homonyms. These words are spelled the same, but they are pronounced differently and they have different meanings in the context of the words that surround them. Children need to understand that words can *look* the same but mean different things and sound different when used in sentences. Grasping this important principle and having a large repertoire of examples help them check their own understanding more carefully. It will also help them be more accurate in pronunciation when reading aloud and achieve more accurate spelling.

Explain the Principle

"Some words look the same, have a different meaning, and may sound different."

CONTINUUM: WORD MEANING — RECOGNIZING AND USING HOMOGRAPHS (SAME SPELLING, DIFFERENT MEANING, AND MAY HAVE DIFFERENT PRONUNCIATION)

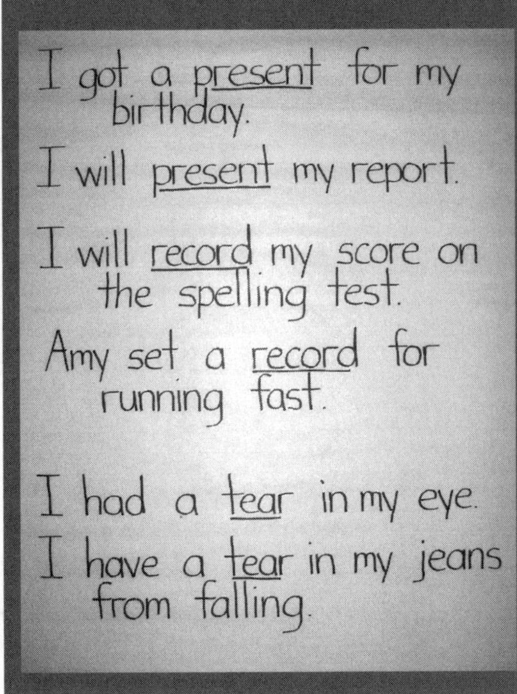
I got a present for my birthday.
I will present my report.
I will record my score on the spelling test.
Amy set a record for running fast.
I had a tear in my eye.
I have a tear in my jeans from falling.

teach

Explain the Principle

“Some words look the same, have a different meaning, and may sound different.”

① Tell the children that they are going to learn a new and interesting thing about certain words.

② Suggested language: “Today you are going to learn about words that look exactly the same, but when you read them in a sentence, you realize they have different meanings; usually you also say them differently.”

③ “I'm going to read the first two sentences.” Demonstrate reading the first pair of sentences. Read them twice if needed, or have one or two children repeat the readings.

④ Suggested language: “What do you notice about the words I have underlined?”

⑤ Discuss the two highlighted words with the children, talking about the meaning and pointing out how the words are pronounced differently. Explain that to know what the word means and how to say it, you have to think about the meaning of the whole sentence. You have to think about making the word “sound right” in the sentence.

⑥ Suggested language: “There are some words that look the same but have different meanings and usually sound different. These words are called *homographs*.” You can have the children say the word, but it is not important to spend a lot of time on the technical language. Your goal is to help them learn the concept and become familiar with some examples.

⑦ Follow the same procedure for the rest of the homographs you are using. To emphasize the concept, have the children try reading the sentences with both the correct and incorrect pronunciation. Help them see that they can check to be sure what they read not only looks right but sounds right and makes sense.

⑧ Tell the children that they will be writing and illustrating sentences that have words that look the same but have different meanings and sound different.

write
illustrate
read

- Have the children choose four homograph word cards. Have them write and illustrate four pairs of sentences on Four-Box Sheets and then read them to a partner.

Go around the circle, each child reading two sentences. Add selected sentences to the class chart if you need more examples.

Link

Interactive Read-Aloud: Read aloud books that increase children's awareness of homographs and help children expand their sense of English syntax. Examples are:

- ***The Dove Dove*** by Marvin Terban
- ***Comes a Wind*** by Linda Arms White

Shared Reading: Read the chart of sentences with homographs together so that the children internalize the examples.

Guided Reading: During word work, help children who need more experience with homographs.

Interactive Writing: As you work with small groups, point out homographs, and ask the children to give both pronunciations of the word and talk about the meaning.

Independent Writing: When you confer with the children, help them untangle any confusion they may have about the use of homographs.

assess

- When sampling oral reading, notice whether the children are accurately pronouncing homographs. Corrections made on their own indicate they are monitoring their reading and thinking about meaning.
- Give children several unfamiliar sentences containing homographs, and ask them to read the sentences quickly; note their pronunciation.

Expand the Learning

Have the children make a "homograph book" by placing the word on the left-hand page and writing and illustrating two sentences, with two different meanings, on the right-hand page.

Connect with Home

Have the children take home Homograph word cards and repeat the activity with family members using different words.

Have them take their homograph books home to share with family members.

Learning about Words with Multiple Meanings

7

Sentence Pictures

Consider Your Children

This lesson establishes the idea that a word can have more than one meaning. Be sure that the children have heard both meanings of the word in oral language or in texts you have read aloud. Work with the high frequency words children already know or those with familiar phonograms. Think about your children's experiences; for example, if they have used a *die* when playing games and they have talked about what it means for someone to *die,* this pair of words would be a good choice for this lesson.

Working with English Language Learners

Pay particular attention to whether English language learners know the words you are using in the lesson and have been exposed to both meanings. You may want to limit the lesson to three or four very simple words. Use pictures and actions whenever possible. Create sentences that the children can read and understand, and have them read them orally several times. You may want to work with these children in a small group as they make their sentences; help them with the sentences, and have them read the sentences several times before they illustrate them.

You Need

- Chart paper.
- Markers.

From *Teaching Resources:*

- Lesson WM 7 Word Cards.
- Four-Box Sheets (two for each child).

Understand the Principle

Children need to understand that a word may have two or more different meanings. When they have learned this concept, they can monitor the meaning of words in their reading, detecting variations in meaning or multiple meanings, thus better comprehending the text. Multiple meaning words are also homographs.

Explain the Principle

" Some words are spelled the same but have more than one meaning. "

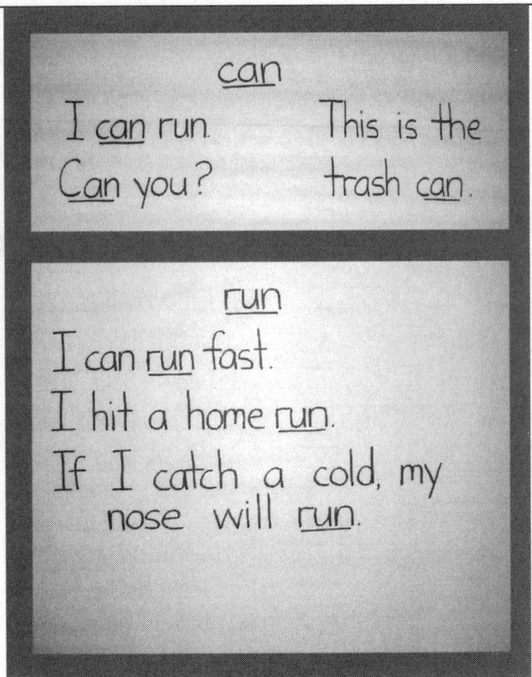

Explain the Principle

“Some words are spelled the same but have more than one meaning.”

① Tell the children that there are certain words that can have more than one meaning.

② Start with a blank chart, writing sentences as you go. (Rather than putting all the examples on a large piece of chart paper, make individual “posters” on smaller paper that you can easily place in different places around the room as reminders.)

③ Suggested language: “Today we are going to look at some of the words you already know, and we are going to think about their meanings. You know this word.” Show the word *can*.

④ Have children talk about the two meanings. Suggested language: “Let’s think about a sentence for each of the meanings of the word *can*.” Have the children suggest sentences, but be sure that the meaning in each is clear and that they are easy for children to read and understand.

⑤ Repeat with two or three other words that you have selected.

⑥ Summarize the lesson by asking the children what they notice about the words they have talked about today. Write a summary statement on the chart; for example, “Some words have more than one meaning.”

⑦ Tell the children that they are going to create sentences for words that have more than one meaning (multiple meanings).

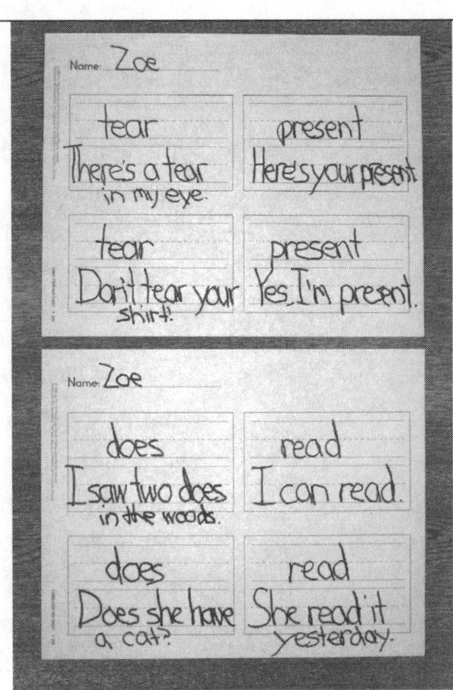

take
write
illustrate

▸ Have the children select four word cards from those for this lesson. Using two Four-Box Sheets, they write and illustrate a sentence for each meaning of the word.

Have children take turns reading some of their sentences. Children may offer words that have variations in meaning but that are not technically *multiple* meanings because they are derived from the same semantic area *(throw a ball, throw a pot, throw up)*. Do not be too concerned about technicalities. The important thing is for children to explore and think about different meanings. You can explain over time how words are *used* in different ways.

Link

Interactive Read-Aloud: Read aloud books that incorporate word play based on multiple meanings. Examples are:

- ***When the Sun Rose*** by Barbara Helen Berger
- ***Mrs. Biddlebox*** by Linda Smith

Shared Reading: As you read poems and other pieces of writing together, help children understand how the context of the sentence helps them know which meaning of a word is intended. Some good examples are "My Love for You" and "I Never Saw a Purple Cow" *(can)*; "Bow-Wow the Dog" and "There's a Hole in My Bucket" *(well)*; and "At the Zoo" and "Big Ship Sailing" *(back)*. See *Sing a Song of Poetry.*

Guided Reading: After reading a text, go back to a word that potentially has two meanings. Have the children talk about how they knew the right meaning.

Interactive Writing: When a word with multiple meanings arises, point it out.

Independent Writing: When you confer with children about their writing, discuss word choice.

Expand the Learning

Repeat the lesson with different multiple-meaning words.

Compile an ongoing classroom chart of words with multiple meanings.

Connect with Home

Send children's sentences and illustrations home so they can share them with family members.

assess

- Notice whether the children can create sentences that reflect alternative meanings of words.
- Give the children a sheet on which you have written a word with multiple meanings. Ask them to write two sentences in which the word is used with a different meaning.

Word Structure

Looking at the structure of words will help children learn how words are related to each other and how words can be changed by adding letters, letter clusters, and larger parts of words. Being able to recognize syllables, for example, helps children break down words into smaller units that are easier to analyze. In phonological awareness lessons, children learn to recognize the word breaks and to identify the number of syllables in a word. They can build on this useful information in reading and writing.

Words often have affixes, parts added before or after a word to change its meaning. An affix can be a prefix or a suffix. The word to which affixes are added can be a *base* word or a *root* word. A base word is a complete word; a root word is a part with Greek or Latin origins (such as *phon* in *telephone*). It will not be necessary for young children to make this distinction when they are beginning to learn about simple affixes, but working with suffixes and prefixes will help them read and understand words that use them as well as use them accurately in writing.

Endings or word parts that are added to base words signal meaning. For example, they may signal relationships *(prettier, prettiest)* or time *(running, planted)*. Principles related to word structure include understanding the meaning and structure of compound words, contractions, plurals, and possessives as well as knowing how to make and use them accurately. We have also included the simple abbreviations that children often see in the books they read and want to use in their writing.

Connect to Assessment

See related WS Assessment Tasks in the Assessment Guide in *Teaching Resources:*

- Recognizing Syllables in Words
- Writing Syllables in Words
- Understanding and Forming Contractions
- Recognizing Compound Words
- Forming Plurals with *s* and *es*
- Forming Plurals of Words Ending in *y*
- Reading Words with Suffixes
- Reading Words with Endings Added to Base Words
- Forming Possessives

Develop Your Professional Understanding

See *Word Matters: Teaching Phonics and Spelling in the Reading/Writing Classroom* by G.S. Pinnell and I.C. Fountas. 1998. Portsmouth, New Hampshire: Heinemann.

Related pages: 97–98.

1 Recognizing Compound Words

Making Words

Consider Your Children

In this lesson, children learn about two words put together to form a compound word. They will generally find the concept easy and will begin to notice the many compound words in books. Start with easy compound words that are in children's speaking vocabularies, or at least in their listening vocabularies. They should have worked with very simple compound words such as *into* before this lesson and should have encountered many of the words in the books you read aloud to them or those they read themselves in guided reading.

Working with English Language Learners

English language learners should have a great deal of experience hearing, reading, and writing compound words before they study them in this formal lesson. Work with shared reading and interactive writing in small groups. Have children repeat text readings and take apart and put together the compound words that are included. During guided reading, write compound words on a small whiteboard, and cover first one part and then another to show children the component parts of words.

You Need

- Pocket chart.
- Markers.
- Chart paper.

From *Teaching Resources:*

- Pocket Chart Card Template.
- List Sheets.
- Lesson WS 1 Word Cards.

Understand the Principle

There are hundreds of compound words, and knowing how to look for the parts helps children read and write these words. Also, the parts often give clues to a word's meaning.

Explain the Principle

"Some words are made up of two words put together and are called compound words."

"You can read compound words by looking at the two words in them."

plan

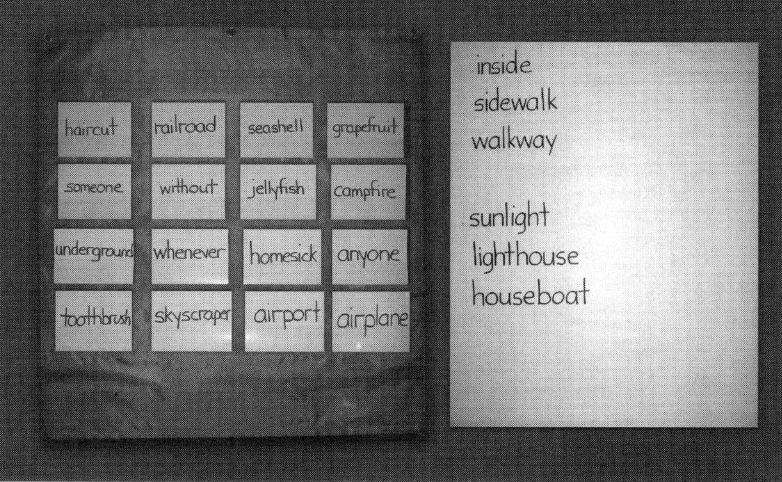

Explain the Principle

"Some words are made up of two words put together and are called compound words."

"You can read compound words by looking at the two words in them."

1. Explain to the children that they are going to learn more about words. Write six to ten compound words on cards for the pocket chart and ask the children what they notice about them. They will likely notice that each is made of two smaller words.

2. Ask them to tell you as many compound words as they can while you list them on the cards.

3. After making a list with many examples, remind the children that the examples are all two words put together and that sometimes the two smaller words help them understand the meaning of the compound word.

4. Make a compound word ladder. Start with one word (*inside,* for example). Invite the children to add a compound word that starts with the second word: *inside, sidewalk, walkway.*

5. Complete a few more ladders so that the children will understand the concept: *sunlight, lighthouse, houseboat.*

6. Explain to the children that today they are going to make compound words with two word cards and then write the compound words on a List Sheet.

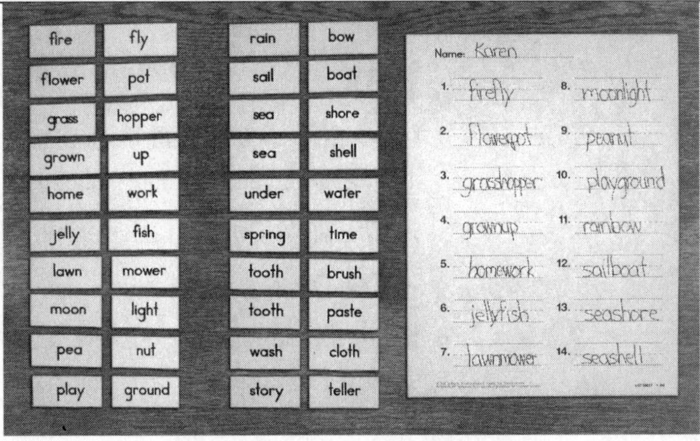

take
match
write
read

▸ Have the children put together two word cards to make one word. Have them make twenty compound words. Be sure to remind them that the words must be real. Ask the children to copy their words onto a List Sheet and read them to a partner.

Have children read their list of compound words to a different partner.

Add a compound word to the word wall as an example.

There may be some discussion of words that *sound* like compound words but really are two single words, for example, *word wall, peanut butter*. You can explain that when words are used together over a long period of time, they may become compound words. Other compound words are "made up" as new words (for example, *minivan*).

Link

Interactive Read-Aloud: Read aloud books that feature compound words, such as

- ***Eli's Night-Light*** by Liz Rosenberg
- ***Gold Fever*** by Verla Kay

Shared Reading: After you have read and enjoyed poems such as "Buttercups and Daisies," "Tree Shadows," and "If All the Little Raindrops" (see *Sing a Song of Poetry*) together, have the children locate compound words with a highlighter marker, highlighter tape, or a masking card.

Guided Reading: After the lesson, have the children turn to particular pages and locate two or three compound words.

Interactive Writing: When working with a small group of writers, point out places where there are compound words.

Independent Writing: When conferring with writers, help them notice compound words.

assess

- Write four or five compound words on cards and have the children read them.
- Dictate four or five compound words and assess the children's ability to write them.

Expand the Learning

Repeat the lesson with other compound words. Use the Word Card Template (see *Teaching Resources*) to create word cards for new compound words.

Give the children one word card and have them generate a second word and write the compound word.

Connect with Home

Have the children search for compound words with family members at home or in the neighborhood. For example, have them find *sidewalk, doorbell, walkway, butterfly, mailman, birdhouse, raindrop, doghouse, bluebird*, and *dishtowel.*

2 Making Compound Words

Word Match

Consider Your Children

This lesson should follow lessons on recognizing and understanding simple compound words such as *into, inside, today,* and *myself.* In this lesson, children apply the same principle to more complex words.

Working with English Language Learners

Compound words can be confusing to English language learners; their meaning may be related to the component words (*sidewalk,* for example) or may not be so obvious (*butterfly,* for example). Help these children understand meaning by discussing the words, using them in sentences, making them with magnetic letters, and acting them out. Use simple examples until your English language learners grasp the principle.

You Need

- Chart paper.
- Markers.

From *Teaching Resources:*

- Lesson WS 2 Word Cards.
- List Sheets.

Understand the Principle

Learning to look at parts helps children read and write many words. Words put together form compound words. (Each part of a compound word must be a word by itself.) Some have easy-to-decode patterns, while others are more complex to read. Often the meaning of a compound word derives from the meaning of the two smaller words, but not always.

Explain the Principle

“Some words are made up of two words put together and are called compound words.”

“You can read compound words by looking at the two words in them.”

plan

every
everything
everyday
everywhere
everybody

head
headache
headband
headphones

sun
sunshine
sunflower

Explain the Principle

"Some words are made up of two words put together and are called compound words."

"You can read compound words by looking at the two words in them."

1. Tell the children that they are going to learn more about compound words.
2. Write the word *every* on the chart. Suggested language: "This is the first part of some compound words, which are words made up of two words put together. This is the first part of *everything*. [Add *thing* to *every*.] Can you think of other compound words that start with *every*?" Children respond: *everyday, everywhere, everybody*.
3. Repeat the demonstration with *head (headache, headband, headphones)* and *sun (sunshine, sunflower)*.
4. Explain to the children that today they are going to find two words that can go together and make a compound word. Demonstrate with the two word cards *pop* and *corn*. Show them how to put the cards together to make *popcorn,* and then write the word on the list sheet. Explain that they should make twenty compound words and then write them on a List Sheet.

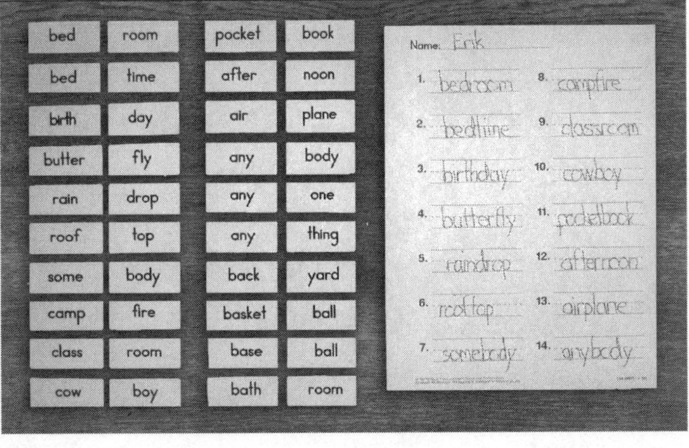

find
match
write
read

▸ Have the children find two word cards that go together and make a compound word. They should make twenty different compound words, record them on a List Sheet, and then read their lists to a partner.

Have each child read a compound word he or she made that someone else has not already mentioned.

Put an example of a compound word on the word wall.

Link

Interactive Read-Aloud: Read aloud books that include several compound words, pointing them out. Examples of appropriate books are:

- ***Wild Bog Tea*** by Annette LeBox
- ***Zachary's Ball*** by Matt Travares

Shared Reading: After you have read and enjoyed a poem such as "A Fuzzy Little Caterpillar," "A Caterpillar Crawled," or "I Hear Thunder" together, have children locate the compound words. (See *Sing a Song of Poetry* for other appropriate poems.) When first reading a poem, cover the second part of a compound word so the children can predict it. Then uncover the word so they can confirm their prediction.

Guided Reading: After reading and discussing a text, have the children use highlighter tape or a masking card to locate two or three compound words.

Interactive Writing: Invite the children to clap the two words in a compound word before trying to write it.

Independent Writing: When you confer with children, point out a compound word they have used.

Expand the Learning

Repeat the lesson and have children make twenty more words.

Use the Word Card Template (see *Teaching Resources*) to create another set of fifty compound words (one hundred individual words) for another lesson.

Post a blank chart on the wall, and challenge the class to find and write one hundred compound words.

Connect with Home

Give children a copy of the word cards to take home and make compound words with family members.

assess

- Have children read a list of five or ten compound words.
- Observe the children's ability to take apart compound words while reading.

3 Forming Possessives

Making Sentences

Consider Your Children

Your children will be using possessives in reading and writing well before you present this lesson, but here you are teaching the principle in an explicit way. This lesson focuses on the singular form of the noun. After the lesson, be sure your children haven't confused possessives with plurals. You can always recognize their thinking if they offer plurals as examples, and you may want to write them on a separate chart. Children may begin to notice that plurals use *s* while possessives have an apostrophe. If the story will be difficult for some of your children to read, you may want to read it with them several times first. Alternatively, make it into a large chart you read to them first. You can also add the missing "apostrophe *s*" as a whole group activity.

Working with English Language Learners

Possessives may be challenging for English language learners. Be sure they have heard and worked with possessives many times in the context of simple texts that they read together or hear you read. Use possessives in sentences with children's names; for example, "This is Brianna's red jacket." Have these students make their own sentences with possessives; write for them or have them write words on cards and let them exchange them. Draw attention to the apostrophe by highlighting it in yellow.

You Need

- Chart paper.
- Markers.
- Magnetic letters.
- Apostrophe magnets (you can make your own with magnetic tape).
- Thin colored markers.

From *Teaching Resources:*

- Copies of the Lesson WS 3 Paragraphs (Lesson Word Cards, Lesson WS 3).

Understand the Principle

An apostrophe and *s* are added to the singular name of a person, animal, place, or thing to show ownership. Children often confuse apostrophes with commas, so you will need to emphasize the placement of the apostrophe. If children ask about words that end with *s* (for example, Charles' lunch) or plural nouns (the pigs' houses), briefly explain the principle of just adding an apostrophe and write the examples on a separate chart. Be aware that children often confuse possessives with plurals.

Explain the Principle

" A person, animal, place, or thing can own something. To show ownership, you add *'s* to a word. "

plan

Explain the Principle

“A person, animal, place, or thing can own something. To show ownership, you add *’s* to a word.”

1. Tell the children you are going to teach them about some punctuation they use in words.
2. Suggested language: “The book belongs to Sam. It is Sam’s book.” Make *Sam’s book* on the easel with magnetic letters or on a chart, showing that you are placing the apostrophe at the top, not at the bottom like a comma.

Sam’s book
Manuela’s coat
Regi’s pencil
Peter’s bag
The dog’s house
The book’s cover

3. Continue the process with sentences such as, “The coat belongs to Manuela. It is ______________ coat. The pencil belongs to Regi. It is __________________ pencil.” Use the names of children in your class at first, and then make the sentences with nouns.
4. After creating a variety of sentences with phrases that show possession, review the principle and have the children say the word *apostrophe* with you. You may want to create a reference chart comparing the comma and its placement with an apostrophe and its placement.
5. Tell the children they are going to read and punctuate some sentences in a short story. You will want to read the sentences to the children first, showing that you will add *s* as you read aloud to make the words possessive. They will need to add an apostrophe and *s* in the written story.

read
mark

▸ Have the children work as partners. One reads the paragraph aloud and they both punctuate the two paragraphs that include several possessives. Have them use their thin colored markers so the apostrophe and *s* stand out.

Sara dog Chip was lost. Sara father and her friend father tried to help, but they could not find him. The dog collar had a tag with Sara phone number. Chip never left Sara yard without her. Where could he be?

The dog food bowl sat in the yard. The cat ball was on the grass. Matt backpack was on the bench, and Erika sweater was on the porch. The sun heat had dried up all the water in the dog little pool, and he was gone.

Invite the children to tell the words to which they added apostrophe and *s* as you write them on a chart.

Link

Interactive Read-Aloud: Read aloud books that include possessives, such as

- ***David's Drawings*** by Catherine Falwell
- ***Tracy's Mess*** by Elise Petersen

Shared Reading: After you have read and enjoyed a poem such as "Old Mother Hubbard" or "Humpty Dumpty" together (see *Sing a Song of Poetry*), have the children locate one or two places where an apostrophe is used to show possession. They can use yellow highlighter tape to make it stand out.

Guided Reading: After reading and discussing a text, have the children turn to one or two pages to locate words that have apostrophes to show possession.

Interactive Writing: Point out the placement of an apostrophe when children write words showing possession.

Independent Writing: When they are editing, be sure children use apostrophes for possessives, *not* plurals.

assess

- Observe the children's use and placement of the apostrophe to show possession in writing texts.
- Dictate two or three sentences with simple possessive forms to determine children's control of the principle.

Expand the Learning

Repeat the lesson with plural possessives (the girls' school), possessives made with words ending in *s* (Marcus' house), and plural nouns not ending in *s* (the children's school).

Connect with Home

Invite the children to write sentences about something that belongs to each of their family members.

4 Recognizing Syllables in Words with Double Consonants

Word Puzzles

Consider Your Children

In order to benefit most from this lesson, your children will need to have good control of simple one-syllable word patterns such as CVC and CVC*e;* they should also be familiar with compound words. For this lesson, they work with two-syllable words that have a short vowel sound in the first syllable (CVC).

Working with English Language Learners

Taking apart multisyllable words is basic to solving them. Provide very explicit demonstrations using magnetic letters, and also let children say and take apart the words themselves. Looking at the words, they will find it easy to divide the word between the double consonants, but it is also necessary for them to know the meaning of each word and to say it, emphasizing the syllable breaks.

You Need

- Magnetic letters.

From *Teaching Resources:*

- Lesson WS 4 Word Cards.
- List Sheets.

Understand the Principle

Children need to learn how to look at parts of multisyllable words. A generalization such as dividing a two-syllable word between the two middle consonants is often helpful. This principle is *usually* true and will give students a good start on dividing words. It doesn't apply to words that have consonant digraphs in the middle *(chicken, catcher).* It does apply to most other words with double consonants or two different consonants.

Explain the Principle

" Divide the syllables between the consonants when a word has two consonants in the middle. "

Explain the Principle

"Divide the syllables between the consonants when a word has two consonants in the middle."

1. Explain to the children that they are going to learn more about dividing words into syllables.
2. Say four or five words with double consonants in the middle, such as *ladder, dollar, saddest,* and *muffin,* and have the children clap the parts with you. You may want to add a few words with two different consonants, such as *helmet, pencil,* or *mistake.*
3. After clapping each word, make the word with magnetic letters on a board. Then divide the word between the consonants and point out the two syllables.
4. Invite the children up to the easel to make a few more two-syllable words with double consonants in the middle. Ask them to divide the words by moving the magnetic letters.
5. Tell the children they are going to put together two word parts to make a whole word (for example, *dol + lar = dollar*). They will take one part and find a second part that makes a real word. Then they will write the word on a List Sheet or in their Word Study Notebook.

early
mid
late

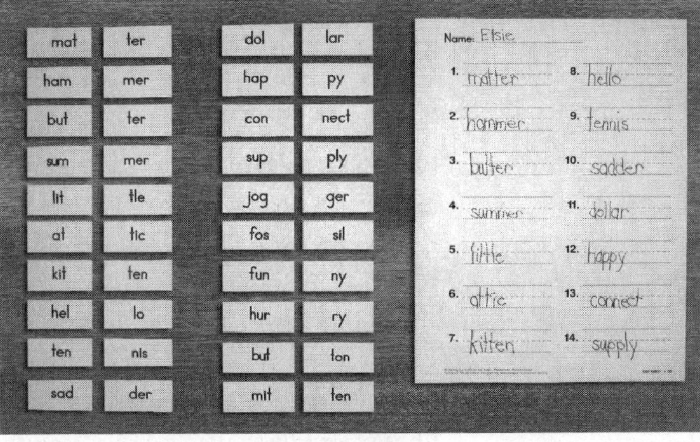

take
find
read
write

- Give children a collection of word parts. They take one part (for example, *muf*) and look for the rest of the word *(fin)*. Then they put the word together, read it, and write it on the List Sheet or in their Word Study Notebooks. They can draw a line to show the syllables in the word *(muf/fin)*.
- Then have them read their words to a partner.

Have children share what they noticed about their words.

Invite a few children to make and divide two or three more examples.

Put an example on the word wall.

WS 4
WORD STRUCTURE

Link

Interactive Read-Aloud: Read aloud books that include many multisyllable words. After enjoying the story, clap two or three words that have double consonants in the middle. Examples of appropriate books are:

- ***Russell's Secret*** by Johanna Hurwitz
- ***McDuff Comes Home*** by Rosemary Wells

Shared Reading: After you have read and enjoyed a poem such as "Once I Saw a Bunny," "Jelly on the Plate," or "If You're Happy and You Know It" together (see *Sing a Song of Poetry*), have the children locate two or three words with double consonants in the middle. Have them make the words with magnetic letters and then divide them into syllables.

Guided Reading: When the children are reading new words with double consonants in the middle, teach them how to cover the last part of the word, including the second consonant, and look at the first part. Then uncover the last part and read the whole word.

Interactive Writing: When the children are going to write words with double consonants in the middle, have them clap and listen for the middle sounds and then write the first and last parts.

Independent Writing: Remind the children to use the pattern of double consonants in the middle when they edit their writing for spelling.

assess

- Dictate four or five words with double consonants or two consonants (not digraphs) in the middle.
- Observe the children's use of the double consonant pattern in words they want to read or write.

Expand the Learning

Repeat the lesson with other words that have double consonants in the middle. Use the Word Card Template (see *Teaching Resources*) to make cards for the parts of the new words you've chosen.

Post a chart for children to list words that fit the pattern; have a goal of finding fifty or one hundred of them.

Connect with Home

Have the children look for words with double consonants (for example, *dollar, mitten, buttons*) in newspapers or in magazines. Give them a goal of finding five to bring to school.

5 Forming the Past Tense by Adding ed 1

Say and Write

Consider Your Children

This is an early lesson for adding *ed* to base words and *d* to base words ending in silent *e* when there is no change in spelling. Children will have had many experiences in reading and writing words in past tense. This lesson incorporates easy examples that most children know so they can focus on this principle. In this lesson children learn how to add the ending and notice the different way the ending can sound.

Working with English Language Learners

Be sure that you use base words that English language learners can understand. Provide many opportunities to say the words and think about the sounds at the end while looking at the words. Make words with magnetic letters and practice putting on the *ed* or *d*. If necessary, work with a small group to help them write the words and then check them.

You Need

- Chart paper.
- Markers.

From *Teaching Resources:*

- Lesson WS 5 Word Cards.
- List Sheets.

Understand the Principle

Affixes are groups of letters added to the beginning or end of a word. A *suffix* is a group of letters added to the end of a word. The *ed* suffix is a word part that changes the meaning (tense) of a word. With the words in this lesson, the spelling does not change, though it sometimes changes with other verbs *(plan, carry).*

Explain the Principle

“Add *ed* to the end of a word to show that you did something in the past.”

“Add *d* to words ending in silent *e* to make the *ed* ending and show it was in the past.”

“When you add *ed* to a word, sometimes it sounds like /d/.”

“When you add *ed* to a word, sometimes it sounds like /ed/.”

“When you add *ed* to a word, sometimes it sounds like /t/.”

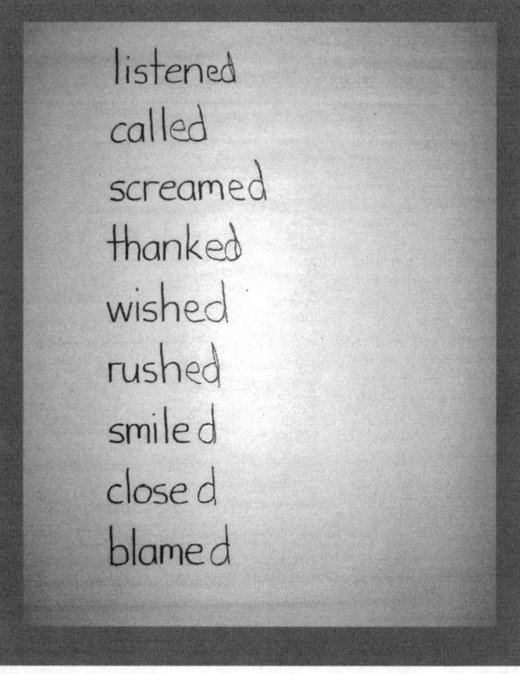

Explain the Principle

“Add *ed* to the end of a word to show that you did something in the past.”

“Add *d* to words ending in silent *e* to make the *ed* ending and show it was in the past.”

“When you add *ed* to a word, sometimes it sounds like /d/.”

“When you add -*ed* to a word, sometimes it sounds like /ed/.”

“When you add *ed* to a word, sometimes it sounds like /t/.”

① Tell the children they are going to learn about adding *ed* to words.

② Have the words *listen, call, scream, thank, wish, rush, smile, close,* and *blame* on the easel.

③ Suggested language: “Read these words with me as I point to them: *listen, call, scream.* To show that something happened in the past, we add *ed* to words: *Today I listen. Yesterday I listened. Today I call. Yesterday I* ________. [Children respond.] *Today I scream. Yesterday I* __________. [Children respond.] What letters do I need to add to each of the words? [Children respond.] Yes, *ed*.” Call on a child to add *ed* to these three words and read them.

④ Suggested language: “Listen for the sound at the end of the words. Yes, they sound like /d/.”

⑤ Repeat the process with *thank, wish,* and *rush,* helping children add *ed* and notice the ending sounds like /t/.

⑥ Continue with *smile, close,* and *blame,* helping children add a *d* (the *e* is already there) and notice the ending sounds like /d/.

⑦ If the children bring up words in which you hear another syllable when adding *ed (melted)* or words for which the spelling changes *(plan, carry),* write them on another chart and tell them that adding *ed* to those words involves something different and they will learn those principles soon. If you feel your children are ready for the challenge, create a column for words that add *ed* and sound like /ed/, such as *wanted.* Then show how to change the *y* to *i* and double the consonant and add *ed* to words such as *carry.* Place the words under the words that sound like /d/ at the end.

⑧ Tell the children that today they will take twenty word cards, write each word on a List Sheet, add *d* or *ed,* and then read their list to a partner.

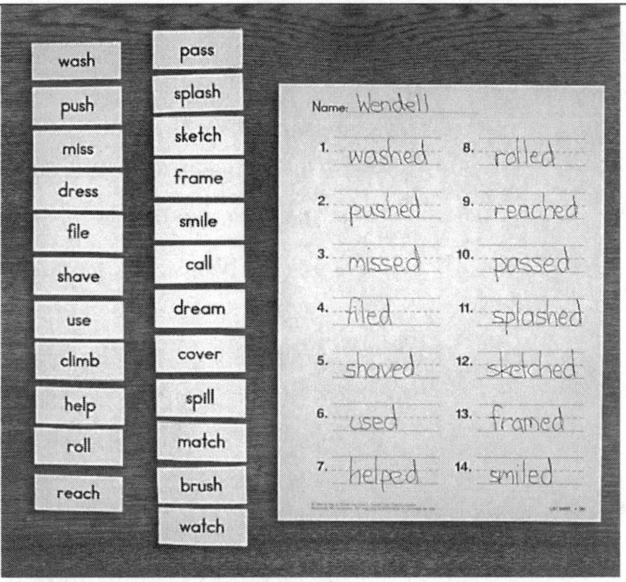

take
say
write
add *d* or *ed*
read

▸ Have the children select twenty words from the pile of word cards, one at a time. Then have them take a card, say it, write the word on a list sheet, and add *d* or *ed*. When they have completed twenty words, and written them on the List Sheet, have them read their lists to a partner.

Have particular children read the words on their list that have *ed* endings that sound like /d/.

Repeat with those that have endings that sound like /t/.

Link

Interactive Read-Aloud: Read aloud books that include many words with suffixes, such as

- ***The Apple Pie Tree*** by Zoe Hall
- ***The Old Woman and the Wave*** by Shelly Jackson

Shared Reading: After you have read and enjoyed a poem such as "A Walk One Day," "Peter Piper," or "Milkman, Milkman" together (see *Sing a Song of Poetry*), have the children give word clues to their classmates regarding words with the *ed* endings: "I'm thinking of a word that means to drop and ends with an *ed* that sounds like /d/ [*spilled*]."

Guided Reading: During word work, write on a whiteboard or make with magnetic letters five or six words, add *d* or *ed,* and have the children read the words quickly.

Interactive Writing: When the children are going to write a new word with an *ed* ending, have them think about whether it sounds like /d/ as in *rained* or /t/ as in *talked* (or /ed/ as in *wanted*).

Independent Writing: Help the children check to be sure they have correctly spelled verb endings in their stories.

Expand the Learning

Repeat the lesson adding words with *ed* pronounced as another syllable *(wanted).*

Repeat the lesson adding a few words in which the spelling changes when *ed* is added *(spy–spied, fry–fried, cry–cried, carry–carried, dry–dried).*

Connect with Home

Have the children take *ed* word cards home to sort by whether they sound like /ed/, /d/, or /t/.

assess

- Have the children read and sort five or six words with *ed* while you observe their speed and accuracy.
- Notice the children's use of *ed* on verbs in their writing.

6 Forming the Past Tense by Adding ed 2

Three-Way Sort

Consider Your Children

Your children should have read many words with the *ed* ending and used the past tense of verbs both in their speech and in their writing. In this lesson, you focus on the simplest principle, adding *ed* when it sounds like a /d/ or /t/ at the end of a word and adding *ed* when it adds another syllable. A simpler lesson on the three ways an *ed* ending is pronounced (for example, Lesson WS 5) should precede this lesson unless children are more sophisticated in their knowledge.

Working with English Language Learners

Inflecting verbs to change tense is a challenging concept when learning another language. Be sure that your English language learners fully understand these simple examples. Work with them in a small group if necessary so that they understand the principle before going on to more complex inflections.

You Need

- Chart paper.
- Markers.
- Magnetic letters.

From *Teaching Resources:*

- Lesson WS 6 Word Cards.
- Three-Way Sort Cards.
- Three-Way Sort Sheets.

Understand the Principle

Affixes are groups of letters added to the beginning or end of words. They include *prefixes* and *suffixes.* The *ed* ending is a *suffix* (technically, an inflectional ending), a group of letters added to a base word to change the meaning and form the past tense. It sounds like /d/ or /t/ or /ed/. When you teach children to add the ending, you are also showing them how to remove it to identify a base word when reading longer words. Sometimes the spelling of the base word changes when you add a suffix (for example, a consonant may be doubled).

Explain the Principle

“ Add *ed* to the end of a word to show that you did something in the past. ”

“ When you add *ed* to a word, sometimes it sounds like /d/. ”

“ When you add *ed* to a word, sometimes it sounds like /ed/. ””

“ When you add *ed* to a word, sometimes it sounds like /t/. ”

plan

Explain the Principle

"Add *ed* to the end of a word to show that you did something in the past."

"When you add *ed* to a word, sometimes it sounds like /d/."

"When you add *ed* to a word, sometimes it sounds like /ed/."

"When you add *ed* to a word, sometimes it sounds like /t/."

1. Tell the children that you are going to teach them about the word ending *ed*. It is called a *suffix*.

2. Make the word *play* with magnetic letters (or on a chart), use it in a sentence (for example, *We play games in the schoolyard*), and then ask the children how you would say the same sentence if it started with *yesterday*. Children will respond, "Yesterday we played games in the schoolyard." Ask a child to come up to the easel and change the word to *played*. The child will add *ed*. Help the children notice the ending sound.

3. Next, make the word *melt* and repeat the process. Help children notice that when you add *ed* to melt, you hear a whole syllable. Have them clap the parts: *melt-ed*.

4. Make the word *walk*. Suggested language: "I walk to school." Ask the children to give the sentence if it started with *yesterday*. Invite a child to make *walk*, add *ed*, and then say *walked*. Suggested language: "What do you notice about *walk*?" Children will notice that the added *ed* sounds like /t/.

5. Summarize by asking the children for one more example in each column. Make the base word with magnetic letters, have a child add the *d* or *ed* ending, and have the class tell whether it sounds like /d/, /t/, or /ed/.

6. Tell the children to place the key words *played*, *melted*, and *walked* at the top of a Three-Way Sort Card. Ask them to take a word card, read it, and place it under the key word that has the same sound at the end. After they have sorted all the word cards, have them read their three columns to a partner. Finally, ask them to copy the three columns on a Three-Way Sort Sheet or in three columns in their Word Study Notebook.

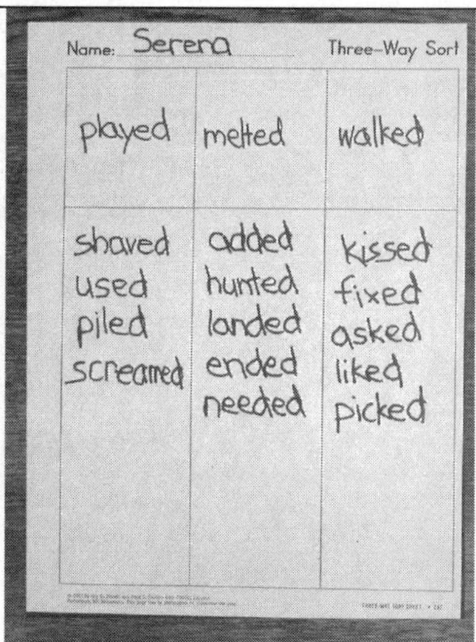

say
sort
read
write

- Have the children say and sort the word cards, read their columns of words to a partner, and write the words on a Three-Way Sort Sheet or in their Word Study Notebooks.

Have the children give one more example for each column on the class chart.

Add an example of each to the word wall.

Link

Interactive Read-Aloud: Read aloud books that include many words that have the *ed* ending. Examples are:

- ***Earthquack*** by Margie Palatini
- ***Dog Days*** by Amanda Harvey

Shared Reading: After you have read and enjoyed one or two poems together, have the children locate words with the *ed* ending and tell whether the ending sounds like /d/, /t/, or /ed/. Some examples to use are "A Mouse in Her Room" (/d/), "New Shoes" (/t/), "Nest Eggs" (/ed/), or "Not a Word" (all three) (see *Sing a Song of Poetry*).

Guided Reading: During word work, write a few words quickly, add *ed,* and have the children read the new words.

Interactive Writing: In texts the children write with you, there will usually be words with the *ed* ending. Prompt children to think about how the ending sounds and how it looks when they write it.

Independent Writing: Teach the children how to check the spelling of words with the *ed* ending when they edit their work.

assess

- Dictate seven or eight words and have the children add the *ed* ending.
- Notice whether the children read words with *ed* endings correctly and spell the words correctly when they write them.

Expand the Learning

Repeat the lesson with a variety of other verbs to give the children more practice. Use the Word Card Template (see *Teaching Resources*) to make cards for the new words you've chosen.

Have the children add more words to the class chart of *ed* endings that make three different sounds.

Connect with Home

Give the children a sheet of word cards (use the Word Card Template in *Teaching Resources*) with verbs that have the *ed* ending to take home and sort on a Three-Way Sort Sheet.

7 Recognizing Syllables in Words

Syllable Sort

Consider Your Children

Most second graders will have had some experience clapping words to indicate syllable breaks and will have no difficulty sorting words by the number of syllables. They may not realize that every syllable has a vowel when you spell it. Check to see whether they can clap syllables, and work with children who have difficulty. Be sure they can read the words they will be sorting. If children have difficulty, you may want to limit the lesson to words of one, two, and three syllables. Use only words the children understand.

Working with English Language Learners

English language learners may be very familiar with the concept of syllables in their own languages. If possible, have them clap a few words from their own languages to identify syllables; the principle is the same. Go over the words you are using and be sure that these children understand their meaning; use pictures if possible. Model saying the words clearly while clapping. Accept approximate pronunciations; working with syllables will help children become more precise in the way they say English words.

You Need

- Chart paper.
- Markers.

From *Teaching Resources:*

- Four-Way Sort Sheets. (Before photocopying them, write the words *bread, cricket, butterfly,* and *pepperoni,* one at the top of each column.)
- Lesson WS 7 Word Cards.

Understand the Principle

Syllables are basic units of words that are easy to hear and that make it possible to break down words into manageable parts. This lesson will help children generalize their knowledge and see the syllable as a unit that they can identify and use to help them decode or spell words. Knowing that every syllable has a vowel is helpful to spellers in structuring words and making more complete attempts.

Explain the Principle

“You can look at the syllables in a word to read it.”

plan

farm	show/er
boat	din/ner
play	ab/sent
skate	crea/ture
beau/ti/ful	pep/per/o/ni
bi/cy/cle	al/li/ga/tor
fan/tas/tic	wa/ter/mel/on
but/ter/fly	cat/er/pil/lar

Explain the Principle

“You can look at the syllables in a word to read it.”

① Explain to the children that they are going to learn about the syllables in words.

② Draw children’s attention to syllables by having them say one-, two-, three-, and four-syllable words. Suggested language: “Listen to the word *hat* [clap once]. Now listen to the word *mother* [clap twice]. Now listen to the word *museum* [clap three times]. When you say these words, you can hear the parts or *syllables*.”

③ Ask the children to say and clap these words as you say each one: *farm, boat, play, skate, shower, dinner, absent, creature, beautiful, bicycle, fantastic, butterfly, pepperoni, alligator, watermelon, caterpillar.*

④ Select a few words to write on the chart, making a slash between the syllables and grouping them according to the number of parts you can hear. Ask the children to discuss what they notice about the words (for example, there is a vowel in every syllable; *dinner* is divided between the *n*s).

⑤ Explain to the children that they are going to say, sort, and write words with one, two, three, and four syllables.

apply

Name: Sandra

bread	cricket	butterfly	pepperoni
boy	playgrond	banana	kindergarten
face	outside	acrobat	watermelon
book	water	everyone	tarantula
desk	believe	magazine	underwater
moon	teacher	bicycle	

take
say
sort
read

▸ Have the children, in pairs, say and sort the syllable word cards. First they place the cards face down. Each child takes a card and says the word aloud to a partner. The partner claps the word. Each child then writes the word under the appropriate column on the Four-Way Sort Sheet. When all the words are listed, have each child add three words of his own to each column. Finally, ask the children to take turns reading their lists to their partner.

Ask the children to share two-, three-, and four-syllable words they added. Add a few more examples to the class chart.

Link

Interactive Read-Aloud: While reading aloud, stop at one or two interesting words and repeat them so the children can listen for the parts. Examples of appropriate books are:

- ***Bill and Pete*** by Tomie de Paola
- ***Little Factory*** by Sarah Weeks

Shared Reading: Invite the children to use a word mask to highlight one-, two-, three-, and four-syllable words. Have the class clap the parts. Poems such as "A, My Name Is Alice," "Caterpillar," and "A Caterpillar Crawled" have examples of one-, two-, three-, and four-syllable words in them.

Guided Reading: When the children have difficulty solving a word, show them how to break it apart. Following the lesson, use the whiteboard or magnetic letters to write or make one-, two-, and three-syllable words. Ask the children to clap the parts; then draw a slash line (or create a space) between the parts.

Interactive Writing: Invite the children to clap words before writing them, particularly two- and three-syllable words.

Independent Writing: Show the child how to use her fingers to "tap" the parts of a word she wants to write. This will help the writer hear the internal sounds.

assess

- Notice whether the children break words into syllables to solve them in reading or writing.
- Notice whether the children, in their writing, are representing a vowel for every syllable (even if the word is not spelled accurately).

Expand the Learning

Repeat the lesson using the first or last names of the children as the examples.

Have the children play Concentration (see *Teaching Resources,* Games) with the syllable word cards for this lesson.

Repeat the lesson with other words. Include only three- and four-syllable words if the children are ready for the challenge. Use the Word Card Template (see *Teaching Resources*) to make cards for the new words you've chosen.

Connect with Home

In a meeting or newsletter, invite family members and children to play a syllable game. Each takes a turn trying to guess a word. The person who thinks up the word gives three clues, the last one telling how many parts the word has. For example, clues for the word *snowballs* might be: *They are white. You make them in the winter. The word has two parts.*

8 Identifying Syllables in Words

Syllable Lotto

Consider Your Children

Use this lesson after your children are able to hear sounds and syllables in words and have control over words with two syllables. CVC and CVC*e* words should also be well under control. The children should be familiar with compound words, words with double consonants, and common affixes such as *ing* and *ed.* They should know how to divide words with open and closed syllables.

Working with English Language Learners

Being able to break words down into syllables is very helpful to English language learners as they develop their ability to pronounce words. Multisyllable words will not be so daunting when they know how to look for the parts. Have them work with cut-up words that they put together and take apart. Be sure the children understand the meaning of the words you select.

You Need

- Whiteboard, chalkboard, or chart paper.
- Markers or chalk.
- Plastic game markers or chips.

From *Teaching Resources:*

- Directions for Lotto.
- Lotto Game Cards (create multiple versions by adding numbers 1 to 4 in various boxes before you photocopy them).
- Word cards from previous lesson (Lesson WS 7 Word Cards).

Understand the Principle

Words are made up of one or more syllables. A syllable is a unit of pronunciation within the word. Each syllable has one vowel sound, although the sound can be represented by more than one vowel *(take, steam).* Helpful principles in taking apart or decoding words with more than one syllable include the following: start by dividing compound words between the two words, remove prefixes and suffixes from the base or root word, and divide syllables between double consonants.

Explain the Principle

“You can look at the syllables in a word to read it.”

plan

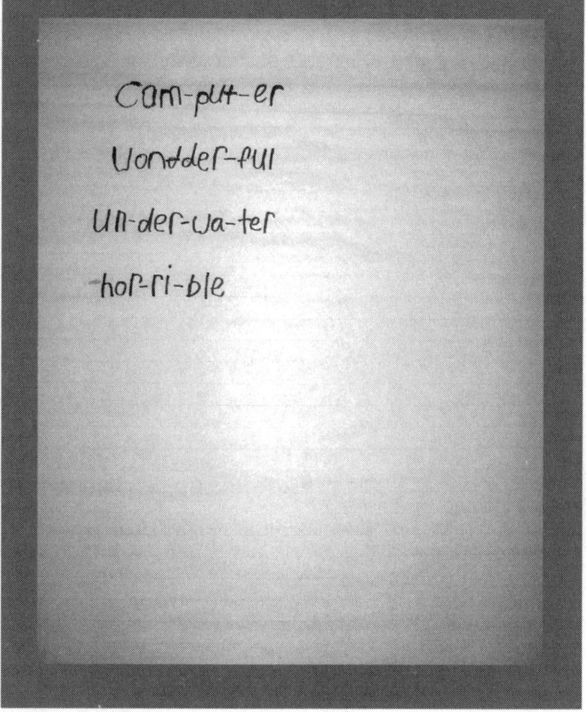

Explain the Principle

“You can look at the syllables in a word to read it.”

① Tell the children that they are going to learn more about syllables.

② Invite them to clap the syllables in a few one- and two-syllable words *(cloth, picnic, basket, napkin).*

③ Then include some three- and four-syllable words *(computer, wonderful, library, underwater).*

④ Have the children say, clap, and then write several three- and four-syllable words on a chart, whiteboard, or chalkboard. Put dashes between the syllables *(un-der-wa-ter).*

⑤ Show the children how to look for a prefix or suffix; explain that these units are also syllables.

⑥ Show the children how to look for syllables in compound words.

⑦ Tell the children they are going to play Syllable Lotto.

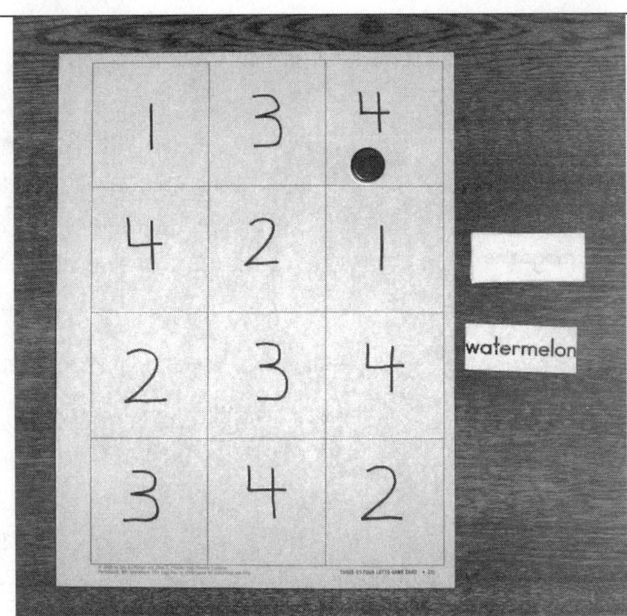

take
say
clap
tell
cover

▸ Have the children play Syllable Lotto in groups of three or four. They take a word card, read it, clap and tell the number of syllables, and cover a game board space with that number (for example, the word *tomato* would allow them to cover a space with the number 3). If they do not have that number on their game board, they can't cover a space. The first player to cover all the spaces on her game board wins the game.

Invite each child to say, clap, and tell a three- or four-syllable word.

Link

Interactive Read-Aloud: Read aloud books that include multisyllable words. Afterward, point out several two-, three-, and four-syllable words. Examples of appropriate books are:

- ***The Story About Ping*** by Marjorie Flack
- ***Liar, Liar Pants on Fire*** by Diane deGroat

Shared Reading: After you have read and enjoyed a poem such as "Away Down East" and "Fuzzy Little Caterpillar" together (see *Sing a Song of Poetry*), have the children locate two-, three-, and four-syllable words.

Guided Reading: When teaching the children how to take new words apart, show them how to identify syllables as a basis for taking words apart. Point out base words with prefixes or suffixes and the parts of compound words.

Interactive Writing: As the children attempt to write new words, encourage them to think about how to write each syllable.

Independent Writing: Prompt the children to look carefully at each syllable in the multisyllable words they write.

assess

- Ask the children to read four or five multisyllable words. Note the way they solve each syllable.
- Read six to ten words on a word list. Have the children look at each word as you say it and draw a slash to show the syllables.

Expand the Learning

Invite the children to add words to a large class chart of three- or four-syllable words on a large wall; set a goal of one hundred words over the next several weeks.

Connect with Home

Have the children look at the print in their neighborhood or home and find five three-syllable words and five four-syllable words.

9 Forming Plurals with s and es

Say and Sort

Consider Your Children

This is the first lesson on looking at how to make singular words plural. Use it after your children are familiar with the concept of plural and can form simple plurals by adding *s*. They should also be skilled in hearing sounds in words.

Working with English Language Learners

Be sure that English language learners have encountered these words in stories they have heard read aloud and read in shared reading. Use concrete objects when necessary to help them understand the concept of plural and link it to the word form. Also, work with them in a small interactive writing group to help them pay attention to the details of plurals and make words plural by coming up to the easel and adding *s* or *es*. Put a number of plural words on a small whiteboard, and ask the children to talk about what they notice.

You Need

- Pocket chart.
- Magnetic letters.

From *Teaching Resources:*

- Pocket Chart Card Template.
- Lesson WS 9 Word Cards.
- Two-Way Sort Sheets.

Understand the Principle

This lesson will help children understand that there are different processes for making nouns plural. For most words, you add *s* or *es*. Children improve their spelling by saying the word and making a connection between the sound of the ending and the spelling. Children learn that *s* does not add a syllable to the word but *es* does add a syllable. They need to look at how the word ends and listen to how they will say the plural form.

Explain the Principle

“ Plural means more than one. ”

“ Add *s* to some words to show you mean more than one (make them plural). ”

“ Add *es* to words that end in *x, ch, sh, s, ss, tch,* or *zz* to make them plural. The *s* at the end sounds like /z/. ”

plan

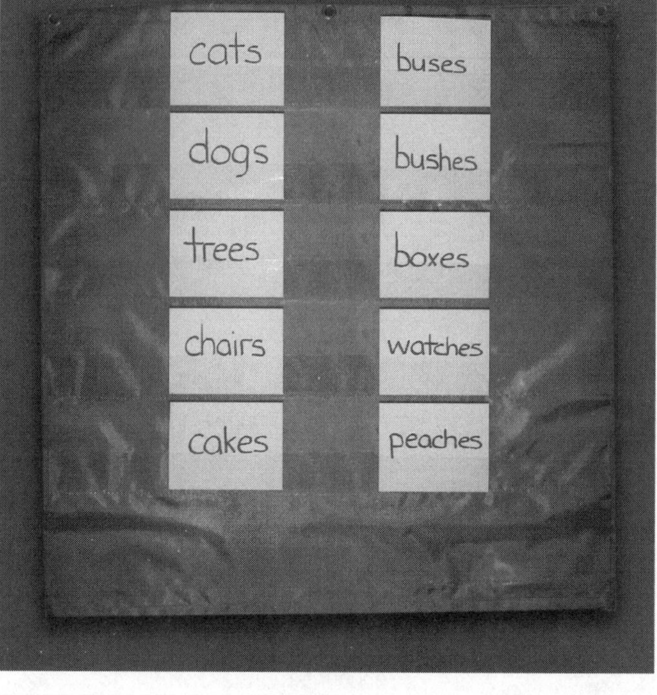

teach

Explain the Principle

“ Plural means more than one. ”

“ Add *s* to some words to show you mean more than one (make them plural). ”

“ Add *es* to words that end in *x, ch, sh, s, ss, tch,* or *zz* to make them plural. The *s* at the end sounds like /z/. ”

① Tell the children that they are going to learn how to write words that mean more than one.

② Start with a collection of word cards showing the two kinds of plurals. Suggested language: “You know that *plural* means more than one. This is one 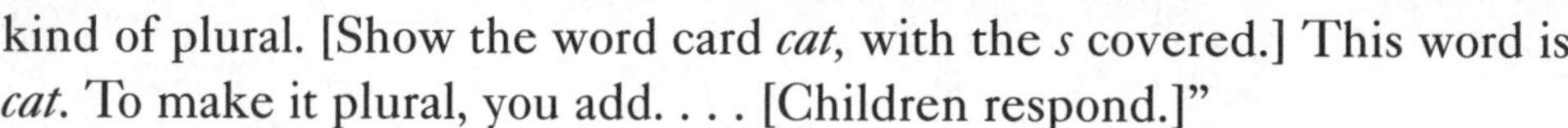kind of plural. [Show the word card *cat,* with the *s* covered.] This word is *cat.* To make it plural, you add. . . . [Children respond.]”

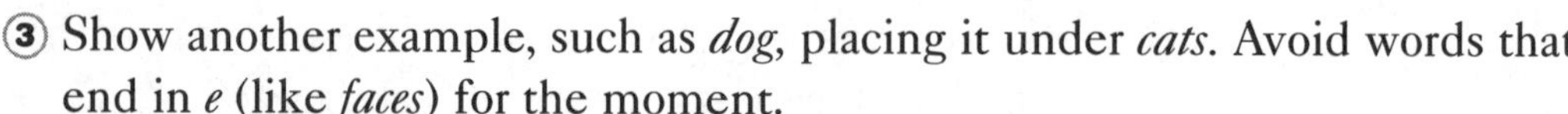

③ Show another example, such as *dog,* placing it under *cats.* Avoid words that end in *e* (like *faces*) for the moment.

④ Then show the children the word *buses.* Suggested language: “Here’s another word, *bus.* I’m going to say the plural—*buses.*” Have the children say the word and think about how it sounds at the end. Show children the word *buses.* “What did I add at the end of this word?” Children may respond.

⑤ Show another example of a plural that ends in *es.* Help the children notice that when you add *es* to a word you can hear another syllable.

⑥ Then show more examples of each kind of plural (*peaches, watches, chairs, cakes, bushes, boxes,* etc.). Ask children to tell you where to place them on the pocket chart—under *s* or under *es.*

⑦ Suggested language: “How are these kinds of plurals different?” Point out some differences yourself if necessary. Comments like these are an indication that children are analyzing words and thinking about the principles:

“One adds *s,* and the other you add *es.*”

“Some sound like /z/, and some sound like /s/.”

“All the ones with *es* sound like /z/, like *boxes,* at the end.”

⑧ Explain to the children that they are going to make words that end in *s* and *es.*

take
say word
make
write
add *s* or *es*
write

- Children take a word card and say the word, make it with magnetic letters, and then write it in the first column of a Two-Way Sort Sheet. Then they make the word plural by adding *s* or *es*. Then they write the plural form in the second column of the sheet.
- Have them create twenty word pairs, writing on the back of the form if necessary.

Ask children to share one pair of words from their list.

Ask them to talk about what they have noticed about plurals.

Place one example of each kind of plural on the word wall.

Link

Interactive Read-Aloud: Read aloud books that include a lot of plural word forms. Point out the *s* and *es* plurals. Examples of appropriate books are:

- ***The Kiss that Missed*** by David Melling
- ***Marvin of the Great North Woods*** by Kathryn Lasky

Shared Reading: Find plural nouns that end in *s* and *es* in the poems you are reading, such as "Where Go the Boats," "Apples, Peaches," and "Wash the Dishes" (see *Sing a Song of Poetry*).

Guided Reading: During word work, make a noun with magnetic letters, and then make it again as a plural. Repeat with three to five words.

Interactive Writing: Call attention to the principle when the children want to write plural nouns. Ask children who are having difficulty with the principle to come up to the easel and write the plural ending.

Independent Writing: Draw attention to the principles for forming plurals while conferring with the children about their writing.

Expand the Learning

Make a summary chart of plurals with *s* and *es.*

Play Concentration (see *Teaching Resources,* Games) with singular and plural forms (*s* and *es*) of nouns.

Connect with Home

Ask family members to help children find examples of plurals with *s* and *es* in newspapers or magazines. The children can bring these examples to school and add them to the class chart.

assess

- Notice whether the children are using conventional plural forms for nouns that require adding *s* or *es.*
- Include four to six plural nouns on a quick spelling test.

10 Understanding Contractions of am, is, and will Phrases

Contraction Lotto

Consider Your Children

Your children will have encountered many contractions in reading and writing and will likely be familiar with the concept from their work in Grade 1. They will probably be able to read most of the words in the lesson easily and will therefore be able to focus on the principle of how contractions are constructed. In this lesson they learn how to omit specific letters in the contracted form and replace them with an apostrophe. Be sure they do not confuse a possessive (apostrophe *s*) with a contraction.

Working with English Language Learners

It's important for English language learners to hear contractions frequently in oral language if they are to use them in their writing. They should also see them often in the texts they read. They will need many demonstrations with simple contractions so they know how to put them together and take them apart. Work with a small group of children who have difficulty with the concept, using magnetic letters to make the demonstration very concrete. Be sure to use the contractions in full sentences.

You Need

- Magnetic letters.
- Cookie sheet.
- Index cards.
- Markers.

From *Teaching Resources:*

- Directions for Lotto.
- Lotto Game Cards (with a contraction of an *am, is,* or *will* phrase in each box).
- Lesson WS 10 Word Cards.

Understand the Principle

Children need to understand how contractions are constructed in order to know what the words mean when they read them and spell them conventionally when they write them. In most contractions, the form of the words in the original phrase doesn't change, but there are some exceptions, such as *will not,* which becomes *won't.* You will need to help children distinguish possessives from contractions.

Explain the Principle

“A contraction is one word made from two words.”

“To make a contraction, put two words together and leave out a letter or letters. Write an apostrophe where the letter(s) are left out.”

plan

Explain the Principle

"A contraction is one word made from two words."

"To make a contraction, put two words together and leave out a letter or letters. Write an apostrophe where the letter(s) are left out."

1. Explain to the children that they are going to learn about some words they see many times when they read and use many times when they write.

2. Using magnetic letters, make the words *I'm, it's, he's, she's, here's, that's,* and *there's* on the cookie sheet. Have the children read the words with you.

3. Ask the children what they notice about all these words. They will likely notice that they all have an apostrophe or that they end with an apostrophe and *s*. Some of the children may know that the words are contractions, a word made from two words.

4. Confirm the correct statements, and help the children see that each word is a shortened form of two words by taking out the apostrophe and making the two complete words (*I am, it is, he is,* for example).

5. Summarize by having the children create contractions from some of the two-word phrases by removing the appropriate letters and putting in the apostrophe.

6. Articulate the principles: "A contraction is one word made from two words. To make a contraction, put two words together and leave out a letter or letters. Write an apostrophe where the letters are left out."

7. Repeat with the contractions *I'll, he'll, she'll, we'll,* and *they'll.*

8. Tell the children that today they have worked with contractions made from phrases that have *am, is,* or *will* in them.

9. Explain to the children that today they are going to play Contraction Lotto with game cards that have a contraction in each box. They will take turns drawing a card, reading the two words, telling the contraction made from

the words, and covering a box (or boxes—some contractions will be repeated) on their cards if the box contains the contraction. The first to cover all the boxes wins the game.

10 Finally, have the children list five contractions made with *is*, *am*, or *will* on an index card to share with the group.

take card
read two words
tell contraction
cover square

- Have the children play Contraction Lotto in groups of three, four, or five. Ask them to read the word cards they pick, say the contractions, and look for them on their game cards.
- Have children write five contractions on an index card.

Have the children read one contraction from the lists on their index cards and tell the two words that make it. Have the children check a partner's index card for the correct spelling of the five contractions. Put an example of each type of contraction on the word wall.

Link

Interactive Read-Aloud: Read aloud books that contain contractions, and have the children tell a few contractions they heard. Examples of appropriate books are:

- ***I'll Always Be Your Friend*** by Sam McBratney
- ***If You Take a Mouse to School*** by Laura Numeroff

Shared Reading: After enjoying poems such as "Five Waiting Pumpkins," "I Hear Thunder," or "Once I Saw a Bunny" together, have the children locate two or three contractions.

Guided Reading: During word work, have the children write three or four two-word phrases and then write the contractions. Alternatively, have the children make the words and contractions with magnetic letters.

Interactive Writing: As the children write contractions, help them notice where the letters are left out and an apostrophe is inserted.

Independent Writing: Have the children reread and edit their writing for correct spelling of contractions.

assess

- Observe the spelling of contractions in the children's writing, making notes about further minilessons needed on the topic.
- Dictate five or six two-word phrases and have the children write the contractions.

Expand the Learning

Have the children play Contraction Concentration (see the Directions for Concentration in *Teaching Resources*).

Have the children play Contraction Lotto a different way. Write two-word phrases in some boxes on the game card and contractions in others. Place the same phrases and contractions on the word cards. Have the children say and look for the contraction if the word card contains a two-word phrase or the two-word phrase if the word card contains a contraction.

Connect with Home

Send home the Contraction Lotto Game Cards and word cards and have the children play the game with family members.

11 Forming Contractions of not and are Phrases

Contraction Concentration

Consider the Children

Use this lesson after the lesson on the easier contractions of *am, is,* and *will* phrases. Contractions of *not* and *are* phrases are also very common, so the children should find them easy to understand. The greater challenges are spelling them correctly and placing the apostrophe correctly. You may want to create a chart with columns and review the types of contractions you've already taught.

Working with English Language Learners

The simple contractions in this lesson help English language learners expand their vocabularies. Be sure to use the contractions in full sentences so the children develop their knowledge of contractions within an appropriate, meaningful syntactical structure. Say the sentence first with the word phrase and then with the contraction and have the children repeat the sentence each time so they hear it and say it before they see the words. You may want to write the whole sentence for a small group of English language learners.

You Need

- Chart paper.
- Markers.

From *Teaching Resources:*

- Directions for Concentration.
- Concentration Game Cards made from WS 11 Word Cards and Deck Card Template.

Understand the Principle

Contractions are used frequently in speaking and writing, and children need to learn how to recognize them quickly while reading and spell them accurately while writing. The contractions with *not* are regular except for *won't.* The contractions with *are* are very consistent in their formation, though *they're* is often confused with its homophones *their* and *there.* You will need to point out frequently that *they're* means *they are.*

Explain the Principle

" To make a contraction, put two words together and leave out a letter or letters. Write an apostrophe where the letter(s) are left out. "

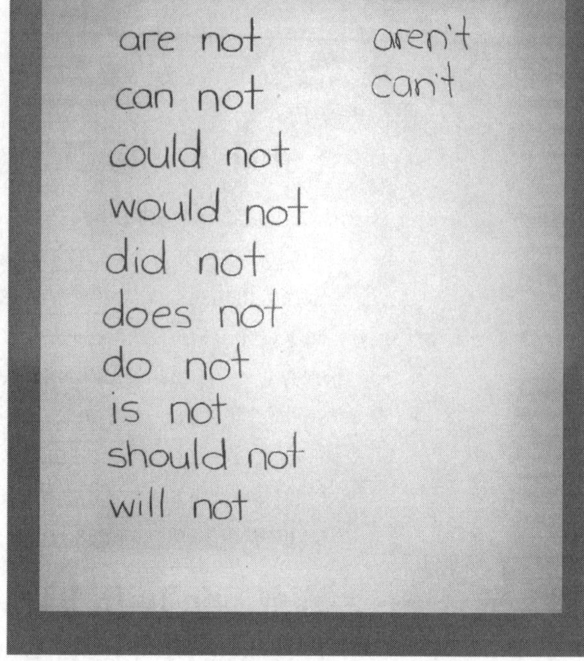

Explain the Principle

"To make a contraction, put two words together and leave out a letter or letters. Write an apostrophe where the letter(s) are left out."

1. Tell the children they are going to learn more about contractions.
2. On a board, in a column on the left, write (or make with magnetic letters) the words *are not, can not, could not, would not, did not, does not, do not, is not, should not,* and *will not.*
3. Explain to the children that they have learned how to make contractions by putting two words together, removing one or more letters, and placing an apostrophe where letters are left out.
4. Read the list of words to the children and have them read them with you to be sure all the words are known. You may want to use them in sentences.
5. Invite one child at a time to the board to make a contraction. Each time, point out the letter or letters that have been removed. Show the children how most of these contractions retain the whole first word and replace the *o* in *not* with an apostrophe. Point out that the word *won't* is an exception.
6. Read the list of contractions with the group and reiterate that each contraction involves the word *not.*
7. Repeat with phrases ending with *are: we are, you are, they are.*
8. Articulate the principle: "To make a contraction, put two words together and leave out a letter or letters. Write an apostrophe where the letter(s) are left out."
9. Have the children play Contraction Concentration by matching two-word phrases with the appropriate contraction.

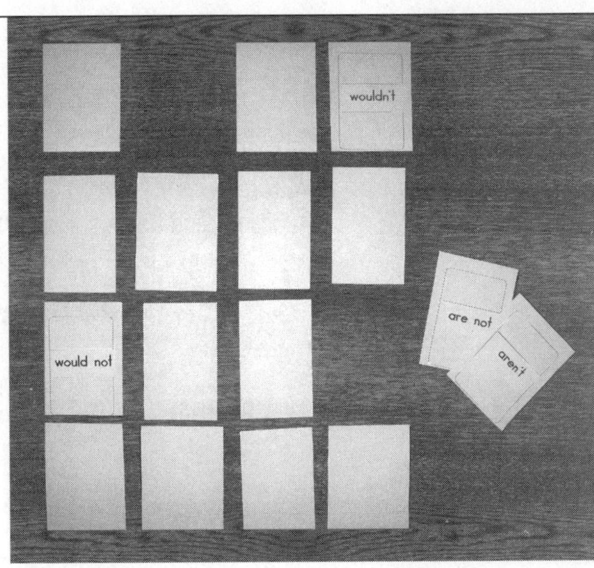

apply

turn
read
turn
read
match

- Have the children play Contraction Concentration with a partner or in a group of three.

Have the children, on a whiteboard, use magnetic letters to make two or three contractions of two-word phrases ending with *not* or *are*. You may want to create a written chart for reference. Place an example of each type of contraction on the word wall.

Link

Interactive Read-Aloud: Read aloud books in which the children will hear a variety of contractions and be able to add them to their vocabularies. Examples are:

- ***You Can't Taste a Pickle with Your Ear*** by Harriet Ziefert
- ***Chicken Soup by Heart*** by Esther Hershenhorn

Shared Reading: Read and enjoy a variety of poems that include contractions, such as "If You're Happy and You Know It" and "Shoo Fly" (see *Sing a Song of Poetry*). Then have the children locate the contractions and tell the two words that form them.

Guided Reading: After reading and discussing a text, have the children locate two or three contractions. During word work, write several two-word phrases on a whiteboard and have the children tell the contracted form of each phrase.

Interactive Writing: Help the children notice contractions they are trying to write. Remind them that the apostrophe is usually placed where the letters are left out.

Independent Writing: Remind the children to check the spelling of contractions and the placement of the apostrophe in the editing process.

assess

- Observe the children's spelling of contractions made from two words ending with *not* or *are.*
- Give the children a page of text. Have them circle the contractions and then write the contractions and the two words used to form them.
- Dictate several contractions of two-word phrases ending with *not* or *are* to determine whether the children are able to spell them correctly.

Expand the Learning

Have the children find contractions and list them on a board headed *Contraction Hunt.* Tell them they can only add contractions that are not already listed.

Add the two-word phrases ending with *am, is,* and *are* and the contractions made from them (see Lesson WS 10) to the Contraction Concentration deck.

Repeat the lesson using two-word phrases ending with *have* and *had.*

Have children play Follow the Path with contractions or two-word phrases in each space (see *Teaching Resources* for directions). When they land on each space, children tell the contraction if the space contains a two-word phrase or the two-word phrase if the space contains a contraction.

Connect with Home

Send home the Contraction Concentration cards and have the children play the game with family members.

Send home two sheets of word cards. One sheet has one word of a contractible phrase on each card. The other sheet contains contractions. Have children match two uncontracted words with the appropriate contraction and read them to family members.

12 Summarizing Contractions (am, is, will, not, are, have, had)

Word Sort

Consider the Children

Teach this lesson after the children have worked with each contraction category. This lesson summarizes and consolidates their knowledge. Some of the contractions are easy to decode and construct, while others are more challenging.

Working with English Language Learners

It is important for English language learners to hear the contractions in full sentences so they can associate them with a meaningful context. Once they understand the concept of contractions and understand their structure, they will be able to use what they know in reading and writing. Reviewing the principle and examples on the summary chart will solidify their knowledge, and the chart will serve as a useful reference.

You Need

- Chart paper.
- Markers.

From *Teaching Resources:*

- Lesson WS 12 Word Cards.
- Two-Column Sheets.
- Three-Way Sort Sheets (with three key words added at the top).

Understand the Principle

Contractions appear often in oral and written language. Once children understand that contractions are formed from two other words, they will understand contractions better and use them in writing. Remember that the designation *'d* in a contraction can mean either *had* or *would,* and that the word *is* or *has* can be used with names of people, places, or objects—*Carol's going home* or *Carol's gone home,* for example.

Explain the Principle

"To make a contraction, put two words together and leave out a letter or letters. Write an apostrophe where the letter(s) are left out."

plan

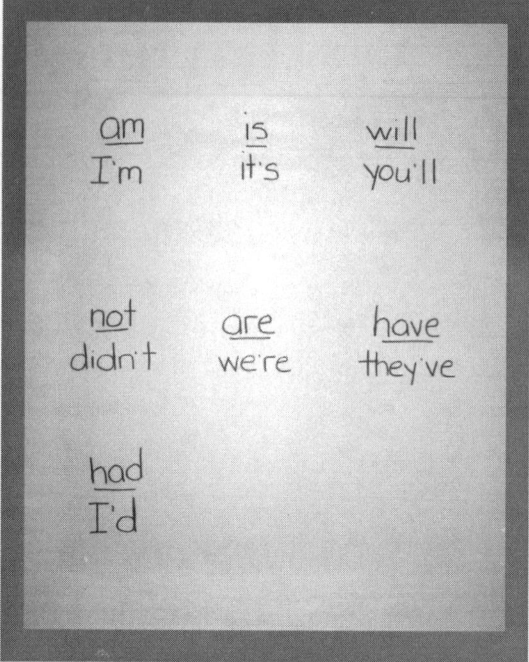

am
I'm
is
it's
will
you'll
not
didn't
are
we're
have
they've
had
I'd

Explain the Principle

"To make a contraction, put two words together and leave out a letter or letters. Write an apostrophe where the letter(s) are left out."

① Explain to the children that they are going to learn about many different contractions.

② On a chart, write the words *am, is, will, not, are, have, had,* each at the top of a column. In each column include one contraction made with that word. (There is only one contraction for *am.*)

③ Invite the children to read the words with you and explain that the word at the top of each column is part of each contraction below it.

④ Ask the children to suggest other examples for each category and tell the two words that form the contraction.

⑤ Alternatively, hold up large contraction word cards and ask the children in which column to place them.

⑥ Continue until you and the children have listed or placed each contraction in the correct category. If the children suggest other contractions that fit, add them to the correct column. If they suggest others that don't fit an existing category, such as *let's*, explain the words that are being contracted and start a new column.

⑦ Review the principle.

⑧ Explain to the children that they will work with a partner to sort contraction word cards into three columns according to the key words (*not, will,* and *is,* or alternatively *are, have,* and *had*). One child sorts the cards, and the partner checks the sort and reads the columns. Then the cards are removed and shuffled, and the other child sorts.

⑨ Finally, each child takes a Two-Column Sheet, selects twenty contraction cards, and writes the contraction in the left column and the two words from which the contraction is formed in the right column.

- take card
- say word
- sort
- check list
- read list
- write contraction
- write two words

- Have the children work in pairs to complete a Three-Way Sort.
- Then have each child write twenty contractions and their two components on a Two-Column Sheet.

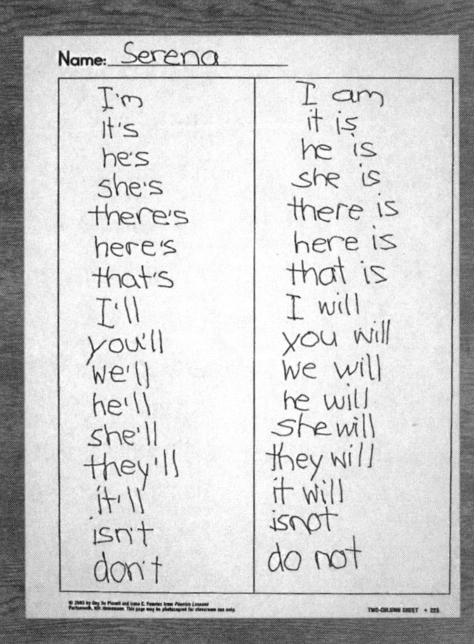

Name: Serena
I'm
it's
he's
she's
there's
here's
that's
I'll
you'll
we'll
he'll
she'll
they'll
it'll
isn't
don't
I am
it is
he is
she is
there is
here is
that is
I will
you will
we will
he will
she will
they will
it will
isnot
do not

Invite the children to read their contraction Two-Column Sheets to a different partner.

Link

Interactive Read-Aloud: Read aloud books that feature many contractions, such as

- ***Farfallina and Marcel*** by Holly Keller
- ***The Burger and the Hot Dog*** by Jim Aylesworth

Shared Reading: After reading poems such as "Take Me Out to the Ballgame" or "Two Little Kittens" (see *Sing a Song of Poetry*) together, have the children circle the contractions or highlight them with colored transparent tape.

Guided Reading: During word work, write two words on the whiteboard and invite the children to tell the contracted form. Repeat for a variety of contractions.

Interactive Writing: Point out instances of two words that can be put together to form a contraction.

Independent Writing: Point out contractions the children use in their writing.

Expand the Learning

Repeat the lesson by reviewing the chart and having the children sort contractions of two-word phrases ending with the three key words not used in the initial sort.

Give the children the Words Around the Room Sheet (see *Teaching Resources*). Write *not, is, will, are, have,* and *had* as the categories. Have the children read around the room and list as many contractions as they can for each category.

Connect with Home

Send home the contraction word cards for children to sort with family members.

assess

- Dictate a sampling of seven or eight contractions of two-word phrases ending with *is, will, not, are, have, had,* in order to assess the children's understanding.
- Use contraction word cards and word cards containing the corresponding two words (use the Word Card Template in *Teaching Resources*) for a matching task. Have the children find the two words that make each contraction and write the equation: for example, *is* + *not* = *isn't.*

13 Forming Comparisons with -er, -est

Word Pictures

Consider Your Children

In this lesson, children learn how to compare two items or show the greatest degree of a characteristic with words that have *-er* or *-est* added to the base word. Your children should have heard comparative forms in spoken language and in the books you've read aloud, so that these structures will be familiar. Use words that are part of the children's oral vocabularies.

Working with English Language Learners

Comparative forms are a challenge to children who are just beginning to learn English. Be sure you have read many books that illustrate comparatives in an engaging way; point out the words the author is using, and have the children repeat them. Repeated readings of appropriate poems in shared reading will also help them become familiar with comparatives. Also use interactive writing (with pictures or concrete objects) to help these children understand *-er* and *-est* endings. For example: "John has a new ball. Sirie has a newer ball. Raji has the newest ball." Let the children come up to the easel to put on the *-er* and *-est* endings.

You Need

- Magnetic letters.
- Chart paper.
- Markers.

From *Teaching Resources:*

- Three-Column Sheets.
- Lesson WS 13 Word Cards.

Understand the Principle

It is important for children to hear, read, and write words in their conventional form. Children need to learn that when you compare or show the most of a characteristic, you add another syllable to the word (*-er* or *-est*). In this lesson, the spelling does not change when the ending is added. So you can focus on the ending without being concerned about the spelling of the base word.

Explain the Principle

"Add *-er* or *-est* to show how one thing compares with another."

Explain the Principle

"Add *-er* or *-est* to show how one thing compares with another."

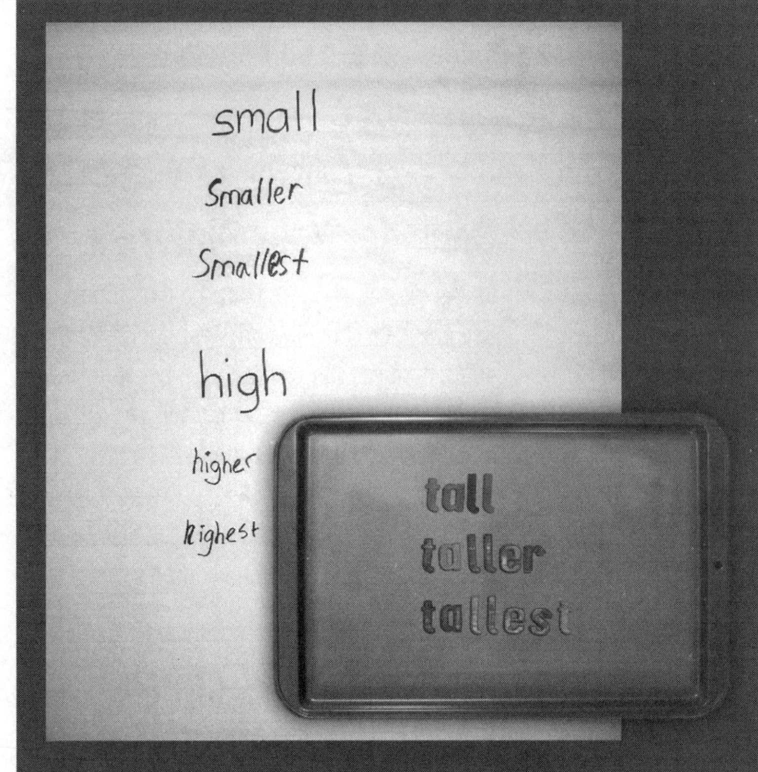

1. Tell the children that today you are going to help them notice something interesting about words.

2. Ask two children, one who is shorter than you are and one who is shorter than both you and the other child, to help you demonstrate the concept. Suggested language: "If I say Erica [the shorter of the two children] is tall, then Matt is tall__. [Children respond, "Taller."] I am the tall___. [Children respond, "Tallest."] Yes, I am the tallest."

3. "Take a look at these words." Put *tall, taller,* and *tallest* on a magnetic cookie sheet with magnetic letters (or on the chart), showing how you start with *tall,* then add *-er,* and then add *-est.*

4. Now write *small* on the chart. Ask the children to come up and write *smaller* and then *smallest.*

5. Repeat with *high, low, young, old.*

6. Summarize by helping the children understand that adding *-er* means more and adding *-est* means most.

7. Also remind them that when they add *-er* or *-est,* they hear an additional word part (have them clap the word to hear the added syllable).

8. Explain to the children that today they are going to add *-er* and *-est* to a number of words.

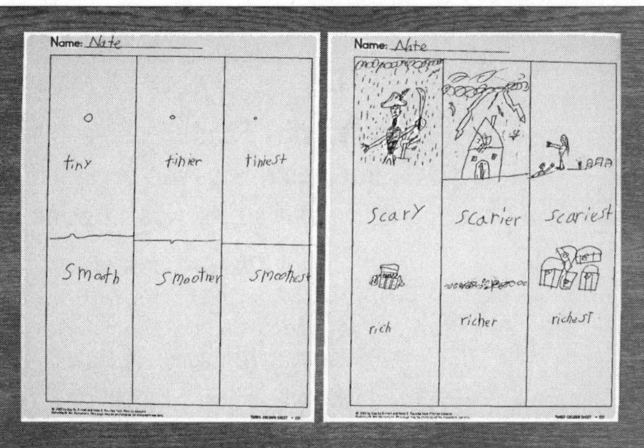

take
draw
write
add
draw
write
add
draw
write

▸ Have the children use word cards to write and illustrate several sets of comparative and superlative word forms on the two sides of a Three-Column Sheet. Ask them to take a word card (*tall,* for example), draw a small picture in the first column of something the word might describe, and label the picture with the word. Then they will add *-er* and *-est* to the word and draw two more pictures, one in the second and one in the third column.

Have the children suggest three more words and tell how to change them to make them first comparative and then superlative.

Place an example of a word with *-er* and one with *-est* on the word wall.

Link

Interactive Read-Aloud: Read aloud books that feature words with comparative and superlative endings. Examples are:

- ***Things That Are Most in the World*** by Judi Barrett
- ***Biggest, Strongest, Fastest*** by Steve Jenkins

Shared Reading: Read poems that involve comparisons such as "Taking Off," "Bunnies Bedtime," and "Good, Better, Best" (see *Sing a Song of Poetry*), and have children use highlighter tape, a highlighter pen, or a masking card to call attention to words with *-er* or *-est.*

Guided Reading: When the children are trying to read words with *-er* and *-est,* show them how they can take off the ending and read the base word and then add the final syllable. During word work, write four or five words on the whiteboard, and then add *-er* and *-est.* Then have the children make two or three words with magnetic letters and do the same.

Interactive Writing: Point out words that compare and have *-er* or *-est* as children attempt to write them.

Independent Writing: When helping writers use description, model how they can compare one object to another by using the *-er* or *-est* ending.

assess

- Notice the children's use of comparisons in their oral language and in their writing.
- Dictate two or three words and have the children add *-er* or *-est.*

Expand the Learning

Repeat the lesson with words ending with a short vowel and one consonant (CVC or CCVC), such as *big* and *thin.*

Repeat the lesson to teach the principle for adding *-er* and *-est* to words ending in *e* (*cute, cuter, cutest,* for example): add *-r* and *-st* to words ending in *e.*

Repeat the lesson to teach the principle for adding *-er* and *-est* to words ending in *y* (*funny, funnier, funniest,* for example): change the *y* to *i* and add *-er* and *-est.*

Use the Word Card Template (see *Teaching Resources*) to make cards for the new words you've chosen.

Connect with Home

Give the children a blank Four-Box Sheet (see *Teaching Resources*) to take home, and ask them to create four different sets of comparative and superlative pictures with family members.

14 Forming Past Tense: Double the Consonant and Add ed

Making Words

Consider Your Children

This lesson introduces a spelling change when adding the *ed* ending and should therefore follow lessons on adding *ed* or *d* to words (verbs) when there is no spelling change to the base word. Select words the children will understand.

Working with English Language Learners

Work with English language learners orally to be sure they can use the past tense for a number of verbs. They should be familiar with the examples and their meanings. Have them work with magnetic letters to emphasize doubling the consonant. Have them write the words and highlight the double consonant in yellow.

You Need

- Chart paper.
- Markers.
- Magnetic letters.

From *Teaching Resources:*

- Lesson WS 14 Word Cards.
- List Sheets.

Understand the Principle

When children are able to notice base words and their affixes (groups of letters added to the beginning or ending), they understand more about what the words mean and how to spell them. A suffix is one kind of affix that is added to the end of a word. The *ed* suffix is added to show past tense. Sometimes the spelling of the base word changes when the suffix is added. Knowing to be alert for changes in spelling when adding a suffix will help children improve their spelling.

Explain the Principle

“You add word parts to the ending of words to show you did something in the past.”

“Double the consonant before adding *ed* to words ending in a short vowel and one consonant. Add *ed* if the word ends with a vowel and a double consonant.”

plan

teach

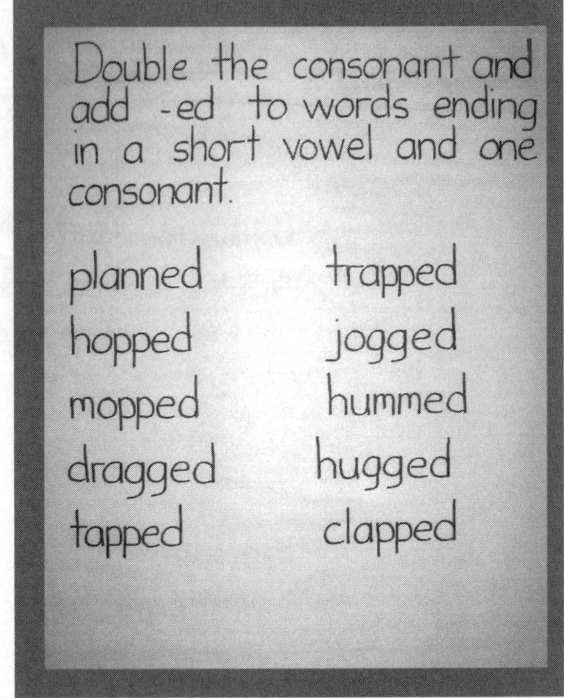

Double the consonant and add -ed to words ending in a short vowel and one consonant.
planned
trapped
hopped
jogged
mopped
hummed
dragged
hugged
tapped
clapped

Explain the Principle

"You add word parts to the ending of words to show you did something in the past."

"Double the consonant before adding *ed* to words ending in a short vowel and one consonant. Add *ed* if the word ends with a vowel and a double consonant."

① Explain to the children that they are going to learn more about how words are spelled when *ed* is added to show something happened in the past.

② Have the words *planned, hummed, trapped, dragged, hopped, hugged, jogged, tapped, mopped*, and *clapped* written on a chart.

③ Suggested language: "Read these words with me. What do you notice about all of them?" Children will notice:

"They all end in *ed*."

"*ed* sounds like /d/ or /t/."

"They have two consonants before *ed*."

"They all tell something done in the past."

"They are all things you can do (verbs)."

④ Ask the children to point out the base word, the word to which the *ed* ending was added. With a colored marker or highlighter tape (or by underlining), highlight the base word. Help the children see that there was one vowel and the vowel sound was short.

⑤ Guide the children to notice how the spelling changed when *ed* was added. They will notice that the final consonant was doubled.

⑥ To summarize, write the heading, *Double the consonant before adding* ed *to words with a short vowel and one consonant at the end.*

⑦ Demonstrate the process of changing the spelling. Make a word with magnetic letters on an easel—*sip*, for example. Add another *p* and *ed*.

⑧ Explain to the children that today they will take a word card and make the word with magnetic letters. Then they will change the spelling by doubling the consonant and adding *ed* if the word ends with a short vowel and one consonant. They will add *d* or *ed* to words that don't need a spelling change. They will do this for twenty words and then write their words on a List Sheet. Finally, they will read the list to a partner.

take
add
write
read

▸ Have the children select twenty word cards, add *ed*, and change the spelling if needed. Then they write the new words on a List Sheet and read their list to a partner.

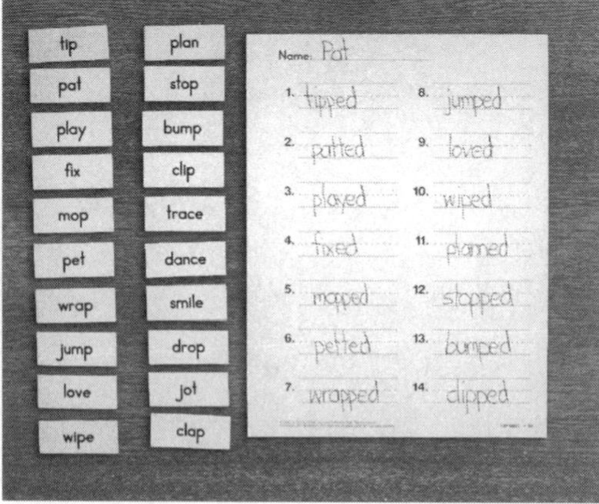

Have the children make two or three words with magnetic letters on the easel and add *ed*. Put an example of a word that requires doubling the consonant on the word wall.

Link

Interactive Read-Aloud: Read aloud books that include many words with suffixes. Examples are:

- ***Bearsie Bear and the Surprise Sleepover Party*** by Bernard Waber
- ***Mean Soup*** by Betsy Everitt

Shared Reading: After you have read a whole text one or two times, such as "The Turtle" or "The Goat" (see *Sing a Song of Poetry*), have the children locate verbs that have double consonants before the *ed.*

Guided Reading: During word work, have the children make or write three or four words with a short vowel and consonant and add *ed.*

Interactive Writing: Help the children notice the pattern in words to which they add *ed.*

Independent Writing: Teach the children to notice the spelling of words ending in *ed* when they are editing.

assess

- Dictate five or six base words and have the children add *ed.*
- Notice the children's spelling of words with the *ed* ending and their ability to read words accurately and quickly when they have *ed* endings.

Expand the Learning

Invite the children to add words with a short vowel, a double consonant, and *ed* to the class chart.

Connect with Home

Send home a sheet of base words for children to practice adding *ed* with family members.

Generative Lesson

15 Adding -er and Doubling the Consonant

Making Words

Consider Your Children

This lesson should follow the lesson on adding *-er* and *-est* to verbs that do not require a spelling change in the base word (Lesson WS 13). In this lesson, the children learn how to change the spelling of a base word when *-er* is added. Children should understand the base words you are using and have worked with adding and removing endings.

Working with English Language Learners

English language learners may have difficulty understanding that not only does a word's spelling (and pronunciation) change when you add the *-er* ending, so does the part of speech and the meaning. Use words in sentences, or put an article such as *the* or *a* in front of the word with *-er* to signal that it is a noun. Have students put the ending on with magnetic letters or highlight it to draw their attention to the added letters. Discuss the changes in the word, and highlight the double letters in a different color.

You Need

- Magnetic letters.
- Chart paper.
- Markers.

From *Teaching Resources:*

- List Sheets.
- Lesson WS 15 Word Cards.

Understand the Principle

The suffix *-er* is added to a base verb to change it to a noun. Adding the *-er* creates a noun representing a person who "does something." When *-er* is added to some words, the spelling is not changed (*painter,* for example). In this lesson, children learn that when *-er* is added to words that end in a short vowel and a single consonant, the consonant is doubled before the ending is added *(rob, robber).*

Explain the Principle

"Double the consonant and add *-er* to words ending in a short vowel and one consonant."

plan

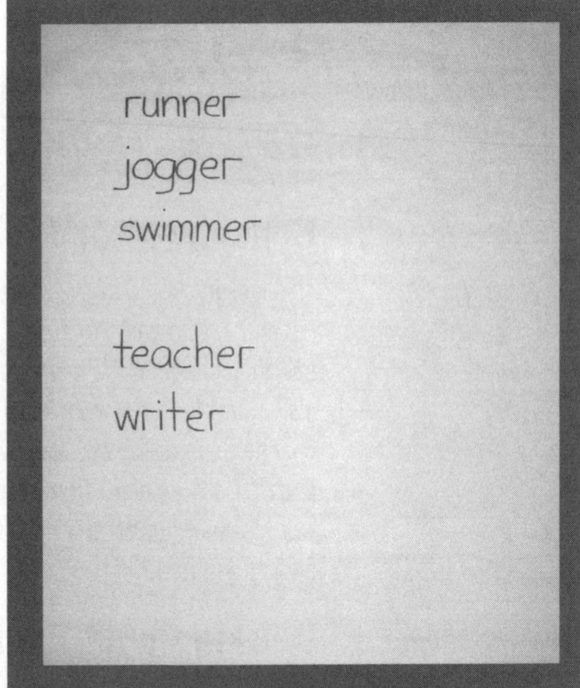

Explain the Principle

"Double the consonant and add *-er* to words ending in a short vowel and one consonant."

① Tell the children that they are going to learn more about adding the suffix *-er* to words.

② Make the words *run, jog,* and *swim* with magnetic letters, or write them on a chart. Read the base word *run* and make it say *runner.* Repeat with *jogger* and *swimmer.*

③ Ask the children what they notice about the words you made. They will likely notice you doubled the consonant and added *-er.*

④ Explain that the base words *run, jog,* and *swim* have a short vowel and one consonant at the end. You may want to contrast them with words such as *teach/teacher* and *write/writer.*

⑤ Summarize the principle and write it at the top of the chart.

⑥ Explain to the children that they are going to make twenty words with *-er.* They will take a word card, make the word with magnetic letters, and add *-er.* They will change the spelling of the base word only if they need to. They will repeat the process until they have made twenty words. Then they will write their words on a List Sheet.

apply

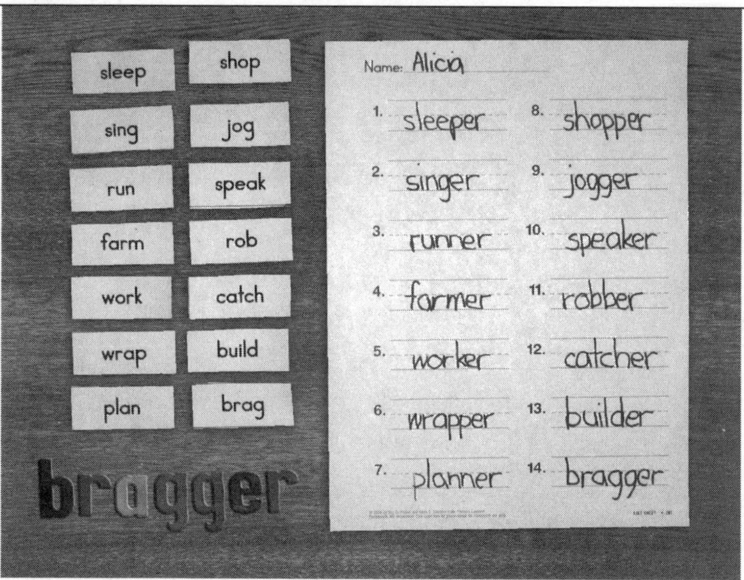

take
make
add
write

- Have the children take a word card, make the word with magnetic letters, add *-er*, and write the word with the suffix on a List Sheet.

Invite the children to read their lists to a partner.

Place an example of a word with a doubled consonant on the word wall.

Link

Interactive Read-Aloud: Read aloud books with verbs that have the *-er* ending, such as

- ***Back to School for Rotten Ralph*** by Jack Gantos
- ***Building a House*** by Byron Barton

Shared Reading: For the first reading of a poem, use stick-on notes to cover two or three words with *-er* endings. Have the children use the language of the sentence to predict the word and tell the spelling.

Guided Reading: When the children are trying to solve words with *-er* suffixes, show them how to use a finger to block out the ending and look at the base word first.

Interactive Writing: When the children are going to write a new word with an *-er* ending, help them think about whether the spelling of the base word should change.

Independent Writing: When the children attempt to write a word with an *-er* ending, demonstrate how to change the spelling of the base word before adding *-er* if needed.

assess

- Dictate five or six words, some of which require a spelling change when *-er* is added, to assess the children's control of the principle.

Expand the Learning

Repeat the lesson with words that have *-or* added *(collector, inventor, survivor, actor, visitor)*. Use the Word Card Template (see *Teaching Resources*) to make cards for the new words you've chosen.

Connect with Home

Send home a list of words for children to make with magnetic letters (or letter cards, see *Teaching Resources*) and add *-er*.

16 Adding Suffixes to Words Ending in y

Make and Write

Consider Your Children

This lesson should follow lessons on adding *es* and *ed* to words requiring no spelling change and words requiring a doubling of the final consonant. Children should be familiar with these forms of words in their oral language and should have worked with simple suffixes, such as adding *s* or *ed*.

Working with English Language Learners

English language learners will need simple examples and many repetitions to understand verb endings. Inflectional endings are often difficult for English learners. Demonstrate and then have them work in pairs to create simple sentences that will help them understand the function of verbs. A few powerful examples will help them build categories for these words. You will want to help them notice the endings in print because they often leave them off in spoken language.

You Need

- Magnetic letters.
- Chart paper.
- Markers.
- Cookie sheet.

From *Teaching Resources:*

- Three-Column Sheets.
- Lesson WS 16 Word Cards.

Understand the Principle

Children need to understand that there are base words to which suffixes are added. *s* and *ed* are suffixes that indicate present and past tense. The *s* is added to show present tense in relation to singular subjects; *ed* is added to show past tense. When these suffixes are added to words, they can sound different, depending on the base word *(walked, melted)* and they can require a change in the spelling of the base word *(cried)*.

Explain the Principle

“You can add word parts to the end of a word to show you did something in the present or in the past.”

“Change the *y* to *i* and add *es* or *ed* to words that end in a consonant and *y*.”

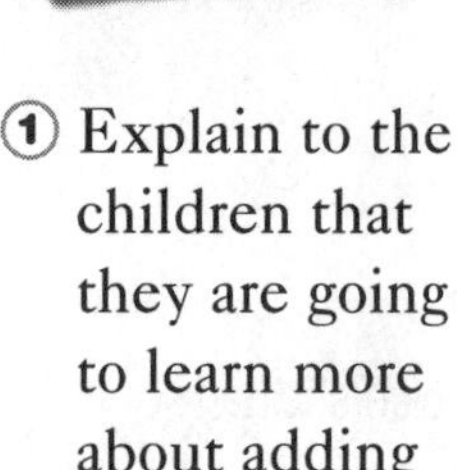

Explain the Principle

“You can add word parts to the end of a word to show you did something in the present or in the past.”

“Change the *y* to *i* and add *es* or *ed* to words that end in a consonant and *y*.”

① Explain to the children that they are going to learn more about adding suffixes to words.

② Have *play, plays, played* and *cry, cries, cried* made in magnetic letters on a board or written on a chart. Read the words.

③ Suggested language: “What do you notice about the endings added to these words?” Children will notice that *s* and *ed* are added to *play,* and that the *y* in *cry* is changed to *i* before *es* and *ed* are added.

④ Make one more example for each (for example, *plan, plans, planned* and *try, tries, tried*), showing how to change or add letters.

⑤ Summarize by helping the children understand and state the principle that adding *s* and *ed* to the end of words can show you did something in the present or in the past.

⑥ Explain to the children that they will add *es* and *ed* to fifteen words. First they take a word card and write the word in the first column of a Three-Column Sheet. Then they will make the word with magnetic letters, add *s* or *es* (changing the spelling if needed), write the word in the second column, then change the ending to *ed,* and write that word in the last column. Finally they will read the last column to a partner.

take
make
write
add
write
write
read

- Have the children take a word card, make and write the word, add *s* or *es*, write the word, change the ending to *ed*, and write the word. Then have them read the last column to a partner.

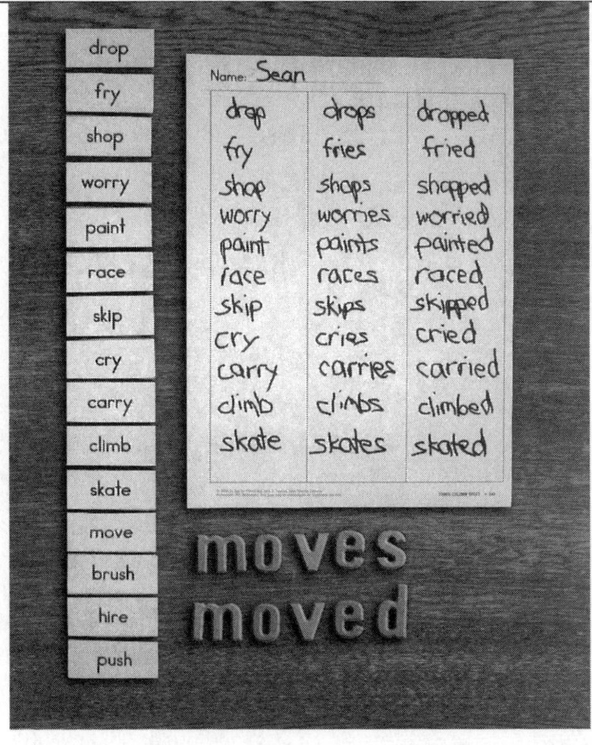

Invite the children to give one or two more examples.

Add an example for *es* and *ed* added to words ending in *y* to the word wall.

Link

Interactive Read-Aloud: Read aloud books that contain many words that have *es* and *ed* added, such as

- ***Where the Big Fish Are*** by Jonathan London
- ***The Big Cheese of 3rd Street*** by Laurie Anderson

Shared Reading: On subsequent readings of poems such as "Fire! Fire! Cried Mrs. McGuire!," have the children locate words that have spelling changes when *es* or *ed* is added.

Guided Reading: During word work, show four or five words ending in *y* and have the children tell how to change the spelling when *es* or *ed* is added. Help children use knowledge of plural structure while problem-solving words in reading.

Interactive Writing: As the children contribute words, help them notice if the spelling changes when a suffix is added.

Independent Writing: Teach the children how to check words that have *es* and *ed* endings when they are editing their writing.

assess

- Observe children's ability to change the *y* to *i* when adding *es* or *ed* as they write.
- Dictate four or five words and have children write the word with *es* or *ed*.

Expand the Learning

Repeat the lesson with other verbs and a variety of principles: include words that require no spelling change, words that require doubling the consonant, and words for which the *y* changes to *i*. Use the Word Card Template (see *Teaching Resources*) to make cards for the words you've chosen.

Connect with Home

Send home a sheet of word cards and two sheets of letter cards (see *Teaching Resources*) and have the children add *es* and *ed* endings to verbs.

17 Forming Past Tense: Summary for ed Words

Three-Way Sort

Consider Your Children

Before you use this lesson, your children should have worked with the past tense and have a good repertoire of examples. They may already understand that *ed* is associated with different sounds. This lesson is a review of the different principles for adding *ed.* It summarizes the spelling and sound changes and will help children systematize their knowledge.

Working with English Language Learners

English language learners may know the present tense form of a verb but be just learning how to change verbs to represent different tenses. Be sure they have heard enough language read aloud to recognize the different verb forms and perhaps use them automatically in known pieces of text. Write contrasting sentences to help them understand better; for example, "I can paint. Yesterday I painted the floor." Don't be concerned if they overgeneralize the rule (I *rided*). Recognize their good thinking and say the correct form. With experience, they will sort out the irregular verbs.

You Need

- Pocket chart.

From *Teaching Resources:*

- Pocket Chart Card Template.
- Lesson WS 17 Word Cards.
- Three-Way Sort Cards.
- Three-Way Sort Sheets.

Understand the Principle

There are three different sounds for the suffix *ed:* /t/, /d/, and /ed/. Within the category of words that have a /d/ sound are words that have a spelling change: doubling the consonant *(hopped)* or changing the *y* to *i.*

Knowing this concept will help children build categories for these words and help them standardize spelling of past tense words.

Explain the Principle

" When you add *ed* to a word, sometimes it sounds like /d/. "

" When you add *ed* to a word, sometimes it sounds like /ed/. "

" When you add *ed* to a word, sometimes it sounds like /t/. "

" Sometimes you change the *y* to *i* and add *ed,* and the ending sounds like /d/. "

plan

Explain the Principle

“ **When you add *ed* to a word, sometimes it sounds like /d/.** ”

“ **When you add *ed* to a word, sometimes it sounds like /ed/.** ”

“ **When you add *ed* to a word, sometimes it sounds like /t/.** ”

“ **Sometimes you change the *y* to *i* and add *ed*, and the ending sounds like /d/.** ”

① Explain to the children that you are going to review all they know about adding the suffix *ed* to words.

② Place three words in each of the three columns in the pocket chart.

③ Invite the children to read the three words in each column with you. Ask them to share what they notice about the words in each column:

Column 1: “All the words end in an *ed* that sounds like /d/.” “*Planned* has a double consonant.” “*Care* has just a *d* added.” “The *y* in *carry* was changed to *i* and then *ed* was added.”

Column 2: “All the words end in an *ed* that sounds like /t/.” “*Walk* has an *ed* added.” “*Chase* has a *d* added.” “*Hop* has a doubled consonant and *ed*.”

Column 3: “All the words end in an *ed* that sounds like /ed/.” “The *ed* makes a second syllable that you can hear.”

④ Explain to the children that they are going to sort word cards on a Three-Way Sort Card according to the end sound they hear. The key words will be *planned*, *walked*, and *wanted*. They should say the word, look for the *ed*, listen for its sound, and put it under the right column. Finally they will write their three columns on a Three-Way Sort Sheet.

say
listen
sort
write
read

- Have the children complete a three-way sort, sorting cards by the sound of *ed* in the word. They write their sorts in three columns on a Three-Way Sort Sheet.
- Have them read their three columns to a partner.

Name: Raquel
Three-Way Sort
planned walked wanted
cleaned sprayed dried turned smelled
polished crashed wiped chased scraped asked
painted floated planted tasted traded

Invite the children to suggest one more word to add to each column of the class chart.

Point out an example of each *ed* sound on the word wall.

Link

Interactive Read-Aloud: Read aloud books that include several words with *ed* endings. Following the reading, add a word to each column of the chart. Examples of appropriate books are:

- ***Winter Shoes for Shadow Horse*** by Linda High
- ***Out to Lunch*** by Peggy Perry Anderson

Shared Reading: When reading a poem such as "There Was a Crooked Man," "Not a Word," or "The House That Jack Built" together (see *Sing a Song of Poetry*), have the children locate an *ed* word that has an ending sound like /d/, /t/, or /ed/.

Guided Reading: Prompt the children to look for base words and *ed* endings when taking new words apart.

Interactive Writing: As the children write words with *ed* endings, prompt them to say the words and listen for the ending sound.

Independent Writing: Remind the children to think about spelling changes when adding *ed* to words.

assess

- Observe the children's use of *ed* when they are reading and writing texts.
- Dictate five or six words with *ed* endings.

Expand the Learning

Repeat the lesson with different words to help the children differentiate further the words that have the sound of /d/ or /t/ or /ed/ at the end. Use the Word Card Template (see *Teaching Resources*) to make cards for the new words you've chosen.

Connect with Home

Send home a sheet of words with *ed* (use the Word Card Template in *Teaching Resources*) for children to sort.

18 Forming New Words: Summary for Adding s, ed, ing

Make and Write

Consider Your Children

Be sure children have had adequate experience with each of these endings before summarizing the information. Use key examples that children already know as single words; they will be looking at them in new ways.

Working with English Language Learners

Inflecting verbs is one of the most difficult aspects of learning another language. You learn a word but then find that it changes form in different contexts to meet syntactic rules and convey meaning precisely. These subtleties of language are complex. Help your English language learners use words in sentences so that they can understand and begin to internalize these rules of syntax. Be explicit in helping them understand tense, making links to their native language if possible (since inflections work differently in different languages, this may be difficult).

You Need

- Chart paper.
- Markers.

From *Teaching Resources:*

- Three-Column Sheets.
- Lesson WS 18 Word Cards.

Understand the Principle

This lesson culminates a sequence of lessons on adding *s, ed,* and *ing* to words, with some requiring spelling or sound changes when the suffix is added. When suffixes are added, they sometimes require a spelling change: doubling the consonant, dropping the silent *e,* or changing the *y* to *i* before adding the suffix.

Explain the Principle

“You can add word parts to the end of a word to show you are doing something now or that you did something in the past.”

Explain the Principle

"You can add word parts to the end of a word to show you are doing something now or that you did something in the past."

① Tell the children that you are going to help them think about all they know about adding *s*, *ed*, and *ing* endings to words.

② Write one word at a time on a chart; then write it with *s*, with *ed*, and with *ing*. As you make each change, ask the children what letters to add and whether the base word requires a spelling change.

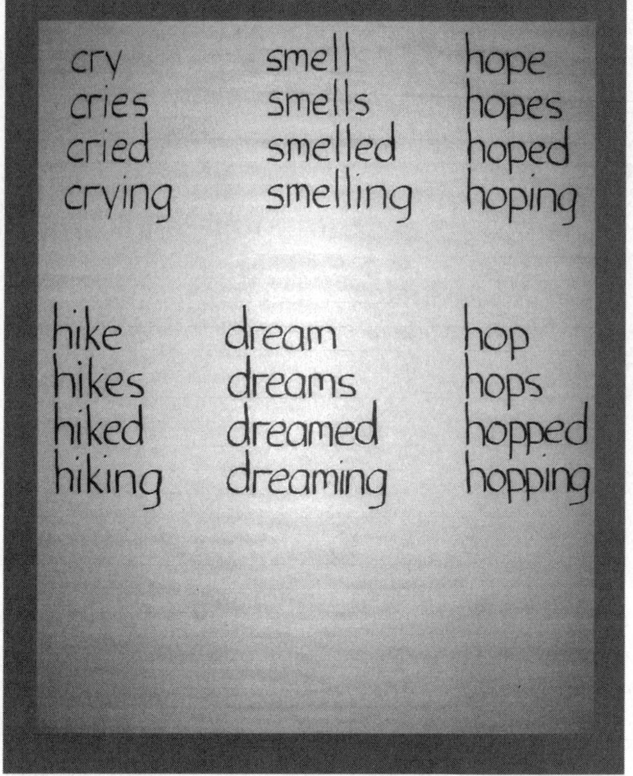

③ Tell the children they are going to use a Three-Column Sheet and word cards with verbs on them. They will say the word on the card and then write it with *s* in the first column of the sheet, with *ed* in the second column, and with *ing* in the third column. Remind them to make spelling changes as needed.

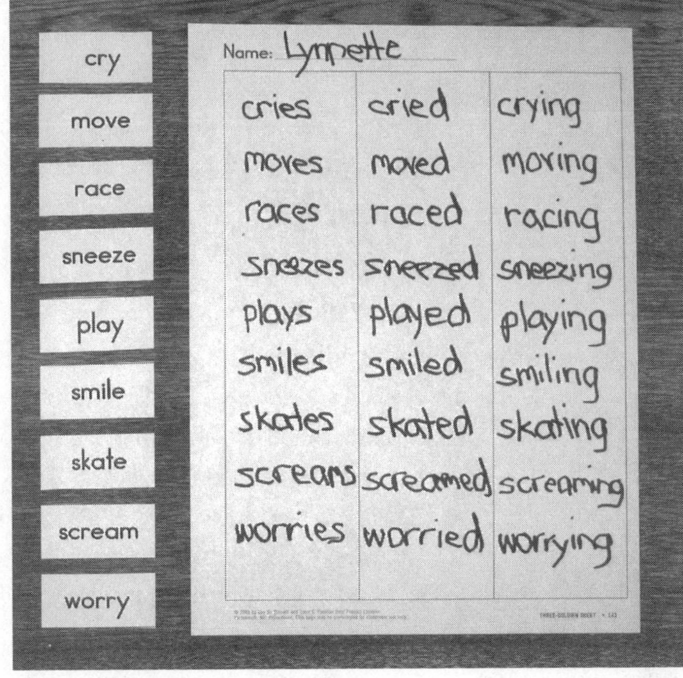

say
add
write
add
write
add
write
read

▸ Have the children take twenty word cards, one card at a time, and write each verb with the suffixes *s*, *ed*, and *ing* in each of the three columns on the Three-Column Sheet. Then ask them to show and read one of their columns to a partner.

cry
move
race
sneeze
play
smile
skate
scream
worry
Name: Lynnette
cries cried crying
moves moved moving
races raced racing
sneezes sneezed sneezing
plays played playing
smiles smiled smiling
skates skated skating
screams screamed screaming
worries worried worrying

Have the children share one or two more examples and add them to the chart.

Link

Interactive Read-Aloud: Read aloud books that include verbs with endings, such as

- ***Lucky Song*** by Vera B. Williams
- ***Dig Dig Digging*** by Margaret Mayo and Alex Ayliffe

Shared Reading: After you have read and enjoyed a poem, have the children use a masking card or highlighter tape to locate words with *s, ed,* and *ing* suffixes. "Silly Simon," "Tree Shadows," and "Someone" have words with all three suffixes (see *Sing a Song of Poetry*). Have them tell if the spelling of the base word has changed.

Guided Reading: As the children read a text, prompt them to notice base words and *s, ed,* and *ing* endings to help them take apart unfamiliar words.

Interactive Writing: After constructing a group text, have the children locate the words with *s, ed,* and *ing.*

Independent Writing: Teach children to check their spelling when they add *s, ed,* and *ing* endings to base words.

assess

- Select and dictate ten base words, several of which require dropping the *e,* doubling the consonant, or changing the *y* to *i* in order to add *s, ed,* or *ing.*

Expand the Learning

Repeat the lesson with other verbs. Use the Word Card Template (see *Teaching Resources*) to make cards for the new words you've chosen.

Connect with Home

Send home a sheet of word cards (use the Word Card Template in *Teaching Resources*) for children to select and write five base words and add *s, ed, or ing.*

19 Forming Plurals with Words Ending in y

Make and Write

Consider Your Children

Use this lesson after your children are familiar with the concept of plural and can form simple plurals by adding *s* and *es.* In this lesson, they learn that they need to look at the last two letters to help them know how to change the spelling. The lesson focuses on words ending in a consonant and *y* and can be repeated for words ending in a vowel and *y.*

Working with English Language Learners

Making words plural is a challenge for English language learners because there are many plural forms in English. Once they learn the most regular plurals (*s* and *es*), which are themselves a challenge, they need to expand the way they look at words to include other variations. Be sure your English language learners have had a chance to see and read the words you use in this lesson. Use shared reading and interactive writing to help them meet and notice these word structures in a meaningful context before they work with them in this direct lesson. For example, you could have a small group compose and write sentences about their families or any other topic that would incorporate these words. Show the children how to remove the *y* and add *ies,* and have them take turns writing the plural on the chart.

You Need

- Chart paper.
- Markers.
- Magnetic letters.

From *Teaching Resources:*

- Lesson WS 19 Word Cards.
- Two-Way Sort Sheets.

Understand the Principle

This widely applicable rule is one that will help children spell the plural forms of a large number of nouns that end in *y.* They need to notice whether there is a vowel or consonant before the *y.* When there is a vowel, they simply add *s.* When there is a consonant and *y,* they change the *y* to *i* and add *es.*

Explain the Principle

“Change the *y* to *i* and add *es* to words that end in a consonant and *y* to make them plural.”

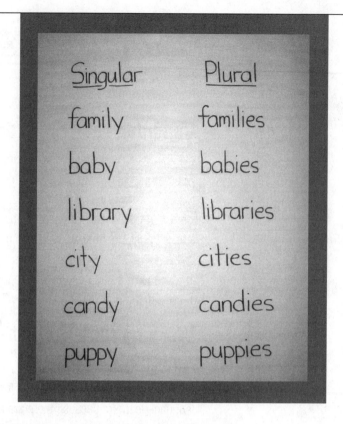

Singular	Plural
family	families
baby	babies
library	libraries
city	cities
candy	candies
puppy	puppies

Explain the Principle

“ Change the *y* to *i* and add *es* to words that end in a consonant and *y* to make them plural. ”

① Tell the children that they are going to learn more about how to spell words that mean more than one (plurals).

② Suggested language: “You know that *plural* means more than one. To make most words plural, you add. . . . [Children respond.] Or you can add *es*. Let’s look at some words that are different. For example, look at the word *family*. What did I do to make it say *families*?” Children respond. Point out the changes on the chart.

③ Have the children provide and explain the plural of *baby* and *library*.

④ Then go over the next examples, moving quickly as the children show that they understand the principle.

⑤ Suggested language: “What do you notice about the letter before the *y* in each of these words?” Children will notice (or you may point out) that the letter before *y* is a consonant.

⑥ Explain to the children that they are going to be using a Two-Way Sort Sheet. They will take a word card, write the word in the left column, make the word with magnetic letters, change it to its plural form, and write it in the right column of the Two-Way Sort Sheet. They will do this for ten words.

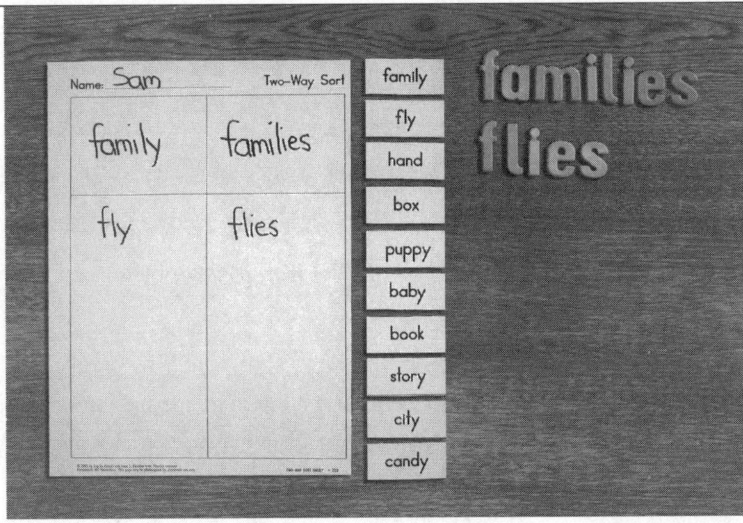

take
make
write
change
write
read

▸ Have the children make and write ten pairs of words on a Two-Way Sort Sheet: a word in its singular form (some that end in a consonant and *y* and some that don't), followed by its plural form. Then have them read their word pairs to a partner.

Ask the children to share a pair of words from their sheet.

Place on the word wall an example of a word that ends in a consonant and *y* and changes to *ies*.

Link

Interactive Read-Aloud: Read aloud books that include many plural forms, such as

- ***New York's Bravest*** by Mary Pope Osborne
- ***The Girl Who Wore Snakes*** by Angela Johnson

Shared Reading: After you have enjoyed a poem together such as "Buttercups and Daisies" or "Curly Locks" (see *Sing a Song of Poetry*), have the children use a masking card or highlighter tape to locate nouns that end with *y* and others that end with *ies.*

Guided Reading: During word work, make a noun with magnetic letters and then make it again as a plural.

Interactive Writing: Call attention to the principle. Ask the children who are having difficulty with the principle to come up to the easel and write the plural ending for a noun that ends in *y.*

Independent Writing: Draw attention to the plural principle while conferring with children about their writing.

assess

- Notice whether the children, in their writing, are using conventional plural forms for nouns that end in *y.*
- Include two to four words that end in *y* in a quick spelling test.

Expand the Learning

Repeat the lesson with nouns that end in a vowel and *y* so the children can learn to make the distinction: *day–days, way–ways, play–plays, key–keys, monkey–monkeys.* Use the Word Card Template (see *Teaching Resources*) to make cards for the new words you've chosen.

Have the children play Concentration (see *Teaching Resources,* Games) with singular and plural forms of nouns, incorporating a variety of the plural principles.

Connect with Home

Give children a sheet of singular and plural words to take home, cut out, and match with family members.

Or send home only the singular forms and have them make and write the plural forms.

20 Forming Abbreviations

Abbreviation Lotto

Consider Your Children

Your children will encounter many common abbreviations in the texts they read. This lesson focuses on the common abbreviations they read and will want to write: *Mr., Mrs., Dr., St., Ave., Rd., Sun., Mon., Tues., Wed., Thurs., Fri., Sat., Jan., Feb., Mar., Apr., Aug., Sept., Oct., Nov., Dec., Lne., Ct., Blvd., hr., min.* Once they understand the concept, it will be easy for them to learn a whole collection of abbreviations.

Working with English Language Learners

While English language learners are still struggling with English words and their meanings, it may be difficult for them to understand the concept of abbreviations. Start with those they have seen before and understand. Also, place abbreviations in appropriate places for them to become familiar with them: on the calendar and on maps, for example.

You Need

- Chart paper.
- Markers.

From *Teaching Resources:*

- Directions for Lotto.
- Lotto Game Cards.
- Lesson WS 20 Word Cards.

Understand the Principle

Abbreviate means to shorten. Abbreviations are shortened forms of particular words. They are followed by a period. Usually abbreviations have five or fewer letters. Abbreviations are used often in reading and writing. You will want to note that *Ms.* represents a title free of reference to marital status in place of *Miss* or *Mrs.*

Explain the Principle

" Some words are made shorter by using some of the letters and a period. They are called abbreviations. "

plan

teach

Explain the Principle

"Some words are made shorter by using some of the letters and a period. They are called abbreviations."

① Explain to the children that they are going to learn about some words that can be made shorter. They will see them when they read and will sometimes use them when they write.

② Write *Mr.*, *Mrs.*, and *Dr.* on the chart in their complete form *(Mister, Mistress, Doctor)*, with a name next to each (*Mister Turner,* for example). Use names the children know. Have the children read the full names with you and then circle the letters used in the abbreviation. Write the abbreviations next to the names.

③ Continue with *St.*, *Ave.*, and *Rd.*, using familiar locations and the complete words: *Street*, *Avenue*, and *Road*. Circle the letters used to write the abbreviation, and write the abbreviations next to the names.

④ Have the children clap and say the word *abbreviation* with you. Explain that a period follows the letters to show it is an abbreviation.

⑤ Next show a list of the days of the week, circle the letters of the abbreviation, and have a child come up to write the abbreviation.

⑥ Repeat with months of the year. Explain that May, June, and July have four or fewer letters and do not have an abbreviation (although sometimes when people do not have much space to write, they may make up an abbreviation, such as *Jun.* for June or *Jul.* for July).

⑦ Tell the children that they are going to play Abbreviation Lotto. The Lotto Game Cards have an abbreviation written in each box. The word cards are complete words. The player takes a word card, reads it, and tells the abbreviation. Then he looks on his Lotto card and covers the abbreviation if he has it. The first player to cover all the spaces on his game card wins the game.

take
read
tell
cover

- Have the children play Abbreviation Lotto in groups of three or four.

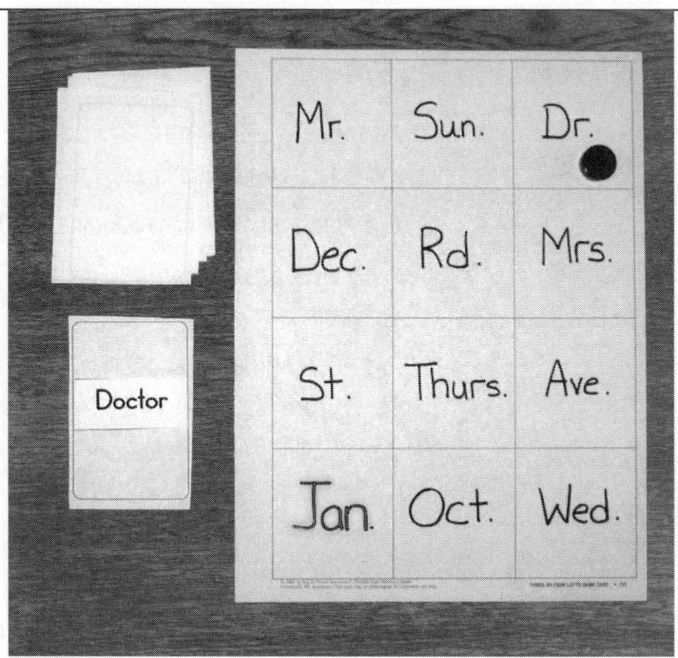

Reread the list of abbreviations on the chart.

Put an example on the word wall.

Link

Interactive Read-Aloud: Read aloud books that include abbreviations, such as

- ***A Fine, Fine School*** by Sharon Creech
- ***Mr. Bear Squash-You-All-Flat*** by Morrell Gipson

Shared Reading: Use poems with abbreviations, such as "'Fire! Fire!' Cried Mrs. McGuire" and "Mr. Crocodile." After reading, make a list of the words and their abbreviations or substitute abbreviations and reread the poem. Use "The Months of the Year" and "Sneeze on Monday" to substitute calendar abbreviations for the full word.

Guided Reading: After reading and discussing a story, have the children locate one or two abbreviations in the text.

Interactive Writing: Look for opportunities for the children to use abbreviations in the stories you compose together.

Independent Writing: Have the children edit their writing to be sure there is a period after each abbreviation.

assess

- Dictate five or ten words and have the children write the abbreviation.
- Observe the children's use of abbreviations in their reading and writing.

Expand the Learning

Have the children play Abbreviation Lotto with the full words on the Lotto Game Cards and the abbreviations on the word cards they draw. Use the Word Card Template (see *Teaching Resources*) to make cards for the abbreviations.

Connect with Home

Have children take copies of word cards and several Lotto Game Cards home, so they can play the game with family members.

21 Adding -er to Words Ending in y

Suffix Lotto

Consider Your Children

This lesson introduces the spelling change to verbs ending in a consonant and *y.* It should follow lessons on adding *-er* to verbs that do not require a spelling change in the base word *(reader, baker)* and on doubling the consonant before adding *-er (runner).* Be sure your children have worked with vowels and vowel combinations and also understand CVC and CVC*e* word structures. This lesson includes all the adding *-er* variations, so that students can summarize and systematize their knowledge.

Working with English Language Learners

English language learners will need a great many opportunities to work with suffixes. Help them say each word as they change it and highlight the part of the word that is changed when they write it. Orally, use words in pairs of sentences to help them get a clearer picture of the meaning: "Jim can *carry* the ball. He is the ball *carrier.*" Play Lotto with a small group to be sure they connect the words successfully.

You Need

- Magnetic letters.
- Cookie sheet.

From *Teaching Resources:*

- Directions for Lotto.
- Lotto Game Cards.
- Lesson WS 21 Word Cards.

Understand the Principle

To add the *-er* suffix to words that end in a consonant and *y,* we first change the *y* to *i.* In these examples, the added *-er* changes the word from a verb to a noun, but the same principle applies to adding the suffixes *-ed* and *-est.*

Explain the Principle

"Change the *y* to *i* and add *-er* to words that end in *y.*"

plan

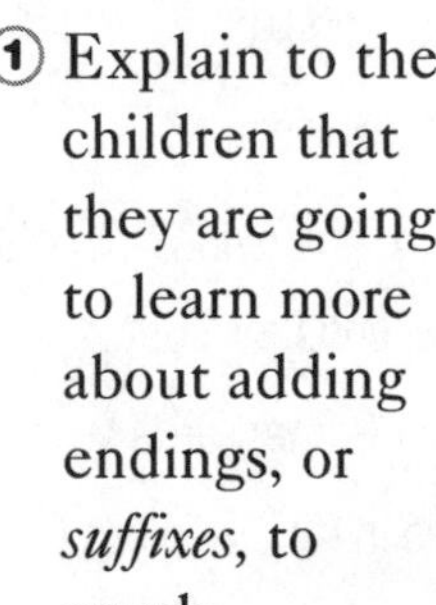

Explain the Principle

“Change the *y* to *i* and add *-er* to words that end in *y.*”

① Explain to the children that they are going to learn more about adding endings, or *suffixes*, to words.

② On the board, have the four words *sing, hike, jog,* and *fly* made with magnetic letters.

③ Tell the children you want to change the word *sing* to *singer.*

④ Suggested language: “What letters should we add?” The children will respond *e-r.*

⑤ Invite a child to add *-er* to *sing,* and then read the word *singer* together.

⑥ Repeat with *hiker* and *jogger.* The children will have already learned when to add just *r* or double the consonant before adding *-er.* This will provide a brief review.

⑦ Demonstrate changing the *y* in *fly* to *i* and then adding *-er.*

⑧ Review one or two more examples that require the spelling change: *supply–supplier, cry–crier, fly–flier.* Children will later learn that if a word ends in a vowel and *y,* the *y* is not changed (*buy* to *buyer*). If they offer these examples, put them on another chart and briefly comment on the principle.

⑨ Explain to the children that today they are going to play Suffix Lotto. They will draw a card and read it. If their Lotto Game Card has the same word with *-er,* they can cover that space with a marker. The first player to cover all the spaces wins the game.

take
read
match
cover

- Have the children play Suffix Lotto in groups of three or four.

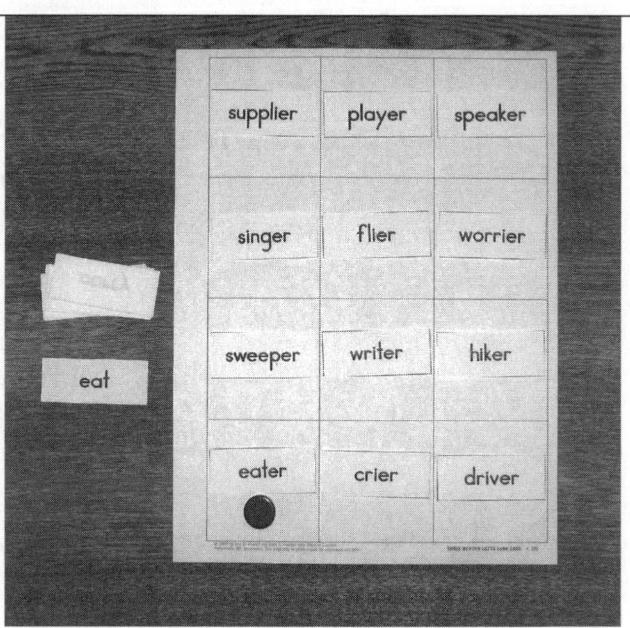

Have the children add *-er* to two or three base words with *y*. Add these words to the class chart.

Link

Interactive Read-Aloud: Read aloud books that contain words with *-er* endings, such as

- ***Much Bigger Than Martin*** by Steven Kellogg
- ***Duck on a Bike*** by David Shannon

Shared Reading: After you have read and enjoyed a poem together, have the children use a masking card or flag to locate words with *-er* suffixes.

Guided Reading: During word work, make four or five words with magnetic letters and have the children add *-er.* Use words that do and do not require spelling changes.

Interactive Writing: Help the children notice base words and *-er* endings in words they want to write. Use the whiteboard to quickly demonstrate those that require spelling changes.

Independent Writing: In the editing process, encourage the children to notice words that have *-er* endings and check to see whether they require a spelling change.

assess

- Observe the children as they read words with the *-er* suffix.
- Dictate four or five base words, some that do and some that do not require spelling changes. Ask the children to write the base word with an added *-er.*

Expand the Learning

Repeat the lesson, using words ending in *y* and a greater variety of suffixes *(-er, -ed, -est).* Use the Word Card Template (see *Teaching Resources*) to make cards for the new words you've chosen.

Connect with Home

Send home word cards and a pair of Suffix Lotto Game Cards so the children can play the game with family members.

early
mid
late

22 Forming Comparatives with -er and -est

Say and Sort

Consider Your Children

Use this lesson after your children's oral vocabularies include the words you will be using and the children are able to hear and notice word parts such as the base word and an ending. They should also have a comfortable knowledge of letter/sound relationships. This lesson incorporates *changing* the spelling of words that end in *y* and doubling the consonant for words that end in a short vowel followed by a single consonant. Be sure children have previously worked with comparisons where the spelling does not change (for example, Lesson WS 13).

Working with English Language Learners

Use pictures, concrete objects, or role play whenever possible to help English language learners understand the concept of comparison. Simple sentences that use comparison will help them understand the meaning of the words in context. Be sure that they both say and see the words as they read the sentences in a shared way. Small-group interactive writing is a very effective approach because the students compose and write sentences as well as reread them; you can focus children's attention on how these words are constructed.

You Need

- Chart paper.
- Markers.

From *Teaching Resources:*

- Four-Box Sheets.
- Lesson WS 22 Word Cards.

Understand the Principle

Understanding the role of affixes helps children analyze words. Instead of learning one word at a time, they learn to look for base words and the additions we make to them to add meaning. Sometimes these additions, or *affixes,* change the type of word—from a noun to a verb, for example. Children use this knowledge of word structure in combination with their sense of meaning and syntax in order to read fluently, predict upcoming words, and check whether their reading "sounds right."

Explain the Principle

“Add *-er* or *-est* to show how one thing compares with another.”

“Add *-r* or *-st* to words that end in silent *e* to make the *-er* or *-est* ending.”

“Double the consonant and add *-er* or *-est* to words that end in a short vowel and one consonant.”

“Change *y* to *i* and add *-er* or *-est* to words that end in *y*.”

WS 22 Word Structure

plan

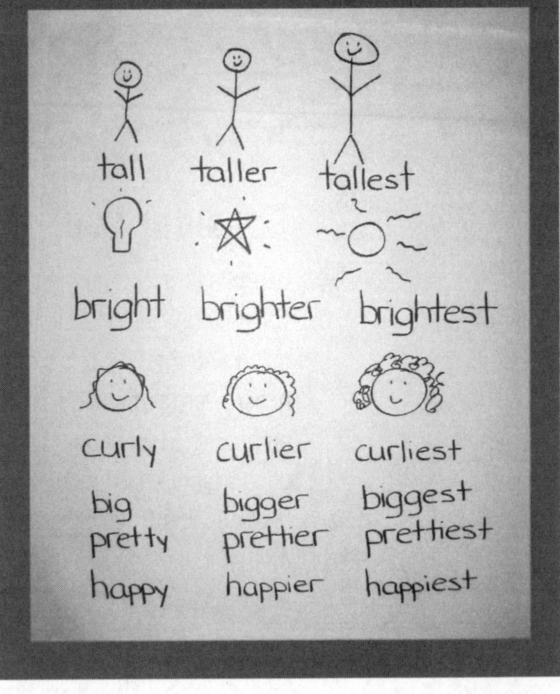

Explain the Principle

"Add *-er* or *-est* to show how one thing compares with another."

"Add *-r* or *-st* to words that end in silent *e* to make the *-er* or *-est* ending."

"Double the consonant and add *-er* or *-est* to words that end in a short vowel and one consonant."

"Change *y* to *i* and add *-er* or *-est* to words that end in *y*."

① Tell the children that they are going to learn more about suffixes.

② Suggested language: "We are going to talk about comparing things today, and we are going to learn some words that help us talk about comparisons." Review the concept of comparatives by noting with children, "This picture is high. This chart is higher. The word wall is highest. Let's say those words—high, higher, highest."

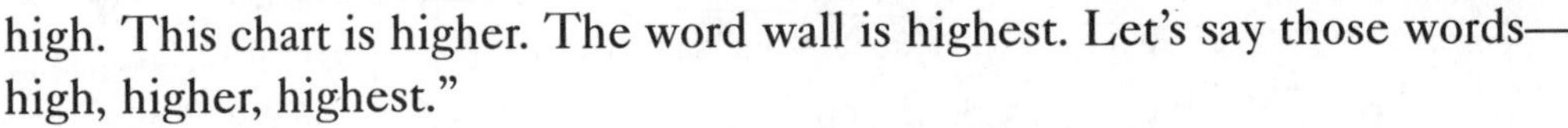

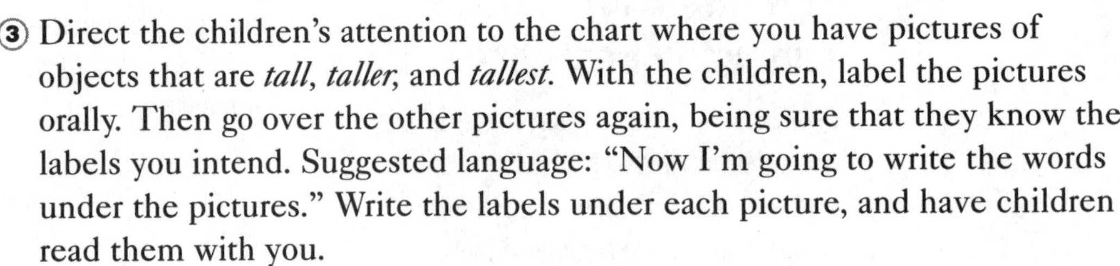

③ Direct the children's attention to the chart where you have pictures of objects that are *tall, taller,* and *tallest.* With the children, label the pictures orally. Then go over the other pictures again, being sure that they know the labels you intend. Suggested language: "Now I'm going to write the words under the pictures." Write the labels under each picture, and have children read them with you.

④ Once the children have the idea, have them generate other examples; draw a quick sketch (or act out) and write the words. For example, *bright, brighter, brightest; curly, curlier, curliest.*

⑤ Ask the children to look at the words and talk about what they notice. They will notice that the words in the central column have an added *-er.* Have the children highlight the *-er* or underline it.

⑥ Suggested language: "So, to show that something is more than another—bigger or shorter—you add *-er.* What about these words?" Indicate the right column and ask children what was added to the words. Children respond with *-est.* Highlight the *-est* at the ends of words.

⑦ Children may also notice that sometimes letters are doubled *(bigger)* or that the *y* is changed to *i (curlier)*. Help them understand the principle that sometimes you double the consonant and add *-er* or *-est* and with words ending in *y* you change the *y* to *i* before adding *-er* or *-est*.

⑧ Tell children that they will be sorting words and show them how.

take
sort
read

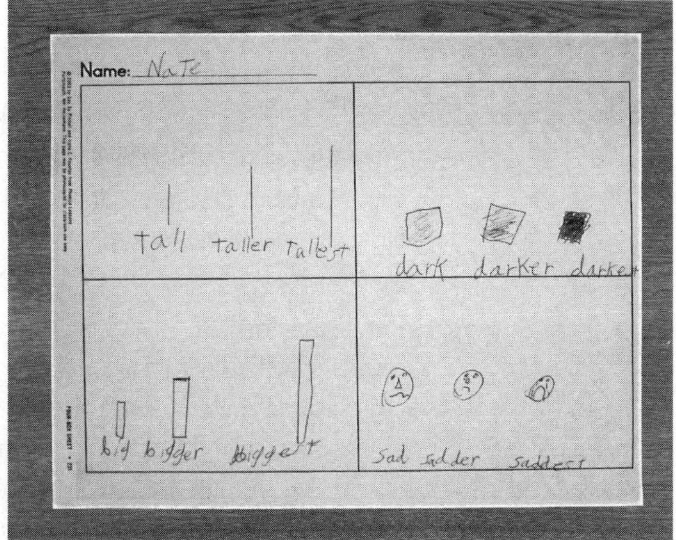

- Have the children sort and say the words that you have arranged in three columns—the base word, the word with *-er,* and the word with *-est*—on the table or desk. The idea is for them to understand the idea of comparatives and superlatives and the fact that endings are added to words to convey this.
- Have children use a Four-Box Sheet. Have them draw and label three small pictures in each box to show a descriptive word (an adjective), the comparative form, and the superlative form (*sad, sadder, saddest,* for example). If needed, post a list of about forty adjectives for children to choose from.

Have the children, in turn, show the drawings and say the words in one box on their sheet.

Put examples of *-er* and *-est* words showing no change in spelling and examples showing the doubled consonant on the word wall.

Link

Interactive Read-Aloud: Read aloud books that emphasize relationships and comparisons. Examples are:

- ***Mr. Gumpy's Motor Car*** by John Burningham
- ***A Pig Is Big*** by Douglas Florian

Shared Reading: After you have read and enjoyed a poem or other text together, have the children use a masking card or highlighter tape to locate words with *-er* and *-est* endings.

Guided Reading: When the children come to difficult or new comparatives and superlatives, have them look at the base word and the *-er* or *-est* ending.

Interactive Writing: Engage the children in some descriptive writing and encourage comparisons (for example, a description of animals seen at the zoo or at the tide pool). After writing and rereading the text, have the children locate the words that compare one thing with another.

Independent Writing: Help the children remember what they learned in the lesson and application activity when they want to write a comparative or superlative word.

Expand the Learning

Repeat the lesson with a greater variety of descriptive words. Use the Word Card Template (see *Teaching Resources*) to make cards for the new words you've chosen.

Create a bulletin board for children's drawings and labels, and title it "Words That Describe."

Connect with Home

Once the children understand the concept, have them create a family chart of drawings and comparison words: *short, shorter, shortest; tall, taller, tallest; young, younger, youngest; old, older, oldest.*

assess

- Dictate six words (two for each principle) and ask children to add *-er* and *-est* to each. Notice whether children are doubling consonants appropriately.

23 Forming Plurals for Words Ending in f

Make and Write

Consider Your Children

Use this lesson after your children are familiar with the concept of plural and can form simple plurals by adding *s* and *es* and plurals for words that end in *y*. It is important for children to hear plural forms in oral language and read-alouds before learning how to spell them.

Working with English Language Learners

Be sure that English language learners understand easier plurals before they encounter plurals for words ending in *f*. The words you use in the lesson should be part of their speaking and listening vocabularies, and it will help a great deal if they have used them in shared reading and interactive writing. If they are unfamiliar with such words, work with them in a small interactive writing group, an ideal situation for helping them understand plurals in context.

You Need

- Chart paper.
- Markers.
- Magnetic letters.

From *Teaching Resources:*

- Lesson WS 23 Word Cards.
- Two-Column Sheets.

Understand the Principle

It helps children to have a useful rule for forming the plural of words ending in *f*. As always, however, there are exceptions to this rule.

Explain the Principle

“Change *f* to *v* and add *es* to words that end in *f, fe,* or *lf* to make them plural.”

CONTINUUM: WORD STRUCTURE — Recognizing and Using Plurals That Change *f* to *v* and Add *es* for Words That End with *f, fe,* or *lf*

plan

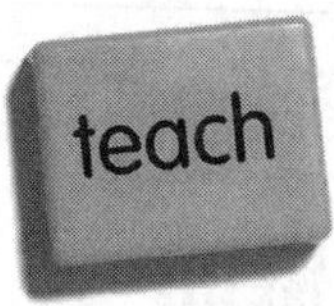

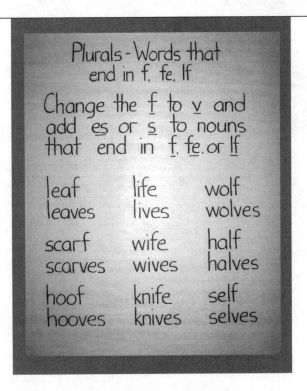

Plurals - Words that end in f, fe, lf

Change the f to v and add es or s to nouns that end in f, fe, or lf

leaf	life	wolf
leaves	lives	wolves
scarf	wife	half
scarves	wives	halves
hoof	knife	self
hooves	knives	selves

Explain the Principle

" **Change *f* to *v* and add *es* to words that end in *f*, *fe*, or *lf* to make them plural.** "

① Tell the children that they are going to learn more about making words plural.

② Suggested language: "We've been looking at different ways to make plurals. Today we are going to look at a special way to make plurals for words that end in *f* or *fe*. For most of those words, you are going to change the *f* to *v* and add *es* or *s*."

③ Read the principle to the children, and then write *leaf–leaves* in the first column of a three-column chart. "This word, *leaf*, ends in *f*. The plural is *leaves*. I changed the *f* to *v* and added *es*."

④ Have the children say the two words and listen for the *f* and *v* difference, which is hard to hear because *f* and *v* are made the same way in the mouth.

⑤ Then write *scarf* and *scarves*, repeating the process. (Sometimes *scarfs* is accepted, but *scarves* is preferred.)

⑥ Write *life* at the top of the second column. Suggested language: "This word is *life*. It ends in *fe*. To make it plural, I change the *f* to *v* and just add *s*. Why don't I have to add *es*?" Children may respond that there already is an *e* at the end.

⑦ Add *wife* and *wives* to the chart and repeat the process, having children say the two words to hear the difference as well as see it.

⑧ Write *wolf* at the top of the third column. Suggested language: "This word, *wolf*, ends in *lf*. To make the plural, I'm going to change the *f* to *v* and add *es*. Demonstrate and then write *half–halves*.

⑨ Ask children to add examples or suggest them yourself. This time, ask them which is the right column for the example.

⑩ Summarize the lesson by repeating the principle.

⑪ Explain to the children that they will be building plurals for words that end in *f*, *lf*, or *fe*. They will make each word and write the singular form on the left and the plural form on the right of a Two-Column Sheet.

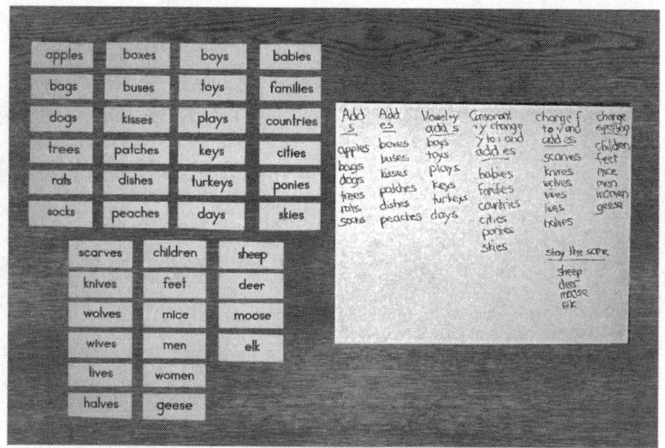

take
make
change
write
read

▸ Children take one word card at a time from a stack. Each child builds the singular word with magnetic letters and then changes the word to form the plural. They write the pairs of words on the Two-Column Sheet, the singular form in the left column and the plural form in the right, until they have made ten pairs of words. Then they read their lists to a partner.

Ask the children to share one pair of words and discuss what they noticed about the words.

Place a plural form of words ending in *f*, *lf*, and *fe* on the word wall as examples.

Link

Interactive Read-Aloud: Read aloud books that contain the plural forms of words ending in *f* or *fe,* such as

- ***Peter's Patchwork Dream*** by Willemien Min
- ***Prudy's Problem and How She Solved It*** by Cary Armstrong-Ellis

Shared Reading: Have the children use highlighter tape or a masking card to find nouns that end with *f, lf,* or *fe,* either in their singular form or those that have been changed to plural.

Guided Reading: During word work, make several nouns ending in *f, lf,* or *fe* with magnetic letters or on a whiteboard and then make them again as plurals.

Interactive Writing: Call attention to the principle when the children are going to write a plural form of a word that ends in *f, lf,* or *fe.*

Independent Writing: Draw attention to the principle for plurals of words ending with *f, lf,* or *fe* while conferring with children about their editing.

assess

- Notice whether children, in their writing, are using conventional plural forms for nouns that end in *f, lf,* and *fe.*
- Include two words that end in *f, lf,* or *fe* in a quick spelling test.

Expand the Learning

Play Concentration (see *Teaching Resources,* Games) with singular and plural forms of nouns.

Connect with Home

Give the children a sheet of singular and plural word cards (use the Word Card Template in *Teaching Resources*) to take home and match with family members.

24 Changing Spelling to Form the Plural

Lotto

Consider Your Children

Use this lesson when your children are very familiar with the concept of plural and have worked with other generalizations for forming plurals. They should also be familiar with the meaning of the words that you use, although they may not be able to spell them accurately. It will be easier for children to grasp the principle if they already have the examples in their oral and reading vocabularies.

Working with English Language Learners

For anyone learning another language, plurals are difficult, especially those that do not follow regular rules. For example, for someone just learning English, it would be natural to assume that the plural of *man* is *mans* instead of the changed form, *men*. Be sure that your English language learners have had many opportunities to hear the selected plural forms in books you read aloud to them. Repeated readings (hearing the same selection read aloud, engaging in shared reading, or rereading familiar texts for themselves) help them become familiar with the forms.

You Need

- Chart paper.
- Markers.

From *Teaching Resources:*

- Directions for Lotto.
- Lotto Game Cards.
- Lesson WS 24 Word Cards.

Understand the Principle

This lesson helps children understand that making some words plural means changing the spelling rather than just adding *s* or *es*. This lesson will help them differentiate between these words and words whose plurals have *s* and *es*.

There are many words that change spelling when they are made plural. The children may also realize that the spelling of some words stays the same, as in *sheep, deer,* and *moose.*

Explain the Principle

“Plural means more than one.”

“Change the spelling of some words to make them plural.”

plan

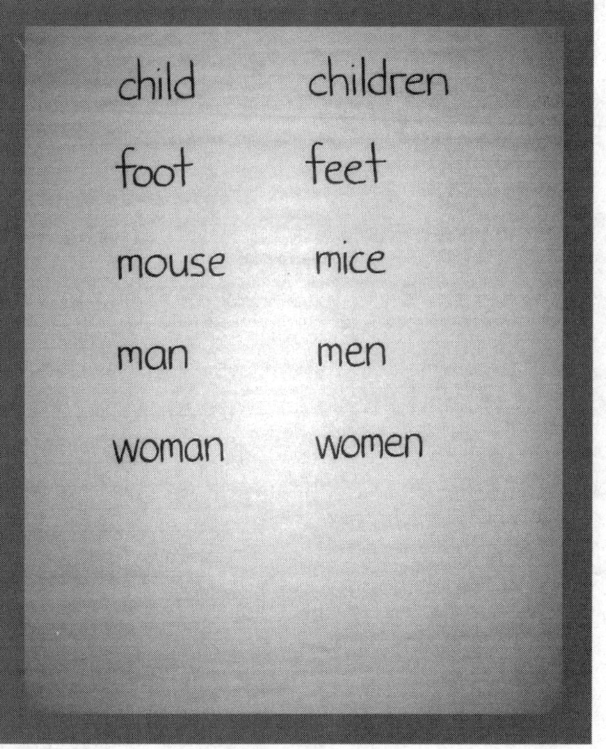

Explain the Principle

“ Plural means more than one. ”

“ Change the spelling of some words to make them plural. ”

① Tell the children that they are going to learn more about making words plural.

② Write the word *child* on the chart and ask the children to read it. Then write the word *children* in the second column. Ask the children to look at the words and tell you what they notice about them. Encourage comments and questions such as:

> “*Child* means one person, but *children* means a lot of young people.”
>
> “They both start with *ch*.”
>
> “*Children* is longer than *child*.”
>
> “Why don’t you add *s* to *child*?”

③ Suggested language: “When you write the plural for some words, you change something about the spelling instead of adding *s* or *es*. You know the words *child* and *children*. You change the spelling of some other words to make them plural.”

④ Write examples such as *mouse–mice*, *man–men*, and *woman–women*. Have children talk about the similarity between *men* and *women*. Suggested language: “With these words, you need to remember the spelling of both the singular noun and the plural noun because they are different from nouns where you add *s* or *es*. We’ll put this chart up in the classroom to help you remember.”

⑤ Tell the children that you are adding a new Lotto game to the class—Plural Lotto. Show them how to play the game by reviewing a few of the words.

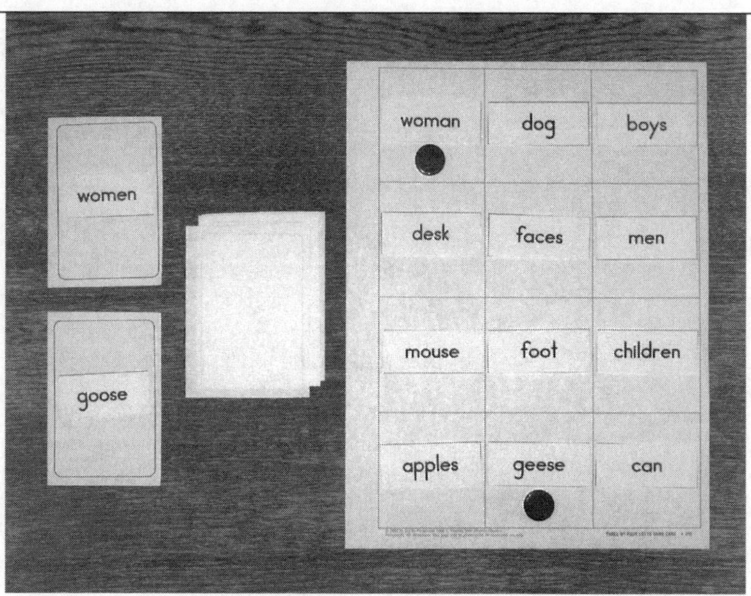

take
say
match
cover

▸ Using Lotto Game Cards and word cards with simple plurals (adding *s* or *es*) and ones that change their spelling in the plural form, have the children play Plural Lotto in groups of three or four.

Ask the children what they noticed about plurals and to tell one pair of words from the game they played.

Place two examples of plurals with changed spelling on the word wall.

Link

Interactive Read-Aloud: Read aloud books that include plural forms with changed spelling, such as

- ***Now One Foot, Now the Other*** by Tomie dePaola
- ***Mice and Beans*** by Pam Munoz Ryan

Shared Reading: After you have read and enjoyed a poem together such as "Good Morning Merry Sunshine" *(child, children)*, "Buffalo Gals" *(foot, feet)*, "Two Little Kittens" *(mouse, mice)*, and "If All the Seas Were One Sea" *(man, men)* (see *Sing a Song of Poetry*), have the children use highlighter tape or a masking card to find plural nouns that are made by changing the spelling of the singular form.

Guided Reading: During word work, make four or five nouns with magnetic letters and then change the spellings to make them plural.

Interactive Writing: Call attention to rare plurals that change the spelling of the base word when they are used in interactive writing.

Independent Writing: Draw attention to plurals that change the spelling of the base word while conferring with children about their writing.

assess

- Notice whether the children are using conventional plural forms for nouns that change the spelling.
- Give the children four or five words and have them tell or write the plural form.

Expand the Learning

Continue playing Plural Lotto with other words so children can gain more practice. Use the Word Card Template (see *Teaching Resources*) to make cards for the new words you've chosen or use word cards from the lessons that address plurals.

Have children play Plural Concentration (see *Teaching Resources*, Games).

Connect with Home

Have children take home word cards and two Plural Lotto Game Cards so that they can play the game with family members.

25 Making Plural Forms: Summary

Sort and Write

Consider Your Children

Use this lesson after your children have studied all the plural forms and can think of examples of each. They should be familiar with the words used, although they may not be able to spell all of them accurately in plural form. Use different examples in the minilesson from those included in the deck of word cards children will sort. This lesson includes all the principles listed in the Continuum for plurals (p. 62), but it is not necessary to write all of them on the chart. You may want to write "Ways to Make Plurals" on the chart above the examples.

Working with English Language Learners

Use words that English language learners know and understand from having met them in other contexts. Since this is a summary lesson, it is important to have very clear examples that children can remember and rely on to help them read and write new plurals. If necessary, work with children in a small group to be sure they suggest examples with which they are very familiar. Teach them to refer to the summary chart as they produce a piece of interactive writing.

You Need

- Chart paper.
- Markers.
- Blank paper or Word Study Notebooks.

From *Teaching Resources:*

- Word Cards drawn from previous lesson (Lesson WS 24).

Understand the Principle

Children need to be able to categorize the kinds of plural forms they have been exploring. This lesson summarizes the principles that will help them move toward conventional spelling of many plural forms.

Explain the Principle

"Add *s* to some words to show you mean more than one (make them plural)."

"Add *es* to words that end with *x, ch, sh, s, ss, tch,* or *zz* to make them plural."

"Add *s* to words that end in a vowel and *y* to make them plural."

"Change the *y* to *i* and add *es* to words that end in a consonant and *y* to make them plural."

"Change *f* to *v* and add *es* to words that end in *f, fe,* or *lf* to make them plural."

"Change the spelling of some words to make them plural."

teach

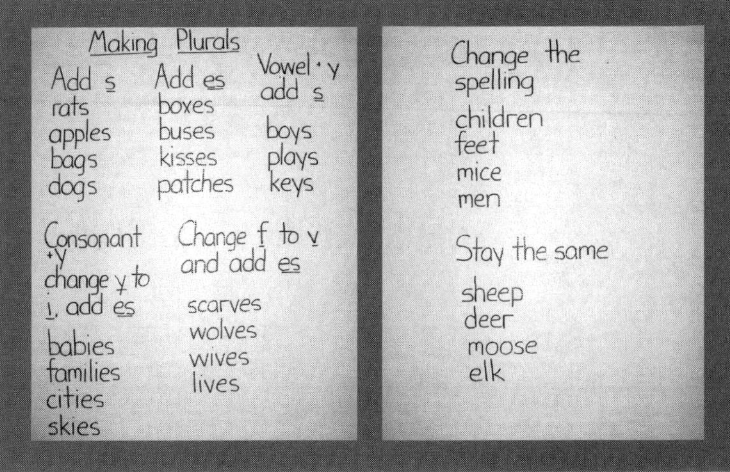

Explain the Principle

“ **Add *s* to some words to show you mean more than one (make them plural).** ”

“ **Add *es* to words that end with *x, ch, sh, s, ss, tch,* or *zz* to make them plural.** ”

“ **Add *s* to words that end in a vowel and *y* to make them plural.** ”

“ **Change the *y* to *i* and add *es* to words that end in a consonant and *y* to make them plural.** ”

“ **Change *f* to *v* and add *es* to words that end in *f, fe,* or *lf* to make them plural.** ”

“ **Change the spelling of some words to make them plural.** ”

① Tell the children that they are going to practice all they know about changing words that are singular into their plural form.

② Start with a blank chart with seven columns (in two rows if necessary). Ask the children to discuss what they have learned about plurals. Demonstrate and encourage comments such as:

“There are a lot of different ways to write plurals.”

“Most of the time you add *s*.”

“You can also add *es*.”

“For some words, you don't add *s*. They just stay the same.”

③ Suggested language: “You know a lot of different ways to make plurals. Today we are going to make a summary chart with all the different kinds of plurals you know. Let's name some plurals, and we'll put them in categories.”

④ Ask children to suggest plural forms. As they do so, place them in a column and label the column. For example, if a student offers *rats*, you might say: “I'll write *rats* in this column. How did you make that plural? [Students respond.] I'll put *add s* at the top. Are there any more examples of this kind of plural?”

⑤ Collect a few more examples, but do not be exhaustive. If a student offers a word in another category, go to another column and then ask the students to talk about how the plural is formed. You will be labeling the columns in response to children's thinking, and the categories can be in any order.

⑥ Work with the children until you complete all the columns. You need only two or three examples in each, but you can write more if children are producing them quickly.

⑦ Summarize by going over the different kinds of plurals they know.

⑧ Explain to the children that today they are going to sort words. They will take cards, read them, and group together the ones whose plurals are formed the same way.

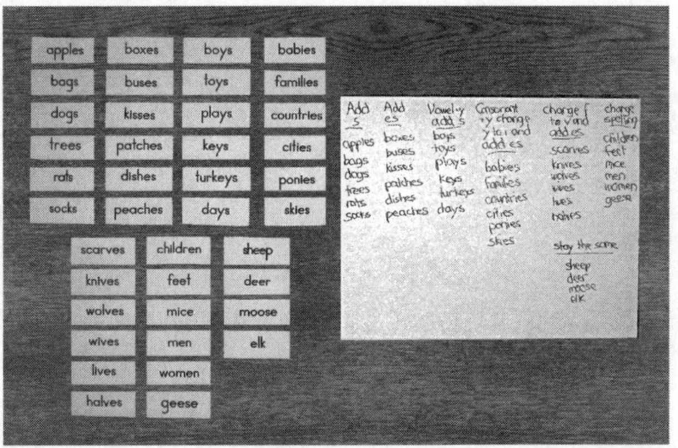

take
read
sort
write

▸ Have the children work with a deck of word cards that includes plurals formed in a variety of different ways. (Many of the words on the cards should be different than those used in the lesson.) Working with a partner, they take turns drawing a card, reading it, placing it in a column, and telling why, until they have sorted twenty words. Then they write the sort in a Word Study Notebook or on a sheet of paper with labels at the top that describe the words in the column (*s or es*, *ends in y*, etc.).

Ask the children what they noticed as they were sorting plurals. Were there any words that were tricky? Discuss how they can think about a plural form to decide how to spell it.

Link

Interactive Read-Aloud: Read aloud books that feature interesting new words that fit into the categories for forming plurals. Examples are:

- ***Pigs Aplenty, Pigs Galore*** by David McPhail
- ***Too Many Tamales*** by Gary Soto

Shared Reading: After you have read and enjoyed a poem or other texts together, have the children use a masking card or highlighter tape to find plural nouns that are made by changing the spelling and those that stay the same.

Guided Reading: During word work, make five or six nouns with magnetic letters and then change the spellings to make them plural. Or quickly write the word pairs on the whiteboard.

Interactive Writing: Working in a small group, help children compose a text in connection with an activity likely to require use of plurals (for example, a mathematics experience). Help children refer to the summary chart to problem-solve the spelling of plurals.

Independent Writing: Draw attention to plural forms while conferring with students about their writing.

assess

- Notice whether the children are using conventional plural noun forms in their own writing.
- Dictate six to ten words in their singular form and ask the children to make each word plural. Be sure to include words reflecting the variety of principles.

Expand the Learning

Play Plural Lotto (see *Teaching Resources,* Games) with words reflecting the variety of plural principles.

Connect with Home

Send home two sheets of word cards (use the Word Card Template in *Teaching Resources*) for children to sort according to plural category with their family members.

26 Recognizing Closed Syllables

Taking Words Apart

Consider Your Children

This lesson can precede or follow the lesson on *open* syllables. It involves teaching the children how to notice and use the vowel sound in the first syllable of two-syllable words, an important principle in syllabication. Be sure to use words the children have in their oral vocabularies.

Working with English Language Learners

Learning how vowels work in English is especially challenging for children who are just learning the language. Paying close attention to vowels and working with good examples are helpful. Use words children are familiar with and understand in oral language when you are reading aloud.

You Need

- Chart paper.
- Markers.
- Magnetic letters.

From *Teaching Resources:*

- Lesson WS 26 Word Cards.
- List Sheets.

Understand the Principle

Syllables are units of pronunciation within words. Every syllable has a vowel sound, and a vowel sound can be represented by more than one letter. Readers and writers use syllables to construct and take apart words. One important generalization about syllabication deals with *open* syllables, syllables ending in a vowel (V or CV), and *closed* syllables, syllables ending with at least one consonant (CVC). When children read two-syllable words, they need to try the first syllable as either short or long; if it doesn't sound right, they then try the remaining option. Some words may have a digraph at the beginning or end (*chicken,* for example).

Explain the Principle

"When a syllable ends with a vowel and at least one consonant, the vowel sound is usually short."

teach

When a syllable ends with a vowel and at least one consonant, the vowel sound usually is short.
pup py
lem on
rab bit
pup py
lem on
rab bit

Explain the Principle

“When a syllable ends with a vowel and at least one consonant, the vowel sound is usually short.”

① Tell the children that they are going to learn more about syllables in words.

② Make *puppy, lemon*, and *rabbit* with magnetic letters on the easel or write them on a chart.

③ Suggested language: “Read these words with me and help me think about the syllables you can hear.”

④ Read the words and have the children tell you the first syllable they hear.

⑤ By separating the magnetic letters, break each word into two syllables *(pup-py, lem-on, rab-bit)*. Suggested language: “What do you notice about the syllables?”

⑥ Children will notice that there are two syllables, each has a vowel sound, the first syllable is a consonant-vowel-consonant (CVC), and the vowel sound in the first syllable is short.

⑦ Explain that when the first syllable ends with a consonant, the vowel sound is usually short and it is called a *closed* syllable. Point out that the mouth is closed when they finish saying the first syllable (the mouth is open when they finish saying an open syllable). Write the principle at the top of the chart.

⑧ Explain to the children that when they want to read a word, they should look at the syllables. When they see one or two consonants in the middle of a word, they can divide the word *after the consonant* that follows the vowel (creating a *closed* syllable) and try the short vowel sound to see whether this sounds like a word (*lem*-on). If they don’t think it does, they should divide the word *after the vowel*, which creates an *open* syllable ending in V or CV and changes the vowel sound to long (*mo*-tel).

9 Summarize by telling the children that a *closed* syllable ends with a consonant (CVC, *cab*-in, or VC, *ab*-sent).

10 Tell the children that they are going to make two-syllable words with magnetic letters. Then they will divide them and write them on a List Sheet, using a dash to show where they divided the word into syllables (*lem*-on).

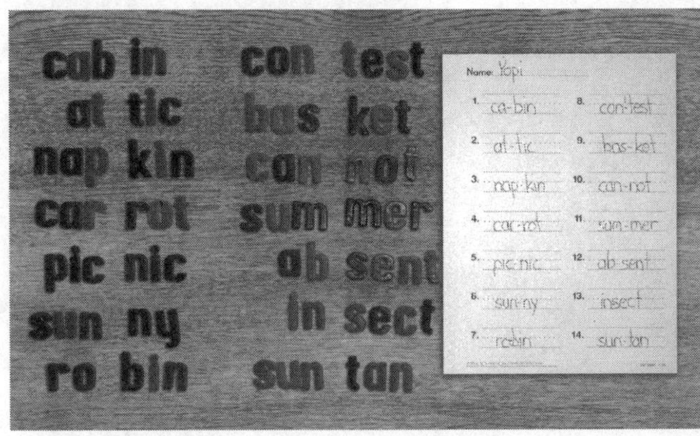

make
divide
write

- Have children use magnetic letters to build the two-syllable words on the word cards, break each word apart into syllables, and write words in parts on a List Sheet.

Make a few words on the easel and have a few children show how they took them apart.

Review the principle that a *closed* syllable ends with at least one consonant (or consonant digraph), and put an example on the word wall.

Link

Interactive Read-Aloud: Read aloud books that include multisyllable words, such as

- ***One Tiger Growls*** by Ginger Wadsworth
- ***Eggday*** by Joyce Dunbar

Shared Reading: After reading a poem such as "Donkey, Donkey" or "Four Seasons" (see *Sing a Song of Poetry*) several times, have the children locate three or four two-syllable words that have a first syllable that is *closed.*

Guided Reading: During word work, write a few words with *closed* first syllables on the whiteboard and have the children tell where to divide them. You may want to mix in a few *open* syllable words and talk about them.

Interactive Writing: When the children are going to write a multisyllable word, encourage them to think about the syllables.

Independent Writing: Prompt the children to say word parts as they try to write multisyllable words. Encourage them to think about each syllable and to be sure it has a vowel.

assess

- Dictate four or five words and have the children write them and divide the syllables.
- Observe children's use of syllabication as they try to read or write new words.

Expand the Learning

Repeat the lesson with other examples of two-syllable words with *closed* syllables. Use the Word Card Template (see *Teaching Resources*) to make cards for the new words you've used.

Have the children find more examples of words with *closed* first syllables.

Connect with Home

Send home a sheet of word cards with two-syllable words (use the Word Card Template in *Teaching Resources*) for children to read with family members.

27 Recognizing Open Syllables

Taking Words Apart

Consider Your Children

Children begin listening for syllables in Kindergarten and Grade 1. In this lesson, they learn one important pattern in syllabication that helps them read and write two-syllable words that have a single consonant in the middle. This lesson can precede or follow the lesson on *closed* syllables. Be sure to use words the children understand. By dividing multisyllable words, they will learn more about the structure of words.

Working with English Language Learners

An important beginning spelling principle is that every syllable has a vowel. Once English language learners know the vowels and can use them in words, they can use this principle to learn about the role of vowels. Provide explicit demonstrations of how to take apart two-syllable words with a single consonant in the middle. Have them perform the action with magnetic letters and say the syllables as they do so. Recognize that pronouncing vowels may be especially challenging to many English language learners.

You Need

- Chart paper.
- Markers.

From *Teaching Resources:*

- Lesson WS 27 Word Cards.
- List Sheets.

Understand the Principle

A syllable is a unit of pronunciation within a word. Every syllable has one vowel sound. The vowel can be a single letter, or it can have other vowels or consonants with it. Some syllables end in vowels (*ho*-tel or *po*-ny) and are called *open* syllables, while others end in consonants (*lem*-on or *cab*-in) and are called *closed* syllables. When they approach an unfamiliar word that has a single consonant in the middle, readers should try alternatives: pronounce the word (1) with the first vowel *long,* as an *open* syllable, or (2) with the first vowel *short,* as a *closed* syllable. The reader can then "match up" each with words known in oral language. Each works about half the time.

Explain the Principle

"When a syllable ends with a vowel, the vowel sound is usually long."

plan

Explain the Principle

" When a syllable ends with a vowel, the vowel sound is usually long. "

A syllable that ends with a vowel usually has a long vowel sound.

baby ba-by
motor mo-tor
hotel ho-tel
open o-pen

① Tell the children that they are going to learn more about syllables in words.

② Write *baby, motor, hotel,* and *open* on the chart.

③ Suggested language: "Read these words with me and help me think about the parts or syllables you hear."

④ Read the words and have the children tell you the first syllable they hear. Rewrite the word with a dash to show the syllable division *(ba-by).*

⑤ Suggested language: "What do you notice about the syllables?" Children will notice that there are two syllables, each has a vowel, and the first syllable ends with a vowel. Encourage them to identify the sound of the first vowel and conclude that it is long. If necessary, briefly review the idea that "long" means you say the name of the vowel.

⑥ Explain that when the first syllable ends with a vowel, it usually has a long vowel sound and is called an *open* syllable. Point out that the mouth is open when they finish saying the first syllable. Write the principle at the top of the chart.

⑦ Explain to the children that when they want to read a word, they should look at the syllables. When they see one consonant in the middle of a word, they can divide the word *after the vowel* (creating an *open* syllable) and try the long sound to see if it is a word (*fe*-ver). If the word doesn't sound right (like a real word), they should divide it *after the consonant* (creating a *closed* syllable), and the vowel will have a short sound (*lem*-on). Point out that the mouth is closed when they finish saying the first syllable.

8. Summarize by telling the children an *open* syllable ends with a vowel (a CV pattern) or can be a single letter (*o*-pen, for example).

9. Tell the children that they are going to read twenty words and cut the syllables apart.

take word
read word
cut parts
write divided word

▸ Show the children how to take the stack of two-syllable word cards and cut them into separate syllable cards. Ask them to take each word, read it, cut it into two syllables, and write the divided word on a List Sheet or in their Word Study Notebook. Have the children do this for up to twenty words.

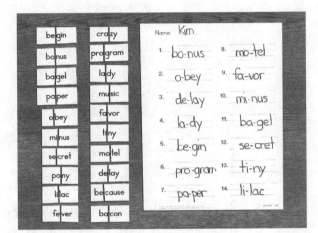

Invite a few children to tell where they divided words.

Review the concept of an *open* syllable, and put an example on the word wall.

Link

Interactive Read-Aloud: Read aloud books with many multisyllable words, such as

- ***Giant Jack*** by Birte Muller
- ***Flamingo Dream*** by Donna Napoli

Shared Reading: After you have read and enjoyed a poem such as "Silly Simon" or "New Shoes" together (see *Sing a Song of Poetry*), have the children locate three or four two-syllable words in which the first syllable is *open.*

Guided Reading: When children come to new two-syllable words with a consonant in the middle, prompt them to say the first part as an *open* syllable, trying the long vowel sound. If it doesn't sound like a word, have them try it as a *closed* syllable, with a short sound. They will have two alternatives to try in the sentence.

Interactive Writing: After you have written a text together, have the children point out two or three words with *open* first syllables (CV).

Independent Writing: Prompt the children to say words and write consecutive sounds. Point out words in their writing that have *open* (CV) and *closed* (CVC) syllables.

Expand the Learning

Repeat the lesson with other two-syllable words.

Have children look for other words that fit the syllabication pattern.

Repeat the lesson with two-syllable words with *closed* syllables (CVC).

Use the Word Card Template (see *Teaching Resources*) to make cards for the new words you've chosen.

Connect with Home

Have the children take home a sheet of word cards to read with family members.

assess

- Create a word grid (see *Teaching Resources*) with ten two-syllable words that have *open* first syllables and have the children read them.
- Observe the children as they take apart new words while reading to see if they are noticing the first *open* syllable.
- Notice improvement in spelling as children become more aware of syllables and the role of vowels.

28 Recognizing Open and Closed Syllables

Say and Sort

Consider Your Children

This lesson should follow lessons on recognizing and using *open* syllables and recognizing and using *closed* syllables. Your children should have good control of reading and writing CVC, CVC*e*, and compound words, as well as words with double consonants in the middle.

Working with English Language Learners

Work with a small group of English language learners to help them pronounce the words and think about the syllables. Accept approximations. This work with vowels will help them in pronouncing English words and, consequently, make it easier for them to read and spell words. Remember that there will always be variations in pronunciation among *all* speakers. Help children use magnetic letters or write the words, highlighting the *open* or *closed* syllables so that they can attend to the sound of the vowel.

You Need

- Pocket chart.

From *Teaching Resources:*

- Pocket Chart Card Template.
- Two-Way Sort Sheets.
- Lesson WS 28 Word Cards.

Understand the Principle

Syllables are units of pronunciation. *Closed* syllables end in at least one consonant (*nap*-kin), and the vowel sound is usually short. *Open* syllables end in a vowel, and the vowel sound is usually long (*ho*-tel). These principles help readers and writers as they read and write.

Explain the Principle

“When a syllable ends with a vowel, the vowel sound is usually long [*ho*-tel].”

“When a syllable ends with a vowel and at least one consonant, the vowel sound is usually short [*lem*-on].”

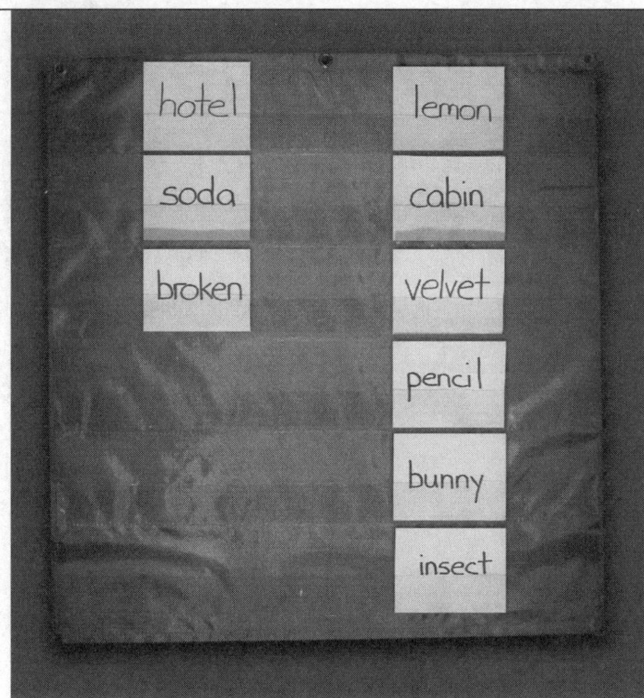

Explain the Principle

“When a syllable ends with a vowel, the vowel sound is usually long [*ho-tel*].”

“When a syllable ends with a vowel and at least one consonant, the vowel sound is usually short [*lem-on*].”

① Tell the children that you are going to help them think about words with *open* and *closed* syllables.

② Put the key words *hotel* and *lemon* at the top of two columns in the pocket chart. Read the two key words with the children.

③ Say another word, ask the children to clap the syllables with you, and then show the word card. Suggested language: “*Cabin: cab*[clap]-*in*[clap]. Show me where to put *cabin*. [Children will tell you to put it under *lemon*.] Yes, *cabin* has a *closed* first syllable like *lemon*, so we put it there.”

④ Continue with *velvet, soda, broken, pencil, bunny,* and *insect.*

⑤ Explain to the children that they will place the two key word cards *lemon* and *hotel* next to each other on their desk or table. They will take a word card, read it, and put it under the key word it resembles until they have sorted ten words with *open* first syllables and ten with *closed* first syllables. If a word begins with an *open* syllable like *hotel*, they will put it in that column. If a word begins with a *closed* syllable like *lemon*, they will put it in that column. Then they will write the words on a Two-Way Sort Sheet.

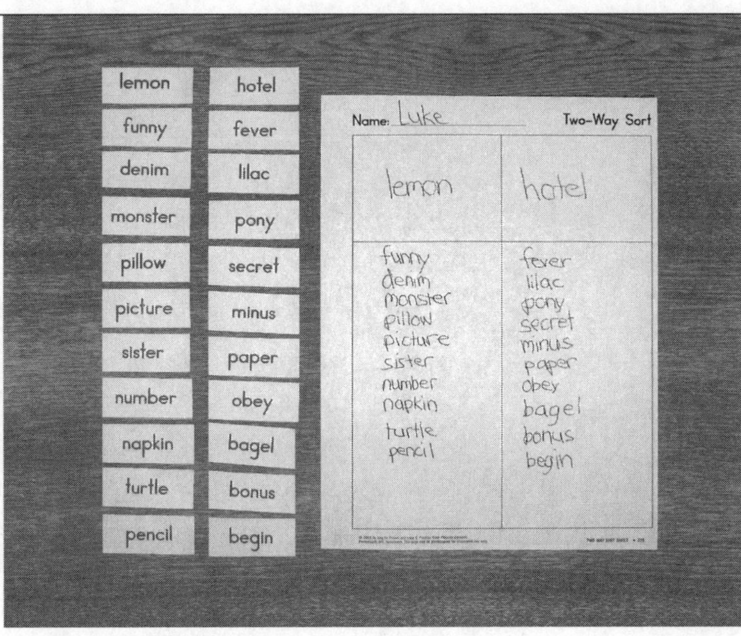

read
sort
write
read

- Have the children say and sort twenty words that begin with *open* and *closed* syllables. Then have them write the sort on the Two-Way Sort Sheet and read the columns to a partner.

Have the children read their sort to a different partner.

Invite them to give another word that begins with an *open* or *closed* syllable.

Review the examples on the word wall.

Link

Interactive Read-Aloud: Read aloud books containing multisyllable words and call attention to one or two. Examples of appropriate books are:

- ***Elinor and Violet*** by Patti Murphy
- ***Crocodile: Disappearing Dragon*** by Jonathan London

Shared Reading: After you have read and enjoyed a poem together, have the children use highlighter tape or a masking card to locate one or two words that begin with *open* and *closed* syllables.

Guided Reading: When the children come to a difficult word, prompt them to say the first part: "Try the first part." "Do you see a part that can help you?" "Look at the first part."

Interactive Writing: Prompt the children to say the syllables in a word prior to writing it. Help them think about writing syllables and being sure each syllable has a vowel.

Independent Writing: When the children are editing their writing, help them to be sure each syllable in their words has at least one vowel.

assess

- Have the children read and sort six words that begin with *open* or *closed* syllables.
- Have the children draw a slash between the syllables of five words.
- Notice improvement in spelling as children attend more closely to syllables and vowels.

Expand the Learning

Have children draw a slash between the two syllables of the words on their Two-Way Sort Sheet.

Repeat the lesson with other words with *open* and *closed* syllables.

Use the Word Card Template (see *Teaching Resources*) to make cards for the words you've chosen.

Connect with Home

Send home a pile of word cards in an envelope for children to say and sort with family members.

Word-Solving Actions

Word-solving actions are the strategic moves readers and writers make when they use their knowledge of the language system to solve words. These strategies are "in-the-head" actions that are invisible, although we can infer them from some overt behavior. The principles listed in this section represent children's ability to *use* the principles in all previous sections of the Continuum.

All lessons related to the Continuum provide opportunities for children to apply principles in active ways, for example, through sorting, building, locating, reading, or writing. Lessons related to word-solving actions demonstrate to children how they can problem-solve by working on words in isolation or while reading or writing continuous text. The more children can integrate these strategies into their reading and writing systems, the more flexible they will become in solving words. The reader/writer may use knowledge of letter/sound relationships, for example, either to solve an unfamiliar word or to check that the reading is accurate. Rapid, automatic word solving is a basic component of fluency and important for comprehension because it frees children's attention to focus on the meaning and language of the text.

Connect to Assessment

See related WSA Assessment Tasks in the Assessment Guide in *Teaching Resources:*

- Sorting Names
- Sorting Words
- Using Known Words to Read or Spell New Words
- Using Letter, Sound, and Word Knowledge to Solve Words and Monitor Reading
- Making New Words by Using What You Know

Develop Your Professional Understanding

See *Word Matters: Teaching Phonics and Spelling in the Reading/Writing Classroom* by G.S. Pinnell and I.C. Fountas. 1998. Portsmouth, New Hampshire: Heinemann.

Related pages: 46–47, 63–64, 90–93, 95, 222–228, 237–244.

1 Learning How to Learn Words: Buddy Study 1

Choose, Write, Build, Mix, Fix, Mix

Consider Your Children

Each five-day Buddy Study cycle highlights a principle your children can apply to spelling many words like those examples selected. Combine this lesson on routines with a lesson on a particular principle from the Continuum. Usually, you would use this first Buddy Study lesson very early in the year, but if your children have not had enough hands-on work with spelling principles, you may want to build a little more expertise first. Prior to this lesson, give high frequency word tests to help children create an ongoing list of words they need to learn. In addition, they will list (or you will add to their lists) words each week that they misspell in their writing and need to learn. The number of words children choose for the five-day cycle will vary (usually between five and ten). Since they are learning a principle, only a few examples are necessary. Since this is the first lesson on a series of new routines, feature a spelling principle that will be easy for your students.

Working with English Language Learners

Your class will be studying these words for five days, so it is important that the words your English language learners choose are meaningful to them. Avoid confusing words that they find difficult to pronounce. Easy high frequency words they do not yet know are always appropriate.

You Need

- Blank index cards.
- Magnetic letters.
- Buddy Study Pocket Chart for cards (see *Word Matters*).

From *Teaching Resources:*

- Words-to-Learn Lists.

Understand the Principle

Attending closely to letter patterns (and how they are related to sounds) helps children learn new words. Even more important, children need to learn the principles that explain how words are structured. They do this by examining words in categories. Powerful examples of words that illustrate the principle help them internalize "rules" they can apply to solving similar words. In this lesson, children use magnetic letters to help them attend to the visual features of words that illustrate a particular principle. In the process, they practice looking at words and noticing errors.

Explain the Principle

" You can make a word several times to learn the sequence of letters. "

plan

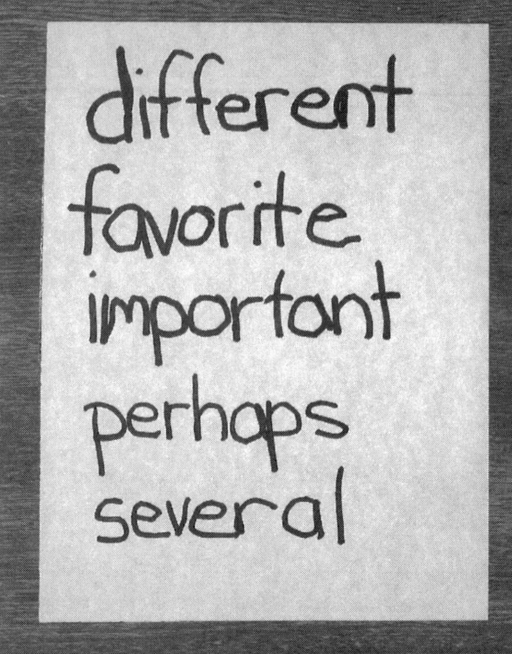

Explain the Principle

"You can make a word several times to learn the sequence of letters."

① Select and present a short lesson on a principle the children will be able to understand easily. Be sure there is a clear list of words that illustrate the principle.

② Explain to the children that you are going to show them how to learn new words. Suggested language: "Today you are going to select three [four, five] words from the lesson we have just completed. Write your words carefully on an index card." Have children choose words from the lesson and write them on the cards.

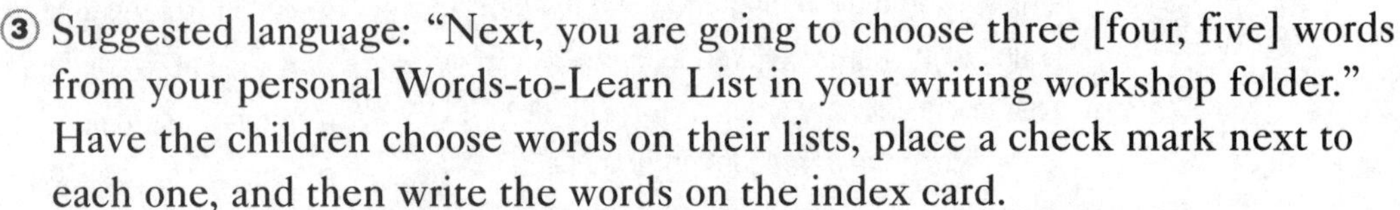

③ Suggested language: "Next, you are going to choose three [four, five] words from your personal Words-to-Learn List in your writing workshop folder." Have the children choose words on their lists, place a check mark next to each one, and then write the words on the index card.

④ Suggested language: "I will be checking your words." Check one student's words for accuracy and place your initials on the index card. "When I put my initials on your card, you know that your words are spelled right. That's important because you are going to use this index card to work on your words all week."

⑤ Show the children where their index cards will be kept (usually in a Buddy Study Pocket Chart; each child has a pocket with his or her name on it).

⑥ Suggested language: "Next, you are going to build each word three times with magnetic letters and check it letter by letter. You check each letter on the card with each letter in the word you made, and you say the names of letters aloud as you check them—s-s, t-t, a-a, y-y." Demonstrate building a word and checking it letter by letter with the word on the index card. Then mix the letters and quickly build and check it two more times.

⑦ Show the children how to put the index cards back in the Buddy Study Pocket Chart so they will be available next time.

choose
write
build
mix
fix
mix

- Have the children choose the specified number of words from the minilesson list and the same number from their personal Words-to-Learn List and build them each three times. Rotate as they write their words to review each child's index card and initial the right corner to show you have checked the words for correct spelling.
- Have the children place their cards in the Buddy Study Pocket Chart so they will be available for the cycle of learning activities. You may want children to make a second set to take home for practice.

Ask the children to talk about the principle presented in the lesson and share more examples.

Ask them to tell how building the words is helping them.

Answer any questions they have about selecting and building words.

Link

Interactive Read-Aloud: Read aloud books that invite children to inquire about words. Examples are:

- ***Goose's Story*** by Cari Best
- ***Little Clam*** by Lynn Reiser

Shared Reading: Using a familiar poem or other text, have children find words that have similar patterns.

Guided Reading: During word work, have the children build words that fit the lesson principle. Building words quickly may be important for children who are not noticing visual features or who are working slowly.

Interactive Writing: Point out patterns as the children construct words. Remind them of the lesson principle when appropriate. If you are working with a small group of inexperienced second graders, have them practice checking letter by letter a word they have written. They can use a word from the word wall or one you write. This will help them learn to use resources in the room.

Independent Writing: Remind the children to check their writing to see that their Buddy Study words are spelled correctly.

Expand the Learning

Repeat the lesson if needed to reinforce the routine.

Connect with Home

Have the children practice making their Buddy Study words at home with magnetic letters or letter cards.

assess

- Notice whether the children are building words accurately and quickly.
- Look at writing samples over several weeks to determine whether the children are using the lesson principle in their daily writing.

2 Learning How to Learn Words: Buddy Study 2

Look, Say, Cover, Write, Check

Consider Your Children

Previously you taught your children a principle, and they selected words from the lesson as well as some personal words. They are ready to use the study method Look, Say, Cover, Write, Check when they are able to select their own words and keep records of their learning. Each child needs a "spelling buddy"; be sure that the pairs of children are able to read each other's words. Form pairs of children similar in their spelling development. It is very important to work with the children until they have habituated the routine and can use it quickly and efficiently. Demonstrate, have them use the routine, and then have them self-evaluate. Some teachers have found it helpful to set a timer in the beginning so children know they are working with limited time.

Working with English Language Learners

Look, Say, Cover, Write, Check is an easy technique to use, but it takes a little practice to do efficiently. Work in a small group with English language learners to be sure they are doing the steps in order and with some precision. Demonstrate the routine as often as necessary.

You Need

- Index cards with Buddy Study words.
- Highlighters.
- File folders with one side cut in three or four strips (see illustration).

From *Teaching Resources:*

- Look, Say, Cover, Write, Check Sheets (select from two different forms).
- Large version of Look, Say, Cover, Write, Check Sheet (for your demonstration).

Understand the Principle

Remembering the details of words requires looking at them closely and noticing the features that make them different from every other word. Children need to learn how to look at words and then test their memory of those features. The deliberate moves in Look, Say, Cover, Write, Check build strategies for remembering and checking that children can use to learn new words thoroughly and quickly. This "slowed-down" way of considering the word ultimately becomes automatic.

Explain the Principle

"You can look at a word, say it, cover it, write it, and check it to help you learn to spell it correctly."

Explain the Principle

"You can look at a word, say it, cover it, write it, and check it to help you learn to spell it correctly."

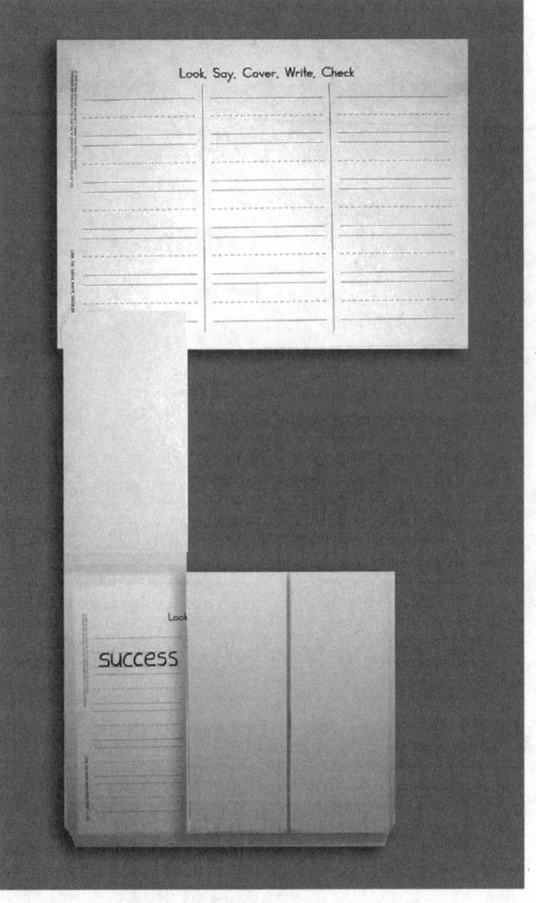

① Briefly review the lesson from day one. Suggested language: "Yesterday you chose words and made them. Today you are going to learn a way to study your words."

② Place a representation of a Look, Say, Cover, Write, Check Sheet on the easel as an enlarged model.

③ Hold up a regular-size Look, Say, Cover, Write, Check Sheet, and then place it in a precut file folder with all the flaps open.

④ Suggested language: "You are going to write one of your Buddy Study words in the first column on the left. Then you check it with the same word on your index card letter by letter. I'm going to do this on my sheet." Demonstrate, and then ask a child to come up to demonstrate.

⑤ Suggested language: "Then you are going to look carefully at the word and cover the word with the flap. Write the word in the next column and then check it letter by letter with the word that you know is correct." Demonstrate.

⑥ Show the children how to look at the word in the left column again and write it in the third column (and fourth column, depending on which sheet you are using). They check the word each time and notice any mistakes.

⑦ Finally, if a word is still misspelled in the last column, show the children how to highlight the part to remember (turned-around letter, wrong letter, omitted letter, etc.). Then tell them to make the misspelled word three times with magnetic letters and check it with the word on the Buddy Study index card.

apply

look
say
cover
write
check

- Have the children use Look, Say, Cover, Write, Check with their spelling buddies.

Ask the children to talk about the principle being highlighted in this Buddy Study cycle.

Explain that they will be using Buddy Study each week to focus on their spelling.

Link

Interactive Read-Aloud: Read aloud books that invite children to inquire about words. Examples are:

- ***No More Kissing*** by Emma Clarke
- ***Slim and Jim*** by Richard Egielski

Shared Reading: Model locating and checking a word in a familiar text.

Guided Reading: Encourage the children to look at a difficult word closely and check it. During word work, have the children look at a word, cover it, build it with magnetic letters, and then check it. Work with children who are having difficulty learning to use the routine smoothly and quickly.

Interactive Writing: When the children want to write a word, demonstrate looking carefully at the same word in another text or on the word wall, writing it, and checking it. Remind children to check a word after writing it on the chart.

Independent Writing: When the children use words that are on the word wall or in their personal word banks, encourage them to use a quick version of Look, Say, Cover, Write, Check. They will not be using the folders but will be looking closely, writing the word without looking, and checking it.

Expand the Learning

Repeat the lesson as needed to reinforce the routines.

Connect with Home

Have the children take their Buddy Study index cards home in order to practice the words with family members.

assess

- Notice whether the children are applying the principle highlighted in this Buddy Study cycle in their daily writing.
- Ask children to proofread their writing to be sure they have correctly spelled the words they have been learning.

3 Learning How to Learn Words: Buddy Study 3

Buddy Check

Consider Your Children

In this lesson, children learn how to notice and correct spelling errors using the check-and-try-it-again technique. Your children will need to have a spelling partner. Be sure partners have about the same spelling ability, so that they can read each other's words and use them in sentences.

Working with English Language Learners

Buddy Check offers English language learners a systematic way of checking their own learning of words. Be sure that partners know how to pronounce the words and use them in sentences. You may need to work with some pairs to be sure that they are using words correctly in sentences.

You Need

- Highlighters.
- Markers.
- Magnetic letters.
- Cookie sheet.
- Index cards with Buddy Study words.

From *Teaching Resources:*

- Buddy Check Sheets.
- Large version of Buddy Check Sheet.

Understand the Principle

Children need to learn that looking at a word can help them arrive at the correct spelling. When they notice a word seems wrong, they can try other letter sequences until the pattern "looks right."

Explain the Principle

"You can write a word, look at it, and try again to make it 'look right.'"

"You can notice and think about the parts of words that are tricky for you."

"You can write words to see if you know them."

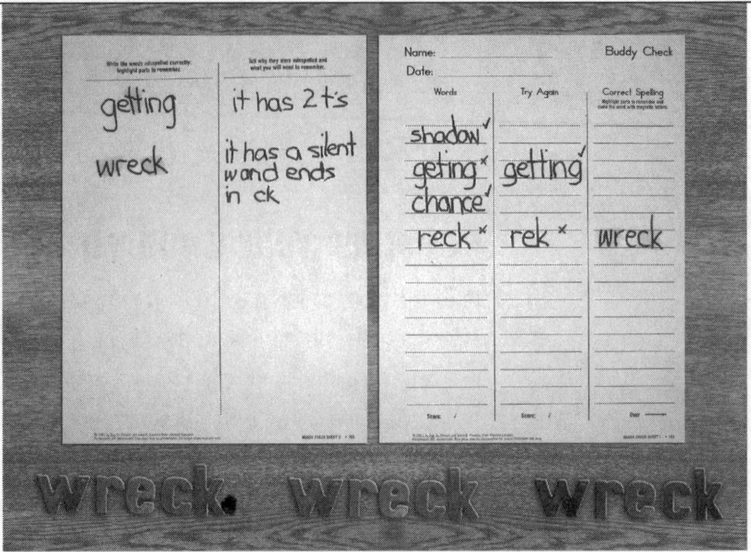

Explain the Principle

"You can write a word, look at it, and try again to make it 'look right.'"

"You can notice and think about the parts of words that are tricky for you."

"You can write words to see if you know them."

1. If necessary, refer briefly to the day one lesson.
2. Suggested language: "Yesterday you used Look, Say, Cover, Write, Check to study words. Today you are going to do Buddy Check to see which words you know. I am going to show you a good way to fix your own spelling errors."

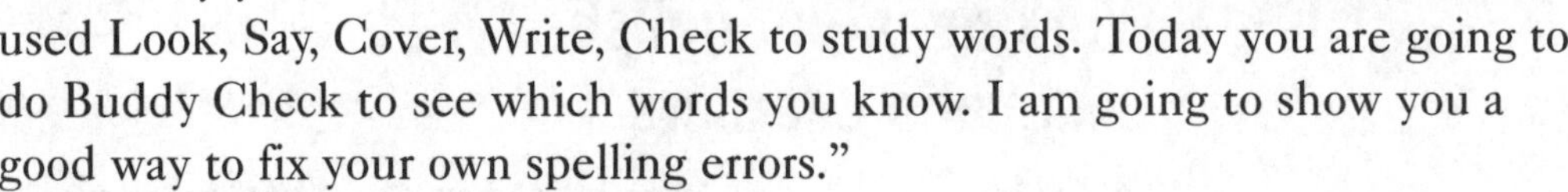

3. Have a child write her words, which you say one at a time and use in a sentence, in the first column of the enlarged Buddy Check Sheet. (Arrange with the demonstration child beforehand to make at least one error so that you can show the other children what to do.)

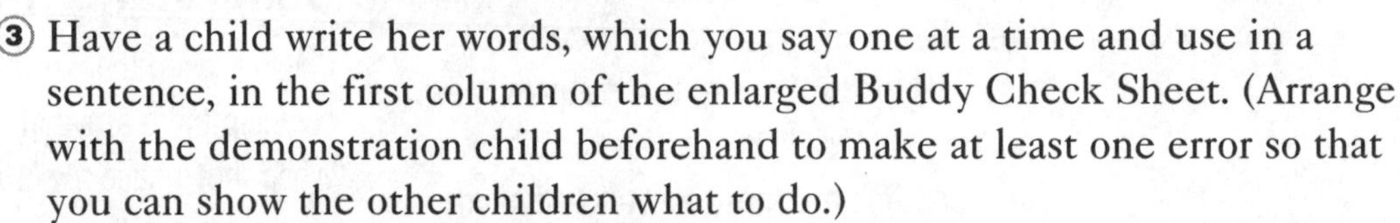

4. When the child has finished writing the words in the first column, check them one at a time and make a check mark by every word written correctly. Make an X next to any incorrect words, and ask the child to try them again. If there are any words still wrong, write these words correctly in the last column.
5. Ask the child to look at the correct spelling of the word(s) in the last column and say what she wants to remember about the word(s). Have her write the word(s) in the bottom section of the sheet and highlight the tricky part with a highlighter marker or to circle it.
6. Have her make the word three times with magnetic letters and then write what she wants to remember (for example, there are two *t*s in *getting*).
7. Explain to the children that they will do Buddy Check with their spelling partners.

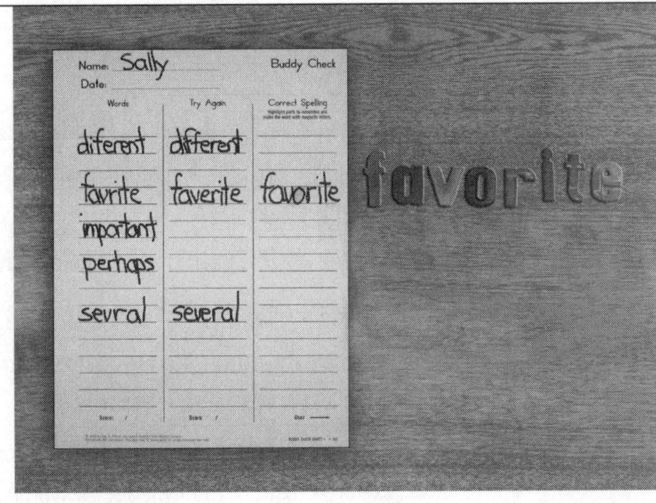

write
try again
mark
write

- Have partners complete the Buddy Check.

Have the children share some of the statements they made on their sheets about the tricky words.

Link

Interactive Read-Aloud: Read aloud books that invite children to inquire about words. Examples are:

- ***Dig, Wait, Listen*** by April Pulley Sayre
- ***Wish, Change, Friend*** by Ian Whybrow

Shared Reading: Model locating and checking a word in a familiar text.

Guided Reading: During word work, have the children test their knowledge of words by quickly writing some familiar words that you dictate. Have partners check each other's words. Have the children write the words they miss and highlight the parts they need to remember.

Interactive Writing: When working with small groups, have the children write high frequency words quickly and then check them. Have them highlight the parts that are tricky.

Independent Writing: Have the children proofread their writing to be sure they have correctly spelled the words they have been studying.

assess

- Observe the children's self-correction strategies when they are writing independently.
- Ask children to proofread their writing to be sure they have correctly spelled the words they have been learning.

Expand the Learning

Repeat the lesson featuring a different principle to reinforce the routines.

Connect with Home

Have the children take their Buddy Check Sheets home. Family members can dictate and check the words.

Learning How to Learn Words: Buddy Study 4

4

Making Connections

Consider Your Children

Your children need to "overlearn" the strategies for decoding words and developing a formal approach to accurate spelling. Throughout the first Buddy Study cycle, observe the children to see how they are using the word learning techniques. You will probably need to go through the cycle again, demonstrating and reminding, three or four times. No time will be lost for instruction because you will be teaching a new minilesson on a principle. You will be demonstrating and reminding children of the Buddy Study routines in addition.

In this minilesson, you will be using the simplest Making Connections Sheet and helping children think of one or two simple ways to connect words.

Working with English Language Learners

Making connections requires English language learners to notice features of the words they are studying and link them with other words they know. Doing so helps them form personal word networks. Work with them in small groups to be sure they understand the concept of making connections and remind them that they can transfer features of words they know to words they don't yet know.

You Need

- Magnetic letters.
- Index cards with Buddy Study words.

From *Teaching Resources:*

- Making Connections Sheets.
- Large version of Making Connections Sheet.

Understand the Principle

Children need to develop a network of knowledge about language. Rather than learning each word separately, good word solvers learn principles, strategies, and patterns that help them use old knowledge to create new knowledge. Establishing the habit of looking for common patterns and making connections among words by how they look or sound or what they mean helps children form categories of words.

Explain the Principle

"You can use parts of words you know to read or write new words."

"You can use what you know about words to read new words."

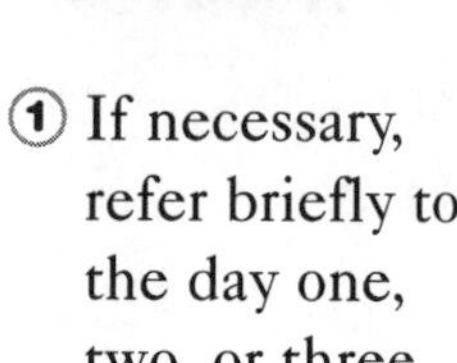

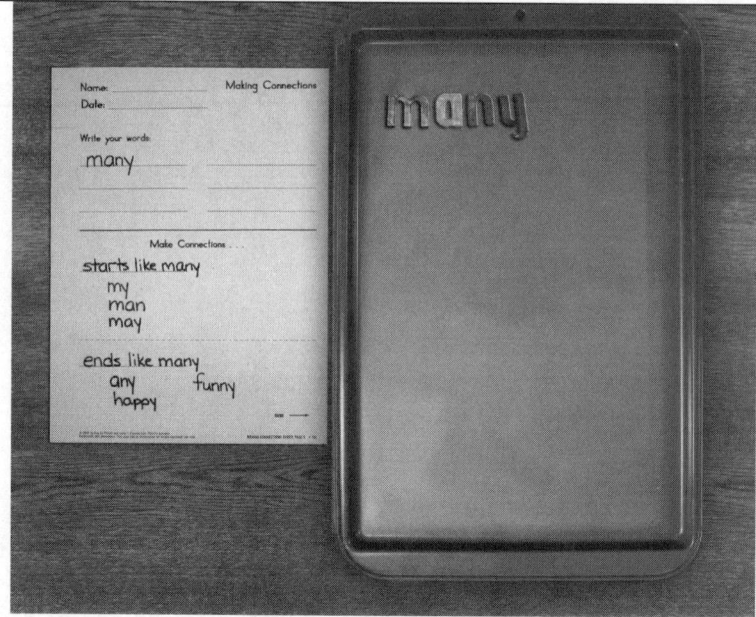

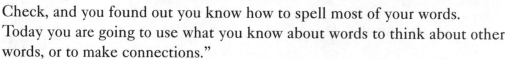

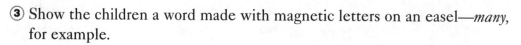

Explain the Principle

“You can use parts of words you know to read or write new words.”

“You can use what you know about words to read new words.”

① If necessary, refer briefly to the day one, two, or three lesson.

② Suggested language: “Yesterday you did Buddy Check, and you found out you know how to spell most of your words. Today you are going to use what you know about words to think about other words, or to make connections.”

③ Show the children a word made with magnetic letters on an easel—*many*, for example.

④ Ask if they know another word that starts like *many*. Children may suggest words such as *my, man, may.*

⑤ Then ask the children if they know any words that end like *many*. Children may suggest words like *any, happy, funny*.

⑥ Suggested language: “Today you are going to think of words that start like and end like your Buddy Study words. You can use the word wall and your own word lists as resources. I’m going to show you how to record your connections.”

⑦ Show the children the enlarged Making Connections Sheet and demonstrate filling it out.

⑧ Explain that as the year goes on, they will be making many different kinds of connections among words, but for today they should try to think of three words that start like and three words that end like each of their Buddy Study words.

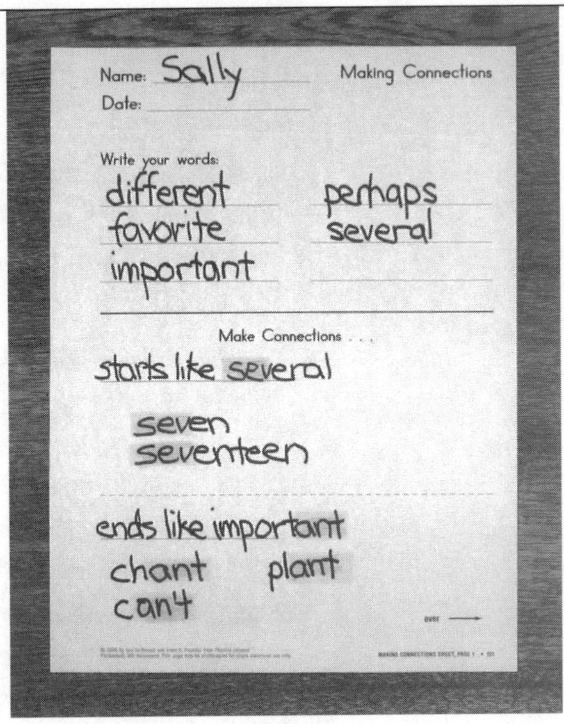

write
connect x 3

▸ Have the children use their Buddy Study words to make connections. Ask them to write each word on their list and then write three words that start the same and three words that end the same.

Have the children share one connection they have made for each word, using language like this (which you may need to demonstrate):

"*Both* starts like *big*."

"*Both* ends like *with*."

Post a chart that lists the kinds of connections children have learned how to make: start the same, end the same. As you teach children to make other connections and as they discover more ways, you can add them to the chart.

Link

Interactive Read-Aloud: Read aloud books that invite children to make connections among words. Examples are:

- ***The Perfectly Orderly House*** by Ellen Kindt McKenzie
- ***October Smiled Back*** by Lisa Westberg Peters

Shared Reading: After you have enjoyed a poem or story together, ask the children to find words that start or end the same, using a masking card or highlighter tape to mark them.

Guided Reading: When reading a new text, prompt the children to solve a new word by thinking about whether they know words that are similar in some way.

Interactive Writing: When the children want to write a new word, ask them to think of words they know that start or end like it.

Independent Writing: Prompt the children to spell a new word by thinking of a similar word they know.

assess

- Dictate a few easy words to the children. Ask them to write each word and make one connection between that word and another word.

Expand the Learning

Repeat the lesson to reinforce the routine.

Teach the children how to make other connections:

words with the same middle sound
words with the same vowel sound
words that start or end the same
words that rhyme
words with the same consonant clusters
words that have the same endings
words that mean about the same
words that mean about the opposite
words that are related in meaning

Connect with Home

Have the children take their Making Connections Sheets home to share with family members.

Encourage them to think of more connections at home and bring them back to share with the rest of the class.

5 Learning How to Learn Words: Buddy Study 5

Buddy Test

Consider Your Children

It is important for children to be successful on this final Buddy Test. Observe your students closely over the four days of work in the cycle. They should spell almost all of the words correctly by the third and fourth days. If they do not, you may need to reduce the number of words, help them choose less difficult words, or evaluate how well they have engaged with each of the ways of learning words. The teacher will evaluate the test and use the information for planning future lessons.

Working with English Language Learners

English language learners particularly need to experience success. You can predict their performance on the Buddy Test by looking at their Making Connections Sheets. If children are having a great deal of difficulty, work with them in a small group, helping them make their words with magnetic letters and talking about word features. You may need to make the experience more meaningful. Help them use the words in sentences during interactive writing.

You Need

- Index cards with Buddy Study words.
- Word Study Notebooks.

From *Teaching Resources:*

- Words-To-Learn Sheet.

Understand the Principle

Good writers spell words accurately in a largely unconscious way, paying attention to what they want to communicate. Ultimately, spellers must call to mind the features of a word and produce it in writing without a model, fluently and automatically. When spellers try new words, they get an idea of what they control and what they need to learn and remember. Therefore, after five days of learning a set of words, spelling partners or buddies dictate each word and use it in a sentence.

Explain the Principle

“You can write words to see if you know them.”

teach

Explain the Principle

"You can write words to see if you know them."

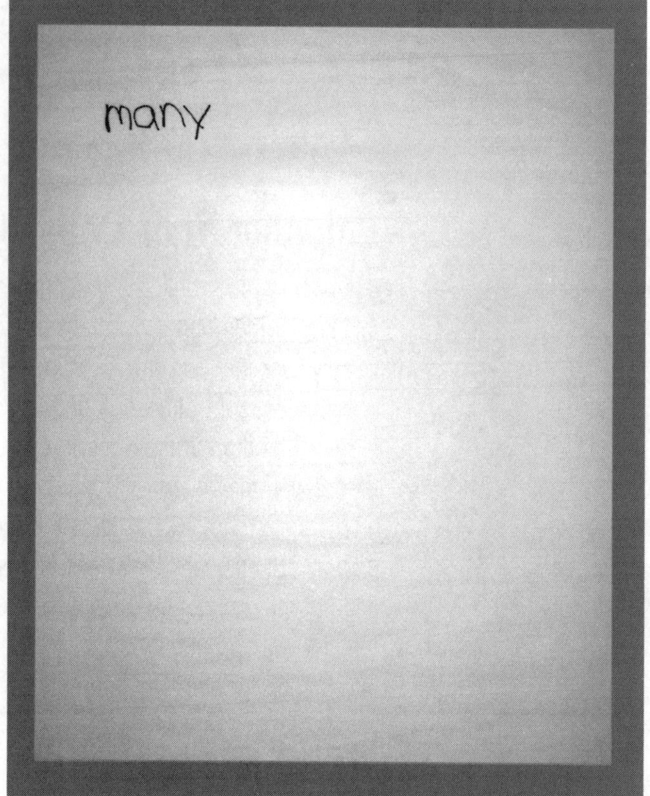

1. Suggested language: "Yesterday you made connections with your Buddy Study words. Today you are going to test your knowledge of the words. Your buddy is going to read each of your words to you and use it in a sentence, just like on the Buddy Check. You are going to write your words in your Word Study Notebook and put the notebook in the basket for me to check." Show the children the designated place where they are to turn in their Word Study Notebooks.
2. Ask a child to come up to the chart and demonstrate saying a word and using it in a sentence: "*Many*. I have *many* friends at school."
3. Tell the partners who are taking the test to say *ready* when they are ready to hear the next word. Encourage the partners who are giving the test to let the writers take the time they need to think about and write the word.
4. Suggested language: "After you give your buddy the test, then your buddy gives you the test. Buddies don't check each other's words, so this won't take a lot of time."

say
write

- Have partners administer the Buddy Test.
- Check the children's work to determine how effective the week of study has been. When you return the Word Study Notebooks, have the children make any words they misspelled with magnetic letters. Ask the children to circle the checks next to the words on their Words-to-Learn Lists (in their writing workshop folders) to show they have learned them. Any misspelled words should be selected again later.

You may want to organize your sharing to focus on the principle you have used for your initial minilesson. Have children talk about what they have noticed about words (from the application activity).

Another alternative for sharing is to have children talk about the features of words that they will remember after the Buddy Test.

Link

Interactive Read-Aloud: Read aloud books that invite children's curiosity and expand their listening vocabularies, such as

- ***Looking Out for Sarah*** by Glenna Lang
- ***Beto and the Bone Dance*** by Gina Freschet

Shared Reading: After you have read and enjoyed a text together, invite the children to share what they notice about any of the words in the text. Model some interesting comments, such as "I see *y* at the end of *my* and it sounds like *i*."

Guided Reading: If the children need to give greater attention to features of words, spend one or two minutes building words with magnetic letters and checking them with the same words in the book.

Interactive Writing: Have the children check the accuracy of a word they have written by checking it with the word wall or a word card.

Independent Writing: Remind the children that they are expected to spell accurately all the words they have successfully written on the Buddy Test.

assess

- Observe the children's accurate spelling in their independent writing.
- Keep records of the words children have spelled successfully on the weekly test.

Expand the Learning

Repeat the Buddy Study cycle to be sure the children have learned the routines.

Connect with Home

Invite the children to take copies of their Buddy Tests home to show family members the words they have learned to spell.

6 Recognizing and Using Syllables

Syllable Race

Consider Your Children

Use this lesson after your children have good control of letter/sound relationships, are familiar with many spelling patterns, and know a lot of one-syllable words. In this lesson, they learn how to take apart new multisyllable words by noticing word parts. Be sure the words you use are within your children's oral language vocabularies.

Working with English Language Learners

Breaking words apart into syllables helps English language learners zero in on the details of English words. They hear clear, slowed-down pronunciations, as well as the breaks indicating different parts. Use words that you can make meaningful by using pictures, actions, or sentences. Provide repeated opportunities for these children to work with syllables, and accept approximate pronunciations.

You Need

From *Teaching Resources:*

- Directions for Follow the Path, which you can adapt for the Syllable Race.
- Follow the Path Game Cards made from Lesson WSA 6 Word Cards and Deck Card Template.

Understand the Principle

A syllable is a unit of pronunciation; it enables readers and writers to take apart longer (multisyllable) words. The number of syllables in a word is also equal to the number of times the speaker opens his mouth or moves his jaw down. Syllables help readers think about the number of vowel sounds they hear in a word. They also help readers separate the base word from any affixes.

Explain the Principle

"You can divide a word into syllables to read it."

plan

teach

Explain the Principle

"You can divide a word into syllables to read it."

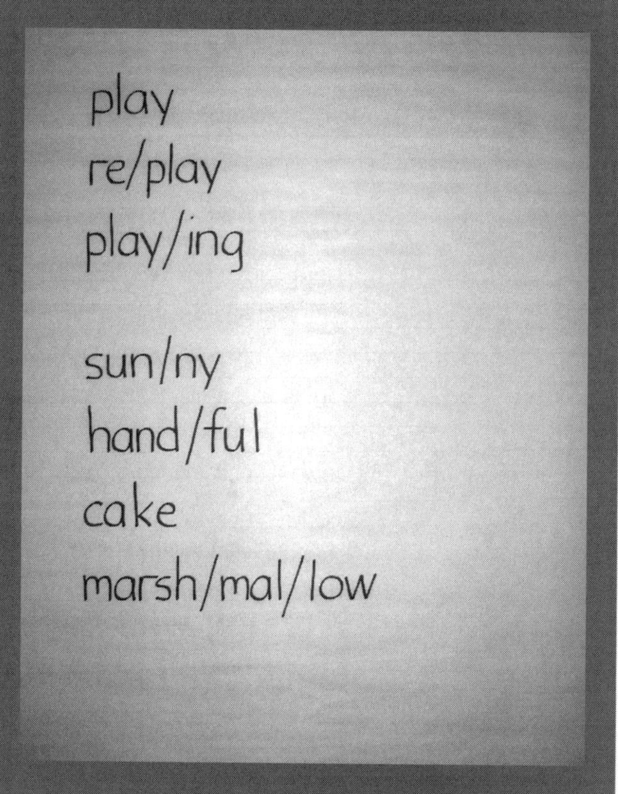

play
re/play
play/ing
sun/ny
hand/ful
cake
marsh/mal/low

① Tell the children that they are going to learn how to read longer words.

② Write the words *play*, *replay*, and *playing* on a chart. (It helps to start with examples that have the same base word.) Have the children say the words with you and listen for the parts they hear.

③ Point out that the word *play* is one syllable and that it is the base word in *replay* and *playing*. The prefix and suffix both form a syllable, and you can hear one vowel sound in each syllable. You may also point out that your jaw drops two times when you say *replay* and *playing* and only once when you say *play*.

④ Repeat with the words *sunny*, *handful*, *cake*, and *marshmallow*. Have the children listen for and notice parts that help them take the words apart.

⑤ Explain that you divide a word into syllables to read it.

⑥ Tell the children that today they are going to play Syllable Race. Demonstrate the game. They will take a card, read it, tell the number of syllables, and say the word in syllable parts. They will move their marker the same number of spaces as syllables in the word.

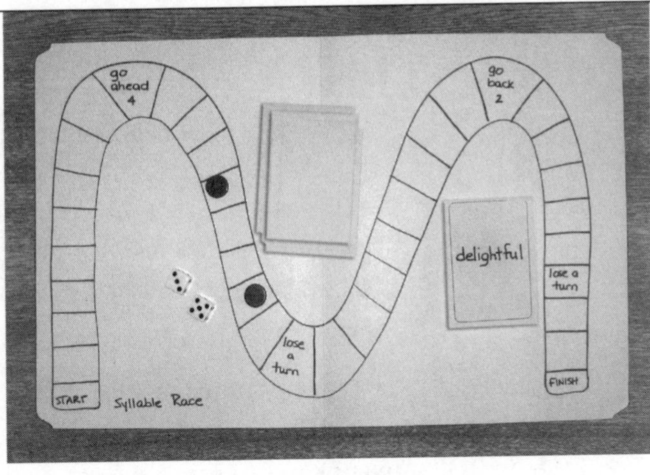

take
read
tell
divide
move

- Have the children play Syllable Race. The spaces on the path are blank except for a few spaces that say "Go ahead 4" or "Go back 2." Each player places her marker at start, takes a word card, reads the word, tells the number of syllables, and pronounces the word again slowly so that each syllable can be heard (for example, "Party, two, par-ty"). The player then moves her piece the number of syllables that are in the word. The first player to reach the end wins the game.

Have the children name a few objects in the classroom while you add the words to the chart. Then ask them to tell where they hear the break in these words.

Link

Interactive Read-Aloud: Read aloud books with multisyllable words. After doing so, have the children say two or three words and divide them into syllables as you write them on a chart. Examples of appropriate books are:

- ***Clams All Year*** by Maryann Cocca-Letter
- ***I Love You Like Crazy Cakes*** by Rose Lewis

Shared Reading: After you have read and enjoyed a poem such as "The Animal Fair," "Gregory Griggs," "Moses Supposes," or "The Months of the Year" together (see *Sing a Song of Poetry*), have the children locate three or four words with two or three syllables using a masking card or highlighter tape. Have them say the word in parts.

Guided Reading: When the children come to new words as they read text, prompt them to notice parts so they can break the word down smoothly and efficiently. Use language such as "Do you see a part that can help?" "What do you know that can help?" or "Look at the first part."

Interactive Writing: When the children are writing longer words on the group chart, have them say the parts and write one part at a time.

Independent Writing: As the children write new words, have them say each part by itself.

assess

- Observe the children's ability to take apart longer words as they read texts.
- Have the children read four or five multisyllable words; note how efficient they are in taking words apart.

Expand the Learning

Repeat the lesson with different words, and provide a different set of word cards for the Syllable Race game.

Teach the children to play the Word Grid game with syllables (see *Teaching Resources,* Word Grid).

Connect with Home

Send the Syllable Race game and word cards home so the children can play the game with family members.

Generative Lesson

7 Making Connections Between Words That Start the Same

Making Connections

Consider Your Children

This lesson should follow lessons that help your children notice various word parts. Assess their ability to connect words that start the same, focusing on the beginning letters only; they may not be able to spell the rest of the words conventionally.

Working with English Language Learners

Children who are learning English words for the first time may find it difficult to notice connections among them. This explicit lesson helps them see obvious connections and communicates the idea that connections will be helpful in solving words. Work with a small group if necessary; have the children make words with magnetic letters so that they can take them apart and put them back together.

You Need

- Magnetic letters.
- Chart paper.
- Markers.

From *Teaching Resources:*

- Lesson WSA 7 Word Cards.
- Word Link Sheet.

Understand the Principle

Children need to notice similarities among words and use them to solve new words. Words can start with the same vowel, consonant, consonant cluster, or digraph. They can also begin with the same syllable (*be*-fore, *be*-gan).

Explain the Principle

"You can connect the beginning of a word with a word you know."

plan

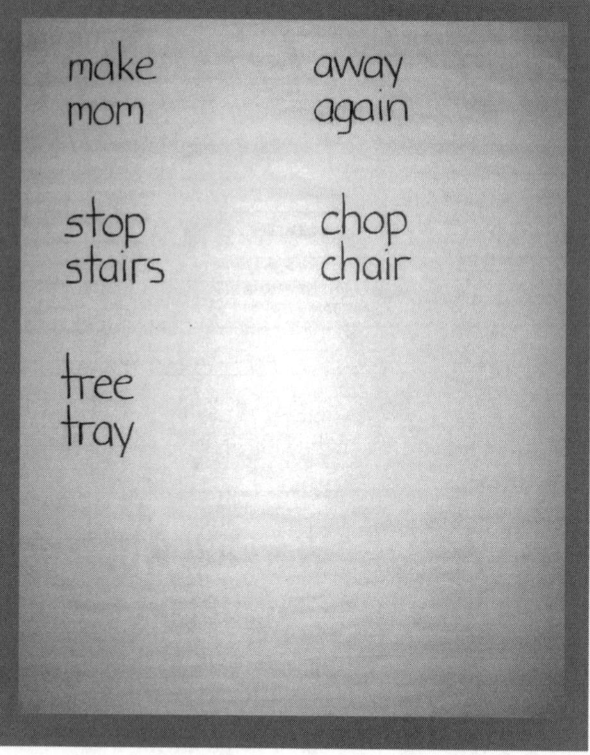

teach

Explain the Principle

"You can connect the beginning of a word with a word you know."

1. Explain to the children that you are going to help them notice more about how words are alike.
2. Have the words *make/mom, stop/stairs, chop/chair, tree/tray, away/again* written on a chart.
3. Suggested language: "What do you notice about these words?" Read the words with the children. They will notice that the words start the same. Some start with the same first letter or first two letters.
4. Add other words that begin with two- or three-letter clusters.
5. Explain to the children that when they know the first part of one word, they can notice it in other words.
6. Summarize like this: "You can connect the beginning of the word with a word you know."
7. Explain to the children that today they are going to select six word cards that start with a different letter or letter cluster, make each word with magnetic letters, and then write the words, one in each box of a Word Link Sheet. Underneath each word, they will write two more words that start like that word.

take card
make with letters
write word
write two more words

▸ Have the children take six word cards, make the words with magnetic letters, enter the words on a Word Link Sheet, and write two other words that start the same.

Have the children choose one box of words to read to a partner.

Link

Interactive Read-Aloud: Read aloud books that feature sound substitutions at the beginning of words, such as

- ***Aster Aardvark's Alphabet Adventures*** by Steven Kellogg
- ***The Hungry Thing*** by Jan Slepian

Shared Reading: After you have read and enjoyed a poem such as "Clouds" or "One Misty, Moisty Morning" (see *Sing a Song of Poetry*), have the children find several words that start with a particular letter or letters and have the class think of another word that starts the same way. Make the words with magnetic letters.

Guided Reading: When the children come to a new word, prompt them to connect what they know: "Do you know a word that starts like that?" or "Do you see a part you know?"

Interactive Writing: Prompt the children to think of words they know to help them start to write a new word.

Independent Writing: Encourage the children to make connections to words they know in order to write new words.

Expand the Learning

Repeat the lesson with words beginning with other consonant clusters and digraphs.

Have the children play Follow the Path with words that start the same (see *Teaching Resources*). Write words with consonant clusters, consonant digraphs, or beginning vowels on each space. They take a word card, read it, and move to the next space that has a word that starts the same. Alternatively, they roll a die, move the number of spaces, read the word, and tell another word that starts the same.

Connect with Home

Give the children other word cards and a Word Link Sheet to take home and complete with family members.

assess

- Observe how the children connect the beginning letters or letter clusters they know as they read or write new words.
- Dictate four or five words; then ask the children to write other words that start like these words do. Are the beginnings the same?

8 Making Connections Between Words That End the Same

Make and Write

Consider Your Children

This lesson should follow a lesson on making connections between words that start the same. If your children have difficulty noticing and using the last parts of words they know to figure out new words, help them identify connected words for several days.

Working with English Language Learners

Being able to connect words they know will make English language learners' word solving more flexible and efficient. Many of these children try to learn words as isolated units; instead, they should search for connections. Have the children write some of the words, highlighting the ending parts that are alike.

You Need

- Chart paper.
- Markers.
- Magnetic letters.
- Highlighters.

From *Teaching Resources:*

- Lesson WSA 8 Word Cards.
- Word Pairs Sheets.

Understand the Principle

Words can end with the same letter, letter cluster, or rime (pattern). Noticing and using ending parts such as these helps children solve unfamiliar words. They learn to use parts they know to figure out a word they don't know.

Explain the Principle

"You can connect the ending of a word with a word you know."

plan

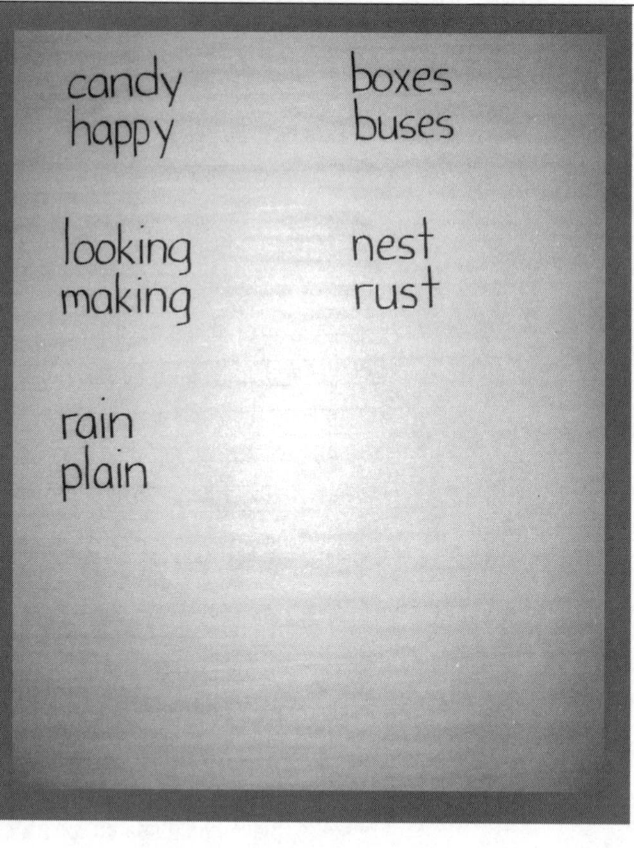

candy
happy
boxes
buses
looking
making
nest
rust
rain
plain

Explain the Principle

"You can connect the ending of a word with a word you know."

1. Remind the children that they have learned how to connect the beginning parts of words they know to other words. Tell them you are now going to help them notice and use the ending parts of words.
2. Have five pairs of words that end the same on the chart.
3. Have the children read each pair with you. Suggested language: "What do you notice about these two words?" Children respond that they end the same and tell the letters that are the same.
4. Explain to the children that they are going to make words that end the same.

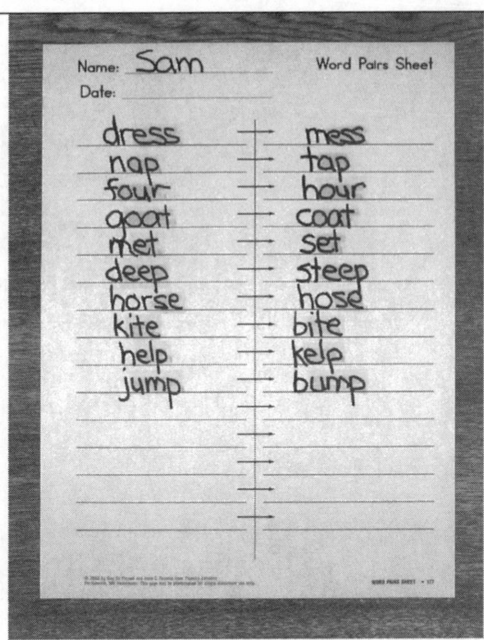
Name: Sam Word Pairs Sheet
Date:

dress	mess
nap	tap
four	hour
goat	coat
met	set
deep	steep
horse	hose
kite	bite
help	kelp
jump	bump

take card
make word
write word
make new word
write new word
highlight same part

▸ Have the children select ten word cards, one at a time. Ask them to take the card, make the word with magnetic letters, write it on the left side of a Word Pairs Sheet, make a new word that ends the same, and write it on the right side of the sheet. (Remind them that *ends the same* means the same ending letter, letter cluster, or rime.) Then have them use a highlighter pen to highlight or underline the ending part that is the same in both words.

Have children read their ten pairs to a partner.

Link

Interactive Read-Aloud: Read aloud books that feature words that end the same, such as

- ***Barnyard Song*** by Rhonda Gowler
- ***Monkey Do!*** by Allen Ahlberg

Shared Reading: After you have read and enjoyed a poem such as "The Brook," "Susie Moriar," or "Little Robin Redbreast" together (see *Sing a Song of Poetry*), have the children use a masking card, highlighter tape, or flag to find pairs of words that end the same.

Guided Reading: After reading a text, have the children locate two or three words that end the same. In word work, write three or four unfamiliar words on a whiteboard. Ask the children to think of a word that ends the same as each word.

Interactive Writing: Prompt children to think about a word they know when writing the ending of a new word.

Independent Writing: When conferring with writers, point out words that end the same.

assess

- Observe whether the children apply word endings they know to new words.
- Dictate four or five words and have children write other words that end the same.

Expand the Learning

Repeat the lesson using words with other endings.

Repeat the lesson, inviting the children to connect a word with two other words, one that starts the same and another one that ends the same.

Have children play the Word Grid game. They cross out words on their grid that end the same as the word card.

Connect with Home

Send home a Word Pairs Sheet and a list of words. Have the children make the words with magnetic letters or letter cards, write each word, and make and write a new word that ends the same.

9 Making Connections Between Words with the Same Pattern

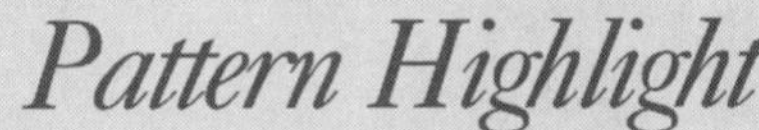

Consider Your Children

To benefit from this lesson, your children should have good control of basic letter patterns, common phonograms, consonant clusters, and consonant digraphs. As they connect words through letter sequences, they will be able to use these connections to solve new words.

Working with English Language Learners

Making connections among words helps English language learners make sense of written English. Instead of learning each word in isolation, they begin to form word categories and are able to recognize patterns more quickly. Use words they understand and, for the most part, can read. The important learning here is to notice word patterns and actively search for connections among those patterns.

You Need

- Chart paper.
- Markers or highlighter tape.

From *Teaching Resources:*

- Lesson WSA 9 Word Cards.
- Word Pairs Sheets.

Understand the Principle

Children need to develop a network of strategies for solving words. By connecting letter sequences or patterns they know with new words they are trying to solve, they will be able to solve these new words more efficiently and better attend to the meaning of the text.

Explain the Principle

" You can connect words that have the same letter patterns. "

Explain the Principle

"You can connect words that have the same letter patterns."

① Tell the children that they are going to learn how to look for letter patterns that are the same.

② Write *light* and *might* on the chart and invite a child to highlight with a marker or highlighter tape the letters that are the same. Do the same with *running, sitting; play, tray; race, trace; unpack, untie.*

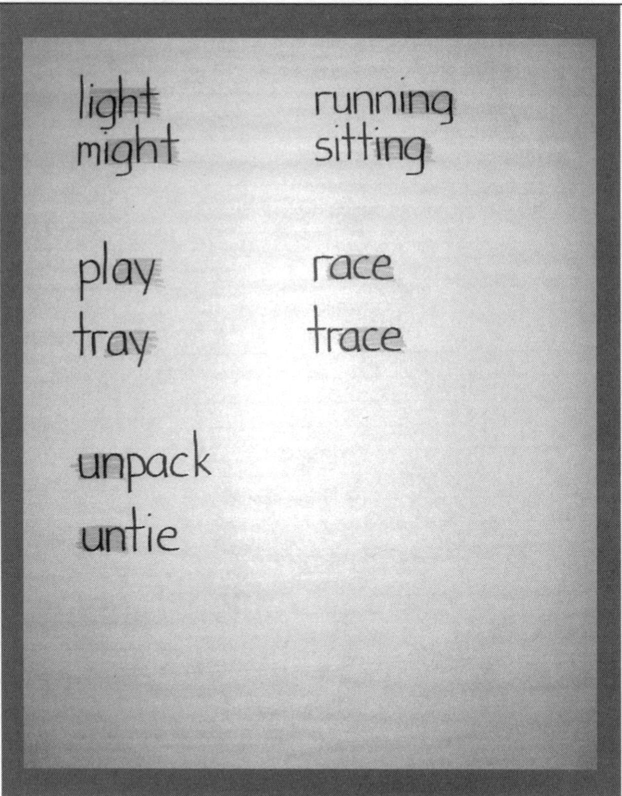

③ Explain that you can connect words that have the same letter pattern.

④ Tell the children that today they are going to create ten word pairs that have the same letter pattern. They will select a word and then write another word that has the same pattern. They will then underline (or highlight with a marker) the parts that are the same.

take
write
connect
highlight

▸ Have the children take a word card, write the word on a Word Pairs Sheet, and then write another word that has same letter pattern. Have them create ten pairs of words. Ask them to highlight or underline the letter sequence that is the same.

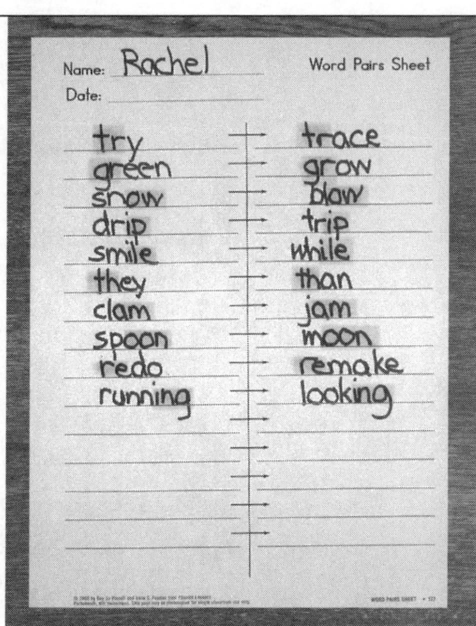

Name: Rachel
Word Pairs Sheet
Date:
try — trace
green — grow
snow — blow
drip — trip
smile — while
they — than
clam — jam
spoon — moon
redo — remake
running — looking

Invite the children to share two or three pairs of words they connected. Add the pairs of words to the class chart.

Link

Interactive Read-Aloud: Read aloud books that feature word connections, such as

- ***Quilt Counting*** by Lesa Cline-Ransome
- ***Little Fish, Lost*** by Nancy Van Laan

Shared Reading: After you have read and enjoyed a poem or song together, have a child select a word and call on another child to write a word that has the same letter pattern.

Guided Reading: When the children are problem-solving new words, prompt them to use patterns they know: "Do you know a word like that?"

Interactive Writing: Prompt the children to use letter sequences or parts from words they know as they attempt to write new words.

Independent Writing: Point out letter sequences or patterns in familiar words as children write so they can see how to make connections.

assess

- Observe whether the children use known patterns as they read and write.
- Dictate two or three words and ask the children to write another word that has the same letter pattern.

Expand the Learning

Repeat the lesson with different word cards.

Have the children play a game with a partner. They tell a word to their partner, who makes it with magnetic letters, connects it with another word with the same pattern, and makes the second word. Then the partners switch roles.

Connect with Home

Invite each child to write five names of objects in a room in his home (the kitchen, for example) and think of a word with the same letter pattern for each. Have them bring their lists to school to share.

Send home a Words Around the Room Sheet (see *Teaching Resources*) on which you have entered a category such as words that start the same, words that end the same, or words that have the same pattern. Ask the children to pick a room and write down everything they see that fits the category.

10 Using Word Parts to Solve Words

Word Ladders

Consider Your Children

This lesson should follow many basic lessons on using what you know about words to solve new words. Work with easy examples. At first, be sure the children not only know the words you are using parts of but also know the new words you make; then move on to solving less familiar words. Teach the strategy in the clearest way possible, letting the children know the potential resource they have in known words.

Working with English Language Learners

If English language learners think of words as isolated items, they won't learn new words efficiently. Help them use the store of words they have learned to make connections with new words. If their reservoir of English words is limited, you can still help them use what they know.

Decrease the difficulty of the task by changing the stipulations; for example, they can make word ladders by changing *all but* one or two letters. Alternatively, give children words or cards and have them arrange them into word ladders.

You Need

- Chart paper.
- Cookie sheet.
- Whiteboard.
- Magnetic letters.
- Highlighters or markers.

From *Teaching Resources:*

- Word Ladder Sheets.

Understand the Principle

Children can use a core of known words to figure out many new words. They need to learn that parts (beginnings, middles, endings, prefixes, suffixes, syllables) of words they know can help them figure out new words. Keeping this principle in mind will make them active word solvers.

Explain the Principle

"You can use what you know about words to read new words."

plan

Explain the Principle

“ You can use what you know about words to read new words. ”

① Explain to the children that they have learned a lot about words and that today they will learn how to use many different word parts to figure out new words.

② Make the word *my* with magnetic letters. Ask the children to make another word like *my*. They will likely make a word that starts or ends the same (for example, *my–mom* or *my–by*).

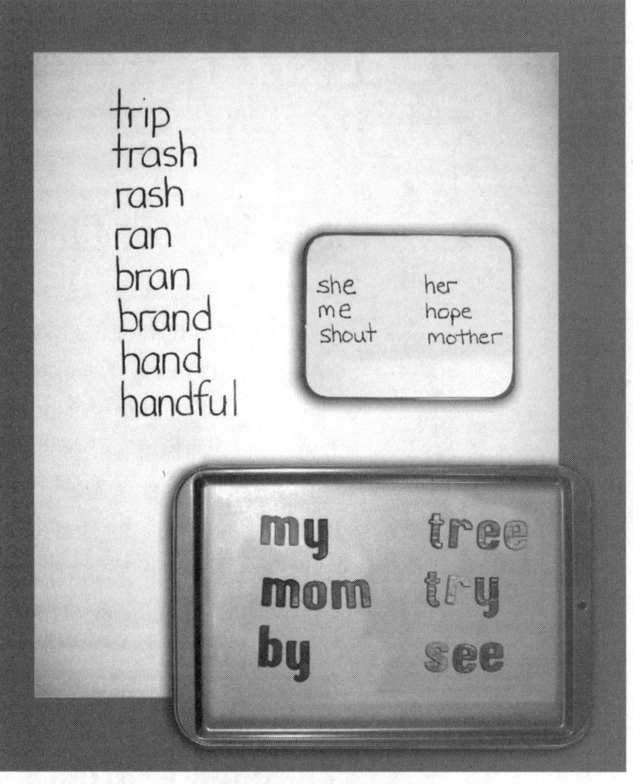

③ Repeat for *tree (try–see), she (me–shout),* and *her (hope–mother).*

④ Select other words, make each on a whiteboard, and make a similar one below it.

⑤ Next show the children how to make word ladders. Write one word and change, add, or remove one or two letters to make a new word, make another new word by changing, adding, or removing one or two letters, and so on, for as many words as you can. See photograph.

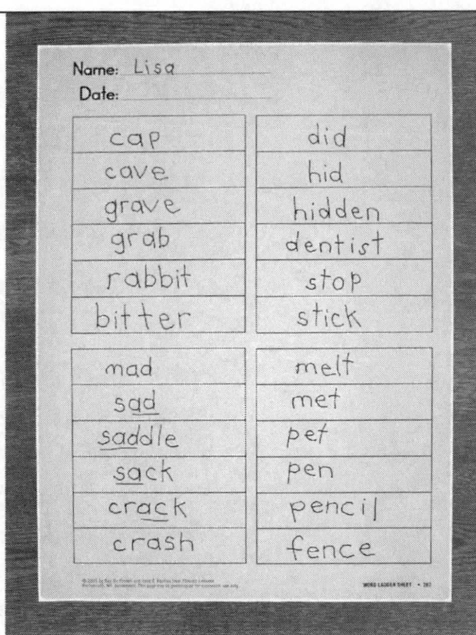

write word
make word
write word
change letters
write new word
highlight similar parts

- Have the children make a minimum of four word ladders on a Word Ladder Sheet. Ask them to make a word with magnetic letters, write it in one of the boxes on the sheet, change, add, or remove one or two letters, and write the new word. When they have finished a ladder, have them highlight the word parts in each word that they used from the word above on the ladder to make the new word.

Have the children read one word ladder to a partner.

Show two or three ladders so the children can see a great variety of connections.

Link

Interactive Read-Aloud: Read aloud books that feature word changes, such as

- ***The Fish Who Could Wish*** by John Bush
- ***The Tale of Three Trees*** by Angela Elwell Hunt

Shared Reading: Enjoy poems together that encourage connections between words such as "A Nonsense Alphabet" or "Four Seasons" (see *Sing a Song of Poetry*). *Teaching Resources,* Rhymes, Alliteration, and Language Play bibliographies provide more examples.

Guided Reading: When the children come to new words, prompt them to use word parts: "Do you see a part you know?" "What part can help you?" "Look at the first part." "The last part is like ____________." "That word is like __________."

Interactive Writing: Prompt the children to use a word or word part they know to help them write a new word.

Independent Writing: Help the children use their core of known words as resources for writing new words. Encourage them to use the word wall as a resource.

Expand the Learning

Repeat the lesson with other words.

Connect with Home

Send home a Word Ladder Sheet and have the children make word ladders with family members.

assess

- When you prompt children to use word parts, note their speed and success.
- Give the children a list of four or five words and ask them to write words that are connected to these words in some way.

11 Using What Is Known to Solve Words

Word Race

Consider Your Children

Your children should have worked with consonant clusters, consonant digraphs, and a variety of phonograms prior to this lesson on onsets (word beginnings) and rimes (the vowel-bearing part of a syllable).

Working with English Language Learners

English language learners may be thinking of words as whole entities, and they need to learn to look at the parts. If these children have difficulty breaking words into parts, work with them in a small group, using magnetic letters to build words and divide them into first and last parts. Be sure the children understand the words used as examples.

You Need

- Pocket chart.

From *Teaching Resources:*

- Pocket Chart Card Template.
- Category Word Cards, Onsets and Rimes as a resource for words for making the game board.
- Follow the Path Game Board.
- Directions for Follow the Path, which you can adapt for the Word Race game.

Understand the Principle

Readers need to focus on clusters of letters: reading words letter by letter is inefficient. This lesson focuses on noticing and using the *onset* (the consonant or consonants that make up the first part of a word or syllable) and the *rime* (the vowel-bearing part of the word or syllable). The children work with one-syllable words to learn how to take words apart.

Explain the Principle

“You can use word parts to solve a word.”

“You can look at the first and last parts of a word to read it.”

Explain the Principle

"You can use word parts to solve a word."

"You can look at the first and last parts of a word to read it."

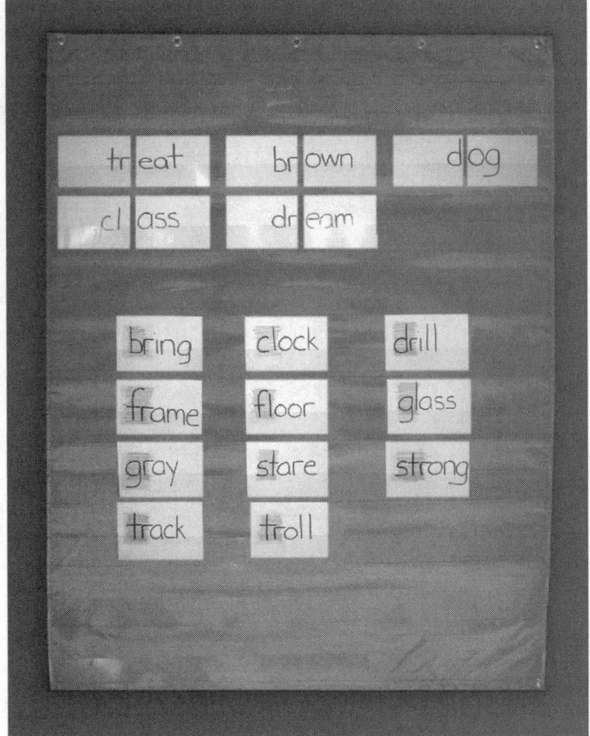

1. Tell the children that they are going to learn how to use word parts to read and write words quickly.
2. Place a consonant cluster onset card (*tr*, for example) in the pocket chart. Tell the children it is the first part of a word. Then add a phonogram or rime (*eat*, for example). Tell them it is the last part of a word and that you now have a complete word, *treat*. Repeat with *br–own, d–og, cl–ass, dr–eam, fl–ake, gr–een, pr–ince, st–ore, str–ipe*.
3. Explain to the children that you can look at the first and last parts of a word to read it.
4. Remove the combined onset and rime cards and place whole words *(bring, clock, drill, frame, floor, glass, gray, stare, strong, track, troll)* in the pocket chart one at a time.
5. Ask the children to come up to the chart to highlight the first part and read the word.
6. After working with four or five words, have them find and highlight the last part of the words you place in the chart.
7. Tell the children that today they are going to play Word Race.

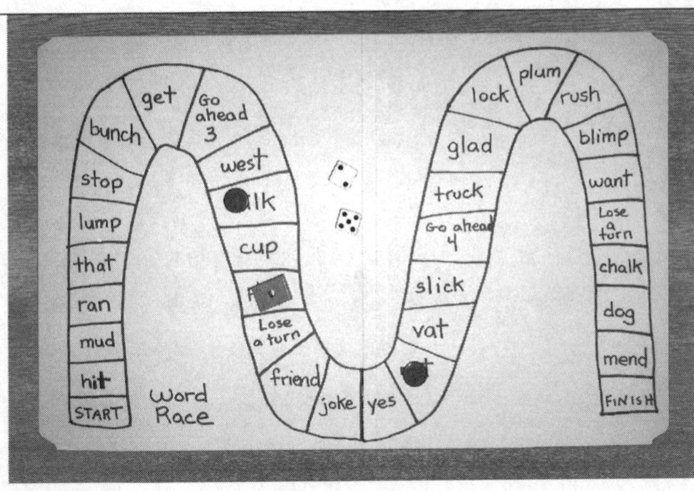

apply

throw
move
read
tell

- Have the children play Word Race in groups of two, three, or four. They place their colored markers at Start, throw a die, move the number of spaces, read the word written on the space, and tell the first and last parts. The first player to get to the end wins.

Hold up a few one-syllable word cards and have the children read them and tell the parts.

Link

Interactive Read-Aloud: Read aloud books with rhymes so the children can hear and notice word parts. (See *Teaching Resources,* Rhyme Books Bibliography for many examples.) Examples are:

- ***Hey, Little Ant*** by Phillip and Hannah Hoose
- ***Word Wizard*** by Cathryn Falwell

Shared Reading: After you have read and enjoyed a poem such as "Bed in Summer" or "The Squirrel." For an example of this type of wordplay, share "Eletelephony" (see *Sing a Song of Poetry*). Have the children use a masking card, flag, or highlighter tape to locate the first and last parts of a few words.

Guided Reading: As the children read a text and come to a new word, show them how to use their finger to cover the last part of a word so they can attend to the first part. Then show them how to uncover the rest of the word and look at the last part.

Interactive Writing: As the children write a word, prompt them to think about the first part and the last part.

Independent Writing: Prompt the children to think of word parts as they try to spell new words.

Expand the Learning

Repeat the lesson with other examples.

Have children play Word Race a different way. When they land on a space, they read the word and tell another word that starts with the same first part. Or they can give another word that has the same last part.

Connect with Home

Send home some colored markers, a block with numbers on it to use as a die, and a Word Race Game Board, so the children can play Word Race with family members.

assess

- Dictate four or five words and ask the children to mark the first and last part of each.

12 Using Letter Clusters to Solve Words

Word Grid Game

Consider Your Children

This lesson helps the children learn how to use two- or three-letter word parts to take apart new words. They should have worked with initial letter clusters or onsets and be able to recognize and say the first and last parts of words.

Working with English Language Learners

Developing the ability to take words apart to solve them gives English language learners power over words and helps them notice the details of written language. Have these children work with magnetic letters so they will see explicitly how letter clusters work. You may want to repeat this lesson for your English language learners using different examples.

You Need

- Pocket chart.
- Die with six consonant clusters or digraphs written on the sides.
- Simply drawn picture cards (glove, clock, skate, shoe).

From *Teaching Resources:*

- Lesson WSA 12 Word Cards.
- Directions for Word Grid game.
- Word Grid Sheets made from the Word Card Template and the Word Lists for Lesson WSA 12.

Understand the Principle

There are many groups of letters or letter clusters that often appear together. They include consonant clusters (blends such as *pl* and consonant digraphs such as *sh*). Being able to recognize and use these word parts helps children take words apart when they read.

Explain the Principle

“You can use word parts to solve a word.”

“You can look at the first and last parts of a word to read it.”

plan

Explain the Principle

“You can use word parts to solve a word.”

“You can look at the first and last parts of a word to read it.”

1. Tell the children that you are going to help them learn more about using word parts.
2. Have pictures of a glove, a clock, a skate, and a shoe in the pocket chart. Hold up word cards that name these pictures, one at a time, and ask the children to notice the first part and place the word card next to the correct picture.
3. Explain that the letter cluster at the beginning of each word is a word part that they will see in many words. Underline or highlight the letter cluster.
4. Explain to the children that today they are going to play the Word Grid game.

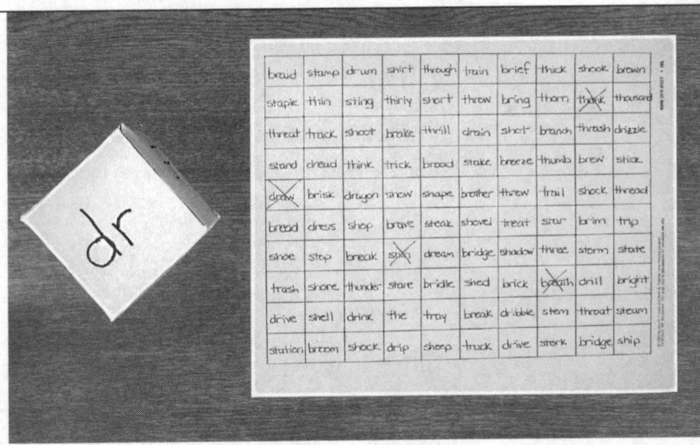

take
write
mark

- Give each child a Word Grid Template on which there are words beginning with a consonant cluster or digraph. Taking turns, each child throws a die, looks for a word on the grid that starts with the same letter cluster, says the word, and crosses it out. The first child to cross out all the words on the sheet wins the game.

Have the children read their Word Grid Game Sheets to a partner.

Add a few more words to the pocket chart and have children highlight the beginning letter cluster.

Link

Interactive Read-Aloud: Read aloud books that feature many words with consonant clusters and digraphs, such as

- ***One Duck Stuck*** by Phyllis Root
- ***Puddles*** by Jonathan London

Shared Reading: Use poems and songs such as "Combinations" (see *Sing a Song of Poetry*) that include words that start with letter clusters and digraphs.

Guided Reading: Demonstrate how to cover the last part of the word with your finger while you look at the first part. Then uncover the whole word.

Interactive Writing: Prompt the children to think of words that start like the words they want to write.

Independent Writing: Prompt the children to use their knowledge of letter clusters to write new words.

assess

- Notice the children's ability to take words apart while reading text.
- Show the children a list of four or five new words and observe their ability to take them apart using the initial letter cluster.

Expand the Learning

Repeat the lesson with words that begin with other consonant clusters or digraphs. Place other consonant clusters or digraphs on the die. Alternatively, write six rimes on the die and have children connect the words with the same rime.

Connect with Home

Send home a sheet of pictures that represent words that begin with consonant clusters and digraphs. Have the children write the words and underline the initial letter cluster.

Send home a block or die and Word Grid Sheets for children to play the Word Grid game with family members.

13 Adding Letters to the Beginning and End of Words

Making New Words

Consider Your Children

To benefit most from this lesson, your children need to be familiar both with changing the beginning and end of words and with adding letters to the beginning or end. This lesson will increase their flexibility in word solving.

Working with English Language Learners

This lesson helps English language learners look closely at the details of words and develop the ability to manipulate them. Repeat words as many times as necessary to help these children connect the sounds with the letters and distinguish between words. Work with your English language learners in a small group so that they can practice making new words with magnetic letters.

You Need

- Magnetic letters.
- Cookie sheets.

From *Teaching Resources:*

- Lesson WSA 13 Word Cards.
- Word Pairs Sheets (two for each child).

Understand the Principle

Knowing about adding word parts *(h + and = hand)* or deleting word parts *(stop – s = top)* helps children become more resourceful in taking apart new words. The word part can be a letter, a cluster, a prefix, a suffix, or an inflectional ending.

Explain the Principle

" You can add letter clusters to the beginning or end of a word to make a new word. "

Explain the Principle

“You can add letter clusters to the beginning or end of a word to make a new word.”

1. Tell the children that today they are going to learn how to add or take away parts of words to make new words.
2. Make the word *in* with magnetic letters. Have the children read the word. Add *th* to the beginning and have the children read the word.
3. Repeat with *eat/treat* and *ill/still.*
4. Make the word *play* with magnetic letters. Have the children read the word. Add *ing* at the end and have the children read the word.
5. Repeat with *cat/catch*, *can/candy.*
6. Explain to the children that they can add letter clusters to the beginning and to the end of words they know to make new words. They can also remove letters from the beginning in words such as *plan*, *an* or *pitch*, *itch*.
7. Tell the children that they are going to add to or remove letters from twenty words to make new words.

Name: Mort | Word Pairs Sheet
Date:

chair	hair
at	fat
glow	low
speak	peak
it	spit
on	won
lip	flip
flower	lower
ground	round
eat	pleat

choose
write
make
add or take away
write

- Give the children a batch of fifteen to twenty word cards. Ask them to choose ten words and write them on a Word Pairs Sheet. Have them make each word with magnetic letters, add or remove letters from the *beginning,* and write the new word next to the first one.
- Then give them a second batch of word cards. Ask them to select ten words and write them on the left side of another Word Pairs Sheet. Have them make each word with magnetic letters, add letters to the *end,* and write the new word next to the first one. Let them come up with their own words if they choose.

Have the children make a few words with magnetic letters and show how they changed them by adding letters to the beginning or the end to make new words.

Link

Interactive Read-Aloud: Read aloud books that promote play with words, such as

- ***Waffle*** by Chris Raschka
- ***Muncha! Muncha! Muncha!*** by Candace Fleming

Shared Reading: After you have read and enjoyed a poem together such as "I Like Silver" or "The Boy Who Stood in the Supper Room" (see *Sing a Song of Poetry*), have the children place small stick-on notes over the beginning or end of a few words to show how they can make a new word.

Guided Reading: During word work, make a few words quickly, adding or removing letters to make new words.

Interactive Writing: As the children write new words, point out how they can add letters to words they know.

Independent Writing: As the children try to spell new words, show them how to add letters to the beginning or end of words they know.

assess

- Notice the children's flexibility in adding or removing letters to known words as they try to read or write new words.
- Give the children four or five words and ask them to add letters to the beginning or end of these words and make new words.

Expand the Learning

Repeat the lesson with other examples and word lists.

Have the children come up with their own examples to which they will add letters to the beginning or end.

Connect with Home

Have the children, with family members, use magnetic letters (or letter cards; see *Teaching Resources*) to make five new words from words they know.

14 Removing Letters from the Beginning and End of Words

Word Pairs

Consider Your Children

This lesson should follow the lesson on adding letters to the beginning or end of words. It provides a little more challenge and helps increase learners' flexibility. If your children get confused using both operations, you may want to focus only on beginnings or endings until they are more fluent.

Working with English Language Learners

Learning to manipulate words in this way is easier if English language learners are working with known words and recognize the connections between them. Be sure these children are very familiar with the words you are using for this lesson. They should understand them in oral language and be able to read and write them.

You Need

- Magnetic letters.
- Cookie sheet.

From *Teaching Resources:*

- Lesson WSA 14 Word Cards.
- Word Pairs Sheets.

Understand the Principle

Children become flexible word solvers when they learn how to use word parts to figure out other words. With practice, this strategy becomes quick and automatic and greatly increases reading efficiency.

Explain the Principle

“You can take away letters from the beginning of a word to make a new word.”

“You can take away letters from the end of a word to make a new word.”

plan

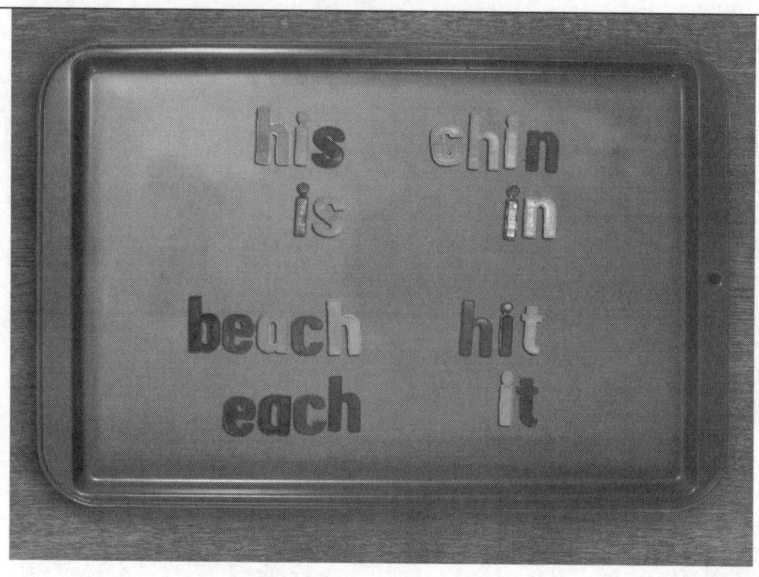

Explain the Principle

"You can take away letters from the beginning of a word to make a new word."

"You can take away letters from the end of a word to make a new word."

① Tell the children that you are going to help them learn more about using word parts to figure out new words.

② Put the word *his* on the board with magnetic letters. Invite a child to take away a letter or letters and tell the word that is left.

③ Repeat with *chin, beach, hit, charm, fall, stack.*

④ Ask the children to remove a letter or letters from the end of *ant, drops, falling, desks, candy, catch, zoom, think.*

⑤ Ask the children what they have noticed about word parts. They will explain that you can add or remove letters from the beginning or end of words to make new words.

⑥ Tell the children that they are going to make new words by removing beginning or ending letters from other words.

apply

choose
make
write
take away
write

▸ Have the children select ten word cards, make each word with magnetic letters, write the word on a Word Pairs Sheet, remove a letter or letters from the beginning or end, and then write the new word.

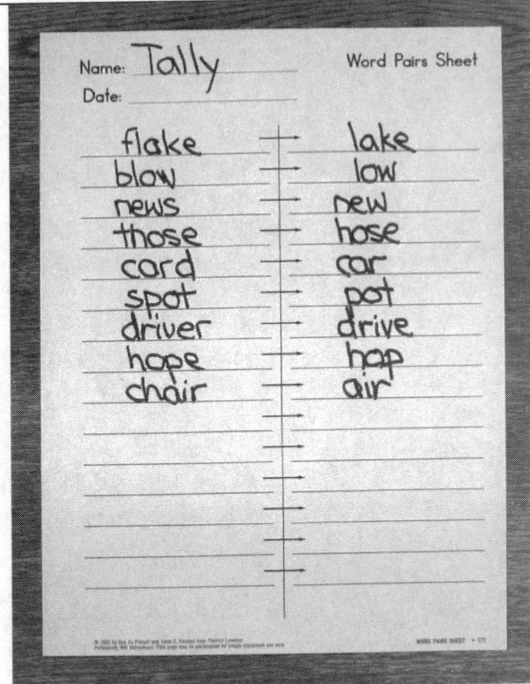
Name: Tally
Date:

Word Pairs Sheet

flake	lake
blow	low
news	new
those	hose
card	car
spot	pot
driver	drive
hope	hop
chair	air

Invite a few children to make a word with magnetic letters and call on other children to remove some letters from the beginning or end to make a new word.

Link

Interactive Read-Aloud: Read aloud books that involve word play, such as

- ***Brave Potatoes*** by Toby Speed
- ***In the Small Pond*** by Denise Fleming

Shared Reading: After you have read and enjoyed a poem such as "My Old Hen," "Bring the Wagon Home, John," or "A Peanut Sat on a Railroad Track" together (see *Sing a Song of Poetry*), have the children locate a word and cover the beginning or end with a stick-on note to make a new word.

Guided Reading: Write a few words on the whiteboard, erase the beginning or end of each, and have the children say the new words.

Interactive Writing: As the children try to write a new word, point out how they can think of a word they know and remove some letters.

Independent Writing: As the children write, show them word parts they can notice in words.

assess

- Dictate four or five words and ask the children to cross out letters at the beginning or end to create new words.
- Observe the children's flexibility in noticing and using word parts.

Expand the Learning

Repeat the lesson with other words.

Have the children come up with their own words from which they can remove letters to make new words.

Connect with Home

Have the children make a list of five words they have seen written in their home or neighborhood. Then have them find words on the list from which they can take away some letters to make new words. Ask them to bring their list to school to share with their classmates.

Generative Lesson

Connecting Words That Sound the Same but Look Different

15

Homonym Lotto

Consider Your Children

In this lesson, your children learn about words that sound the same and have different spellings. Technically they are homophones, one form of homonym. The children should have good control of spelling patterns and letter/sound relationships and have been introduced to synonyms and antonyms.

Working with English Language Learners

Homonyms are especially difficult for children who are learning English and learning to read at the same time. Use the words in sentences and, when possible, use pictures or act out words to help these children understand the different meaning of the two words you are saying. Presenting the written words while saying them helps English language learners distinguish between them. Give them many opportunities to say the words and talk about them.

You Need

- Chart paper.
- Markers.

From *Teaching Resources:*

- Directions for Lotto.
- Homonym Lotto Game Cards.
- Lesson WSA 15 Word Cards.

Understand the Principle

The word *homonym* applies to homophones (words that are pronounced the same but are spelled differently and mean different things) and homographs (words that look the same but mean different things and are sometimes pronounced differently; when they are pronounced differently they are called *heteronyms*). There are easier-to-spell and more-difficult-to-spell homophones. The spelling of homophones provides a clue to their meaning, so children need to notice the different spellings.

Explain the Principle

“You can read words by noticing that they sound the same but look different and have different meanings.”

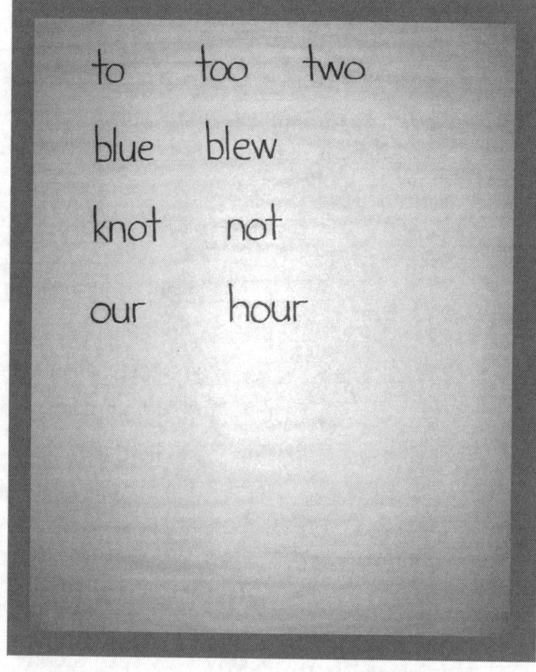

to too two
blue blew
knot not
our hour

Explain the Principle

"You can read words by noticing that they sound the same but look different and have different meanings."

1. Tell the children that they are going to learn about words that sound the same but have different spellings and meanings.
2. Write the words *to, too, two* on the chart. Invite the children to use them in a sentence.
3. Repeat with *blue/blew, knot/not,* and *our/hour.*
4. Ask the children what they noticed. They will conclude that the words sound the same but have different spellings and meanings.
5. Explain that these words are called *homonyms.* When they read them, they will need to notice not only how they sound but how they are spelled in order to figure out the meaning.
6. Tell the children that they are going to play Homonym Lotto.

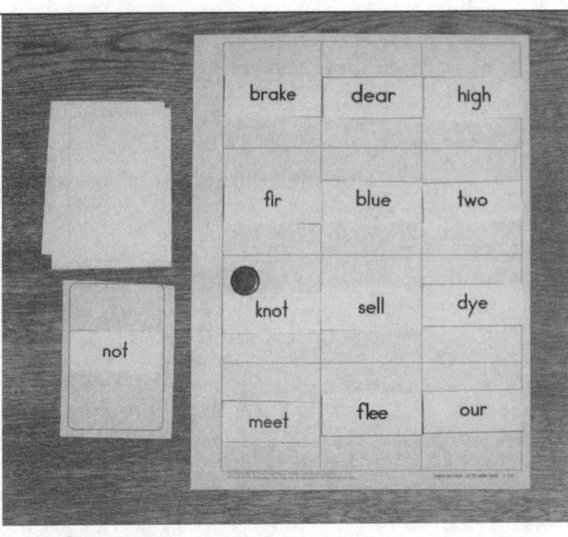

take
read
say in sentence
match
say in sentence
cover

- Have the children play Homonym Lotto in groups of three or four. They take a word card, read the word, use it in a sentence, look for a matching word (one that sounds the same) on their game card, use the matching word in a sentence, and cover the space. The first player to cover all the spaces wins the game.

Invite the children to give a few more homonym pairs to add to the chart.

Link

Interactive Read-Aloud: Read aloud humorous books that feature homonyms, such as

- ***The King Who Rained*** by Fred Gwynne
- ***A Chocolate Moose for Dinner*** by Fred Gwynne

Shared Reading: After you have enjoyed poems such as "In the Morning" *(our, way, so, in)* and "Silly Simon" *(fair, to, your, ware, were, not, for, whole, in, pail, which, made, poor, through)* or "How Much Wood Would a Woodchuck Chuck" together (see *Sing a Song of Poetry*), have the children find two or three words and tell a homonym for each.

Guided Reading: Point out homonyms in texts the children read (or ask them to find some). Work with a few homonym pairs on the whiteboard during word work.

Interactive Writing: As the children compose texts, point out words that are homonyms.

Independent Writing: Help the children look for words that are correctly spelled but have the wrong spelling for their intended meaning (*their, there,* and *they're,* for example).

assess

- Dictate two or three word pairs, using each word in a sentence. Select common homonyms that children often use in writing.
- Observe the children's correct spelling of homonyms.

Expand the Learning

Repeat the lesson with different homonyms. (See *Word Matters,* Appendix 26, for an extensive list of homonym pairs.)

Start a "homonym search" board or chart in the classroom and have children add homonyms as they find them. Review the list at the end of each week.

Connect with Home

Send home the Homonym Lotto Game Board and Word Cards so the children can play Homonym Lotto with family members.

Generative Lesson

Connecting Words: Same Spelling, Different Meanings

16

Concentration

Consider Your Children

Your children should be very familiar with a variety of spelling patterns so they can recognize these words early on and focus on their meanings. They will also build their vocabularies if some of the words, particularly in their second meaning, are new.

Working with English Language Learners

Words that look the same but mean something different and sometimes sound different are a challenge for English language learners. Use the words in sentences, use pictures, and/or act out the meaning of words to help them understand this concept. Tell them explicitly that the sequence of letters (the written word) looks the same but the word can mean completely different things. If you can, find a word or two in their own languages to use as examples; however, they may not yet have encountered such words in writing, so while they may have heard these words, the concept may be new to them.

You Need

- Pocket chart.
- Sentence strips.

From *Teaching Resources:*

- Pocket Chart Word Cards for *bat, fly, drop, wind, read* (use the Pocket Chart Card Template).
- Directions for Concentration.
- Concentration Game Cards made from Lesson WSA 16 Word Cards and Deck Card Template.

Understand the Principle

Words can have the same spelling and have different meanings (*he has a baseball and a* bat; *there was a* bat *in the barn*). Words can also be spelled the same but sound different (*I like to* read; *she* read *a book*). These words are often called homographs, but you should not be concerned about children learning the term.

Explain the Principle

“You can read words by remembering that some words look the same but sometimes sound different and have different meanings.”

plan

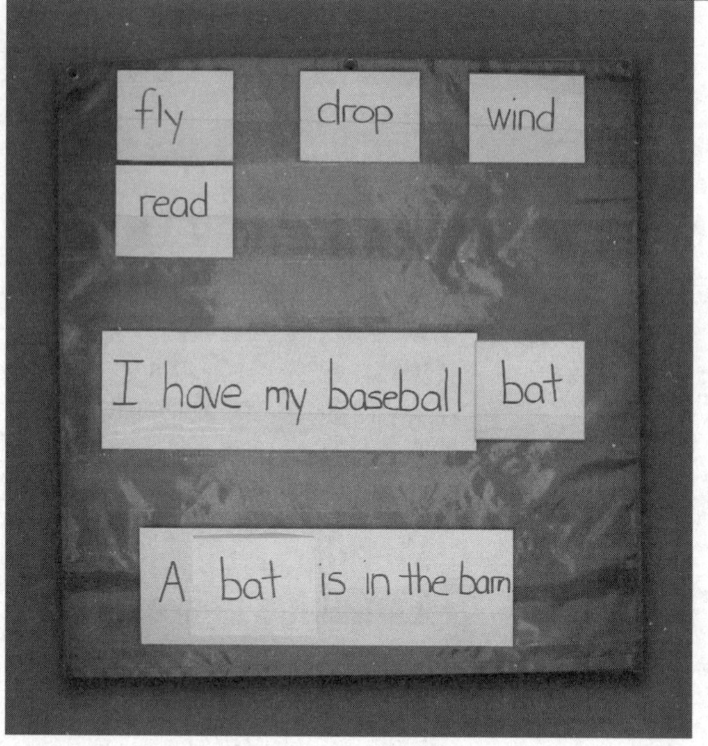

Explain the Principle

“You can read words by remembering that some words look the same but sometimes sound different and have different meanings.”

1. Explain to the children that they can read words by thinking about how they look and what they mean.

2. Tell them you are going to show them something interesting about words they know. Have *bat, fly, drop,*
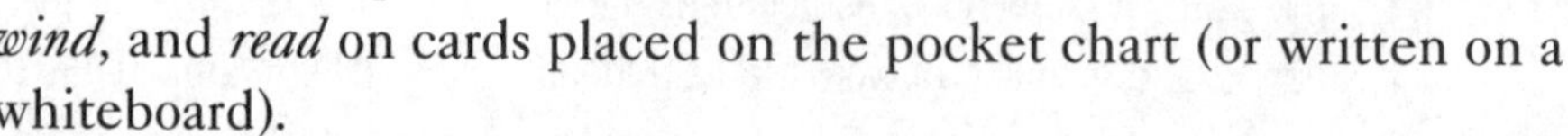
wind, and *read* on cards placed on the pocket chart (or written on a whiteboard).

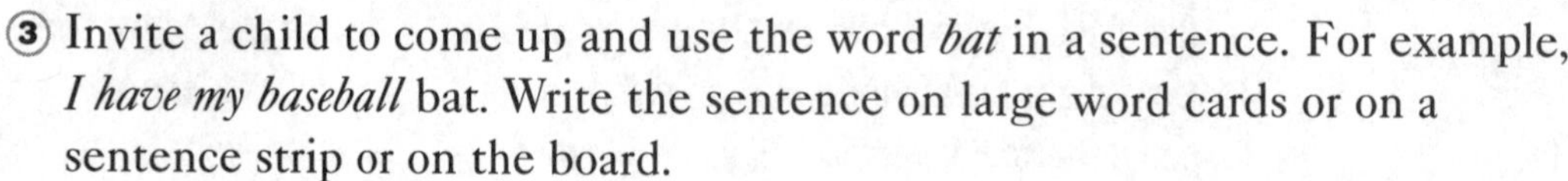

3. Invite a child to come up and use the word *bat* in a sentence. For example, *I have my baseball* bat. Write the sentence on large word cards or on a sentence strip or on the board.

4. Ask another child to create a sentence using the other meaning of *bat.* For example, *A* bat *is in the barn.*

5. Explain to the children that they can read words such as this by remembering that they look the same but can mean something different.

6. Repeat with *fly* and *drop.*

7. Do the same with *wind* and *read.* At this point explain that words can look the same, mean something different, and also sound different.

8. Tell the children that they are going to play Concentration with words that look the same but have different meanings and sometimes also sound different.

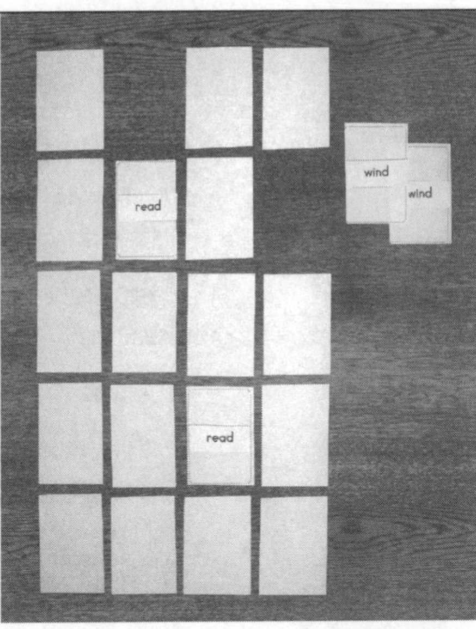

turn
say
use in sentence
turn
say
match
say
use in sentence

- Have the children play Concentration in groups of two, three, or four. They take turns turning over one card, saying it, using it in a sentence, turning over a second card, and if it matches, using it in a sentence and claiming the pair of cards. If they don't match, they turn both cards face down again.

Have the children share three or four more words that look the same and add them to the class chart.

Link

Interactive Read-Aloud: Read aloud humorous books that feature words with multiple meanings, such as

- ***Amelia Bedelia Goes Camping*** by Peggy Parish
- ***Amelia Bedelia*** by Peggy Parish

Shared Reading: Read poems such as "Rock-a-Bye Baby" *(wind, rock, will, fall),* "The Orchestra" *(can, play, bass, boom, drum),* or "I Saw Esau" *(saw)* together (see *Sing a Song of Poetry*). Have children find two or three words that can have different meanings. Have them tell whether the pronunciation changes.

Guided Reading: During word work, make two or three words on the whiteboard that can have different meanings and sound different, such as *present* (a gift, to make a presentation, the current time).

Interactive Writing: As you write with the children, point out words that can look the same and mean something different.

Independent Writing: As you confer with writers, point out homographs.

assess

- Observe the children's ability to notice and use different pronunciations of a word to fit its meaning.

Expand the Learning

Repeat the lesson with other homographs and word cards.

Have children use both sides of a Four-Box Sheet (see *Teaching Resources*) to illustrate and label pairs of homographs.

Connect with Home

Send home the Concentration Game Cards so the children can play the game with family members. Invite the children to have their family members help them search for three more examples of homographs.

Glossary

Affix A part added to the beginning or ending of a base or root word to change its meaning or function (a *prefix* or *suffix*).

Alphabet book A book for helping children develop the concept and sequence of the alphabet by showing the letters and people, animals, or objects that have labels related to the letters (usually the labels begin with the letters).

Alphabetic principle The concept that there is a relationship between the spoken sounds in oral language and the graphic forms in written language.

Analogy The resemblance of a known word to an unknown word that helps you solve the unknown word.

Antonym A word that has a different sound and opposite meaning from another word (*cold* vs. *hot*).

Assessment A means for gathering information or data that reveals what learners control, partially control, or do not yet control consistently.

Automaticity Rapid, accurate, fluent word decoding without conscious effort or attention.

Base word A whole word to which you can add affixes, creating new word forms *(washing)*.

Blend To combine sounds or word parts.

Buddy Study A word study system for learning conventional spelling strategies.

Closed syllable A syllable that ends in one or more consonants *(lem-on)*.

Comparative form A word that describes a person or thing in relation to another person or thing (for example, *more, less; taller, shorter*).

Compound word A word made up of two or more other words or morphemes *(playground)*. The meaning of a compound word can be a combination of the meanings of the words it comprises or can be unrelated to the meanings of the combined units.

Concept book A book organized to develop an understanding of an abstract or generic idea or categorization.

Connecting strategies Ways of solving words that use connections or *analogies* with similar known words (knowing *she* and *out* helps with *shout*).

Consonant A speech sound made by partial or complete closure of the airflow that causes friction at one or more points in the breath channel. The consonant sounds are represented by the letters *b, c, d, f, g, h, j, k, l, m, n, p, q, r, s, t, v, w* (in most of its uses), *x, y* (in most of its uses), and *z*.

Consonant blend Two or more consonant letters that often appear together in words and represent sounds that are smoothly joined, although each of the sounds can be heard in the word *(trim)*.

Consonant cluster A sequence of two or three consonant letters that appear together in words *(trim, chair)*.

Consonant digraph Two consonant letters that appear together and represent a single sound that is different from the sound of either letter *(shell)*.

Consonant-vowel-consonant A common sequence of sounds in a single syllable (*hat*, for example).

Contraction A shortening of a syllable, word, or word groups usually by the omission of a sound or letters *(didn't)*.

Decoding Using letter/sound relationships to translate a word from a series of symbols to a unit of meaning.

Dialect A regional variety of a language. In most languages, including English and Spanish, dialects are mutually intelligible; the differences are actually minor.

Directionality The orientation of print (in the English language, from left to right).

Distinctive letter features Visual features that make every letter of the alphabet different from every other letter.

Early literacy concepts Very early understandings related to how print works.

English language learners People whose native language is not English and who are acquiring English as an additional language.

Fluency Speed, accuracy, and flexibility in solving words.

Grammar Complex rules by which people can generate an unlimited number of phrases, sentences, and longer texts in that language. *Conventional grammar* refers to the accepted conventions in a society.

Grapheme A letter or cluster of letters representing a single sound, or phoneme *(a, eigh, ay).*

Graphophonic relationship The relationship between the oral sounds of the language and the written letters or clusters of letters.

Have a try To write a word, notice that it doesn't look quite right, try it two or three other ways, and decide which construction looks right; to make an attempt and check oneself.

High frequency words Words that occur often in the spoken and written language *(the).*

Homograph One of two or more words spelled alike but different in meaning, derivation, or pronunciation (the *bat* flew away, he swung the *bat;* take a *bow, bow* and arrow).

Homonym (a type of *homograph*) One of two or more words spelled *and* pronounced alike but different in meaning (we had *quail* for dinner; I would *quail* in fear).

Homophone One of two or more words pronounced alike but different in spelling and meaning (*meat* vs. *meet, bear* vs. *bare*).

Idiom A phrase with meaning that cannot be derived from the conjoined meanings of its elements *(raining cats and dogs).*

Inflectional ending A suffix added to a base word to show tense, plurality, possession, or comparison *(darker).*

Letter knowledge The ability to recognize and label the graphic symbols of language.

Letters Graphic symbols representing the sounds in a language. Each letter has particular distinctive features and may be identified by letter name or sound.

Lexicon Words in a language.

Long vowel The elongated vowel sound that is the same as the name of the vowel. It is sometimes represented by two or more letters *(cake, eight, mail).*

Lowercase letter A small letter form that is usually different from its corresponding capital or uppercase form.

Morpheme The smallest unit of meaning in a language. Morphemes may be *free* or *bound.* For example, *run* is a unit of meaning that can stand alone. It is a *free morpheme.* In *runs* and *running,* the added *s* and *ing* are also units of meaning. They cannot stand alone but add meaning to the free morpheme. *s* and *ing* are examples of *bound morphemes.*

Morphemic strategies Ways of solving words by discovering *meaning* through the combination of significant word parts or morphemes *(happy, happiest; run, runner, running).*

Morphological system Rules by which morphemes (building blocks of vocabulary) fit together into meaningful words, phrases, and sentences.

Morphology The combination of morphemes (building blocks of meaning) to form words; the rules by which words are formed from free and bound morphemes—for example, root words, prefixes, suffixes.

Multiple-meaning words Words that mean something different depending on the ways they are used (*run*—home run, run in your stocking, run down the street, a run of bad luck).

Onset In a syllable, the part (consonant, consonant cluster, or consonant digraph) that comes before the vowel *(cr-eam).*

Onset-rime segmentation The identification and separation of onsets (first part) and rimes (last part, containing the vowel) in words *(dr-ip).*

Open syllable A syllable that ends in a vowel sound *(ho-tel).*

Orthographic awareness The knowledge of the visual features of written language, including distinctive features of letters as well as spelling patterns in words.

Orthography The representation of the sounds of a language with the proper letters according to standard usage (spelling).

Phoneme The smallest unit of sound in spoken language. There are approximately forty-four units of speech sounds in English.

Phoneme addition Adding a beginning, middle, or ending sound to a word *(h + and, an + t).*

Phoneme blending Identifying individual sounds and then putting them together smoothly to make a word *(c-a-t = cat).*

Phoneme deletion Omitting a beginning, middle, or ending sound of a word *(cart – c = art).*

Phoneme-grapheme correspondence The relationship between the sounds (phonemes) and letters (graphemes) of a language.

Phoneme isolation The identification of an individual sound—beginning, middle, or end—in a word.

Phoneme manipulation The movement of sounds from one place to another.

Phoneme reversal The exchange of the first and last sounds of a word to make a different word.

Phoneme substitution The replacement of the beginning, middle, or ending sound of a word with a new sound.

Phonemic (or *phoneme*) awareness The ability to hear individual sounds in words and to identify particular sounds.

Phonemic strategies Ways of solving words that use how words *sound* and relationships between letters and letter clusters and phonemes in those words *(cat, make).*

Phonetics The scientific study of speech sounds—how the sounds are made vocally and the relation of speech sounds to the total language process.

Phonics The knowledge of letter/sound relationships and how they are used in reading and writing. Teaching phonics refers to helping children acquire this body of knowledge about the oral and written language systems; additionally, teaching phonics helps children use phonics knowledge as part of a reading and writing process. Phonics instruction uses a small portion of the body of knowledge that makes up *phonetics*.

Phonogram A phonetic element represented by graphic characters or symbols. In word recognition, a graphic sequence composed of a vowel grapheme and an ending consonant grapheme (such as *an* or *it*) is sometimes called a *word family.*

Phonological awareness The awareness of words, rhyming words, onsets and rimes, syllables, and individual sounds (phonemes).

Phonological system The sounds of the language and how they work together in ways that are meaningful to the speakers of the language.

Plural Of, relating to, or constituting more than one.

Prefix A group of letters that can be placed in front of a base word to change its meaning *(preplan).*

Principle In phonics, a generalization or a sound/spelling relationship that is predictable.

R-controlled vowel sound The modified sound of a vowel when it is followed by *r* in a syllable *(hurt).*

Rhyme The ending part (rime) of a word that sounds like the ending part (rime) of another word *(mail, tale).*

Rime The ending part of a word containing the vowel; the letters that represent the vowel sound and the consonant letters that follow it in a syllable *(dr-eam).*

Root The part of a word that contains the main meaning component.

Schwa The sound of the middle vowel in an unstressed syllable (for example, the *o* in *done* and the sound between the *k* and *l* in *freckle*).

Segment To divide into parts *(to-ma-to).*

Semantic system The system by which speakers of a language communicate meaning through language.

Short vowel A brief-duration sound represented by a vowel letter *(cat).*

Silent *e* The final *e* in a spelling pattern that usually signals a long vowel sound in the word and does not represent a sound itself (*make,* for example).

Suffix An affix or group of letters added at the end of a base or root word to change its function or meaning *(handful, running).*

Syllabication The division of words into syllables *(pen-cil).*

Syllable A minimal unit of sequential speech sounds composed of a vowel sound or a consonant-vowel combination. A syllable always contains a vowel or vowel-like speech sound *(to-ma-to).*

Synonym One of two or more words that have different sounds but the same meaning *(chair, seat).*

Syntactic awareness The knowledge of grammatical patterns or structures.

Syntactic system Rules that govern the ways in which morphemes and words work together in sentence patterns. Not the same as *proper grammar,* which refers to the accepted grammatical conventions.

Syntax The study of how sentences are formed and of the grammatical rules that govern their formation.

Visual strategies Ways of solving words that use knowledge of how words *look,* including the clusters and patterns of the letters in words *(bear, light).*

Vowel A speech sound or phoneme made without stoppage of or friction in the airflow. The vowel sounds are represented by *a, e, i, o, u,* and sometimes *y* and *w.*

Vowel combinations Two vowels that appear together in words *(meat).*

Vowel digraph Two successive vowel letters that represent a single vowel sound *(boat),* a vowel combination.

Word A unit of meaning in language.

Word analysis The breaking apart of words into parts or individual sounds in order to parse them.

Word family A term often used to designate words that are connected by phonograms or rimes (for example, *hot, not, pot, shot*). A *word family* can also be a series of words connected by meaning (affixes added to a base word; for example: *base, baseball, basement, baseman, basal, basis, baseless, baseline, baseboard, abase, abasement, off base, home base; precise, précis, precisely, precision*).

References

Adams, J.J. (1990). *Beginning to Read: Thinking and Learning about Print.* Cambridge, MA: MIT Press.

Allington, R. (1991). Children who find learning to read difficult: School responses to diversity. In E.H. Hiebert (ed.). *Literacy for a Diverse Society.* New York: Teachers College Press.

Armbruster, B.B., Lehr, F., and Osborn, J. (2001). *Put Reading First: The Research Building Blocks for Teaching Children to Read: Kindergarten through Grade 1.* Jessup, MD: National Institute for Literacy.

Ball, E.W., and Blachman, B.A. (1991). Does phoneme awareness training in kindergarten make a difference in early word recognition and developmental spelling? *Reading Research Quarterly* 26 (1): 49-66.

Biemiller, A. (1970). The development of the use of graphic and contextual information as children learn to read. *Reading Research Quarterly* 6: 75-96.

Blachman, B. (1984). The relationships of rapid naming ability and language analysis skills to kindergarten and first grade reading achievement. *Journal of Educational Psychology* 76: 614-622.

Blanchard, J.S. (1980). Preliminary investigation of transfer between single-word decoding ability and contextual reading comprehension of poor readers in grade six. *Perceptual and Motor Skills* 51: 1271-1281.

Bradley, L., and Bryant, P.E. (1983). Categorizing sounds and learning to read—a causal connection. *Nature* 301: 419-421.

Bryant, P.E., Bradley, L., Camlean, M., and Crossland, J. (1989). Nursery rhymes, phonological skills and reading. *Journal of Child Language* 16: 407-428.

Bryant, P.E., MacLean, M., Bradley, L.L., and Crossland, J. (1990). Rhyme and alliteration, phoneme detection, and learning to read. *Developmental Psychology* 26 (3): 429-438.

Ceprano, M.A. (1980). A review of selected research on methods of teaching sight words. *The Reading Teacher* 35: 314-322.

Chall, J.S. (1989). Learning to read: The great debate. 20 years later. *Phi Delta Kappan* 70: 521-538.

Clay, M.M. (1991). *Becoming Literate: The Construction of Inner Control.* Portsmouth, NH: Heinemann.

Clay, M.M. (1998). *By Different Paths to Common Outcomes.* York, ME: Stenhouse Publishers.

Clay, M.M. (2001). *Change over Time in Children's Literacy Development.* Portsmouth, NH: Heinemann.

Daneman, M. (1991). Individual difference in reading skills. In R. Barr, M.L. Kamil, P. Mosenthal, and P.D. Pearson (eds.). *Handbook of Reading Research* (Vol. II, pp. 512-538). New York: Longman.

Ehri, L.C. (1991). Development of the ability to read words. In R. Barr, M.L. Kamil, P. Mosenthal, and P.D. Pearson (eds.). *Handbook of Reading Research* (Vol. II, pp. 383-417). New York: Longman.

Ehri, L.C., and McCormick, S. (1998). Phases of word learning: Implications for instruction with delayed and disabled readers. *Reading and Writing Quarterly* 20: 163-179.

Fountas, I.C., and Pinnell, G.S. (1996). *Guided Reading: Good First Teaching for All Children.* Portsmouth, NH: Heinemann.

Fountas, I.C., and Pinnell, G.S. (eds.) (1999). *Voices on Word Matters: Learning about Phonics and Spelling in the Literacy Classroom.* Portsmouth, NH: Heinemann.

Fox, B., and Routh, K.D. (1984). Phonemic analysis and synthesis as word-attack skills: Revisited. *Journal of Educational Psychology* 76: 1059-1064.

Hohn, W., and Ehri, L. (1983). Do alphabet letters help prereaders acquire phonemic segmentation skill? *Journal of Educational Psychology* 75: 752-762.

Holdaway, D. (1987). *The Foundations of Literacy.* Portsmouth, NH: Heinemann.

Hundley, S., and Powell, D. (1999). In I.C. Fountas and G.S. Pinnell (eds.). *Voices on Word Matters* (pp. 159-164). Portsmouth, NH: Heinemann.

Juel, C. (1988). Learning to read and write: A longitudinal study of 54 children from first through fourth grades. *Journal of Educational Psychology* 80: 437-447.

Juel, C., Griffith, P.L., and Gough, P.B. (1986). Acquisition of literacy: A longitudinal study of children in first and second grade. *Journal of Educational Psychology* 78: 243-255.

Lesgold, A.M., Resnick, L.B., and Hammond, K. (1985). Learning to read: A longitudinal study of word skill development in two curricula. In G.E. MacKinnon and T.G. Walker (eds.). *Reading Research: Advances in Theory and Practice* (Vol. 4, pp. 107-138). New York: Academic Press.

Liberman, I., Shankweiler, D., and Liberman, A. (1985). The Alphabetic Principle and Learning to Read. U.S. Department of Health and Human Services. Reprinted with permission from The University of Michigan Press by the National Institute of Child Health and Human Development. Adapted from Phonology and the problems of learning to read and write. *Remedial and Special Education* 6: 8-17.

Liberman, I.Y., Shankweiler, D., Fischer, F.W., and Carter, B. (1974). Explicit syllable and phoneme segmentation in the young child. *Journal of Experimental Child Psychology* 18: 201-212.

Lundberg, I., Frost, J., and Petersen, O.P. (1988). Effects of an extensive program for stimulating phonological awareness in preschool children. *Reading Research Quarterly* 23: 264-284.

McCarrier, A.M., Pinnell, G.S., and Fountas, I.C. (2000). *Interactive Writing: How Language and Literacy Come Together.* Portsmouth, NH: Heinemann.

Moats, L.C. (2000). *Speech to Print: Language Essentials for Teachers.* Baltimore: Paul H. Brookes.

Nagy, W.E., Anderson, R.C., Schommer, M., Scott, J., and Stallman, A. (1989). Morphological families in the internal lexicon. *Reading Research Quarterly* 24: 262-282.

National Institute of Child Health and Human Development (2001). *Report of the National Reading Panel: Teaching Children to Read: An Evidence-Based Assessment of the Scientific Research Literature on Reading and Its Implications for Reading Instruction. Reports of the Subgroups.* Washington, DC: National Institutes of Health.

New Standards Primary Literacy Committee (1999). *Reading and Writing: Grade by Grade.* Washington, DC: National Center on Education and the Economy and the University of Pittsburgh.

Perfetti, C.A., Beck, I., Bell, L., and Hughes, C. (1987). Children's reading and the development of phonological awareness. *Merrill Palmer Quarterly* 33: 39-75.

Pinneli, G.S., and Fountas, I.C. (1998). *Word Matters: Teaching Phonics and Spelling in the Reading/Writing Classroom.* Portsmouth, NH: Heinemann.

Pinnell, G.S., Pikulski, J., Wixson, K.K., et al. (1995). *Listening to Children Read Aloud: Data from NAEP's Integrated Reading Performance Record (IRPR) at Grade 4.* Report No. 23-FR-04, prepared by the Educational Testing Service. Washington, DC: Office of Educational Research and Improvement, U.S. Department of Education.

Pressley, M. (1998). *Reading Instruction That Works: The Case for Balanced Teaching.* New York: The Guilford Press.

Read, C. (1971). Pre-school children's knowledge of English phonology. *Harvard Educational Review* 41: 1-34.

Snow, C.E., Burns, M.S., and Griffin, G. (eds.) (1989). *Preventing Reading Difficulties in Young Children.* Washington, DC: Committee on the Prevention of Reading Difficulties in Young Children, Commission on Behavioral and Social Sciences and Education, National Research Council.

Treiman, R. (1985). Onsets and rimes as units of spoken syllables: Evidence from children. *Journal of Experimental Child Psychology* 39: 161-181.

Vellutino, F.R., and Denckla, M.B. (1991). Cognitive and neuropsychological foundations of word identification in poor and normally developing readers. In R. Barr, M.L. Kamil, P. Mosenthal, and P.D. Pearson (eds.). *Handbook of Reading Research* (Vol. II, pp. 571-608). New York: Longman.

Vellutino, F.R., and Scanlon, D.B. (1987). Phonological coding, phonological awareness, and reading ability: Evidence from longitudinal and experimental study. *Merrill Palmer Quarterly* 33: 321-363.

Vellutino, F.R., Scanlon, D.M., Sipay, E.R., et al. (1996). Cognitive profiles of difficult-to-remediate and readily remediated poor readers: Early intervention as a vehicle for distinguishing between cognitive and experiential deficits as basic causes of specific reading disability. *Journal of Educational Psychology* 88: 601-638.

phonics lessons

Letters, Words, and How They Work

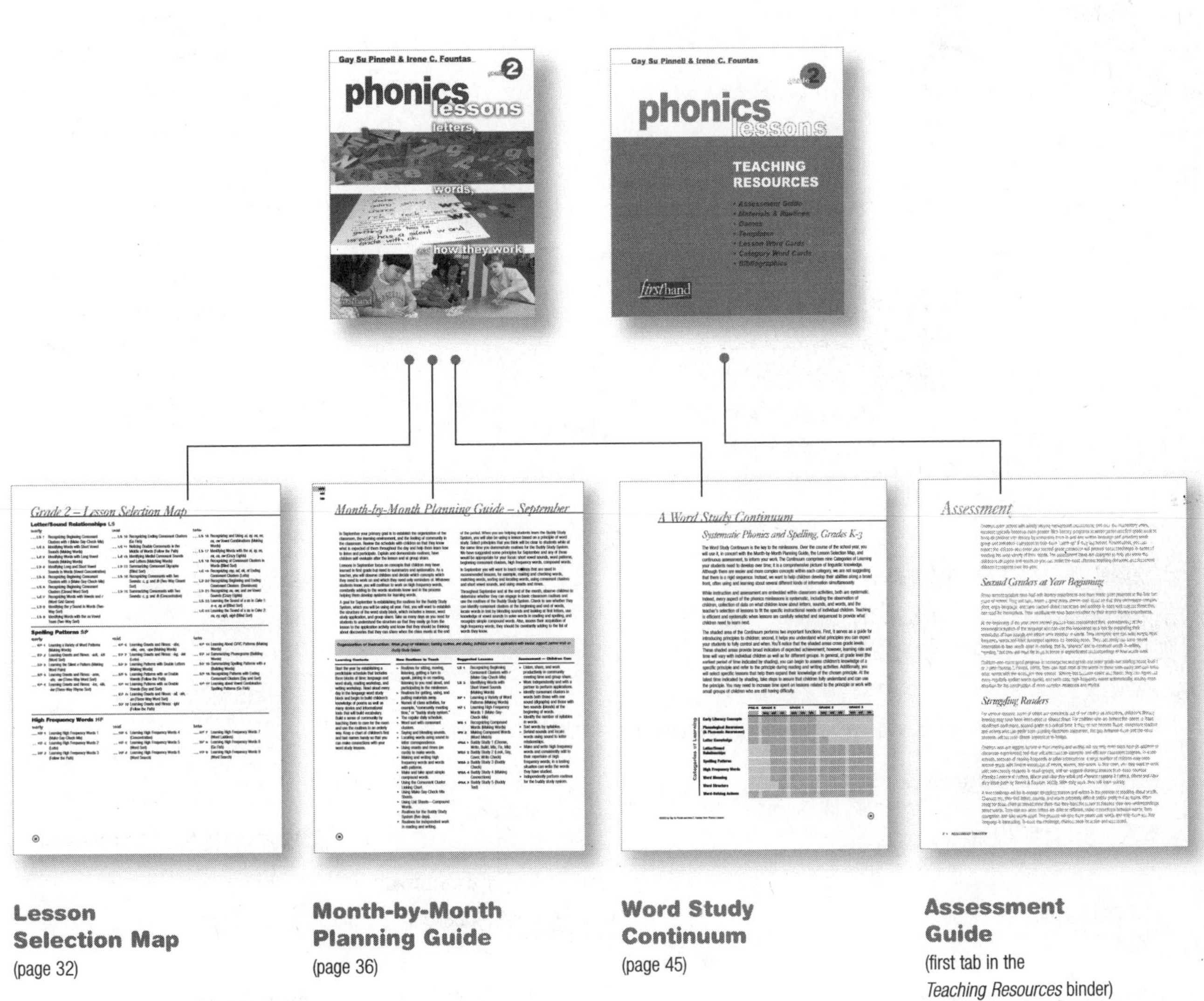

Lesson Selection Map
(page 32)

Month-by-Month Planning Guide
(page 36)

Word Study Continuum
(page 45)

Assessment Guide
(first tab in the *Teaching Resources* binder)

Your Essential Teaching Tools

FirstHand
An imprint of Heinemann
A division of Reed Elsevier Inc.
361 Hanover Street
Portsmouth, NH 03801–3912
www.firsthand.heinemann.com

Offices and agents throughout the world

Library of Congress Cataloging-in-Publication Data

Pinnell, Gay Su.
Phonics lessons : letters, words, and how they work / by Gay Su Pinnell and Irene C. Fountas.
p. cm.
Includes bibliographical references.
Contents: [1] Grade K — [2] Grade 1 — [3] Grade 2.
ISBN 0-325-00562-1
1. Reading — Phonetic method. 2. English language — Phonetics. I. Fountas, Irene C. II. Title.

LB1573.3 .P54 2003 2002190837
372.46'5--dc21

Printed in the United States of America on acid-free paper

07 06 05 04 03 ML 2 3 4 5 6